Immroth's Guide
to the
Library of Congress Classification

LIBRARY SCIENCE TEXT SERIES

Immroth's Guide to the Library of Congress Classification

Third Edition

By

Lois Mai Chan

Libraries Unlimited, Inc. • Littleton, CO • 1980

Based upon Immroth's *Guide to Library of Congress Classification*,
1st and 2d Editions,
© Barbara F. Immroth 1968, 1971
All Rights Reserved

© Libraries Unlimited, Inc. 1980
All Rights Reserved
Printed in the United States of America

LIBRARIES UNLIMITED, INC.
P.O. Box 263
Littleton, Colorado 80160

Library of Congress Cataloging in Publication Data

Immroth, John Phillip.
 Immroth's Guide to the Library of Congress classification.

 (Library science text series)
 Includes bibliographies and index.
 1. Classification, Library of Congress. I. Chan,
Lois Mai. II. Title. III. Title: Guide to the
Library of Congress classification.
Z696.U4I5 1980 025.4'33 80-16981
ISBN 0-87287-224-6
ISBN 0-87287-235-1 (pbk.)

PREFACE TO THE THIRD EDITION

Since the publication of the second edition in 1971 of *A Guide to the Library of Congress Classification* by John Phillip Immroth, certain changes in Library of Congress policies and practice with regard to the classification have taken place, the schedules of several classes have been revised, and a number of new schedules never published before have appeared. The purpose of this edition is to bring this guide up-to-date to reflect current Library of Congress policies and practice and to reorganize the material in the book in such a way as to facilitate use.

The first four chapters of the book have been reorganized and rewritten. Chapter 1 provides a brief overview of the development and the purpose of the Library of Congress Classification. Chapter 2 discusses the general principles and characteristics. All information regarding the notation, including the Cutter number, applicable to the entire system, is given in chapter 3. Chapter 4 explains the use of tables. Practice concerning the notation or tables limited to a special class or a special type of materials is discussed in the appropriate sections in chapters 5 and 6. Chapter 5, discussing individual classes, has been thoroughly revised and enlarged. Chapter 6, on special types of library materials, is a new chapter which did not appear in the previous editions.

Many new examples have been added. Examples retained from the second edition have been checked against the Library of Congress shelflist in order to ensure their validity. The bibliographies at the end of the chapters have been updated to include recent writings on the classification. Tables that are readily available from the schedules have been removed from the appendix, which now contains only those tables that are used throughout the system but printed only in a few schedules, and a number of tables which have undergone considerable revision or changes since the publication of the latest edition of the main schedules of those classes.

As in the case of earlier editions, this book is intended to be an introduction to the Library of Congress Classification. As such, it does not include detailed instructions for every subclass or table, but attempts to provide the reader with basic understanding of the characteristics of the classification, the arrangement within the classes, the format of the schedules and tables, and special problems of use and notation.

Practicing classifiers may also find this book useful. Chapter 3 on notation and chapter 6 on the classification of special types of library materials, in particular, have incorporated current Library of Congress practice and recent policy changes. These are based on announcements appearing in *Cataloging Service Bulletin* and consultation with the staff of the Library of Congress Subject Cataloging Division.

In preparing this edition, I am indebted to many individuals for their assistance. I wish to acknowledge particularly Mary K. D. Pietris, Chief of Subject Cataloging Division, Library of Congress; Mary Ann Ferrarese, Head of Shelflisting Section; Rose Marie Clemandot, Assistant Head of Shelflisting Section; and the staff of the Division for many hours of consultation and their invaluable comments and suggestions. I wish to thank also Melda Fuller and Celia A. Smith for typing the manuscript and Eileen Bell, Mary Stuart, and Shirley DeSimone for proofreading.

Lois M. Chan
University of Kentucky

IN MEMORY OF
John Phillip Immroth

TABLE OF CONTENTS

1　　　INTRODUCTION

A BRIEF HISTORY OF EARLIER
CLASSIFICATION SYSTEMS USED BY THE
LIBRARY OF CONGRESS

Earliest Systems

Prior to the establishment of the Library of Congress, the Congress of the United States used the Library Company of Philadelphia and the New York Society Library. The Library of Congress was established when the American legislature prepared to move from Philadelphia to the new capital city of Washington, D.C. Section five of "An Act Making Further Provision for the Removal and Accommodation of the Government of the United States," signed by President John Adams on April 24, 1800, provided a sum of $5,000 "for the purchase of such books as may be necessary for the use of Congress at the said city of Washington, and for fitting up a suitable apartment for containing them."[1]

Senator Samuel Dexter of Massachusetts was chiefly responsible for the selection of the initial collection of the Library of Congress. He ordered 740 books from the London booksellers Cadell & Davies. These books were sent from London on December 11, 1800, and reached Washington by May 2, 1801. On January 26, 1802, "An Act Concerning the Library for the use of both Houses of Congress" was approved by Congress. It provided for a room for the Library of Congress, the establishment of suitable rules and regulations by the President of the Senate and the Speaker of the House, and the appointment of a librarian by the president. Three days later President Thomas Jefferson appointed John Beckley, the Clerk of the House, as the first Librarian of Congress.

The first classification system or shelf arrangement system used by the Library of Congress is recorded in the first catalog issued by the Library in April of 1802. The books in this catalog were arranged by size—212 folios, 164 quartos, 581 octavos, 7 duodecimos, and 9 maps. Each of these categories was further subarranged by accession number.

The first recorded change in the classification system appears in the third catalog issued by the Library in 1808. In addition to the size-format system of the 1802 arrangement, categories were added for special bibliographic forms. These were plans, state laws, journals of the House of Representatives of the United States, reports of Committees of the House, executive reports and papers, receipts and expenditures, bill books of the House, and gazettes.

Although classification schemes such as the 1802 and 1808 schemes were not uncommon in the early nineteenth century, there were definitely forms of subject classification schemes in existence. In fact, the members of Congress had used or had available for their use a subject classification scheme when Congress was housed in Philadelphia. This subject classification scheme used by the Library Company of Philadelphia since 1789 served as the basis for the Library of Congress' first subject approach in 1812. The Philadelphia scheme had its basis in the system of classification of Francis Bacon as modified by Jean le Rond d'Alembert.

The seventeenth century English philosopher Francis Bacon divided all knowledge into two broad categories:

> HUMAN KNOWLEDGE: "Information derived from the senses."
> THEOLOGY: "Information derived from revelation."

He subdivided Human Knowledge into History, Poesy, and Philosophy, based on three distinct faculties of the human mind: History coming from memory, Poesy from imagination, and Philosophy from reason. In examining Bacon's system, it must be remembered that his is a philosophical system for categorizing knowledge; it was not designed as a library classification system. Bacon's system appeared first in 1605 in his *Advancement of Learning*. In 1751 d'Alembert published the plans for Diderot's *Encyclopédie* in *Discours Préliminaire de l'Encyclopédie*. Included in this work is his system for arranging the *Encyclopédie*; in short, his system for the classification. He cited his debt to Bacon as the model for his system; however, d'Alembert made two major changes in Bacon's system as well as numerous minor ones. The first major change was the removal of Bacon's second major category, Theology or "Revealed knowledge," from its separate location. D'Alembert placed Revealed theology with Natural theology as a subdivision of Philosophy. Bacon's separation of Human knowledge and Divine knowledge thus did not exist in d'Alembert's system. The second major change was the order of the three remaining main classes. D'Alembert changed Bacon's order of History, Poesy, Philosophy to History, Philosophy, Poesy (or "Fine Arts" as he called Poesy).

The Philadelphia scheme, based on Bacon's classification as modified by d'Alembert, comprised 31 classes. The 1812 Library of Congress system represented a reduction of the 31 classes to 18:

1. Sacred history;
2. Ecclesiastical history;
3. Civil history, including chronology, biography, antiquities, etc.;
4. Geography and topography; voyages and travels;
5. Law;
6. Ethics, or the moral system in general; theology and mythology;
7. Logic, rhetoric, and criticism;
8. Dictionaries, grammars and treatises on education;
9. General and local politics; political economy, etc.;
10. Trade and commerce;
11. Military and naval tactics;
12. Agriculture, rural economy, etc.;

13. Natural history; natural and experimental philosophy, etc.;
14. Medicine, surgery, and chemistry;
15. Poetry, and the drama; works on fiction, wit, etc.;
16. Arts and sciences, and miscellaneous literature;
17. Gazettes;
18. Maps, charts, and plans.[2]

Classes 1-4 represent History; 5-14, Philosophy; and 15-16, Fine Arts. The last two classes, "17. Gazettes," and "18. Maps, charts, and plans" are not subject divisions but rather form divisions. Under each of the 18 classes the books were subdivided by size and arranged alphabetically.

Jefferson's System

On August 24, 1814, the Library of Congress, as well as most of the Capitol, was burned by British soldiers. Most of the collection was destroyed in the fire. Thomas Jefferson offered to sell his personal library to Congress. In 1815 Congress voted $23,950 to purchase the Jefferson library of 6,487 books which were classified in Jefferson's own system. Jefferson's system was retained by the Library of Congress with some modifications until the end of the nineteenth century. Forty-four main classes, or "chapters," composed this system, which was also based on the systems of Bacon and d'Alembert. The following summary shows not only the 44 chapters but also Jefferson's subdivisions, including his use of geographic subdivision.

1. History, civil; ancient history. -2. Modern history, foreign, southern: General works, Italy, Rome, Florence, Naples, Venice, Spain, Portugal, France. Northern: General works, Lapland, Russia, Poland, Hungary, Sweden, Denmark, Prussia, Germany, Flanders, United Netherlands, Switzerland, Geneva, Turkey, Asia, Africa. -3. Modern history, British, Scotland, Ireland. -4. Modern history, American, Ante-Revolutionary: General, particular. Post-Revolutionary: General, particular. Newspapers. -5. History, ecclesiastical. -6. History, natural: physics, natural philosophy. -7. Agriculture. -8. Chemistry. -9. Surgery. -10. Medicine. -11. Natural history: Animals, anatomy. -12. Natural history: Animals, zoology. -13. Natural history: Botany. -14. Natural history: Mineralogy. -15. History, Natural: Occupations of man, technical arts. -16. Philosophy, moral: Ethics, (1) moral philosophy, (2) law of nature and nations. -17. Religion. -18. Jurisprudence: Equity. -19. Jurisprudence: Common law, bodies of law, statutes, courts, entries, conveyancing, criminal law, tracts, reports. -20. Jurisprudence: Law, merchant. -21. Jurisprudence: Law, maritime. -22. Jurisprudence: Law, ecclesiastical. -23. Jurisprudence: Foreign law. -24. Politics: General theories of government, special governments. Ancient. Modern. France: Monarchical, revolutionary, imperial, her colonies. England: Constitution, Parliament, dependencies. United States: Colonial, Revolutionary, reconstituted, States. Political economy: General, statistics,

(Summary continues on page 18)

commerce, finance. -25. Mathematics, pure: Arithmetic.
-26. Mathematics, pure: Geometry. -27. Physics-mathematics:
Mechanics, statics, dynamics, phonics, optics. -28. Astronomy.
-29. Geography, general: Europe, Asia, Africa, America. -30. Fine
arts: Architecture. -31. Fine arts: Gardening, painting, sculptur-
ing. -32. Fine arts: Music. -33. Poetry, epic. -34. Romance, tales,
fables. -35. Pastorals, odes, elegies, etc. -36. Didactic. -37.
Tragedy. -38. Comedy. -39. Dialogue, epistolary. -40. Logic,
rhetoric, orations. -41. Criticism: Theory. -42. Criticism: Bibliography. -43. Criticism. Languages, general: Polyglot, Oriental,
Greek, Latin, Italian, Spanish, French, Northern, English, Welsh.
-44. Polygraphical.[3]

Jefferson devotes fifteen chapters, 1-15, to History; fourteen chapters, 16-29, to
Philosophy; and fourteen chapters, 30-43, to Fine Arts. The final chapter, 44, is
provided for those polygraphical works which do not naturally fit into any of the
three major subject categories and their subdivisions. It should be pointed out
that the Librarian of Congress, George Watterston, did not use all of Jefferson's
subdivisions. For example, in "Chapter 2. Modern History: Foreign," Watterston
arranged all the books into a single alphabet, ignoring Jefferson's geographic
subdivisions.[4] Each successive librarian made changes in the system. Most of
these changes were made for practical reasons. While Jefferson's system provided
the basic theoretical framework, later changes and modifications reflect a
pragmatic approach based on the needs of the collection.

Ainsworth Rand Spofford, Librarian of Congress from 1864 to 1897, made
major adjustments in both the classification and the notation. Originally a notation had been developed combining the chapter number and the book number in
a fraction-like arrangement. For instance, 4/27 would have meant chapter 4,
American history, book number 27.

> An inserted book was numbered by adding a letter to the book
> number of the book next preceding, or by renumbering the entire
> class. For example, a Collection of papers relating to the history of
> Massachusetts being number 4/27, the Collections of the
> Massachusetts Historical Society when added to the Library were
> marked 4/27a. As many as a dozen or more insertions, arranged in
> order of accession, were sometimes made and numbered thus by
> the added letters *l*, m, etc.[5]

The notation was revised by Spofford so that the denominator was really a shelf
number, not a book number. For example, 15/9456 might then mean chapter 15,
Technology, shelf 9456, which was the shelf reserved for books on the subject of
Inter-Ocean Canals. Canal and river improvements in general had the number
15/9453. This meant chapter 15, Technology, and shelf number 9453 for books
on canal and river improvements in general. Obviously shelf 9453 precedes shelf
9456 just as the subordination of subject matter from general to specific does in
this case. This device allowed far greater subdivisions within each chapter. This
change meant that the notation denoted a fixed location, not a relative one.
However, as the collection of the Library grew, often the shelf number came to
have only a subject meaning and not a locational one.[6]

THE NEW LIBRARY OF CONGRESS CLASSIFICATION

By the 1890s it was obvious that the Jeffersonian system was no longer adequate. The collection had grown from seven thousand books to nearly one million. The move to the new library building in 1897 made this fact painfully apparent. John Russell Young, the Librarian of Congress at that time, instructed James C. M. Hanson, the Head of the Catalogue Division, and Charles Martel, the Chief Classifier, to study the possibilities of adopting a new classification system for the Library of Congress. In December of 1897 Young gave the following advice:

> As an inflexible rule, no method of classification should be favored which would disintegrate the general collection. The Library of Congress must ultimately be the universal library of the Republic. To that end the most magnificent library edifice in the world has been erected and is destined to be, it is to be hoped, the home of America's literary and artistic genius, supplemented and strengthened by that of all lands and all time. And now, when the work of organization is in a plastic condition, before what is done hardens and consolidates and becomes difficult of undoing, no step should be taken without considering not alone what is most convenient today, but what will be most useful a hundred years from today.
>
> Therefore, in the work of classification, while each department maintains its respective character, the main purpose is the consolidation of the general library. What may have gone from its shelves to strengthen the medical or develop a law library, what may be contemplated in the way of a Congressional library of reference, can and should be replaced. But there must be no invasion of the general library's domain as one of universal reference.[7]

In tracing the initial development of the Library of Congress Classification system, LaMontagne outlines the ideological possibilities existing at the time:

> Three main streams of thought were (1) the educational and philosophic system, which, originating in Greece, followed the development of Western thought and culminated in the French System of Jacques-Charles Brunet; (2) the seventeenth-century divisions of Francis Bacon which, modified and adapted by d'Alembert and Jefferson, were transmitted to Melvil Dewey by Johnston and W. T. Harris; (3) the evolutionary order, in the nineteenth century, of Merlin and Lesley, which Cutter transmuted into his Expansive Classification.[8]

Two courses of action were open to the Library of Congress, LaMontagne continues: "to choose from the classification schemes already existing in printed form the one best suited to the needs of the Library; or, to build up an 'eclectic' system which would profit by the experience of other large reference libraries and utilize the best features of all existing classifications."[9]

Hanson and Martel investigated and evaluated three major published classification schemes: Melvil Dewey's *Decimal Classification*, then in its fifth edition; the first six expansions of Charles Ammi Cutter's *Expansive Classification*; and the *Halle Schema* devised by Otto Hartwig. It is indeed regrettable that the Library of Congress could not adopt Dewey's *Decimal Classification* in 1898. A prime difficulty was Dewey's refusal to allow any major changes in his system at that time; over one hundred libraries had adopted the *Decimal Classification*, and Dewey felt that it would be unfair to these libraries to allow the Library of Congress to make any adjustments in his system. Further, Martel criticized the *Decimal Classification* as a "system bound up in and made to fit the notation, and not the notation to fit the classification."[10] The *Halle Schema* was considered to be too strongly oriented in traditional German philosophical thought to be applicable to the Library of Congress. However, serious consideration was given to Cutter's *Expansive Classification*. Cutter was quite helpful and ready to allow any necessary changes. In 1929, Hanson recalled these early decisions concerning the development of L.C. classification:

> The situation as to classification was fully appreciated by men like Mr. Spofford and Mr. Hutcheson, and little or no opposition was made, therefore, when plans for a new system were submitted. . . .Cutter's *Expansive Classification* was selected as the chief guide, with, however, radical modifications in the notation. For instance, one, or at most two capital letters were to indicate classes, Arabic numerals in integral, not decimal sequence, with gaps (*Springende Nummer*) for subdivisions, and Cutter numbers for individual books. It was Spofford who insisted on the integral, not decimal, sequence of numbers. Mr. Spofford was inexorably opposed to the decimal system, per se, and his opposition was shared in part by other members of the staff, including the chief of the Catalogue Division, who felt that only by supplying a mixed notation and providing many radical changes would it have been possible for the Library of Congress to consider this system.[11]

The appointment of Charles Martel in 1897 to the staff of the Catalogue Division enabled the operation of reclassification to proceed and, for the next two decades, Martel carried the burdens of reclassification and the development of the new system.

At the 1896 congressional hearings on the "Condition of the Library of Congress," Herbert Putnam, then Librarian of the Boston Public Library, was called as a witness. His testimony indicated his interest in classification. When Putnam succeeded Young as the Librarian of Congress in 1899, Hanson lost little time in presenting his plans for reclassification and the development of a new classification to the new Librarian.[12]

Although Putnam strongly supported the plans for reclassification, he questioned whether the Library of Congress should develop its own system, rather than adopt a nationally accepted scheme such as *Dewey Decimal Classification*. Reclassification was held up for two years. In the end, the decision to develop a new system prevailed and reclassification continued in 1901.[13]

Specifically, there are only two direct influences of Cutter's *Expansive Classification* on the new LC classification: first, the outline to the sixth expansion of the *Expansive Classification* was used by Hanson in developing the outline for the LC classification; and, second, the seventh expansion of Class Z, Book Arts, was used by Martel as the basis for Class Z, Bibliography and Library Science.

The Outlines of the New Classification

Before Hanson came to the Library of Congress, he had worked with Cutter's *Expansive Classification* at the University of Wisconsin Library. Cutter's outline of classes consisted basically of subject classes using a single letter. The single letters were to be expanded by adding one or two additional letters. Hanson's revision or adaptation of the *Expansive Classification* used the single letters but expanded them numerically to form the notation. This resulted in the mixed notation of letters and numbers which was to be used for the L.C.Classification:

Cutter's Outline[14]		**Hanson's First Outline (1899)**[15]		
A	Reference and General works	A	1-200	Polygraphy; Encyclopedias; General Periodicals; Societies, etc.
B	Philosophy	A	201-3000	Philosophy
BR	Religion & Religions (except the Christian & Jewish)	A	3001-B9999	Religion; Theology; Church history
C	Christian & Jewish religions			
D	Ecclesiastical history			
E	Biography	C	1-9999	Biography; and studies auxiliary to history
F	History & subjects allied	D	1-9999	General history; periods; & local (except America) with Geography
		E-F		American; history and geography
G	Geography & travels	G		Geography; general; and allied studies (e.g., Anthropology & Ethnology)
H	Social sciences	H	1-2000	Political science
		H	2001-9999	Law
I	Sociology	I	1-8000	Sociology
J	Government, Politics			

(Outline of classes continues on page 22)

Cutter's Outline (cont'd)		Hanson's First Outline (1899) (cont'd)		
K	Legislation. Law. Woman. Societies	I	8001-9999	Women; Societies, clubs, etc.
		J	1-2000	Sports, amusements
		J	2001-9999	Music
		K		Fine arts
		L-M		Philosophy & Literature
L	Science in general, & Physical sciences Includes Science & Arts (treated in the same book), Science (general works), Mathematics, Physics, Chemistry, Astronomy	N		Science; Mathematics; Astronomy; Physics; Chemistry
M	Natural history in general, Microscopy, Geology, Biology	O		Natural history, general; Geology
N	Botany	P		Zoology; Botany
O	Zoology			
Q	Medicine	Q		Medicine
R	Useful arts in general, Metric arts, Extractive and Productive arts, Chemical and Electrical arts, Domestic economy	R		Useful arts; Agriculture
S	Engineering & Building	S		Manufactures
T	Manufactures and Handicrafts	T		Engineering
U	Defensive and preservative arts	U		Military, Naval science; light houses; life saving; fire extinction
V	Recreative arts; Sports; Theatre, Music	V-Y		Special collections
W	Fine arts			
X	Language			
Y	Literature			
YF	Fiction			
Z	Book arts	Z		Bibliography (Book arts)

This outline demonstrates that Cutter's notation was not consistently hierarchical. For example, Religion begins with the double letter BR and the single letters C and D are used as divisions of BR. Also the order of Cutter's main classes shows no direct relationship to the systems of Bacon or d'Alembert. Cutter fully expands Science to a main class separating it from both Philosophy and History. He also brings Technology into close proximity to Science and Medicine. Although his notation is not consistently hierarchical, it is expanded to subject subdivisions by the addition of letters; numbers are used mnemonically for form and place divisions. To a large extent Hanson followed Cutter's outline of classes in his own outline. The only major change in the order of the *Expansive Classification* in Hanson's revision was placing the arts—fine arts, music, and literature—between the social sciences and the sciences. In 1903 Hanson further perfected this outline as the basis for the new L.C. Classification; the nearly final form of the outline was completed the following year.

It is interesting to note the final expansion of Classes A and B. In Hanson's first outline, A1-200 was designed for Polygraphic works, A201-3000 for Philosophy, and A3001-9999 for Religion. In the 1903[16] outline Philosophy was reduced by 300 numbers—Philosophy started with A501 instead of A201. In the 1904 outline Polygraphy was allotted a separate Class—A—and Philosophy and Religion combined into the separate Class B. These changes in the 1904 outline represent the decision to use double instead of single letters as were used for the first classes of L.C. Classification (Classes Z and E-F).

The 1903 outline was:

A (in part)	Polygraphy. General works.
A501-3000	Philosophy.
A3001-B	Religion; & Theology.
C	Biography; Studies auxiliary to History.
D	History (except America).
E-F	America. History and Geography.
G	Geography; & allied studies: Anthropology; etc.
H	Statistics. Economics.

The 1904 outline was:

A	General works. Polygraphy.
B-BJ	Philosophy.
BL-BX	Religion. Theology.
C	History—Auxiliary sciences.
D	History & topography (except America).
E	America General and U.S. General History.
F	U.S. Local and America Outside U.S. History.
G	Geography, Anthropology, Sports
H-HA	Social Sciences. General Statistics.
HB-HJ	Economics

(Outlines continue on page 24)

1903 outline (cont'd)		1904 outline (cont'd)	
J	Sociology	HM-HX	Sociology
		J	Political Science
K	Law	K	Law
L	Education Sports. Amusements	L	Education
M	Music	M	Music
N	Architecture. Graphic Arts	N	Fine arts
P	Philology (Language and literature)	P	Philology (Language and literature)
Q	Science	Q	Science
R	Medicine	R	Medicine
S	Agriculture. Plant and animal industry	S	Agriculture. Plant and animal industry
T	Technology	T	Technology
U	Military Science	U	Military Science
V	Naval Science	V	Naval Science
Z	Bibliography	Z	Bibliography

The Development of Individual Schedules

Class Z, Bibliography and Library Science, was chosen as the first schedule to be developed, as it would contain the bibliographical works necessary for the reclassification project.

In 1898 Martel prepared the first version of Class Z, Bibliography and Library Science, from a revision of the seventh expansion of Cutter's Class Z: Book Arts. The following table[17] shows the close relationship of Cutter's Class Z and the new L.C. Class Z.

Cutter		L.C.	
Z	Books Arts	Z	Bibliography and Library Science

Production ZA-ZK

ZA	Authorship		
ZB	Rhetoric		
ZC	Branches of literature		
		4-8	History of books and bookmaking
ZD	Writing: Paleography	40-115	Writing
ZE	Manuscripts	41-42	Autographs
ZF	Shorthand, Stenography	43-48	Calligraphy Penmanship
ZG	Penmanship, Calligraphy	49-51	Typewriting
		53-100	Shorthand
		103-104	Cryptography
		105-115	Paleography
ZH	Printing	116-550	Book industries and trade
ZI-ZJ	Incunabula and Blockbooks	116-265	Printing
ZK	Binding	266-275	Binding

Distribution ZL-ZM

ZL	Publishing and bookselling	278-550	Publishing and bookselling
ZM	Book Buying		
		551-661	Copyright. Intellectual property

(Lists continue on page 26)

Cutter (cont'd)		**L.C.** (cont'd)	
Storage and Use ZN-ZS		665-997	Libraries and library science
ZN	Private libraries		
ZP-ZS	Public libraries		
		998-1000	Book prices. Booksellers' catalogs
Description and Use ZT-ZZ		1001-8999	Bibliography
ZT	Publications		
ZU	Bibliography in general		
ZV	Anonymous and Pseudo-nymous books	1041-1107	Anonyms and pseudonyms
ZW	Subject and class bibliographies	1201-4941	National bibliography
		5051-7999	Subject bibliography
ZX	National bibliography	8001-8999	Personal bibliography
ZY	Literary history		
ZZ	Selection of reading		

Five subclasses, ZA Authorship, ZB Rhetoric, ZC Branches of literature, ZY Literary history, and ZZ Selection of reading, were not used by Martel. These were to be covered in subclass PN for General literature in Class P, Language and Literature. The remaining subclasses were all used. However, instead of using double letters to represent the subclasses, numerical subdivisions were used. Even Cutter's subclass ZF for Shorthand and Stenography was retained and expanded to include typewriting. This location often concerns the user of LC classification as other works on secretarial training occur in Class H.

Subject specialists at the Library of Congress developed each of the individual schedules, consulting bibliographies, treatises, comprehensive histories and the existing classification schemes in initially determining the scope and content of an individual class and subclass. The actual shelf arrangement of the books often established the final pattern for the sequence. The specialists worked on individual subclasses independently, with an editor in charge of the whole schedule.

The approach used in the development of L.C. Classification is discussed by Richard S. Angell, former Chief of the Subject Cataloging Division, in an article in *Law Library Journal*:

> While in general outline and sequence of topics it has affinity with earlier systems, the Library's schedules basically represent a fresh start in the design of a system for its own particular purposes. The schedules were developed one by one, by specialists working under a central direction, but with considerable independence. They were built up for the most part inductively, that is, by taking account of the collections of the Library as they existed and as they were expected to develop because of the Library's needs for comprehensive collections in all fields of knowledge.
>
> From these origins and impulses the Library of Congress classification has developed into a comprehensive practical system for the arrangement and management of collections of books. With one obvious exception [i.e., Class K, Law] it is a complete system, embracing all of the areas of human knowledge, the various components of this universe of knowledge having been allocated to the respective schedules. The objective in the partitioning of this universe is to secure well-defined areas corresponding to the concepts by which the separate fields are taught and expounded, and on which developmental research is based. Within each area the objective is to provide an orderly and apprehendable arrangement of the volumes in an array which will make direct access to the collections useful and meaningful to qualified students and scholars, and helpful to the staff in the control and servicing of items wanted for reference or circulation. To the extent that this partitioning is successful the classification as a whole becomes a seamless garment in that each of the parts exists basically for its place in the whole structure. At the same time the size and scope of the collections give each of the parts a considerable independence and self-sufficiency within its own field. This is particularly true of the manner in which certain common elements of a general classification scheme are treated in each of the parts of ours. Geographical and chronological arrangements, for example, are framed in accordance with the needs of each subject field; that is, they are not carried out by means of a single division table as is the case in certain other classifications. This feature of the schedules has been both criticized and praised; criticized for resulting in extremely detailed and bulky individual schedules, praised for the freedom allowed in each schedule for development according to its subject field's own intrinsic structure.[18]

One main unifying factor in all the classes is the notation consisting of letters, cardinal numbers, and Cutter numbers. Class D, developed in 1902, was the first schedule in which double letters were used instead of single letters as had been used in Classes Z and E-F. Since then, double letters have been used for subclasses in all schedules except in Classes Z and E-F in which only single letters have been used, and in Classes D and K in which triple letters are also used.

The publication of the individual schedules began in 1901 with Class E-F. By June 1, 1904, the classification of Classes D, E-F, M, Q. R, S, T, U, and Z had been completed. Classes A, C, G, H, and V were in the process of development. By 1948, all schedules, with the exception of those for Class K, had been completed and published. The schedule for Subclass KF, Law of the United States, the first schedule in Class K to be developed, was published in 1969. Since then, the schedules for Subclass K (Law [General]), Subclass KD (Law of the United Kingdom and Ireland), and Subclass KE (Law of Canada) have also appeared.

THE PURPOSE OF THE
LIBRARY OF CONGRESS CLASSIFICATION

The Library of Congress Classification was originally designed and developed as a utilitarian system for the use of the Library of Congress only. L.C. Classification was not based on any philosophical system for classifying knowledge. It was designed to classify the books of the Library of Congress collection and future expansions of the collections. Herbert Putnam emphasized practical consideration as a basis for the development of the L.C. Classification when he wrote in 1901:

> The system of classification thus far applied is one devised from a comparison of existing schemes (including the "decimal" and the "expansive"), and a consideration of the particular conditions in this Library, the character of its present and probable collections, and of its probable use. It is assumed that the departments of history, political and social science, and certain others will be unusually large. It is assumed that investigators will be more freely admitted to the shelves.

> The system devised has not sought to follow strictly the scientific order of subjects. It has sought rather convenient sequence of the various groups, considering them as groups of *books*, not as groups of mere subjects.[19]

This system was not intended for use by any library other than the Library of Congress. As L.C. Classification was being developed, no attempt was made to create a perfect general classification system which would be used by all major American libraries. The original attitude of the Library of Congress may be discerned in the following statement taken from its annual *Report* of 1916:

> In contrast with the card catalogue of the Library which, owing to the sale of the printed cards is a matter of general concern to libraries, the classification of our collections was assumed to be of concern solely to ourselves—that is to the efficient administration of this Library within itself. Upon this assumption the scheme adopted has been devised with reference (1) to the character and probable development of our own collections, (2) to its operation by our own staff, (3) to the character and habits of our own readers, and (4) to the usages in vogue here, a distinguishing feature

of which is the freedom of access to the shelves granted to serious investigators.

With these considerations the resultant scheme, while organic in the sense that certain fundamentals were the basis of each schedule, is unsymmetrical, since each schedule was devised with reference to its own utilities (as applied to that particular group of material) rather than with reference to its proportionate part in an integral whole.

There was therefore no expectation that the scheme would be adopted by other libraries; much less was there any profession that it would be suited to their needs. It is, moreover, still incomplete, and various schedules sufficiently advanced for our own use are yet unavailable in printed form.

Under the circumstances the number of other libraries that are already adopting it in whole or in part is somewhat surprising.[20]

Instead of being a classification of knowledge in the abstract, the L.C. Classification is based on literary warrant. The term literary warrant means that the schedules of a classification system have been developed with reference to the published literature, in other words, based on what the actual literature itself warrants. In the case of the L.C. Classification, literary warrant refers specifically to the Library's collection. Although much of the scheme is based on the literary warrant of the late nineteenth and early twentieth century, with the continuous revisions of the system, current literary warrant is taken into consideration, which causes new areas to develop. As Charles Bead pointed out in 1966,

> The LC classification, being completely based on the Library's collections, is coextensive in scope with the book stock of the Library of Congress. Therefore, the LC classification is comprehensive but not truly universal at the present time. Expansion of the classification is governed by and depends upon the acquisition of new material.[21]

Many of the problems in the use of L.C. Classification by other libraries result from its having been designed and developed for a single library with its specific services and collections. LaMontagne cites legislative reference as one of the services of the Library of Congress that determined the order of the individual classes of the system:

> The primary purpose of the Library, that of legislative reference, determined their order. The Classification, therefore, although universal in scope, is in its organization a special library classification.[22]

Presently a majority of American academic and research libraries as well as some major public libraries use L.C. Classification. A recent survey of libraries in the

United States and Canada revealed that approximately 14.7 percent use the L.C. Classification. Among large libraries, particularly university libraries, L.C. Classification users account for 62.3 percent of the libraries surveyed.[23] Outside of the United States and Canada, the use of the system is limited.

The classification system is directly sponsored and supported by a permanent national governmental organization, the Library of Congress. It is used and expanded daily by the Library's classifiers. Thus the system may be considered as a government-supported organic classification system. The results of the application of the system, i.e., the L.C. call numbers, are regularly included on L.C. cataloging records.

SUMMARY

This chapter has briefly surveyed the basic outlines of the classification systems used at the Library of Congress prior to the development of the present Library of Congress Classification system. The inherent weaknesses in the Jeffersonian system have been demonstrated. The reasons for the development of a new system for the Library of Congress, i.e., the weaknesses of that older system as well as the great physical growth of the Library's collections, were discussed. As a result of study of available classification schemes and systems of notation, and the dissatisfaction with decimal notation in particular, the Library of Congress developed its own unique classification system. Charles Ammi Cutter's *Expansive Classification* was used to develop the first class in the new system, Class Z, Bibliography and Library Science, and was a basis for the general outline of all the classes. A mixed notation of letters and numbers was found to satisfy the requirements of the new classification. The purpose of the L.C. Classification system was discussed with regard to the original intention and the subsequent adoption of the system by other libraries in the United States and Canada.

BIBLIOGRAPHY

History of the Library of Congress Classification

Bead, Charles C. "The Library of Congress Classification: Development, Characteristics, and Structure," in *The Use of the Library of Congress Classification; Proceedings of the Institute on the Use of the Library of Congress Classification*, edited by Richard H. Schimmelpfeng and C. Donald Cook. Chicago: American Library Association, 1968.
Pages 18-32 present a recent official statement on the development, characteristics and structure of L.C. Classification.

Childs, J. B. "Genesis of the Library of Congress Classification," *Herald of Library Science*, 15:330-34, July/Oct. 1976.

Cole, John Y. "The Library of Congress in the Nineteenth Century: An Informal Account," *The Journal of Library History*, 9:222-40, July 1974.
An interesting and readable paper on the history of the Library of Congress in the nineteenth century includes material on classification and is based on primary sources. Another article of Cole's that does not mention classification but describes the same period in relation to the development of the

Library of Congress as the national copyright depository is: "Of Copyright, Men, and a National Library," *Quarterly Journal of the Library of Congress*, 28:114-36, April 1971.

Hanson, J. C. M. "The Library of Congress and Its New Catalogue: Some Unwritten History," in *Essays Offered to Herbert Putnam by His Colleagues and Friends on His Thirtieth Anniversary as Librarian of Congress: 5 April 1929*. Edited by William Warner Bishop and Andrew Keogh. New Haven: Yale University Press, 1929, pp. 178-94.
This article contains much essential information about the beginnings of L.C. Classification as recorded by one of its founders.

Johnston, William Dawson. *History of the Library of Congress, 1800-1864*. Washington: GPO, 1904.
This volume is the first and only volume of a planned comprehensive history of the Library of Congress. The succeeding volumes were never completed or published.

Lacy, Dan. "Library of Congress: A Sesquincentenary Review," *Library Quarterly*, 20:157-79; 235-58, July and October 1950.
This two-part article presents many helpful facts about the history of the Library of Congress.

LaMontagne, Leo E. *American Library Classifications with Special Reference to the Library of Congress*. Hamden, CT: Shoe String Press, 1961.
Pages 27-62 deal with early American classification schemes and especially those at the Library of Congress. Based on primary sources.

Library of Congress in Perspective: A Volume Based on the Reports of the 1976 Librarian's Task Force and Advisory Groups. Edited by John Y. Cole. New York: R. R. Bowker Co., 1978.

Martel, Charles. "Classification: A Brief Conspectus of Present Day Library Practice," *Library Journal*, 36:410-16, Aug. 1911.

Martel, Charles. "Library of Congress Classification," *Bulletin of the American Library Association*, 5:230-32, July 1911.

Mearns, David Chambers. *The Story Up to Now, The Library of Congress, 1800-1946*. Washington: GPO, 1947.
This work is a reprint of the first section of the 1946 *Annual Report of the Librarian of Congress* (pages 13-227 in the Report). Although it is far less detailed than Johnston, it does provide information on the history of the classification systems, including the development of the present Library of Congress system.

Scott, Edith. "J. C. M. Hanson and His Contribution to Twentieth Century Cataloging." Diss., University of Chicago, 1970, pp. 177-228.
Contains discussion on the development of the Library of Congress Classification.

Spofford, Ainsworth Rand. *A Book for All Readers; Designed as an Aid to the Collection, Use and Preservation of Books and the Formulation of Public and Private Libraries.* 3rd ed., rev. New York: Putnam, 1909.
This book by one of the most important Librarians of Congress includes a section on classification of books, pages 362-72. Spofford makes some reference to the development of L.C. Classification as well as comments on other classification systems.

U.S. Library of Congress. *Alphabetical Catalogue of the Library of Congress: Authors.* Washington: GPO, 1864.
This was the first printed author catalog of the Library of Congress. It includes an interesting preface by Spofford.

U.S. Library of Congress. *Catalogue of the Library of Congress: Index of Subjects.* Washington: GPO, 1869. 2v.
This is the second major printed catalog to be issued by Spofford and also includes a useful preface.

U.S. Library of Congress. *Catalogue of the Library of the United States; To Which Is Annexed a Copious Index, Alphabetically Arranged.* Washington: Printed by Jonathan Elliot, 1815.
This is the first Library of Congress printed catalog to be arranged using the Jeffersonian classification system. It was edited by George Watterston.

U.S. Library of Congress. Jefferson Collection. *Catalogue of the Library of Thomas Jefferson.* Compiled with annotations by E. Millicent Sowerby. Washington: The Library of Congress, 1952-59. 5v.
This catalog lists the original Jefferson collection purchased by the Library of Congress. It is arranged in Jefferson's 44 chapters. The introduction to the first volume contains additional information on the Jefferson collection and its organization.

Supplemental Readings on Early Available Schemes
(With Particular Emphasis on Cutter's *Expansive Classification*)

Aldred, Thomas. "The Expansive Classification," *Library Association Record,* 7:207-19, 1905.
Discussion of Cutter's system from a British viewpoint.

American Library Association. *A.L.A. Catalog, 8,000 Volumes for a Popular Library, With Notes, 1904.* Prepared by the New York State Library and the Library of Congress under the Auspices of the American Library Association Publishing Board. Editor: Melvil Dewey. Associate editors: May Seymour and Mrs. H. L. Elmendorf. Part 1: Classed. Part 2: Dictionary. Washington: GPO, 1904.
Pages 5-7 contain an explanation and outline of the *Expansive Classification.* The entire first part consists of a two-column class number approach with the Dewey Decimal number on the left of the entry and Cutter Expansion number on the right. This work can be used as an interesting comparison of the two systems.

American Library Association. *Catalogue of the A.L.A. Library: Five Thousand Volumes for a Popular Library.* Washington: GPO, 1893.
Pages 145-256 show entries arranged according to the *Expansive Classification.* Sample pages of author and subject indexes are also included.

Bliss, Henry Evelyn. *The Organization of Knowledge in Libraries, and the Subject-Approach to Books.* New York: H. W. Wilson Co., 1934.
Pages 230-41 are thoughtful criticisms of the Expansive Classification.

Boston Athenaeum. *How to Get Books, with an Explanation of the New Way of Marking Books,* by Charles Ammi Cutter. Boston: Rockwell and Churchill, 1882.
This and the following nine entries represent a part of Cutter's work on classification in general and his Expansive system in particular.

Cutter, Charles Ammi. *Charles Ammi Cutter: Library Systematizer.* Edited by Francis L. Miksa. Littleton, CO: Libraries Unlimited, 1977.
Contains selections and excerpts of Cutter's writings and outlines of his Expansive Classification.

Cutter, Charles Ammi. "Classification on the Shelves," *Library Journal,* 4:234-43, July-Aug. 1879.
This article written while Cutter was Librarian at the Boston Athenaeum includes an account of the new scheme prepared for use at the Library. Cutter cites the value of relative classification instead of fixed location. He also comments on both the Decimal system of Dewey and his own Expansive system.

Cutter, Charles Ammi. "The Expansive Classification," in *Transactions and Proceedings of the Second International Library Conference, London, July 13-16, 1897.* London: Printed for Members of the Conference by Morrison & Giblex of Edinburgh, 1898, pp. 84-88.
This exposition of the Expansive system serves as an excellent introduction to that system. A synopsis for a special scheme for Shakespeare is included.

Cutter, Charles Ammi. *Expansive Classification.* Part 1: The First Six Classifications. Boston: C. A. Cutter, 1891-1893.
This is the only completed work by Cutter on his classification system. The first six expansions are included with instructions for the use of each.

Cutter, Charles Ammi. *Expansive Classification.* Part 2: Seventh Classification. Ed. by W. P. Cutter. Boston (Northampton, MA): 1896-1911. 2v. with suppl. pages.
Much of the seventh expansion was completed by Cutter's nephew, William P. Cutter, after the elder Cutter's death. This work was issued in parts and is difficult to describe bibliographically.

Cutter, Charles Ammi. *Explanation of the Cutter-Sanborn Author-Marks Three-Figure Tables.* Rev. by Kate Amery Jones. Northampton, MA: Kingsburg Press, 1935.

Cutter, Charles Ammi. *Local List*. Boston: C. A. Cutter, 189?.

Cutter, Charles Ammi. *Subject Divisions under Countries instead of Country Divisions under Subjects*. Boston: C. A. Cutter, 189?.

Cutter, Charles Ammi. "Suitability of the Expansive Classification to College and Reference Libraries," *Library Journal*, 24:C41-49, July 1899.
This is an interesting discussion by Cutter with examples of the uses and especially the notation of his system. He also included some comments on the Decimal system.

Cutter, William Parker. *Charles Ammi Cutter*. Chicago: American Library Association, 1931.

Dewey, Melvil. *Decimal Classification and Relativ Index for Libraries, Clippings, Notes, etc.* 5th ed. Boston: Library Bureau, 1894.
This is the edition of Dewey's *Decimal Classification* that was available for consideration by Hanson and Martel.

Eaton, Thelma. "The Development of Classification in America," in *The Role of Classification in the Modern American Library. Papers presented at an Institute Conducted by the University of Illinois Graduate School of Library Science, November 1-4, 1959*. Champaign, IL: Illini Union Bookstore, 1959. pp. 8-30.
This is a short but sound summary of the history of American library classification.

Halle. Universität. Bibliothek. *Schema des Realkatalogs*. Leipzig: O. Harrassowitz, 1888.
This is the *Halle Schema* primarily developed by Otto Harwig. It, as well as Dewey's fifth edition, was considered and rejected by Hanson and Martel.

Immroth, John Phillip. "Expansive Classification," *Encyclopedia of Library and Information Science*, 8:297-316, 1972.
This is a general review of the Expansive Classification including the entire general outline for the sixth expansion, discussions of Biscoe Date-Letters, Cutter author-marks, criticism, and use.

Lamb, Eliza. "The Expansive Classification in Use," *Library Quarterly*, 4:265-69, April 1934.
The use of the *Expansive Classification* in the twentieth century at the University of Wisconsin Libraries is presented in this article.

LaMontagne, Leo E. *American Library Classification with Special Reference to the Library of Congress*. Hamden, CT: Shoe String Press, 1961.

Phillips, W. Howard. *A Primer of Book Classification*. 5th ed. London: Association of Assistant Librarians, 1961.
Pages 83-94 cover the Expansive Classification.

Sayers, W. C. Berwick. *Canons of Classification, Applied to "The Subject," "The Expansive," "The Decimal," and "The Library of Congress" Classifications: A Study in Bibliographical Classification Method.* London: Grafton, 1915.
The Expansive Classification is discussed on pages 67-93.

Sayers, W. C. Berwick. *An Introduction to Library Classification: Theoretical, Historical and Practical with Readings, Exercises and Examination Papers.* 9th ed. London: Grafton, 1954.
Pages 93-99 deal with the Expansive Classification.

Sayers, W. C. Berwick. *A Manual of Classification for Librarians and Bibliographers.* 3rd ed., rev. with some corrections. London: Andre Deutsch, 1959.
Another similar presentation of the Expansive Classification on pages 141-50.

Tauber, Maurice F., and Edith Wise. *Classification Systems.* Vol. 1, pt. 4 of *The State of Library Art*, edited by Ralph R. Shaw. New Brunswick, NJ: Graduate School of Library Service, Rutgers, The State University, 1961.
Pages 108-139 give a complete survey of material about the Expansive Classification.

A Selected List of
Additional Early Classification Schemes

Edmands, John. *New System of Classification and Scheme for Numbering Books, Applied to the Mercantile Library of Philadelphia.* Philadelphia: Grant, Faires & Rodgers, printers, 1883.

Fletcher, William I. *Library Classification.* Reprinted, with alterations, additions, and an index from his "Public Libraries in America." Boston: Roberts Bros., 1894.

Harris, William T. *Essay on the System of Classification.* St. Louis: Missouri Democrat and Job Printing House, 1870.
This is a reprint from the *Catalogue, Classified and Alphabetical, of the Books of the St. Louis Public School Library* (St. Louis: Missouri Democrat and Job Printing House, 1870), pp. ix-xvi, which also contains Harris' "System of Classification."

Perkins, Fred B. *A Rational Classification of Literature for Shelving and Cataloging Books in a Library.* Rev. ed. San Francisco: Francis, Valentine & Co., printers, 1882.

Schleiermacher, A. A. E. *Bibliographisches System der Gesammten Wissenschaftskunde, mit einer Anleitung zum Ordnen von Bibliotheken . . .* Braunschweig: Vieweg, 1852.

Shurtleff, Nathaniel B. *A Decimal System for the Arrangement and Administration of Libraries.* Boston: Priv. print., 1856.
This is a decimal notation for the fixed location of materials, which was used at the Boston Public Library.

Smith, Lloyd P. *On the Classification of Books. A Paper Read Before the American Library Association, May, 1882.* Boston: Library Bureau, 1882.

Steffenhagen, Emil. *Die Ordnungsprincipien der Universitäts-Bibliothek Kiel . . .* Burg: Hopfer, 1888.

NOTES

[1] *The Library of Congress in Perspective: A Volume Based on the Reports of the 1976 Librarian's Task Force and Advisory Groups*, edited by John Y. Cole (New York: R. R. Bowker, 1978), p. 5.

[2] William Dawson Johnston, *History of the Library of Congress, 1800-1864* (Washington: GPO, 1904), p. 49 and plate 29.

[3] Johnston, *History*, pp. 145-46.

[4] Johnston, *History*, p. 148.

[5] Johnston, *History*, p. 368.

[6] Leo E. LaMontagne, *American Library Classification with Special Reference to the Library of Congress* (Hamden, CT: Shoe String Press, 1961), pp. 55-56.

[7] David Chambers Mearns, *The Story Up to Now, The Library of Congress, 1800-1946* (Washington: GPO, 1947), p. 162.

[8] LaMontagne, *American Library Classification*, p. 218.

[9] LaMontagne, *American Library Classification*, p. 223.

[10] LaMontagne, *American Library Classification*, p. 224.

[11] J. C. M. Hanson, "The Library of Congress and Its New Catalogue: Some Unwritten History," in *Essays Offered to Herbert Putnam by His Colleagues and Friends on His Thirtieth Anniversary as Librarian of Congress: 5 April 1929.* New Haven: Yale University Press, 1929, pp. 186-87.

[12] LaMontagne, *American Library Classification*, p. 227.

[13] Edith Scott, "J. C. M. Hanson and His Contribution to Twentieth Century Cataloging," Diss., University of Chicago, 1970, pp. 177-228.

[14] Charles Ammi Cutter, *Charles Ammi Cutter: Library Systematizer*, ed. by Francis L. Miksa (Littleton, CO: Libraries Unlimited, 1977), pp. 280-82.

[15]LaMontagne, *American Library Classifications*, pp. 228-29.

[16]LaMontagne, *American Library Classifications*, pp. 234-36.

[17]LaMontagne, *American Library Classifications*, pp. 226-27.

[18]Richard S. Angell, "Development of Class K at the Library of Congress," *Law Library Journal*, 57 (Nov. 1964):353-54.

[19]Herbert Putnam, "Manual: Constitution, Organization, Methods, etc.," in *Report of the Librarian of Congress for the Fiscal Year Ending June 30, 1901* (Washington: GPO, 1901), p. 234.

[20]U.S. Library of Congress, *Report of the Librarian of Congress and Report of the Superintendent of Library Grounds for the Fiscal Year Ending June 30, 1916* (Washington: GPO, 1916), p. 103.

[21]Charles C. Bead, "The Library of Congress Classification: Development, Characteristics, and Structure," in *The Use of the Library of Congress Classification; Proceedings of the Institute on the Use of the Library of Congress Classification*, edited by Richard H. Schimmelpfeng and C. Donald Cook (Chicago: American Library Association, 1968), p. 18.

[22]LaMontagne, *American Library Classifications*, p. 253.

[23]John P. Comaromi, Mary Ellen Michael, and Janet Bloom, "A Survey of the Use of the Dewey Decimal Classification in the United States and Canada." Prepared for Forest Press, Lake Placid Foundation, November 1975, pp. 13, 16.

2   PRINCIPLES, STRUCTURE, AND FORMAT

CLASSIFICATION

As discussed in the previous chapter, the basic outline of the Library of Congress Classification was adopted from Cutter's *Expansive Classification.* As typical of nineteenth century American classification systems, the entire field of knowledge is divided into main classes which correspond largely to academic disciplines. The main classes are then divided into subclasses, representing branches of the major disciplines. Within each subclass, further subdivisions are provided to specify form, place, time, and subject (or topical) aspects. The progression is from the general to the specific, forming a hierarchical display of knowledge.

In developing the L.C. Classification, certain assumptions were made. LaMontagne states the basic orientation of the system:

> It was recognized that the classification should, in brief,
>
> 1. be oriented primarily toward the requirements of the Congress and secondarily to those of other government departments and agencies, scholars, and all other users;
> 2. provide for large amounts of diverse material, both scholarly and popular, for which no existing classification was adequate; and
> 3. afford a systematic approach to the Library's resources through the classed catalog and the arrangement of the books on the shelves.[1]

Based on these assumptions and adapted from Cutter's *Expansive Classification,* the structure of the L.C. Classification evolved and resulted in the following:

I.	A	General Works. Polygraphy
II.	B-P	Humanistic Disciplines and the Social Sciences
	B-BJ	Philosophy
	BL-BX	Religion
	C-F	History
	C	Auxiliary Sciences
	D	Universal and Old World
	E-F	America
	G	Geography. Anthropology. Folklore, etc.
	H-L	Social Sciences
	H	General
	HA	Statistics

II.		Humanistic Disciplines and the Social Sciences (cont'd)
	HB-HJ	Economics
	HM-HX	Sociology
	J	Political Science
	K	Law
	L	Education
	M	Music
	N	Fine Arts
	P	Language and Literature
III.	Q-V	Natural Sciences and Technology
	Q	General Science
	QA	Mathematics
	QB-QE	Physical Sciences
	QB	Astronomy
	QC	Physics
	QD	Chemistry
	QE	Geology
	QH-QR	Biological Sciences
	QH	Natural History. General Biology. Cytology
	QK	Botany
	QL	Zoology
	QM	Human Anatomy
	QP	Physiology
	QR	Bacteriology. Microbiology
	R	Medicine
	S	Agriculture
	T	Technology
	U	Military Science
	V	Naval Science
IV.	Z	Bibliography and Library Science

The rationale for the collocation of main classes and subclasses has been articulated by Martel:

> The concept underlying it may be stated as follows: (1. Class A) General works: Periodicals, Societies, Collections, Encyclopedic works, etc. (2. Class B) Theory, or theories, of man concerning the universe: Philosophy and Religion. (3.-6. Classes C-F) History and auxiliary sciences. (7. Class G) Geography and Anthropology: G, Descriptive and physical geography—man's abode and source of his means of subsistence; GF, Anthropogeography—man as affected by and affecting his physical milieu; GN, Physical anthropology and ethnology and Primitive or Prehistoric man; GR, Folklore, Tradition—mind and soul of man in transition from primitive to advanced culture; GT, Manners and customs; and GV, Amusements, sports, etc., related to GR; as a class, G may be therefore regarded as supplementary to History and leading to groups (8.-9. Classes H-J) Economic and Social evolution of man,

(10. Class K) Law, (11. Class L) Education, and (12. Class M), (13. Class N), and (14. Class P) Fine arts and Letters—the esthetic and intellectual development and state of man. Together, classes B-P form the group of the Philosophico-historical and philological sciences. The second group embraces the Mathematico-physical, Natural, and Applied Sciences: (15. Class Q) Science, (16. Class R) Medicine, (17. Class S) Agriculture, (18. Class T) Technology, (19. Class U) Military science, and (20. Class V) Naval science. Bibliography, which in many libraries is distributed through the different classes, is kept together in the Library of Congress and forms together with Library science (21. Class Z).[2]

NOTATION

The notation is a mixed system utilizing letters in the alphabet and arabic numerals. Main classes are denoted by single capital letters. Double or triple capital letters represent subclasses. One notes that the classes in history and in the area of social sciences occupy a larger amount of space (Classes C-L) within the notational structure, as compared to natural sciences and technology (Classes Q-V). It has been assumed from the beginning that the Library serving the Congress would possess an extensive collection in history and social sciences.

Within each main class or subclass, the integers 1-9999 (some with decimal extensions) are used for subdivisions. The earlier decision not to use decimal numbers was rescinded later, and decimal extensions of integers are used where there are no available integers for new subjects.

After the first combination of letter(s) and numerals, another combination follows. This is called a Cutter number, based on the book numbering system devised by Charles Ammi Cutter. The Cutter number is always preceded by a period (.) and the number following the period is treated decimally.

Details concerning the notation will be presented in chapters 3 and 4.

ENUMERATIVE DISPLAY

The L.C. Classification is essentially an enumerative scheme in that aspects of a subject are pre-coordinated and enumerated. Relatively little notational synthesis exists in the system. Even form divisions and common divisions are enumerated under each subject. Auxiliary tables are used for the purpose of pinpointing specific numbers within a range of numbers provided in the main schedule, rather than for the purpose of providing additional notational segments to be added to the main number in order to render it more specific, as in the case of *Decimal Classification*, *Bliss Bibliographic Classification*, and *Colon Classification*. As a result of enumeration, the schedules are more voluminous than any of the other systems.

GENERAL CHARACTERISTICS AND COMMON FEATURES

Because the individual schedules of the L.C. Classification have been developed separately by different groups of persons working more or less independently, the system has been viewed as a "series of special classifications."[3] Nonetheless, there are certain unifying characteristics common to all the schedules, namely, the physical format of each schedule, internal arrangement of classes and subclasses, the notation, and auxiliary tables. These are discussed in detail below.

Physical Format

The Individual Schedules

The schedules for L.C. Classification published so far comprise 34 individual volumes for the main classes and subclasses. A full set of schedules contains over 10,000 pages. The individual schedules are:

A   General works: 4th ed. (1973)

B   Philosophy. Psychology. Religion.
      Part I. B-BJ: Philosophy. Psychology. 3rd ed. (1979)
      Part II. BL-BX: Religion. 2nd ed. (1962)

C   Auxiliary Sciences of History. 3rd ed. (1975)

D   History: General and Old World. 2nd ed. (1959) Reissue with supplementary
      pages, 1966

E-F   History: America. 3rd ed. (1958) Reissue with supplementary pages, 1965

G   Geography. Anthropology. Recreation. 4th ed. (1976)

H   Social Sciences. 3rd ed. (1950) Reissue with supplementary pages, 1965

J   Political Science. 2nd ed. (1924) Reissue with supplementary pages, 1966

K   Law
      K: Law [General] (1977)
      KD: Law of the United Kingdom and Ireland (1973)
      KE: Law of Canada (1976)
      KF: Law of the United States. Prelim. ed. (1969)

L   Education. 3rd ed. (1951) Reissue with supplementary pages, 1966

M   Music, Books on Music. 3rd ed. (1978)

N   Fine Arts. 4th ed. (1970)

P   Philology and Literature.
      P-PA: General Philology and Linguistics. Classical Languages and Literatures (1928) Reissue with supplementary pages, 1968
      PA Supplement: Byzantine and Modern Greek Literature. Medieval and Modern Latin Literature. (1942) Reissue with supplementary pages, 1968
      PB-PH: Modern European Languages. (1933) Reissue with supplementary pages, 1966
      PG: Russian Literature. (1948) Reissue with supplementary pages, 1965

(Schedule continues on page 42)

P   (cont'd)

    PJ-PM: Languages and Literatures of Asia, Africa, Oceania. American Indian Languages; Artificial Languages. (1935) Reissue with supplementary pages, 1965

    P-PM Supplement: Index to Languages and Dialects. 2nd ed. (1957) Reissue with supplementary pages, 1965

    PN, PR, PS, PZ: General Literature. English and American Literature. Fiction in English. Juvenile Literature. 2nd ed. (1978)

    PQ, Part 1: French Literature. (1936) Reissue with supplementary pages, 1966

    PQ, Part 2: Italian, Spanish, and Portuguese Literatures. (1937) Reissue with supplementary pages, 1965

    PT, Part 1: German Literature. (1938) Reissue with supplementary pages, 1966

    PT, Part 2: Dutch and Scandinavian Literatures. (1942) Reissue with supplementary pages, 1965

Q   Science. 6th ed. (1973)

R   Medicine. 3rd ed. (1952) Reissue with supplementary pages, 1966

S   Agriculture, etc. 3rd ed. (1948) Reissue with supplementary pages, 1965

T   Technology. 5th ed. (1971)

U   Military Science. 4th ed. (1974)

V   Naval Science. 3rd ed. (1974)

Z   Bibliography. Library Science. 4th ed. (1959) Reissue with supplementary pages, 1965

Besides these schedules, there is an outline (4th ed., 1978) for the entire system. Class K, Law, is only partially completed and published.

Format of Each Schedule

Each schedule has a similar if not identical format. The usual elements making up each schedule are 1) a prefatory note, containing a brief history of the schedule as well as concise remarks on the scope of the schedule; 2) a synopsis*, consisting of a list of all double letters covered in the schedule; 3) an outline, in greater detail than the synopsis of the portion of the classification covered in the schedule; 4) the schedule, containing the main classification tables; 5) any necessary auxiliary tables; 6) a detailed index; and 7) any supplementary pages of additions and changes to the schedule. Not all schedules have auxiliary tables; and some do not have an index (e.g., Subclass PQ, pt. 1 or pt. 2). Usually, if there is no index to a schedule, there is an extensive outline at the beginning of the schedule.

The following is an example of the synopsis to Class Q. The synopsis is simply a list of all the double letters or subclasses appearing in the individual schedules.

---

*This has been left out of some of the recently published schedules.

SYNOPSIS

Q   SCIENCE (GENERAL)

QA   MATHEMATICS

QB   ASTRONOMY

QC   PHYSICS

QD   CHEMISTRY

QE   GEOLOGY

QH   NATURAL HISTORY (GENERAL). BIOLOGY (GENERAL)

QK   BOTANY

QL   ZOOLOGY

QM   HUMAN ANATOMY

QP   PHYSIOLOGY

QR   MICROBIOLOGY

Synopsis for each of the classes in the L.C. Classification is included in chapter 5 of this guide.

A small portion of the outline to Class Q is given below to demonstrate the greater detail represented in the outline. The outlines to the schedules can be most useful to the beginning classifier. Any logical or hierarchical order of the schedule may be readily discerned.

OUTLINE

Q   **SCIENCE**

1-295	General
300-380	Cybernetics
350-380	Information theory

QA   **MATHEMATICS**

1-99	General
76-76.8	Computers. Computer science
101-141.8	Arithmetic
150-271	Algebra
273-280	Probabilities. Mathematical statistics
300-433	Analysis
440-699	Geometry. Trigonometry. Topology
801-939	Analytic mechanics

(Outline continues on page 44)

QB		**ASTRONOMY**
	1-139	General
	145-237	Practical and spherical astronomy
	275-343	Geodesy
	351-421	Theoretical astronomy and celestial mechanics
	500-903	Descriptive astronomy
	981-991	Cosmogony. Cosmology

QC		**PHYSICS**
	1-75	General
	81-114	Weights and measures
	120-168	Descriptive and experimental mechanics
	170-197	Atomic physics. Constitution and properties of matter
		Including relativity, quantum theory, and solid-state physics
	221-246	Acoustics. Sound
	251-338.5	Heat
	310.15-319	Thermodynamics
	350-467	Optics. Light
	450-467	Spectroscopy
	474-496.9	Radiation physics
	501-766	Electricity and magnetism
	501-718.8	Electricity
	669-675.5	Electromagnetic theory
	676-678.6	Radio waves (Theory)
	717.6-718.8	Plasma physics
	750-766	Magnetism
	770-798	Nuclear and particle physics. Atomic energy. Radioactivity
	793-793.5	Elementary particle physics
	794.95-798	Radioactivity
	801-809	Geophysics. Cosmic physics
	811-849	Geomagnetism
	851-999	Meteorology. Climatology
		Including cloud and weather modification
	974.5-976	Meteorological optics
	980-999	Climatology and weather
	994.95-999	Weather forecasting

The main portion of the schedule, listing the class numbers and captions, appears next. The following example is a small section of the first page of the schedule for Class Q. For instance, a general scientific periodical in the German language would be assigned the basic notation of "Q3." A general yearbook in science would be classed in "Q9."

Q   **SCIENCE (GENERAL)**

For applied science and technology, *see* T

	Periodicals. By language of publication
1.A1A-Z	Polyglot
.A3-Z	English
2	French
3	German
4	Other languages (not A-Z)
9	Yearbooks
	Collected works (nonserial), *see* Q111-113
	Societies
	Including works about societies, serial publications of societies
10	International
	America
11	United States
21	Canada
22	Latin America
23	Mexico
25	Central America
29	West Indies
33	South America
	Europe
41	Great Britain
44	Czechoslovak Republic

The next example shows a partial section of one of the tables in Class G. The use of tables is discussed in chapters 4 and 5.

TABLE IV

REGIONS (UNITED STATES)

.A1-19	Regions
.A11	New England
.A115	Northeastern States
.A12	Middle Atlantic States
.A124	Potomac Valley
.A13	South
.A135	Tennessee Valley
.A137	Ozark Mountain region

In most of the schedules, a detailed index of the individual schedule follows the main classification section and the auxiliary tables. Schedules PB-PH, PG (in part), PJ-PM, PQ parts 1 and 2, and PT parts 1 and 2 have no indexes. There are some references from one schedule to another in the indexes, but in most cases the indexes refer only to the individual schedules of which they are a part. The following example is taken from Class Q.

INDEX

A

ACTH, *see* Adrenocorticotrophic hormone
Aardvarks (Zoology): QL737.T8
Abacus (Mathematics): QA75
Abdomen (Human anatomy): QM543
Abelian functions (Mathematical analysis): QA345
Aberration
    Astronomy: QB163
    Electromagnetic theory: QC671
Abietaceae (Botany): QK494.5.P66
Abrocomidae (Zoology): QL737.R62
Abscission (Plant physiology): QK763
Absolute differential calculus (Mathematical analysis): QA433

Acarina
    Paleozoology: QE826.A2
    Zoology: QL458-458.2
Acarophilism (Plant ecology): QK924
Acceleration (Physiological effect): QP82.2.A2
Acceleration, Heart (Physiology): QP113
Accelerators, Electron (Nuclear and particle physics): QC787.P3
Accelerators, Linear (Nuclear and particle physics): QC787.L5
Accelerators, Particle: QC787.P3
Accelerators, Plasma: QC718.5.M36
Accelerators, Van de Graaff (Nuclear and particle physics): QC787.V3
Accentors (Zoology): QL696.P266

The seventh part of the format of each schedule is the possible inclusion of a section of additions and changes to the individual class numbers in the schedule. A brief extraction of the additions and changes to Class J may be seen below. In most cases there are far more additions to the schedules than there are changes.

ADDITIONS AND CHANGES TO OCTOBER 1965

J

(Under "British possessions," *add or revise as indicated.)* p. 51

705	**Union of South Africa.**
707	Cape of Good Hope.
708	Special divisions, A−Z.
	e.g. .T7 Transkeian Territories.
709	Basutoland.
721	**Central Africa.**
723	Bechuanaland.
725	Rhodesia. Federation of Rhodesia and Nyasaland.
.3	Northern Rhodesia.
.5	Southern Rhodesia.
	Mashonaland.
	Matabeleland.

Divisions

Initially, the arrangement of divisions within a class, subclass, or subject followed a general pattern, often called "Martel's seven points." In developing the individual schedules, the subject specialists made use of these seven points or appropriate parts of them. They are:

1) General form divisions: Periodicals, Societies, Collections, Dictionaries, etc.
2) Theory, Philosophy
3) History
4) Treatises, General works
5) Law, Regulation, State Relations*
6) Study and teaching
7) Special subjects and subdivisions of subjects progressing from the more general to the specific and as far as possible in logical order.

In practice today, no attempt is made to follow Martel's seven points precisely. Each schedule now has its own model for the breakdown of the discipline. Any number of categories of divisions may appear in a particular schedule, but are not necessarily in the order above. The following is a discussion of general types of division with examples.

General Form Divisions

In addition to periodicals, societies, collections, and dictionaries, general form divisions may consist of congresses, exhibitions, museums, yearbooks, documents, or any general form division peculiar to a specific class or subclass. An example of this is shown in the following extract from the beginning of Subclass CR.

CR HERALDRY

1	Periodicals. Societies. Serials
2	Congresses
	Collected works (nonserial)
4	Several authors
5	Individual authors
9	Museums. Exhibitions
	Subarranged by city or other place of exhibition
11	Directories
13	Dictionaries. Encyclopedias

Unlike other classification systems which usually have a standard set of form subdivisions applicable to all subjects, in the L.C. Classification, form divisions are

---

*Since the development of the K schedules, legal topics relating to specific subjects have been moved to Class K.

developed individually under each subject, based largely on literary warrant. Generally, broader subjects on which there is a larger amount of library material are provided with more form divisions. Many narrow subjects do not have any form divisions at all.

Although the general form divisions usually precede all other divisions, this is not an absolute rule. For instance, "CN 70 Dictionaries. Encyclopedias" is separated from the other general form divisions by the elements "CN 40 Philosophy. Theory," "CN 44 Methodology. Technique," "CN 50 Study and teaching," and "CN 55-62 History," as may be seen in the following example.

CN EPIGRAPHY

1	Periodicals. Societies. Serials
15	Congresses
	Collected works (nonserial)
20	Several authors
.5	Individual authors
25	Museums, libraries, and other institutions. By place, A-Z
30	Private collections
40	Philosophy. Theory
41	Relation to archaeology, history, etc.
	Relation to architectural decoration, *see* NA4050.I5
42	Relation to religion
44	Methodology. Technique
46	Photographic methods
50	Study and teaching
55	History of epigraphy (General)
	Biography of epigraphists
61	Collective
62	Individual, A-Z
70	Dictionaries. Encyclopedias

Theory, Philosophy

This second element of the general principle of arrangement is used primarily in the main classes and subclasses. It is often only a single number, such as "CN 40, Philosophy. Theory." However, this element, like all the other elements, may be expanded to many numbers in some instances. The theory and philosophy of literature, PN 45-57, receives 13 numbers (see page 49). This particular element may be compared to the standard subdivision "01" in *Decimal Classification*.

PN LITERATURE

Theory. Philosophy. Esthetics

45	General works. Ideals, content, etc. Plots, motives
.5	Forms of literature
	General special. Relation to and treatment of special elements, problems, and subjects
46	Inspiration
47	Life
48	Nature
	Cf. PN56.F5, Fishing
	PN56.G3, Gardens
	PR143, English literature
	PR508.N3, English poetry
	PQ145.3, French literature
	PQ473, French poetry
	etc.
49	Philosophy, ethics, religion, etc.
	Cf. PN1077, Poetry
	PN1647 +, Drama
	PN3347 +, Prose
50	Relation to history
51	Relation to sociology, economics, political science, etc. (social ideals, forces, etc. in literature)
52	Relation to education
53	Relation to art
54	Relation to language
55	Relation to science
	Other special
56	Topics, A-Z
	. . . . . .
	Characters
56.5	Special classes of people
	. . . . . .
57	Individual characters, A-Z

History

The history element of a class or subject is most commonly divided chronologically. This may be seen in Subclass JV6021-6033 for the history of emigration and immigration (see page 50).

JV EMIGRATION AND IMMIGRATION

History

6021	General.

By period.

Under each: (1) General.
(2) Special.

6023-4	Ancient.
6026-7	Medieval to 1800.
6029-30	19th century.
6032-3	20th century.

When period divisions are provided under a topic and the work being classified covers several of the time spans listed, the class number which corresponds to the earliest period on which the work focuses is assigned. If the work also contains material pertaining to even earlier periods which is offered only to introduce briefly the principal time periods under discussion, this introductory material is ignored for classification purposes.

In classifying other editions of the same work, the same class number is used, if the time period covered in each edition remains essentially the same. The same class number is assigned even though the time span covered by a new edition is substantially enlarged, as long as the earliest period covered on which the new edition focuses remains unchanged. On the other hand, if in a new edition the time span covered is enlarged so as to focus first on a later time period provided in the schedule, the number for the later period is assigned. In such cases, the new edition will not stand with the old on the shelves.

Frequently, the history division is combined in some manner with a provision for individual regions and countries.

Treatises, General Works

This element is used for comprehensive works covering a particular class, subclass, or subject. The caption used with this element may be "Treatises," "General works," or "General."

The provision for "General" or "General works" often appears in sequence with the provision for "General special," which means special aspects relating to the subject as a whole and does not include any hierarchical divisions or branches of the subject. In some of the recent editions of L.C. schedules, the caption "Special aspects of the subject as a whole" accompanies, or appears in place of, the caption "General special."

CS GENEALOGY

General works

9	American and English
10	French
11	German
12	Other languages (not A-Z)
14	General special

For example, L. G. Pine's *Trace Your Ancestors*, a general work on genealogy, is classed in "CS 9," and B. H. Kidd's *Using Maps in Tracing Your Family History*, which deals with a special aspect of genealogy, is classed in "CS 14."

Occasionally, there are provisions for "Epitomes," "Outlines," and "Minor works" in this sequence. An epitome may be defined as an annotated outline or chronology. An outline is frequently used to mean a skeletal structure. A minor work means one covering a comprehensive subject but not in a comprehensive fashion. Pamphlets and "addresses, essays, lectures" (if not specifically provided for) are often classed as "minor works."

Often, the element of "Treatises, General works" is subdivided chronologically. "Early works through 1800" and "1801- " are the most common chronological divisions, although others are used also.

CN EPIGRAPHY

	General works
74	Early works through 1800
75	1801-
77	General special
86	Juvenile works
90	Addresses, essays, lectures

In chronological arrangements of this type, the class number which corresponds to the imprint date of the work being cataloged is used.

Under certain subjects, chronological division both by period covered and by date of publication may be provided. Following is an example of provision for this kind of division under a particular subject.

QA MATHEMATICS

	History
21	General
22	Ancient
23	Medieval
	Modern
	General, *see* QA21
24	16th-18th centuries
26	19th-20th centuries
27	By region or country, A-Z
	Biography
28	Collective
29	Individual, A-Z
	e.g. .G3 Gauss
	.J2 Jacobi
	.N2 Napier
30	Directories
	Early works through 1800
31	Greek
	Including translations and commentaries
	For Euclid's Elements as school textbooks, *see* QA451
32	Medieval
33	1501-1700
35	1701-1800
	General works
36	Comprehensive treatises
	Textbooks
.5	Series of textbooks
	Advanced
37	1801-1969
.2	1970-
	Intermediate (without calculus)
39	1801-1969
.2	1970-
	Elementary, *see* QA101-107
40	Handbooks, manuals, etc.
	Popular works, *see* QA93
.5	Juvenile works
41	Formulas, notation, abbreviations
43	Problems, exercises, examinations

Law, Regulation, State Relations

This particular element, which was previously most widely used in the social sciences and is still found in some of the earlier schedules, is disappearing as Class K, Law, is being completed. The provisions for legal topics in subject classes are being cancelled as the schedules are revised. All legal publications are now classed in Class K, Law, and Subclass JX, International law.

Study and Teaching

This element often occurs as a single number as it does in "CN 50, Study and teaching" of epigraphy. Just as in the case of "Theory, Philosophy," "Study and Teaching" may be said to parallel a standard subdivision in *Decimal Classification*, "07." Occasionally, "Study and Teaching" will use more than a single number as in the case of "PR 31-55, Study and teaching of English literature," in which the whole number PR 55 is devoted solely to biographies of teachers of English literature.

PR   ENGLISH LITERATURE

	Study and teaching
	Study and teaching
31	Periodicals. Serials
33	General works. Treatises, etc.
	Outlines, syllabi, etc., *see* PR87 +
35	General special
37	Addresses, essays, lectures
	By period
41	Middle ages to 1600
43	17th-18th centuries
45	19th century
47	20th century
51	By region or country, A-Z
53	By school, A-Z
55	Biography of teachers of English literature, A-Z

In one instance, "MT 1-950," study and teaching of music, an entire subclass is devoted to this element.

Subjects and Subdivisions of Subjects

This last element describes the bulk of the individual developments or expansions of classes, subclasses, and subjects. Insofar as possible, a logical order is employed. "JN 1291-1381," the numbers for civil and political rights in Scotland, may be used as an example of this. The logical subdivisions of this particular subject are Citizenship, Naturalization, Suffrage, Electoral system, Contested elections, and Corrupt practices. Obviously, one subdivision naturally or logically precedes the other. For example, one cannot have a contested election until an electoral system is present. See example on page 54.

JN   CONSTITUTIONAL HISTORY – GREAT BRITAIN

Scotland.

Civil and political rights.
                Citizenship
        1291   General.
        1295   Law.
        1299   Special topics.
                Naturalization.
        1305   General.
        1309   Law.
        1311   Special topics.
                Suffrage.
                General.
        1321   Documents.
        1325   History.
        1329   Other.
        1333   Special.
                Electoral system.
        1341   General.
        1346   Law, by date.
        1351   Contested elections.
        1361   Corrupt practices.

The specialists responsible for each subject attempted to develop this point appropriately and independently for all classes, subclasses, and subjects. Geographic division often naturally occurs in this last element of Martel's Seven Points.

Geographic Division

The geographic division in L.C. schedules follows one of two general patterns. Continents and countries are either arranged in a preferred order or arranged alphabetically. Major geographic areas are generally arranged in the following preferred order for American users.

America.
    North America.
        United States.
        British North America. Canada.
        Mexico.
    Central America.
    West Indies.
    South America.
Europe.
    Great Britain.
    Continental Countries.
Asia.
Africa.
Australia and New Zealand.
Pacific Islands.
Arctic regions.
Antarctic regions.

Within each region further subdivision is made either naturally or alphabetically. The alphabetical geographic division is used when one class number is assigned to the geographic division, e.g., "By region or country, A-Z."[4]

The use of geographic division by preferred order allows a particular geographic area to have its own specific and even unique subject subdivisions. This application of geographic division may be called subject division under country.

Subject Division under Country

Often in the L.C. Classification, especially in the social sciences, subject division under country is used instead of country division under subject. In *Decimal Classification* a subject is usually subdivided fully before adding any geographic division; in the L.C. Classification, however, a class or subclass may be divided geographically and then have further subject subdivisions. It is most obvious in Classes C-G (History and Geography) and in the newly developed Class K in which laws of individual nations are classed first by jurisdiction, then by subject and form. Another example of this is the division of "Constitutional History and Administration" in Class J (Political Science). Subdivisions by country occur before further subdivisions of the subject, i.e., Subclasses JK, United States; JL, British America, Latin America; JN, Europe; and JQ, Asia, Africa, Australia, etc. This process of subdividing a subject first by country and then using specific subject divisions appropriate to that country allows greater specific and appropriate enumeration for each country.

The following example from Subclass GR for Folklore may be used to review the patterns of general divisions.

GR FOLKLORE

1	Periodicals. Societies. Serials
10	Congresses
	Collected works (nonserial)
15	Several authors
20	Individual authors
35	Dictionaries. Encyclopedias
37	Directories
40	**Philosophy. Relation to other topics. Methodology**
42	Relation to psychology
43	Relation to special classes of persons, A-Z
	.C4 Children
44	Special methods, A-Z
	.C3 Cartography
	.S7 Structural analysis

(Example continues on page 56)

GR   FOLKLORE (cont'd)

	Study and teaching. Research
45	General works
.5	Fieldwork
	By region or country
46	United States
47	Other regions or countries, A-Z
	Museums. Exhibitions, *see* GN35 +
48	History
	Folklorists
49	Folklore as a profession
	Biography
50	Collective
55	Individual, A-Z
	General works, treatises, and textbooks
60	Early through 1800
65	1801-1974
66	1975-
67	General special (Special aspects of the subject as a whole)
68	Outlines, syllabi
.5	Popular works
69	Juvenile works
71	Addresses, essays, lectures
	Folk literature (General)
72	General works
73	Collections of texts
	By form
	Folktales
74	General works
	Themes, motives, etc.
.4	General works
.6	Classification, indexes, etc.
75	Individual folktale themes and motives, A-Z

The range of numbers GR 1-37 are examples of General form divisions. Philosophy is represented by GR 40-44. "Study and teaching" appear as the next element receiving three numbers, GR 45-47. The use of geographic division alphabetically may be seen in GR 47, Other regions or countries, A-Z. It may be noted that GR 46 is reserved for the United States. This technique allows the U.S., or the favored country, to receive preferred treatment without using the full preferred order. History is represented by GR 48. Biography of Folklorists is collocated to follow History. General works is a good example of the previous discussion. The common chronological subdivisions of "Early through 1800," "1801-1974," and "1975-" are denoted by GR 60-66. GR 67 is reserved for General special. This is followed by a span of numbers for minor forms — Outlines, syllabi; Popular works; Juvenile works; and Addresses, essays, lectures — in GR 68-71. following these is the major portion of the subclass, namely, subject subdivisions.

Notes in Classification Schedules

The class numbers and captions (i.e., headings and subheadings) are often accompanied by notes. The notes generally fall into one of the following categories.

Scope Notes

These notes are used to explain what goes under a particular caption. In most cases, a scope note is used to explain LC's separation of the material, if the topic in question is very similar in nature to a topic located in another area, e.g.,

> **Inorganic chemistry**
> Special elements. By chemical symbol, A-Z
> Class here works on the origin, properties, preparation,
> reactions, isotopes, and analytical chemistry of
> individual elements and their inorganic compounds.
> For the determination of atomic and molecular weights,
> *see* QD464

Explanatory See Notes

The second sentence of a scope note (see example above), when used alone, is called an "explanatory *see* note." Such a note is used to identify certain concepts which are understood by the caption immediately above the note but are to be classed elsewhere under a different number. In the past, "prefer notes" (which have been discontinued) were used for the same purpose.

Example:

> **By language**
> European
> For inscriptions of particular countries in modern
> European languages, *see* the country, CN900+

Confer Notes

A confer note informs the user that information related to the topic in question is also found under another number or other numbers in the system, or that (going down hierarchically) the list of subtopics under the caption in question is not complete and additional subtopics are found under another class number. The note consists of a class number with a statement of what the class number represents. In recently revised editions, a span of numbers is indicated by the initial number with a plus sign.

> **Flags, banners, and standards**
> Cf. CR191+, Public and official heraldry
> JC345+, Political theory
> UC590+, Military standards

See Notes

A *see* note is used most often in a case when a decision has been made to relocate a topic in the scheme. The existing class number is parenthesized or removed and a *see* reference is added at the end of the caption.

TH	**Water supply**
6523	General special. Specifications, etc.
(6525)	Rural domestic water supply, *see* TD927

TX	
585	Tea
	Milk, *see* SF254 +

Including Notes

These notes are used to indicate by example the kinds of topics subsumed under the caption, e.g.,

MACHINERY EXCLUSIVE OF PRIME MOVERS
Including millwork, i.e., the shafting, gearing and
other driving machinery of mills and factories

Frequently, they help to identify concepts which the reader would not ordinarily assume to be included within the scope of the caption.

Divide Like Notes

These notes, which refer from a range of numbers to another range of numbers, are used for the purpose of saving space in the printed schedules. For example:

TN	**Mercury ore deposits and mining**
463-469	Special countries
	Divided like TN403-409

AG	**Dictionaries. Minor encyclopedias**
5-90	Other
	Divided like AE5-89.9

Parenthesized Numbers

Within the L.C. schedules, certain numbers are enclosed in parentheses. The parentheses indicate that the number enclosed is not used by the Library of Congress. A number is placed in parentheses when the Library of Congress cancels the number but wishes to leave it in the schedule for other libraries which may prefer to use it.

Z SUBJECT BIBLIOGRAPHY

7291	Riddles
7295	Roads. Highways
(7298)	Rubber, *see* Z 6297

HD

*(58.5) **Managerial economics,** *see* HD30.22   p. 29
  (*Parenthesize* number; *change* line to
    reference.)

[69 Other . . .] p. 29
  *(.D4) Decisionmaking, *see* HD30.23
      (*Parenthesize* number; *change* line to
        reference.)
  *(.F58) Forecasting, *see* HD30.27
      (*Parenthesize* number; *change* line to
        reference.)

As shown in the examples above, all parenthesized numbers are accompanied by *see* references. Currently, as cumulative editions are being prepared, the parenthesized numbers are usually removed. The *see* references, if appropriate, often remain in the schedule. In a few exceptional cases, a parenthesized number may be left in the new schedule as a "pivotal" number for the purpose of appending special notes or directions.

Alternative Class Numbers

On many L.C. cataloging records, in addition to the regular L.C. call number, one or more alternative class numbers enclosed in brackets are provided when the work may be classed in more than one number. Alternative class

---

*Example taken from *L.C. Classification — Additions and Changes.*

numbers are generally provided for incunabula, subject bibliographies regularly classed in Z, analytics in series or sets classed as a whole, and, until recently, for fiction in English regularly classed in PZ. On cataloging records for works in medicine produced through the cataloging program shared between the National Library of Medicine and the Library of Congress, alternative class numbers based on the National Library of Medicine Classification scheme are given in addition to the L.C. call numbers. Details of alternative class numbers appear in chapters 5 and 6.

SUPPLEMENTARY AIDS TO THE USE OF LIBRARY OF CONGRESS CLASSIFICATION

An Index to L.C. Classification

Although most of the individual L.C. schedules include detailed indexes, there is no general index to the entire classification issued by the Library of Congress. In 1947 work toward a general index was begun by the Library of Congress. All existing individual indices were cut and mounted on cards; Class K, Law, was not included as this schedule is still in the process of completion. It was decided to wait until Class K was completed to publish the general index. Presently, there is no plan to resume this project.

Two unofficial general indices have been published recently. *An Index to the Library of Congress Classification*,[5] published by the Canadian Library Association, is a cumulation of the indexes to the individual schedules. *Combined Indexes to the Library of Congress Classification Schedules*,[6] compiled by Nancy B. Olson and published by the U.S. Historical Institute, is a much more elaborate work. It consists of five sets in fifteen volumes:

Indexes by Person

> Set I. Author/Number Index, 1974
> Two volumes

> Set II. Biographical Subject Index, 1974
> Three volumes

> Set III. Classified Index to Persons, 1974
> Three volumes

Index by Place

> Set IV. Geographical Name Index, 1974
> One volume

Subject Index

> Set V. Subject Keyword Index, 1974
> Six volumes

In addition, a cumulative supplement in three volumes covering 1975-78 is being prepared.

A Manual to L.C. Classification

There is no manual issued by the Library of Congress explaining the classification. One was begun by Cecil K. Jones and Leo LaMontagne but was never completed. Leo LaMontagne's *American Library Classification with Special Reference to the Library of Congress* (1961) contains many helpful statements on the history, theory, and use of L.C. Classification. This book is particularly valuable as it contains many citations from material available only in Library of Congress departmental reports, etc. All students of classification should carefully read this book. Catherine W. Grout's *Explanation of the Tables Used in the Schedules of the Library of Congress Classification* (1940) is useful as a manual on the auxiliary tables. However, Grout did not cover all the auxiliary tables. Also, many of her examples are taken from earlier editions of the Library of Congress Classification schedules and are thus somewhat dated and occasionally invalid. *A Manual on KF: The Library of Congress Classification Schedule for Law of the United States* (1972), prepared by Patricia Luster Piper and Cecilia Hing-Ling Kwan, provides detailed explanation with numerous examples for Subclass KF. There are additional sources in various books on classification as included in the bibliography at the end of this chapter.

ABRIDGMENTS OF L.C. CLASSIFICATION

Although there is no standard abridgment of L.C. Classification as there is of the *Dewey Decimal Classification* in the *Abridged Dewey Decimal Classification*, there are a few abridgments of individual parts of L.C. Classification schedules. The bibliography at the end of this chapter lists some of these abridgments.

USE OF L.C. CATALOGING RECORDS

One major factor persuading many libraries to convert to L.C. Classification is the existence of the complete L.C. call numbers on the L.C. cataloging records. The L.C. number has a great advantage over the suggested *Decimal Classification* number; the *Decimal Classification* number is only a class number and not a whole call number. One disadvantage of complete acceptance of the whole L.C. call number is the problem of assigning original Cutter numbers to those works for which L.C. cataloging records are not available. The recent appearance of the Library of Congress shelflist on microform (filmed in 1978-1979) has alleviated part of the problem for libraries using L.C. Classification. Further, all L.C. call numbers should be carefully checked before being automatically accepted. Typographical errors do occur; some material may need to be reclassified. The classifier will also find the Library of Congress *Catalog of Books Represented by Library of Congress Printed Cards*, its successor, the *National Union Catalog*, the *Library of Congress Catalog, Books: Subjects*, and LC MARC tapes to be invaluable aids in establishing and verifying actual Library of Congress classifying practice.

REVISIONS AND EXPANSIONS

The individual schedules are kept current by 1) *L.C. Classification—Additions and Changes*, which is published quarterly by the Library of Congress; 2) the addition of supplementary pages of *Additions and Changes* to the later printing of an individual schedule; and 3) periodic new editions of the individual schedules. Both the quarterly *Additions and Changes* and the supplementary pages are printed on leaves, i.e., with alternate pages blank, to allow the possibility of clipping and tabbing into the original schedules. Over the years, a good many issues of *Additions and Changes* have been published. It can be a rather time-consuming effort to go through these issues in search of a new number or to verify an existing number. Fortunately, the Gale Research Company of Detroit has been issuing *Library of Congress Classification Schedules: A Cumulation of Additions & Changes*. There are separate volumes for each schedule, bringing together all additions and changes pertaining to that particular class or subclass which have occurred since the publication of the latest edition of the schedule.

Publication of Schedules

The L.C. Classification schedules have been issued in four types of editions:

1) **New schedules.** This refers to a schedule for a class or subclass which has never been published before. Examples are the schedules for the subclasses of Class K, Law.

2) **Reissues with supplementary pages.** During the 1960s, when the stock of a particular schedule was exhausted, a reprint edition would be issued which included additions and changes up to the time of reprinting interfiled in one alphanumeric sequence which is separated from the main schedule and index. Most of the older schedules which have been reissued appear in this format, e.g., the schedules for Classes D, E-F, L, S, etc.

3) **Cumulative editions.** A cumulative edition represents mainly a cumulation of the previous edition and the additions and changes incorporated into one file. The preparation of such an edition is normally performed by the editorial staff of the Subject Cataloging Division. Because relatively little revamping or rethinking of the classification is involved, the preparation is fairly mechanical and speedy. The recently published second edition (1978) of Schedule PN, PR, PS, PZ was the first schedule prepared in this manner, as was the third edition (1979) of Schedule B-BJ. Other cumulative editions being prepared are the schedules for R and Z.

4) **Revised editions.** These are new editions which have undergone considerable revamping and revision. The process involves rethinking and reviewing of much of the entire schedule. Many numbers are changed and terminology updated. The preparation of such an edition involves not only individual catalogers but also the Principal Subject Cataloger and his staff. Because of the thorough

revision, it requires a great deal more time and effort to prepare such an edition. The recent editions of schedules Q, T, and M belong to this type, and the schedule for Subclasses H-HJ is undergoing such a process.

It should be pointed out that there is no fixed time schedule for revision. Each classification schedule is revised as needed, depending on the availability of the necessary personnel and time. Class Q is already in the sixth edition and Class T in the fifth. Classes A, G, N, U, and Z are in fourth editions. Classes C, E-F, H, L, M, R, S, and V are all in third editions. The remaining classes are all in second editions with the exception of Class P (excluding PN, PR, PS, PZ) and subclasses K, KD, KE and KF, which are in first editions.

Procedure for Revision and Expansion

Revisions and changes in the L.C. Classification occur continuously in the form of addition of new numbers or revision of existing numbers. Welsh has summarized the procedure for revision:

> First of all, it should be noted that the schedules are being revised constantly, literally every day. It is incumbent on members of the subject cataloging staff, in dealing with the materials being added to the collections, to propose any changes necessary to accommodate a new work. After approval by the Editorial Committee of the Subject Cataloging Division, these changes are put into effect at once and published in due course in the quarterly *L.C. Classification—Additions and Changes* and finally in supplements to or new editions of the respective schedule.[7]

The proposal of a new number by a subject cataloger at the Library of Congress normally consists of the proposed number, the caption, the exact location in the schedules where the new number will be inserted, a previously existing pattern (if any) on which the proposed number is based, and the cataloger's explanation (if any). Approximately fifty percent of all new class number proposals are based on analogous situations in other portions of the same schedule. The proposals are reviewed at the weekly editorial meeting attended by the Chief and the Assistant Chief of the Subject Cataloging Division, at least one representative from the Principal Subject Cataloger's office, the Editor of Classification Schedules, and an assistant editor. Once a proposal is approved, it is incorporated into the system and prepared for publication. Revisions and changes to existing numbers or notes follow a similar procedure.

Methods for Expansion

There are six methods for possible expansion of L.C. Classification:

1)   By using the unused letters I, O, W, X, and Y. (It should be noted that the letter W has been used by the National Library of Medicine for its classification schedule for medicine, which may be used by libraries adopting L.C. if Class R is not used.)

2)   By adding a third capital letter or even a fourth to the existing double letters, e.g., CNA, CNB, CNC, etc. This device is presently being used in Classes K and D. (This use is discussed in chapter 5.)

3)   By the assignment of the unused numbers and double letters in the present schedules.

4)   By extending the present numbers decimally.

5)   By further use of Cutter numbers.

6)   By further use of workmarks.

Only the last five methods of expansion have been used generally by the Library of Congress. Obviously, the first method would cause major reclassification within the L.C. schedules; hence it has not yet been used.

Updating Schedules

Because revision of L.C. Classification is a continuous process and because there may be a relatively long period of time between editions of a schedule, it is important to keep the schedules up-to-date for use in classification of library materials. To avoid the necessity of checking through each issue of *L.C. Classification—Additions and Changes* every time a class number is needed, many libraries maintain an official copy of each schedule by incorporating all additions and changes into the main schedule. The updating may be achieved by handwritten annotations, cutting and pasting sections of additions and changes, or retyping the pages. Figures 1-4 illustrate a few of the methods used by the Library of Congress and other libraries for updating the L.C. schedules. Figure 1 shows an original page from the H schedule. Figure 2 (page 66) illustrates the old-style method of handwritten annotations. Figure 3 (page 67) demonstrates the combination of handwritten annotations and cutting and pasting from *L.C. Classification—Additions and Changes*. Figure 4 (page 68) shows the current method of updating schedules which is used by the Library of Congress: the official copy of the schedule is retyped, incorporating all additions and changes. Further changes may be inserted by hand.

Figure 1. Original Page from H Schedule

HD	ECONOMIC HISTORY	**HD**

Classes of labor.
    Woman labor—Continued.

6091–6220   By country.   Table V.[1]
         Under each:
           4 nos. 1 no.
             (1) .A1–5 Collections, documents, etc.
             (2) .A6A–Z Statistics.
             (3) .A7–Z5 General works.
             (4) .Z6A–Z Local, A–Z.

Child labor.
        For night labor of children, *see* HD 5113.

6228   Periodicals. Societies. Collections.
6229   Congresses.
6231   General works.
      Law and legislation.
        Cf. HD 6250, subdivision (1), under each country.
6241   General works.
6243   By country, A–Z.
        .U5–6 United States, arranged like HD 6083.U5–6.
6247   By industry or trade, A–Z.[2]
        Under each:
          (1) General works.
          (2) By country, A–Z.
6250   By country, A–Z.
        Under each (using successive Cutter numbers):
          (1) Documents.
          (2) General works.
          (3) Local, A–Z.
6270   Junior labor.
6280   Middle-aged and older workers.
6300   Immigrant labor.
        Cf. HD 8081, Immigrant labor in the United States.
          HD 8101–8942 (Table VIII, nos. 18 and 8.5), Im-
            migrant labor in other countries.
6305   Other classes of labor, A–Z.
        e. g. .A4, Alien commuters; .A8, Asiatic; .J3, Jewish;
         .N4, Negro (Negro labor, U. S., *see* E 185.8).
6331   Labor and machinery.
6335   Labor and the trusts.
6338   Labor and the church.
6339   Labor and the intellectuals.
      Employers' and workingmen's associations.   Trade-
        unions.   Labor unions.
        For women in trade-unions, *see* HD 6079.
        For American Federation of Labor, Congress of Industrial
         Organizations, etc., *see* HD 8055.

---

[1] For Table V, *see* p. 527–532.   Add country number in Table to 6090.
[2] For List of industries and trades, *see* p. 78–83.

Figure 2. Old-Style (Handwritten) Annotation at L.C.

HD   ECONOMIC HISTORY   HD

Gar 57-60
& Ju. 70-73

Classes of labor.
Woman labor—Continued.

6091–6220   By country.   Table V.[1]
Under each:
4 nos.   1 no. →

Cutter no. 2
p. x A1-4
  (1)   .A1–5   Collections, documents, etc.
  (2)   .A6A–Z   Statistics. *(including legal documents)*
. x A5–Z
  (3)   .A7–Z5   General works.
. x 2
  (4)   .Z6A–Z   Local, A–Z.

6223   Child labor. → *6223 Underdeveloped areas.*
    For night labor of children, *see* HD 5113.

6228   Periodicals.   Societies.   Collections.
6229   Congresses.
6231   General works.
    Law and legislation.
      Cf. HD 6250, subdivision (1), under each country.
6241   General works.
6243   By country, A–Z.
      .U5–6 United States, arranged like HD 6083.U5–6.
6247   By industry or trade, A–Z.
     Under each:
      (1) General works.
      (2) By country, A–Z.
6250   By country, A–Z.
     Under each (using successive Cutter numbers)·
      (1) Documents.
      (2) General works.   *For employment of middle-aged and older*
      (3) Local, A–Z.   *women, see HD 6056.*

See below 6270   Junior labor.   *For employment of the older worker in the U.S.*
6277-6278   → *see opp.*   *federal service, see JK 723. 04.*
6279   6280   Middle-aged and older workers.

6280-
6283,
see
p. 64a   6300   Immigrant labor.
     Cf. HD 8081, Immigrant labor in the United States.
      HD 8101–8942 (Table VIII, nos. 18 and 8.5), Im-
      migrant labor in other countries.
6303 6305   Other classes of labor, A–Z. *6303 Native labor (Indigenous populations).*
    e. g. .A4, Alien commuters; .A8, Asiatic; .J3, Jewish; *By country, see HD 8701-8942*
     .N4, Negro (Negro labor, U. S., *see* E 185.8). *M5 Minorities.*
                           F7 Frontier workers
6331   Labor and machinery.
6335   Labor and the trusts.   *Cf. BR115.E3, Christianity in relation*
see p. 64a 6338   Labor and the church.   *to economics and labor.*
6339.3   Labor and the intellectuals.   → *6338.3 Labor and Judaism.*

Employers' and workingmen's associations. Trade-
unions. Labor unions.
    For women in trade-unions, *see* HD 6079.
    For American Federation of Labor, Congress of Industrial
    Organizations, etc., *see* HD 8055.

---

[1] For Table V, *see* p. 527–532.   Add country number in Table to 6090.
[3] For List of industries and trades, see p. 78–83. *Use in so far as applicable.*
[4] *See footnote 4, p. 23, for interpretation of Cutter number table.*

64
6270   *Youth labor. x A HQ 799.9. D9, Dropouts (social problem).*
     JK923.S8 Federal employment of college students.
   ◯ By country, region, etc.
6273   *United States.*
6274   *By state or region, A-Z.*
6275   *By city, A-Z.*
6276   *Other countries, regions, etc., A-Z.*

Figure 3. Use of Handwriting and Information from "Additions and Changes" by Another Library to Demonstrate "Cut & Paste & Write" Method

HD	ECONOMIC HISTORY	**HD**

Classes of labor.
    Woman labor—Continued.
6091–6220   By country.   Table V.[1]
        Under each:

        4 nos.   1 no.
            (1) .A1–5   Collections, documents, etc. *Including local document.*
            (2) .A6A–Z Statistics.
            (3) .A7–Z5 General works.
            (4) .Z6A–Z Local, A–Z.
    Child labor.
        For night labor of children, *see* HD 5113.

6228   Periodicals. Societies. Collections.
6229   Congresses.
6231   General works.
        Law and legislation.
            Cf. HD 6250, subdivision (1), under each country.
6241   General works.
6243   By country, A–Z.
            .U5–6 United States, arranged like HD 6083.U5–6.
6247   By industry or trade, A–Z.[2]
            Under each:
               (1) General works.
               (2) By country, A–Z.
6250   By country, A–Z.
            Under each (using successive Cutter numbers):
               (1) Documents.
               (2) General works.
               (3) Local, A–Z.
6270   ~~Junior~~ *Youth* labor.
~~6280~~ *6279*   Middle-aged and older workers.
6300   Immigrant labor.
        Cf. HD 8081, Immigrant labor in the United States.
            HD 8101–8942 (Table VIII, nos. 18 and 8.5), Im-
            migrant labor in other countries.
6303   *Native labor (Indigenous population) by country, see HC P101 etc.*
6305   Other classes of labor, A–Z.
        e. g. .A4, Alien commuters; .A8, Asiatic; .J3, Jewish; *.F7 Frontier workers.*
            .N4, Negro (Negro labor, U. S., *see* E 185.8).
6331   Labor and machinery.
6335   Labor and the trusts.   Cf. BR 115.E3, Christianity in relation to economics and labor.
6338   Labor and the church. *Labor and Judaism.*
6339   Labor and the intellectuals.
    Employers' and workingmen's associations. Trade-unions. Labor unions.
        For women in trade-unions, *see* HD 6079.
        For American Federation of Labor, Congress of Industrial Organizations, etc., *see* HD 8055.

---

[1] For Table V, *see* p. 527–532. Add country number in Table to 6090.
[2] For List of industries and trades, *see* p. 78–83.

6270 Youth labor.
    Cf. JK 723.S8, Federal employment of college stu-
      dents.   Cf. HQ799.9.D7, Dropouts (Social
                        problem).
    By country, region, etc.
6273   United States.
6274   By state or region, A–Z.
6275   By city, A–Z.
6276   Other countries, regions, etc., A–Z.

*6279 Middle-aged and older workers.
    (*Not* "6280")
    For employment of middle-aged and older
      women, *see* HD6056.
    For employment of the older worker in the
      U. S. federal service, *see* JK723.O4.
    By country, region, etc.
*6280   United States.
6281   By state or region, A–Z.
6282   By city, A–Z.
6283   Other countries, regions, etc., A–Z.

Figure 4. Current Method of Updating Schedules in L.C.-1

HD	ECONOMIC HISTORY	HD

```
                    Classes of labor
                      Middle-aged and older workers - Continued
                        By country, region, etc.
6280                      United States
6281                        By state or region, A-Z
6282                        By city, A-Z
6283                      Other countries, regions, etc., A-Z
6300                    Immigrant labor
                          Cf. HD8081, Immigrant labor in the United States
                              HD8101-8942 (Table VIII, nos. 18 and 8.5),
                                  Immigrant labor in other countries
6303                    Native labor. (Indigenous populations)
                          By country, see HD8101-8942
6305                    Other classes of labor, A-Z
                          .A4    Alien commuters
                          .A8    Asiatic                   .B56 Black
                          .F7    Frontier worker               For the United States,
                          .J3    Jewish                            see E185.8
                          .M5    Minorities____HD6057+,-Minority women
                                    Cf. HF5549.5.M5, Personnel management
                                 Negro, see .B56; E185.8
                          ├──> 6331 - 6331 2, see p. 64 b
6335                    Labor and the trusts
6338                    Labor and the church
                          Cf. BR115.E3, Christianity in relation to economics
                              and labor
6338.2                  By country, A-Z
                            Under each:
                              (1)  General works
                              (2)  Local, A-Z
6338.3                  Labor and Judaism   6338.4  Labor and Islam
6339.4                  Labor and the intellectuals
                      Employers' and workingmen's associations.  Trade-
                          unions.  Labor unions
                        For women in trade-unions, see HD6079
                      ( For American Federation of Labor, Congress of
                          Industrial Organizations, etc., see HD8055
                        For government employees unions, see HD8005+


                    College students
6276.5                General works
    .52                 By region or country, A-Z
                            Under each country:
                              .x     General works
                              .x2    Local, A-Z
6277                    College graduates
```

Figure 4. (cont'd)

HD   ECONOMIC HISTORY   HD

```
                              Classes of labor
                                Woman labor - Continued.
6091-6220.7                       By region or country.  Table V¹
                                     Under each:
        Cutter no.¹²                    4 nos.   1 no.
          .xA1-4                         (1)   .A1-5    Collections, documents, etc.
                                                          Including local documents
                                         (2)   .A6A-Z   Statistics
          .xA5-Z                         (3)   .A7-Z5   General works
          .x2                            (4)   .Z6A-Z   Local, A-Z
6223                                  Underdeveloped areas
                                  Child labor
                                     For night labor of children, see HD5113
6228                                 Periodicals.  Societies.  Collections
6229                                 Congresses
6231                                 General works
                                     Law and legislation
                                        Cf. HD6250, subdivision (1), under each country
6241                                    General works
6243                                    By country, A-Z
                                          .U5-6 United States, arranged like HD6083.U5-6
6247                                 By industry or trade, A-Z²
                                        Under each:
                                           (1)  General works
                                           (2)  By country, A-Z
6250                                 By country, A-Z
                                        Under each (using successive Cutter numbers):
                                           (1)  Documents
                                           (2)  General works
                                           (3)  Local, A-Z
6270                                  Youth labor
                                        Cf. HQ799.9.D7, Dropouts (Social problem)
                                            JK923.S8, Federal employment of college
                                               students
                                     By country, region, etc.
6273                                    United States
6274                                       By state or region, A-Z
6275                                       By city, A-Z
6276                                    Other countries, regions, etc., A-Z
6277                                  College graduates
6278                                  By country, A-Z
                                        Under each:
                                           (1)  General works
                                           (2)  Local, A-Z
6279                                  Middle-aged and older workers
                                        For employment of middle-aged and older women,
                                           see HD6056
                                        For employment of the older worker in the U.S.
                                           federal service, see JK723.04
```

Handwritten annotations: HD6490.Y65 Labor unions; 6276.5 — .52 see p. 64a; Cf. HD6053.S4, Employment of women college graduates; Cf. HF5549.5.O44 Personnel management

---

¹ For Table V, see p. 527-532. Add country number in Table to 6090
² See footnote I, p. 23, for interpretation of Cutter number table
³ For list of industries and trades, see p. 78-83. Use in so far as
applicable

Figure 4. (cont'd)

HD   ECONOMIC HISTORY   HD

```
                Labor and machinery.  Technological unemployment
  6331              General works
     .18            By industry or trade, A-Z
                       Under each:
                          .x      General works
                          .x2     By region or country, A-Z
     .2             By region or country, A-Z
                       Under each country:
                          .x      General works
                          .x2     Local, A-Z
  ⌐6335             Labor and the trusts⌐
```

BIBLIOGRAPHY

General Articles and Works on L.C. Classification

Angell, Richard S. "On the Future of the Library of Congress Classification," in *Classification Research. Proceedings of the Second International Study Conference held at Hotel Prins Hamlet, Elsinore, Denmark, 14th to 18th September 1964.* Edited by Pauline Atherton. Copenhagen: Munksgaard, 1965, pp. 101-112.
This is a recent statement by the then Chief of the Subject Cataloging Division summarizing the scope, notation, principle of class construction, and provisions for revision of L.C. Classification. Various modern problems of classification are discussed.

Bakewell, K. G. B. "Library of Congress Classification," in *Classification and Indexing Practice.* Hamden, CT: Shoe String Press, 1978, pp. 55-75.

Cataloging Service, 1-125, June 1945-Spring 1978. (Washington: Library of Congress, Processing Department).

Cataloging Service Bulletin, 1- , Summer 1978- . (Washington: Library of Congress, Processing Services).

Curwen, Anthony G. "Revision of Classification Schemes: Policies and Practices," *Journal of Librarianship*, 10:19-38, January 1978.
Discussion of Library of Congress Classification appears on pages 21-23.

Davison, Keith. *Theory of Classification: An Examination Guidebook.* London: Clive Bingley, 1966.
Pages 18-20 offer a short general summary of L.C. Classification.

Doyle, Irene M. "Library of Congress Classification for the Academic Library," in *The Role of Classification in the Modern American Library. Papers Presented at an Institute Conducted by the University of Illinois Graduate School of Library Science, November 1-4, 1959.* Champaign, IL: Illini Union Bookstore, 1959, pp. 76-92.
This article discusses the adoption and use of L.C. Classification at the University of Wisconsin Libraries, the long-time home of the *Expansive Classification.*

Foskett, A. C. "The Library of Congress Classification," in *The Subject Approach to Information.* 3rd ed. Hamden, CT: Linnet Books, 1977, pp. 359-67.

Goodrum, Charles A. *The Library of Congress.* New York: Praeger, 1974.
A recent monograph describing the Library of Congress with a few comments on the classification, cf. pp. 96-97, 147-50.

Hanson, J. C. M. "Library of Congress Classification for College Libraries," *Library Journal*, 46:151-54, February 15, 1921.
Hanson discusses the advantages and disadvantages of the use of L.C. Classification by college libraries.

Hawkes, A. J. "Library of Congress Classification," *Library Association Record*, 16:188-89, April 15, 1914.
This is a synopsis of a paper by a British librarian who was using L.C. Classification in its early days.

Hicks, Frederick C. "Library of Congress Classification and Its Printed Catalogue Cards," *Library Journal*, 31:255-56, June 1906.
Hicks, the Librarian of the U.S. Naval War College at Newport, RI, discusses the reasons for using L.C. Classification at the U.S. Naval War College Library in 1906.

Hoage, A. Annette Lewis. "The Library of Congress Classification in the United States: A Survey of Opinions and Practices, with Attention to Problems of

Structure and Application." Unpublished doctoral dissertation, Columbia University, 1961.
This 233-page work is one of the few books devoted mainly to Library of Congress Classification. Hoage's work is now available in a University Microfilms edition. chapters on "Development and Application of the Schedules," "Opinions of the Classification," "Acceptance of the Classification," "Use of the Classification by Patrons," and a description of the classification in the "Appendixes" are included in this important work. This should be carefully read by all students of L.C. Classification.

Immroth, J. P. "Library of Congress Classification," in *Classification in the 1970s: A Second Look*. Rev. ed., edited by Arthur Maltby. London: Clive Bingley; Hamden, CT: Linnet Books, 1976.

LaMontagne, Leo E. *American Library Classification with Special Reference to the Library of Congress*. Hamden, CT: Shoe String Press, 1961.
Pages 221-333 present a complete study of the background, theory, and structure of L.C. Classification.

Langridge, Derek. *Approach to Classification for Students of Librarianship*. Hamden, CT: Linnet Books, 1973.
Pages 91-92 contain a brief, critical analysis of L.C. Classification by this British teacher of classification at North London Polytechnic.

"Library of Congress Classification," *Library World*, 17:45, July 1914.
This is simply an outline of the schedules available in 1914 and their prices.

"Library of Congress Classification," *Library World*, 18:355-59, June 1916.
This second article in *Library World* contains short summaries and a few critical remarks on Classes A, C, GR, GT, HT, PN-PZ.

Library of Congress Classification (filmstrip). Wichita, KS: Library Filmstrip Center, 1972.
54 frames (18 minutes) in color.

Library of Congress Shelflist: A User's Guide to the Microfiche Edition. Edited by Linda K. Hamilton. Ann Arbor, MI: University Microfilms International, 1979- .

Martel, Charles. "Classification," in *Report of the Librarian of Congress, and Report of the Superintendent of the Library Buildings and Grounds for the Fiscal Year Ending June 30, 1911*. Washington: GPO, 1911, pp. 58-64.
Martel presents the basic objectives and purposes of L.C. Classification.

Martel, Charles. "Classification: A Brief Conspectus of Present Day Library Practice," *Library Journal*, 36:410-16, August 191ſ.
Pages 414-16 contain a brief summary of the structure of L.C. Classification.

Martel, Charles. "Classification: Present Tendencies," *Library Journal*, 29: C132-34, December 1904.
This article on "present tendencies in classification" written in 1904 makes no reference to L.C. Classification. Obviously in 1904 the development of L.C. Classification was not considered to be of major interest to other libraries.

Martel, Charles. "Library of Congress Classification," *ALA Bulletin*, 5:230-32, July 1911.
This is virtually the same summary of L.C. as contained in the previously cited "Classification: A Brief Conspectus of Present Day Library Practice."

Martel, Charles. "The Library of Congress Classification," in *Essays Offered to Herbert Putnam by His Colleagues and Friends on His Thirtieth Anniversary as Librarian of Congress: 5 April 1929*. Edited by William Warner Bishop and Andrew Keogh. New Haven: Yale University Press, 1929, pp. 327-32.
This is an attempt by Martel to justify the practical development of L.C. Classification.

Metcalfe, John. *Subject Classifying and Indexing of Libraries and Literature*. New York: Scarecrow Press, 1959.
Pages 113-17 are a brief modern analysis of L.C. Classification with seven points of comparison to the *Decimal Classification* and the other systems listed.

Mills, Jack. *A Modern Outline of Library Classification*. London: Chapman and Hall, 1960.
Pages 89-102 are a careful summary of L.C. Classification by a scholar of faceted classification. This is an excellent analysis.

Needham, C. D. *Organizing Knowledge in Libraries: An Introduction to Information Retrieval*. 2nd rev. ed. London: Andre Deutsch, 1971.
Pages 163-68 present a brief summary of L.C. Classification.

Perley, Clarence W. "Recent Developments in the Library of Congress Classification," in *Proceedings of the Catalog Section, American Library Association, Washington, D.C., Conference May 13-18, 1929*. Chicago: Catalog Section, American Library Association, 1929.
One of the editors of the classification schedules presents a short historical note on L.C. Classification in 1929. This article also appeared in an abbreviated form in *ALA Bulletin*, 23:300-301, August 1929.

Phillips, W. Howard. *A Primer of Book Classification*. 5th ed. London: Association of Assistant Librarians, 1961.
Pages 96-109 present another brief summary of L.C. Classification.

Roberts, M. A. *The Library of Congress in Relation to Research*. Washington: GPO, 1939.
Pages 33-34 contain a brief introductory summary of L.C. Classification. Mann quotes it in her "Explanation of the system" on pages 72-73 of her *Introduction to Cataloging and the Classification of Books*.

Robertson, David Allen. "The LC Classification as an Aid to Research," *Proceedings of the Catalog Section, American Library Association, Washington, D.C., Conference May 13-18, 1929*. Chicago: Catalog Section, ALA, 1929.
This is a short paper advocating the use of L.C. Classification instead of the *Decimal Classification* in university libraries.

Sahaya, S. "Library of Congress and Its Classification," *Modern Librarian*, 15: 82-86, 1945.
This is a discussion of L.C. Classification by an Indian librarian.

Savage, Ernest Albert. *Manual of Book Classification and Display for Public Libraries*. London: Allen & Unwin and the Library Association, 1946.
Savage advocates the "Principles of Book Classification" of E. Wyndham Hulme and thus the use of L.C. Classification (pages 15-52).

Sayers, W. C. Berwick. *Canons of Classification, Applied to "The Subject," "The Expansive," "The Decimal," and "The Library of Congress" Classifications: A Study in Bibliographical Classification Method*. London: Grafton, 1915.
Pages 127-61 represent the first writing on L.C. Classification by this famous British scholar of classification. This material is revised and expanded in each of the following entries.

Sayers, W. C. Berwick. *An Introduction to Library Classification: Theoretical, Historical, and Practical with Readings, Exercises and Examination Papers*. 9th ed. London: Grafton, 1958.
Pages 99-114 present a general introductory summary of L.C. Classification typical of British examination guide books.

Sayers, W. C. Berwick. *A Manual of Classification for Librarians and Bibliographers*. 3rd ed., rev. London: Andre Deutsch, 1963.
Pages 151-74 present one of the better discussions and summaries of L.C. Classification. It should be read by all students of L.C. Classification. Pages 333-35 contain Sayers' bibliography for L.C. Classification.

Sayers, W. C. Berwick. *A Manual of Classification for Librarians*. 4th ed. completely rev. and partly rewritten by Arthur Maltby. London: Andre Deutsch, 1967.
Maltby updates and rewrites Sayers' section on L.C. Classification on pages 194-211 of this edition.

Sayers, W. C. Berwick. *Sayers' Manual of Classification for Librarians*. 5th ed. by Arthur Maltby. London: Andre Deutsch, 1975.
Section on L.C. Classification appears on pages 174-89.

Schimmelpfeng, Richard H., and C. Donald Cook, eds. *The Use of the Library of Congress Classification. Proceedings of the Institute on the Use of the Library of Congress Classification, Sponsored by the American Library*

Association, Resources and Technical Services Division, Cataloging and Classification Section, New York City, July 7-9, 1966. Chicago: ALA, 1968.
The 13 papers and two appendices which comprise this work should all be carefully read. Many of the individual papers will be cited in the following chapter bibliographies.

Smither, Reginald Ernest. "Library of Congress Classification," *Library World* 16:130-36, November 1913.
This article includes brief sections on history, description, a critical survey, and notation of L.C. Classification. Smither is critical of the lack of a scientific or logical approach to the L.C. outline.

Tauber, Maurice F., and Edith Wise. *Classification Systems.* Vol. 1, pt. 3 of *The State of Library Art.* Edited by Ralph R.Shaw. New Brunswick, NJ: Graduate School of Library Science, Rutgers — The State University, 1961.
Pages 140-88 give a complete bibliographical survey of writings about L.C. Classification with pertinent sections of quotations.

Tauber, Maurice F. *Technical Services in Libraries.* New York: Columbia University Press, 1953.
Pages 200-208 give another summary introduction to L.C. Classification. This is one of the most helpful introductions to the student of L.C. Classification.

U.S. Library of Congress. *Annual Report of the Librarian of Congress.* Washington: GPO, 1901- .
Each of the annual Reports contains sections on the classification.

U.S. Library of Congress. *The Library of Congress and Its Activities.* Washington: GPO, 1926.
In both this and the following entry are brief official statements on L.C. Classification.

U.S. Library of Congress. *The Library of Congress and Its Work.* Washington: GPO, 1907.

U.S. Library of Congress. *The Library of Congress Shelflist.* Microfiche ed. Ann Arbor, MI: University Microfilms International, [1978-79].

U.S. Library of Congress. "Manual: Constitution, Organization, Methods, etc.," in *Report of the Librarian of Congress for the Fiscal Year Ending June 30, 1901.* Washington: GPO, 1901, pp. 177-357.
Herbert Putnam presents many valuable policy statements in this manual.

U.S. Library of Congress. Catalog Division. Card Section. "An Account of the Catalogs, Classifications, and Card Distribution Work of the Library of Congress," *Bulletin*, No. 7, June 15, 1904.
There are useful historical facts in this publication.

"United States Library of Congress Classification," *Library Association Record*, 8:663-64, 1906.
This is another brief review of the L.C. outline and selected schedules.

Welsh, William J. "Considerations on the Adoption of the Library of Congress Classification," *Library Resources & Technical Services*, 11:345-53, Summer 1967.

Wilson, M. "Library of Congress Classification," *Australian Institute of Librarian's Proceedings*, 2:113-17, 1939.

Wynar, Bohdan S. *Introduction to Cataloging and Classification*, 6th ed. Prepared with the assistance of Arlene T. Dowell and Jeanne Osborn. Littleton, CO: Libraries Unlimited, 1980, pp. 429-58.

General Special Articles on L.C. Classification

Ambartsumian, Z. N. "Russian View of Library of Congress Classification," *Library of Congress Information Bulletin*, 7:12-13, September 7-13, 1948.

Auld, Larry. "KWOC Indexes and Vocabulary Comparisons of Summaries of LC and DC Classification Schedules," *Journal of the American Society for Information Science*, 22:322-25, September 1971.

Birket-Smith, K. *Local Applicability of the Library of Congress Classification: A Survey with Special Reference to Non-Anglo-American Libraries*. Copenhagen: Danish Centre for Documentation, 1970.

Bushnell, G. H. "Notes by a British Librarian on the Library of Congress Classification Scheme," *Special Libraries*, 24:41-48, March 1933.

Clemons, H. "D.C. vs. L.C.," *Libraries*, 35:1-4, January, 1930.

Fellows, Dorcas, "Library of Congress Classification vs. Decimal Classification," *Library Journal*, 50:291-95, April 1, 1925.

Fuldauer, D. *Long Subject Files and the L.C. Classification, 1960-1964*. Kent, OH: Kent State University, 1969.

Hoage, A. Annette L. "Librarians Rate L.C. Classification," *Special Libraries, 53:484-85,* October 1962.
This is an abstract of the findings of one section of Hoage's dissertation.

Hoage, A. Annette L. "Patron Use of the L.C. Classification," *Library Resources & Technical Services*, 6:247-49, Summer 1962.
This article represents the findings of another part of Hoage's dissertation.

Hulme, E. Wyndham. "Principles of Book Classification," in *Readings in Library Cataloguing*. Edited and introduced by R. K. Olding. Hamden, CT: Shoe String Press, 1966, pp. 108-40.
Hulme represents a theoretical position on classification different from that of Bliss and Sayers. He strongly advocates the use of L.C. Classification in opposition to the use of philosophically based systems. Olding includes

a three-page biographical sketch, pages 105-107, on Hulme. The original publication of "Principles of Book Classification" was in *Library Association Record*, 13:354-58, 389-94, 444-49, 1911; 14:39-46, 174-81, 216-21, 1912. This was also reprinted as A.A.L. Reprints, No. 1, London: The Association of Assistant Librarians, 1950.

Immroth, John Phillip. *Analysis of Vocabulary Control in Library of Congress Classification and Subject Headings*. Introduction by Jay E. Daily. Littleton, CO: Libraries Unlimited, 1971. Research Studies in Library Science, No. 3.
This is the author's revised doctoral dissertation, which deals with a comparison of L.C. Classification, the indexes to L.C. Classification, and L.C. subject headings. Rules for chain indexing L.C. Classification are included.

"LC Card Division to Distribute Classification Schedules," *Library Journal*, 90: 4312, October 15, 1965.

Mann, Margaret. "Use of Library of Congress Classification." Chicago, 1927. (Mimeographed).
This is the first use study of L.C. Classification.

Matthis, Raimund E. *Adopting the Library of Congress Classification System: A Manual of Methods and Techniques for Application on Conversion*. New York: Bowker Company, 1971.

Mogk, H. "Das System der Kongressbibliothek in Washington," *Beiträge zur Sachkatalogisierung*. O. S. Runge, ed. Sammlung bibliothekswissenschaftlicher Arbeiten, no. 45, ser. 2, no. 28. Leipzig: Harrassowitz, 1937, pp. 51-62.

Perreault, Jean M. *Re-Classification: Some Warnings and a Proposal*. Urbana: University of Illinois, Graduate School of Library Science, 1967.

Rodríguez, Robert D. "Use of Alternative Class Numbers for Bibliography in the Library of Congress Classification System," *Library Resources & Technical Services*, 23:147-55, Spring 1979.

Samore, T. "Form Division in L.C. and D.C. Classification Schemes," *Library Resources & Technical Services*, 6:243-46, Summer 1962.

Shoyinka, P. H. "Adoption of the Library of Congress Classification at the University of Ibadan: Decisions and Practices," *Nigerian Libraries*, 11:65-85, April/August 1975.

Stevenson, Gordon. "The Library of Congress Classification Scheme and Its Relationship to Dewey," in *Major Classification Systems: The Dewey Centennial*. Papers presented at the Allerton Park Institute. Edited by Kathryn Luther Henderson. Urbana-Champaign, IL: University of Illinois, Graduate School of Library Science, 1976, pp. 78-98.

Tauber, Maurice F., and Hilda Feinberg. "The Dewey Decimal and Library of Congress Classification: An Overview," *Drexel Library Quarterly*, 10:56-74, October 1974.

Taylor, G. M., and J. F. Anderson. "It Will Cost More Tomorrow: An Economically Feasible Scheme for Reclassification," *Library Resources & Technical Services*, 16:82-92, Winter 1972.

Indexes

Boston University Libraries. *Index to the Classed Catalog of the Boston University Libraries: A Relative Index Based on the Library of Congress Classification*. Compiled by Mary Darrah Herrick. 2nd ed., rev. and enl. Boston: G. K. Hall, 1964. 2v.

Dewton, J. L. "Subject Index According to Library of Congress Classification," *Library of Congress Information Bulletin*, 8:12-13, December 27, 1949-January 2, 1950.

Edinburgh. Public Library. *Subject and Name Index of Books Contained in the Libraries*. 3rd ed. Edinburgh: Published by Edinburgh Public Libraries Committee, 1949.

Elrod, J. McRee, Judy Inouye, and Ann Craig Turner, eds. *An Index to the Library of Congress Classification: With Entries for special Expansions in Medicine, Law, Canadiana, and Nonbook Materials*. Preliminary ed. Ottawa: Canadian Library Association, 1974.

Immroth, John Phillip. *Analysis of Vocabulary Control in Library of Congress Classification and Subject Headings*. Introduction by Jay E. Daily. Littleton, CO: Libraries Unlimited, 1971.
Pages 49-82 contain a detailed analysis and criticism of the individual L.C. indices.

Newman, Lois, *A General Index to the Library of Congress Classification*. Santa Monica, CA: Rand Corp., 1969. (12 p.).

Nitecki, Andre. *Index to the Library of Congress Classification Outline*. Syracuse, NY: Syracuse University, School of Library Science, 1967.

Olson, Nancy B., comp. *Combined Indexes to the Library of Congress Classification Schedules*. Washington: U.S. Historical Documents Institute, 1974. 15 vols.

Quebec (Province) Bibliothèque nationale. Service du catalogue. *Index alphabétique du catalogue systématique selon la classification de la Library of Congress*. 2nd ed. Montréal: Bibliothèque nationale du Québec, 1968.

U.S. Library of Congress. Subject Cataloging Division. *Library of Congress Subject Headings*. 8th ed. Washington: Library of Congress, 1975. 2 vols.

Williams, James G., Martha L. Manheimer, and Jay E. Daily, eds. *Classified Library of Congress Subject Headings*. Volume 2: Alphabetic List. New York: Marcel Dekker, Inc., 1972.

Abridgments and Adaptations

Abrégé de la Classification Library of Congress, version française provisoire. Traduit de l'américain par David Belley [et autres]. La Pocatière, Quebec: Stage en bibliothéconomie, Collège Saint-Anne-de-la-Pocatière, 1970.

Inglewood Public Library, Inglewood, California. *Library of Congress Classification Adapted for Children's Library Materials.* Produced by J. W. Perkins and others. 3rd ed. Inglewood, CA: Inglewood Public Library, 1976.

Perkins, John W. "An Adapted Library of Congress Classification for Children's Materials," *Library Resources & Technical Services*, 22:174-78, Spring 1978.

Perry, F. C. "Library of Congress Classification Adapted for School Libraries," *School Library Review*, 1:68-73, Christmas term 1936.
This is an adaptation of Classes D, G, H, J, and P.

Rovelstad, Betsey. "Condensation of the Library of Congress M Classification," [n.p.], 1953.
This is an abridgment of Class M: Music, which was reprinted in 1963 as Supplement No. 34 to Music Library Association's *Notes*.

Tiffy, Ethel. "Library of Congress Classification Simplified for Use in the Smaller College Library." Unpublished master's thesis, Columbia University, 1935.
This is simply an abridgment of the history Classes C, D, and E-F. An abstract of this thesis appears in the *ALA Cataloging and Classification Yearbook*, 5:95, 1936.

LC Cataloging Records

U.S. Library of Congress. *Catalog of Books Represented by Library of Congress Printed Cards ...* Ann Arbor, MI: Edwards, 1942-1955. 191v. (Title varies).

U.S. Library of Congress. *The National Union Catalog: A Cumulative Author List Representing Library of Congress Printed Cards and Titles Reported by Other American Libraries. Jan. 1956- .* Washington: GPO, 1956- . (Title varies).

U.S. Library of Congress. *Library of Congress Catalog, Books: Subjects, 1950-1954.* Ann Arbor, MI: Edwards, 1955. 20v.

U.S. Library of Congress. Library of Congress Catalog, Books: Subjects, 1955-1959. Paterson, NJ, Pageant Books, 1960. 22v.

U.S. Library of Congress. *Library of Congress Catalog, Books: Subjects, 1960-1964.* Ann Arbor, MI: Edwards, 1965. 25v.

U.S. Library of Congress. *Library of Congress Catalog, Books: Subjects, 1965- .* Washington: GPO, 1965- .

NOTES

[1]Leo E. LaMontagne, *American Library Association with Special Reference to the Library of Congress* (Hamden, CT: Shoe String Press, 1961), p. 253.

[2]LaMontagne, *American Library Classification*, p. 254.

[3]Arthur Maltby, *Sayers' Manual of Classification for Librarians,* 5th ed. (London: André Deutsch, 1975), p. 175; also J. Mills, *A Modern Outline of Library Classification* (London: Chapman & Hall, 1967), p. 89.

[4]For details, see chapter 3.

[5]J. McRee Elrod, Judy Inouye, and Ann Craig Turner, eds. *An Index to the Library of Congress Classification*, Preliminary ed. (Ottawa: Canadian Library Association, 1974).

[6]Nancy B. Olson, comp., *Combined Indexes to the Library of Congress Classification Schedules*, (Washington: U.S. Historical Documents Institute, Inc., 1974), 15 volumes.

[7]William J. Welsh, "Considerations on the Adoption of the Library of Congress Classification," *Library Resources & Technical Services* 11:348 (Summer 1967).

FORM OF THE NOTATION

The L.C. Classification uses a mixed notation of one, two, or three capital letters, integral or whole numbers from 1 to 9999 with possible decimal extensions, one or two Cutter numbers, and, if appropriate, the year of publication. L.C. call numbers, like *Dewey Decimal* call numbers, consist in general of two principal elements — class number and book number — to which may be added, as required, symbols designating a particular work and a particular edition.

The following two patterns of call numbers are the most common in the L.C. Classification:

Class number:
    One, two, or three capital letters
    Whole numbers 1 to 9999
    Possible decimal extensions
One Cutter number (book number)
Year of publication, if appropriate

Class number:
    One, two, or three capital letters
    Whole numbers 1 to 9999
    Possible decimal extensions
    One Cutter number
A second Cutter number (book number)
Year of publication, if appropriate

The main classes in the L.C. Classification are designated by single capital letters, as shown in the outline in chapter 2. Subclasses are represented by one, two, or three capital letters. A single letter denotes a main class as well as the first subclass — usually the subclass of general works — in that class, e.g., Class N, Fine arts; Subclass N, Visual arts (General); Class P, Language and literature; Subclass P, Philology and linguistics (General). The double letters are the most common symbol for subclasses. In Classes E-F and Z, only the single capital letter is used, and there are no double or triple letter combinations. So far, the triple letter combinations have been used in Classes K and D.

Under each subclass, divisions and subdivisions are denoted by integral numbers in ordinal sequence ranging from 1 to 9999, each of which may be extended decimally.

The Cutter number consists of an initial capital letter followed by arabic numerals. It is preceded by a period and treated decimally. The Cutter number is normally the book number, used to distinguish between different works on the same subject. It is generally based on the main entry of the work. It is sometimes called the author number because most works are entered under the author. Frequently, the Cutter number may form part of the class number, usually as a form, geographic, or topical subdivision. In such cases, a second Cutter number is added as the book number.

The 1976 edition of Carl M. White's *A Historical Introduction to Library Education* has the following call numbers in L.C. Classification and *Decimal Classification*.

	L.C. Classification	Decimal Classification
Class number:	Z668	020.711
Book number:	.W54	W582h
Publication date used to indicate later edition	1976	1976

In the example above, the class number "Z668" in L.C., as well as the *Decimal Classification* number "020.711," means library education in the United States. See also the following card.

White, Carl Milton, 1903-
    A historical introduction to library education : problems and progress to 1951 / by Carl M. White. — Metuchen, N.J. : Scarecrow Press, 1976.
    v, 296 p. ; 23 cm.
    Edition for 1961 published under title: The origins of the American library school.
    Includes bibliographical references and index.
    ISBN 0-8108-0874-9

    1. Library schools—United States—History. 2. Library education—United States—History. I. Title.

Z668.W54   1976   020'.7'11   75-28086
                                                      MARC

Library of Congress   75

".W54" is the book number in L.C., while "W582h" is the book number if the work is classed in the *Decimal Classification.*

Z	The main class letter for bibliography and library science
668	The subdivision by integral number meaning library education in the United States
.W54	The Cutter number for the main entry, White
1976	The date of publication used to indicate an edition

Z688 comes directly from the schedule for Class Z, Bibliography and Library Science. As there are no further directions for cuttering at this point in the schedule, the first Cutter number is used for the main entry, the author's surname. This is an example of a simple L.C. call number in which the class number and book number are easily separable.

The class number consisting of the letter(s) and integral number is assigned from the classification schedules. The Cutter number is based on a set of simple Cutter tables and fitted into the existing sequence of Cutter numbers already assigned under the particular class number in the shelflist. The process of assigning Cutter numbers is called shelflisting. At the Library of Congress, this is performed by a shelflister rather than the subject cataloger who assigns the class number.

CUTTER TABLES

The L.C. notation does not make use of the three-figure or Cutter-Sanborn Author Tables for book numbers. As L.C. is a very close classification, the use of three-figure Cutter numbers would often cause the notation to contain unnecessary elements. The tables for L.C. Cutter numbers are designed in a very simple and easy-to-use fashion. They allow the easy assignment of one or two figures to the initial letter of the main entry. Longer Cutter numbers are used only when necessary.

The following explanation of L.C. Cutter numbers has been provided by the Library of Congress.[1]

Library of Congress call numbers consist in general of two principal elements: class number and book number, to which are added as required symbols designating a particular work.

Library of Congress book numbers are composed of the initial letter of the author's name or the title, followed by Arabic numerals representing the succeeding letters on the following basis:

_. After initial vowels
    for the second letter: b d l,m n p r s,t u-y
           use number: 2 3 4 5 67 8   9

2. After the initial letter S
    for the second letter: a ch e h,i m-p t u
           use number: 2 3 4 5   6 7-8 9

3. After the initial letters Qu
    for the third letter: a e i o r y
          use number: 3 4 5 6 7 9
    for names beginning Qa-Qt
            use: 2-29

4. After other initial consonants
    for the second letter: a e i o r u y
           use number: 3 4 5 6 7 8 9

5. When an additional number is preferred
    for the third letter: a-d e-h i-l m n-q r-t u-w x-z
           use number: 2* 3   4   5 6   7   8   9
          (*optional for third letter a or b)

Letters not included in the foregoing tables are assigned the next higher or lower number as required by previous assignments in the particular class.

The arrangements in the following examples illustrate some possible applications of these tables:

1. Names beginning with vowels:

Abernathy	.A2	Ames	.A45	Astor	.A84
Adams	.A3	Appleby	.A6	Atwater	.A87
Aldrich	.A4	Archer	.A7	Austin	.A9

2. Names beginning with the letter S:

Saint	.S2	Simmons	.S5	Steel	.S7
Schaefer	.S3	Smith	.S6	Storch	.S75
Seaton	.S4	Southerland	.S64	Sturges	.S8
Shank	.S45	Springer	.S66	Sullivan	.S9

(Example continues on page 85)

3. Names beginning with the letters Qu:

Qadriri	.Q2	Quick	.Q5	Qureshi	.Q7
Quabbe	.Q3	Queist	.Q6	Quynn	.Q9
Queener	.Q4				

4. Names beginning with other consonants:

Carter	.C3(7)	Cinelli	.C5(6)	Cullen	.C8(4)
Cecil	.C4(2)	Corbett	.C6(7)	Cyprus	.C9(6)
Childs	.C45	Croft	.C7(6)		

( ) = if using two numbers

5. When there are no existing conflicting entries in the Shelflist, the use of a third letter author number may be preferred:

Cabot	.C3	Callahan	.C34	Carter	.C37
Cadmus	.C32	Campbell	.C35	Cavelli	.C38
Caffrey	.C33	Cannon	.C36	Cazalas	.C39

The numbers are decimals, thus allowing for infinite interpolation on the decimal principle.

Since the tables provide only a general framework for the assignment of numbers, it should be noted that the symbol for a particular name or work is constant only within a single class. Each entry must be added to the existing entries in the Shelflist in such a way as to preserve alphabetical order in accordance with Library of Congress filing rules.

The purpose of using Cutter numbers is to maintain alphabetization whenever an alphabetical array is desirable. They may be used for personal names, corporate names, geographic names, topics, titles of works, etc.

As the above tables demonstrate, Cutter numbers are to be treated decimally and not ordinally. They may be expanded decimally as far as necessary. Also, the user should be advised to take care in the use of either "1" or "9" in Cutter numbers. Either of these numbers, if used, can result in unnecessary decimal extensions. In fact, it is the policy of the Library of Congress to avoid using a Cutter number which ends with the numeral "1" except in special situations designated in the schedules. In assigning original Cutter numbers, a user outside of the Library of Congress is advised not to rely solely on the Cutter tables. It is always preferable to examine the Cutter numbers already used by the Library of Congress under a particular class number.

DOUBLE CUTTER NUMBERS

The term "double Cutter numbers" refers to the use of two Cutter numbers for a particular work or subject. In double Cutter numbers, the first Cutter number becomes an extension of the class number, used to bring out an aspect (form, period, place, or subtopic) of the main subject. The second Cutter number usually stands for the main entry which is often the author's name. Following is an example of the use of double Cutter numbers in classifying *Libraries for Small Museums* (Columbia: Museum of Anthropology, University of Missouri-Columbia, 1975), by Linda Anderson and Marcia R. Collins.

Anderson, Linda M
    Libraries for small museums / by Linda Anderson, Marcia R.
Collins. — 2d ed. — Columbia : Museum of Anthropology,
University of Missouri-Columbia, 1975.

    iii, 48 p. ; 28 cm. — (Miscellaneous publications in anthropology ; no. 4)

    Bibliography: p. 48.
    ISBN 0-913134-96-1

    1. Museum libraries.   I Collins. Marcia R., joint author. II. Title. III.
Series.

    Z675.M94A53 1975   026'.069   76-353333
                                                    MARC

    Library of Congress   76

Z	The letter for the class, Bibliography and library science
675	The subdivision by integral numbers meaning classes of libraries
.M94	The first Cutter number used for further subdivision meaning museum libraries
A53	The second Cutter number for the main entry, Anderson
1975	The date of publication

In this case, the class number continues through the first Cutter number and the book number does not begin until "A53."

    In a few exceptional cases, both Cutter numbers may be used for further subdivisions of the class number, e.g.,

Muzea Wrocławskie: Przewodnik (a work about museums in Breslau)

AM	The double letters for the subclass, Museums
70	The integral number assigned to "Other European countries, A-Z "
.P63	The first Cutter number meaning a city or town in Poland
B735	The second Cutter number meaning Breslau

In such a case, no further book number is assigned because, in the L.C. system, with the exception of call numbers for maps in Class G, call numbers contain no more than two Cutter numbers. If there were more than one work about the museums in Breslau, it would be necessary to add a distinguishing feature (e.g., an additional digit) to the second Cutter number to differentiate between them.

This use of double Cutter numbers may confuse the classifier accustomed to *Decimal Classification* class numbers and Cutter-Sanborn author numbers with work marks. When both Cutter numbers are used as further subdivisions of the subject, the shelflisting of L.C. numbers becomes a process more closely related to the classification than the shelflisting process in *Decimal Classification*.

Topical Cutter Numbers

The use of Cutter numbers to bring out subtopics under a subject results in an alphabetical arrangement of these subtopics. Ordinarily, in a classification scheme, concepts should be logically, not alphabetically arranged. Therefore, wherever possible, subtopics of a discipline in the L.C. Classification are designated by class numbers rather than Cutter numbers. However, where a systematic sequence of coordinate subdivisions is not feasible or cannot be accommodated due to a shortage of integer or decimal numbers, the classification schedules frequently provide for an alphabetical order which is indicated by Cutter numbers designating the individual topics, e.g.,

HF
5549   **Personnel. Employment management.**

.5   By topic, A-Z
          e.g.   .R44   Recruiting of employees
                   .S8   Suggestion systems
                   .T7   Training of employees

The device of "By topic, A-Z" or "Special topics, A-Z" is not used to present a breakdown of a discipline into its component parts unless the area in the notation allotted for the topic is tight and there is no room available for expansion, or unless the nature of the topic is such that there is no possibility of introducing hierarchy into the breakdown and the subtopics to be listed will require no further breakdown of their own into subtopics.

Subdivisions which lend themselves particularly to alphabetical arrangement are personal or corporate names that are part of the subject. Typical cases are individual biographies and works about individual corporate bodies, e.g.,

QA MATHEMATICS

          Biography
28   Collective
29   Individual, A-Z
          e.g.   .G3   Gauss
                .J2   Jacobi
                .N2   Napier

AS ACADEMIES AND LEARNED SOCIETIES

          British North America. Canada
40   General works
42   Individual societies and institutions, A-Z

Cutter Numbers as Geographic Subdivisions[2]

Geographic subdivisions are frequently represented by Cutter numbers following the class number which designates the subject. The caption used in the schedules is normally one of the following:

> By place, A-Z
> By region or country, A-Z
> By region or state, A-Z
> By region or province, A-Z
> By individual island or group of islands, A-Z
> By city, A-Z

The caption, "By country, A-Z," found in many schedules is now obsolete, the current form being "By region or country, A-Z,"[3] unless there are specific provisions in the particular schedule to the contrary. The obsolete form is being replaced gradually during the course of major revisions or at the time an entire schedule is issued in a new edition.

When the classification schedules call for cuttering by region or country, A-Z, but no regions or countries are individually listed, a Cutter number is assigned for a region larger than a country or for a country, but not for a locality within a country—even if the subject heading assigned to the work is subdivided by the specific locality.[4] For example, for works dealing specifically with England, Northern Ireland, Scotland, or Wales, only the Cutter "G-" for Great Britain is used.

For jurisdictions which have undergone name changes, a Cutter number is normally assigned for the latest form of the name, regardless of the name used within the work. If a locality in question was formerly located within the territorial boundaries of another country, a Cutter number is used only for the country in which it is presently situated, even if the work in hand describes conditions applicable to its earlier status, unless there is provision to the contrary in the printed schedule. However, if there are more than ten works in the LC shelflist which have been cuttered under an earlier form of the name, the number for the earlier form may continue to be used.

"A" AND "Z" CUTTER NUMBERS*

Frequently, under a class number, a span of Cutter numbers at the beginning ("A" Cutter numbers) or at the end ("Z" Cutter numbers) of the alphabetical sequence is set aside for special purposes. The "A" Cutter numbers are used most frequently for form divisions such as periodicals or official publications, and the "Z" Cutter numbers are often assigned to special divisions of the subject, e.g., biography and criticism of a literary author, certain corporate bodies associated with the field, etc.

---

*These were called "reserved Cutter numbers" in earlier editions of this book. The term, "reserved Cutter numbers," is not used by the Library of Congress.

UA ARMIES: ORGANIZATION, DISTRIBUTION, ETC.

	By region or country
	Europe
	France
	Army
	Artillery
705.A1-5	Documents
.A6-Z4	General works
.Z5A-Z	Bataillons d'artillérie à pied
.Z6	Regiments. By number

TK ELECTRICAL ENGINEERING. ELECTRONICS. NUCLEAR ENGINEERING

	Computer engineering. Computer hardware
7885.A1A-Z	Periodicals, societies, congresses, etc.
.A2A-Z	Dictionaries and encyclopedias
.A3A-Z	Symbols and abbreviations
.A4A-Z	Directories
.A5A-Z	History
.A6-Z	General works

In the example above, the Cutter numbers ".A1-.A5" have been assigned special meanings. The general works on computer engineering will not be assigned any Cutter number between ".A1-.A5." In other words, a treatise on this subject by an author named Abell which is normally cuttered ".A2" will receive a Cutter number greater than ".A6."

In the past, the Library of Congress used "A" Cutter numbers for government or official publications and periodicals under many class numbers even when there were no explicit instructions in the schedules to do so. The use of these nonprint "A" Cutter numbers has been discontinued. Now, the "A" Cutter numbers are used only when there are specific instructions in the schedules for their use.

SUCCESSIVE CUTTER NUMBERS

The term "successive Cutter numbers" refers to a series of Cutter numbers (e.g., .C5, .C6, .C7) or decimal extensions of a Cutter number (e.g., .C54, .C55, .C56, .C57) in an established succession or order. Successive Cutter numbers are generally used for logical subarrangement of materials classed in the same number. In the past, the use of successive Cutter numbers was often announced in the schedules in the manner shown in the following example from the third edition of the R schedule:

RA   PUBLIC ASPECTS OF MEDICINE

By country.
984   Other American countries, A-Z
Under each (using successive Cutter numbers):
(1) General works
(2) Government hospitals
(3) States, provinces, etc., A-Z
(4) Cities, etc., A-Z
e.g.   Mexico
.M3   General works
.M4   Government hospitals
.M5   States, A-Z
.M6   Cities, A-Z

In this case, the successive Cutter numbers are indicated by (1), (2), (3), and (4) which become .M3, .M4, .M5, and .M6 when applied to Mexico. Both this method of announcing successive Cutter numbers and the use of single-digit Cutter number sequence (except those already established in the shelflist) are now obsolete.

Successive Cutter numbers are now announced in the manner shown below (example from the revised R schedule being prepared):

RA   PUBLIC ASPECTS OF MEDICINE

984   **Other American regions or countries, A-Z**
Under each country:
.x   General works
.x2   Government hospitals. By author
.x3   By state, province, etc., A-Z
.x4   By city, A-Z
e.g.   .C9-94   Cuba
.C9A-Z   General works
.C92A-Z   Government hospitals.
By author
.C93A-Z   By province, A-Z
.C94A-Z   By city, A-Z
.C94H2-49   Havana
.C94H2-29   General works
.C94H3-49   Special institutions.
By name
.C94H36-369   Havana. Dispensario
"Tamayo"

In this case, the successive Cutter numbers are .x, .x2, .x3, and .x4 which become .C9, .C92, .C93, and .C94 when applied to Cuba. In such an instruction, .x stands for the Cutter number assigned to the topic, place, person, or corporate body in question. Note that the Cutter number .x1 is not used because the use of a Cutter number ending in 1 is generally avoided.

Successive Cutter numbers are frequently used in tables. For further discussion and examples, *see* chapters 4 and 5.

DATE IN L.C. CALL NUMBERS

Date as Edition Mark

As mentioned earlier, the date of imprint or copyright is often added to the Cutter number(s) to indicate a variant edition of a work.* Procedures for assigning the edition mark will be discussed later in the section entitled "Distinguishing Editions of a Work."

Date as Part of Class Number

Occasionally, the date is used as a subdivision of the class number and precedes the Cutter number(s), e.g.,

D. M. Kovenock's *Explaining the Vote: Presidential Choices in the Nation and the States, 1968.* 1973-

JK	The double letters for the subclass, Constitutional history—United States
1968	The subdivision by whole numbers meaning statistics of elections and election returns
1968	The date of the election
.K68	The Cutter number for the main entry, Kovenock

In the following example, the date is brought out in the form of a decimal extension of the class number.

QB544
.54
.U6

QB	The double letters for the subclass, Astronomy
544	The subdivision by whole numbers meaning solar eclipses from 1900 to 1999
.54	The decimal number bringing out the year of the eclipse, 1954
.U6	The Cutter number for the main entry

In Class P, Literature, the date of edition or publication is often represented by a date letter, e.g., ".F37" (meaning 1937) which takes the place of the Cutter number. For detailed discussion, *see* chapter 5.

In the classification of maps in Class G, the date of map situation is included as part of the class number. In this case, the date precedes the book number. For example:

---

*The date is also added to a monograph entered under a corporate heading regardless of edition. For details, *see* chapter 6.

G3821
.P2
1946
.P4

G	The subclass single letter meaning Geography (general)
3821	The subdivision by whole numbers meaning Maps of Pennsylvania dealing with a particular subject
.P2	The subject letter-number meaning the particular subject, Roads, i.e., this is a road map of Pennsylvania
1946	The date of map situation
.P4	The Cutter number for the main entry

In some cases, a call number may contain two dates, one as part of the class number, and the other as an edition mark, e.g.,

P. Temin's *Did Monetary Forces Cause the Great Depression?*, 1976.

HB	The double letters for the subclass, Economic theory
3717	The integral number meaning history of crises
1929	The date of the crisis
.T45	The Cutter number for the main entry, Temin
1976	The date of publication

Congressional quarterly's *Guide to 1976 Elections*, 1977.

JK	The double letters for the subclass, Constitutional history — United States
1968	The integral number meaning statistics of elections and election returns
1976	The date of the election
.C65	The Cutter number for the main entry, *Congressional ...*
1977	The date of publication

For procedures of assigning edition marks in these cases, *see* later discussion entitled "Distinguishing Editions of a Work" in this chapter.

DISTINGUISHING WORKS BY THE SAME AUTHOR

In the L.C. Classification, work marks based on the titles of the works used for the purpose of distinguishing different works by the same author on the same subject, like those used with the *Dewey Decimal Classification*, are not used, except in the classification of juvenile belles lettres (*see* chapter 6). Works by the same author on the same subject (i.e., with the same class number) are differentiated by adjusting the book number.

The following guidelines have been provided by the Library of Congress for cuttering of works by one author.[5]

Unless there are provisions to the contrary in the particular schedule, the works of an individual author under a single class number are arranged by category of publication in the order indicated below, using a series of successive Cutter numbers.

Collected works.	By date
Translations.	By date
Selected works.	By date
Translations.	By date
Separate works.	By title
Under each:	
Original editions.	By date
Translations.	By date
Selections.	By date
Translations.	By date
Adaptations.	By adapter, A-Z (Used only for works cataloged during ALA era. Adaptations now classed with works of adapter.)
Criticism.	By author of criticism, A-Z.
Biography and criticism.	By author, A-Z.

It must be emphasized that the above table should be applied only when it does not conflict with any instructions or provisions in the particular schedule. Often it will be possible to use only a portion of the table in any one number. For example, if biography in connection with a particular topic has been given a separate number, the biography provision of the table should be ignored. In the P subclasses the table is unusable since the subclasses normally make use of their own special tables for arranging the works of individual authors.

An example to illustrate the application of the table is given below, as it applies both to alphameric numbers and topical Cutter numbers. Possible Cutter ranges for publication categories are shown, as well as specific author numbers for individual works. The theoretical author Cutter is .C65; the topical Cutter is .R4.

Publication categories	Alphameric number	Topical Cutter
Collected works	.C65 1974	.R4C65 1974
Translations	.C6512-6519*	.R4C6512-6519
An English translation	.C6513 1975	.R4C6513 1975
Selected works	.C66 1974	.R4C66 1974
Translations	.C6612-6619*	.R4C6612-6619
An English translation	.C6613 1975	.R4C6613 1975
Separate works	.C67-679	.R4C67-679
An original edition with title: B. . .	.C673 1975	.R4C673 1975
Translations	.C67312-67319*	.R4C67312-67319
An English translation	.C67313 1976	.R4C67313 1976
Selections	.C6732 1975	.R4C6732 1975
Translations	.C673212-673219*	.R4C673212-673219
An English translation	.C673213 1976	.R4C673213 1976
Criticism	.C6733, A-Z	.R4C6733-67339
A criticism by Smith	.C6733S8	.R4C67338
Biography and criticism	.C68, A-Z	.R4C68-689
A biography by Brown	.C68B76	.R4C683

*See Table for Translations on page 100.

DISTINGUISHING EDITIONS OF A WORK[6]

The Library of Congress prepares a new record for each new edition of a work. The word "edition" refers to issues and reprints as well as revised or updated editions (but not adaptations) for which separate cataloging entries have been prepared. Normally, the same class number assigned to the original edition of a work is used for the new edition, so long as the contents of the new edition do not vary significantly from the original.

However, variations occur in some instances because of various provisions involving dates and languages in the classification system. The following provisions, for example, require different class numbers for new editions of works from those assigned to the original edition:

1) special provisions in the classification schedules for classification by date of publication,

2) special provisions in the classification schedules for classification by the language of the text in hand,

3) special chronological subdivisions specifying imprint date, e.g., "Mathematics — 1961-   ."

When all editions of a work are classed in the same number, their sub-arrangement is based on the following provisions:

General Provisions

Preferred order for the shelf	Device for achieving preferred order
1. Original edition.	1. Assigned first Cutter number. [*See* Figure 1.]
2. Facsimile or photocopy editions of the original.	2. Same Cutter number as the original, plus the imprint date of the original followed by "a," e.g., 1859a; additional facsimile or photocopy editions are assigned "aa," "ab," "ac," etc.
3. Successive editions and reprints in chronological order by the imprint date of the publication being shelflisted. Such words as 2d ed., new ed., rev. ed., improved ed., enl. ed., 1st American ed. indicate another edition exists.	3. Imprint date added to the call number of the original. If two or more editions are published in the same year, the second received is assigned [date]b, the third [date]c, etc. [*See* Figure 2.]
4. Any facsimile or photocopy edition of one of these succeeding editions to follow immediately after its original.	4. Imprint date of the original successive edition followed by "a," "aa," "ab," etc.
5. Translations.	5. Original Cutter number followed by a number from the special table for translations,* preceded normally by number 1, e.g., original: .A4; translation into English: .A413.
6. Abridgments, selections of a single work, or condensed versions.	6. Original Cutter number expanded preferably by a 2, e.g., .A42.
7. Translations of abridgments, selections of a single work, or condensed versions.	7. Cutter of the abridgment, etc., followed by a number from the special table for translations,* e.g., abridgment: .A42; translation into English: .A4213.
8. Criticism.	8. Original Cutter expanded preferably by a 3, e.g., .A43.

Identifying Successive Editions

If there is any indication, however doubtful, that other editions have been published, it is LC practice to process the work as an edition. The following guidelines are used in determining when a date is added to the call number:

---

*See page 100.

1)   The imprint date is added to the call number if there is some indication in the work—usually on the verso of the title page—that it has also been published by another publisher. Since certain publishers, such as Pergamon Press and Asia Publishing House, are known to publish both American and foreign English editions, the imprint date is added to the call number of the edition that is cataloged first as well as to subsequent editions. [*See* Figure 3.]

2)   If a work is published after an author's death, the imprint date is added to the call number unless it can be readily established that the work was published posthumously.

3)   If the work has an American imprint but the author is known to be British, the imprint date is added to the call number.

4)   If a British publication has been copyrighted in the United States, the imprint date is added to the call number in anticipation of an American edition.

Selecting the Appropriate Date

1)   If the imprint date of an edition is uncertain and is bracketed, use the date provided: e.g., for [1892?] and [ca. 1892] use 1892 in both cases.

2)   If the imprint date of an edition is uncertain and two dates are bracketed, use the earlier date provided: e.g., for [1892 or 1893] use 1892, and for [between 1906 and 1912] use 1906.

3)   If the imprint date of an edition cannot be determined beyond the decade or century, use the earliest date of the decade or century plus the letter "z," which places the work after any editions that might have been actually published during that year: e.g., for [196-] and [196?] use 1960z, and for [19--] and [19--?] use 1900z. [*See* Figure 4.]

4)   If the imprint date of an edition contains a date of publication and a copyright date, use the date of publication: e.g., for 1966 [c1964] use 1966. However, if the date of the first impression of the edition cannot be ascertained and the imprint date contains the copyright date and the date of a later impression, use the copyright date: e.g., for c1971, 1977 printing, use 1971.

5)   If the imprint date of an edition contains a date of publication and a printing date, use the date of publication: e.g., for 1969, 1971 printing use 1969, and for 1970, t.p. 1973 use 1970.

6)   If the imprint date of an edition contains a date of publication that has been corrected, use the corrected date of publication: e.g., for 1966 [i.e. 1965] use 1965; and for 1966 [i.e. 1965, c1962] use 1965; and for 1975, cover 1976, use 1976.

7)   If the imprint date of an edition of a multivolume work covers more than one year, e.g., 1826-1828, use the earlier date.

8)   If the imprint date of an edition is an open entry, e.g., 1826-   , use the date provided.

Compilations

If a work is a compilation of individual works already published, the compilation is treated as a separate work and is given its own call number. A new or reprinted edition of a compilation is processed according to the above procedures.

Class Numbers with Dates
Date of imprint as part of the class number:

If the imprint date is assigned in the schedules as part of the class number, this date usually changes from one edition to another. Therefore the editions of a work are not necessarily kept together, depending on what is already filed in the shelflist. Works are grouped into categories by this first date. As a result the Cutter numbers for the editions may vary from edition to edition and a second date is usually not needed in the call number to distinguish editions.

For example:

1st ed.	2d ed.	3d ed.	4th ed.	5th ed.	6th ed.
JK4825	JK4825	JK4825	JK4825	JK4825	JK4825
1949	1952	1956	1960	1964	1968
.M3	.M3	.M3	.M3	.M2	.M2

Date of period, policy, etc. as part of class number:

If the date of period, policy, etc. forms part of the class number, this date usually remains the same for each edition. Therefore it is possible to keep the editions together by using the same Cutter number and adding the imprint date as a second date to each new edition.

For example:

In shelflist	New edition
HB3717	HB3717
1929	1929
.K55	.K55
	1975

In the past when the first date remained the same from edition to edition, successive Cutter numbers rather than double dates were often used to distinguish editions.

For example:

In shelflist	New edition
JN7228	JN7228
1949	1949
.N6	.N62

In these instances, the Cutter number of the most recent edition shelflisted under former procedures is now used and the imprint date of the new edition is added.

For example:

In shelflist:		New edition
JN7228	JN7228	JN7228
1949	1949	1949
.N6	.N62	.N62
		1976

Figure 1. Original Edition.

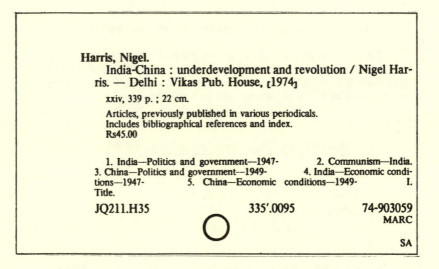

> **Harris, Nigel.**
> India-China : underdevelopment and revolution / Nigel Harris. — Delhi : Vikas Pub. House, [1974]
>
> xxiv, 339 p. ; 22 cm.
>
> Articles, previously published in various periodicals.
> Includes bibliographical references and index.
> Rs45.00
>
> 1. India—Politics and government—1947-   2. Communism—India.
> 3. China—Politics and government—1949-   4. India—Economic conditions—1947-   5. China—Economic conditions—1949-   I. Title.
>
> JQ211.H35   335'.0095   74-903059
>   MARC
>
>   SA

Figure 2. A Variant Edition Published in the Same Year.

Harris, Nigel.
    India-China : underdevelopment and revolution / Nigel Harris. — Durham, N.C. : Carolina Academic Press, c1974.

xxiv, 339 p. ; 23 cm.

"Contains a selection of essays already published in Britain."
Includes bibliographical references and index.
ISBN 0-89089-017-X : $9.00

1. Communism—India.   2. India—Politics and government—1947-   .
3. China—Politics and government—1949-1976.   4. India—Economic conditions—1947-   5. China—Economic conditions—1949-1976.   I. Title.

JQ211.H35   1974b   320.9′51′05   74-30894
                                                                                            MARC

Figure 3. First Edition with an Edition Mark.

Steiner, Stanley.
    Fusang, the Chinese who built America / by Stan Steiner. —
1st ed. — New York : Harper & Row, c1979.

xii, 259 p. ; 22 cm.

Bibliography: p. [239]-251.
Includes index.
ISBN 0-06-014087-9 : $11.95

1. Chinese Americans—History.   2. America—Discovery and exploration—
Chinese.   I. Title.

E184.C5S76   1979   970′.004′951   78-2172
                                                                                          MARC

Figure 4. Date of Publication Uncertain.

Gilhofer, H., & Ranschburg, H., firm, booksellers, Lucerne.
  Landmarks : a choice of important books (1502-1930) including a section Psychology, psychoanalysis, psychiatry, neurology, and an autograph manuscript by Albert Einstein. — Luzern : Gilhofer & Ranschburg GmbH, [197-]
   120 p. : ill. ; 27 cm. — (Catalogue-Gilhofer & Ranschburg GmbH ; 67)
                                                                    Sw***
   Cover title.
   Includes bibliographical references and indexes.
   1. Bibliography—First editions—Catalogs.   2. Bibliography—Rare books—Catalogs.   3. Catalogs, Booksellers'—Switzerland—Lucerne.   4. Gilhofer, H., & Ranschburg, H., firm, booksellers, Lucerne—Catalogs.   I. Title.   II. Series: Gilhofer, H., & Ranschburg, H., firm, booksellers, Lucerne.   Katalog ; 67.
Z999.G46   1970z   016.094'4   78-318650
                                                                    MARC

TRANSLATIONS

Translations of a work normally follow the original text in an alphabetical arrangement by language. This is achieved by using successive Cutter numbers. The numeral 1 is inserted in order to avoid interference with other titles by the same author. The following table provides a general guide for arranging translations. A translation in a language not listed here may be assigned a Cutter number which will place it in the proper place in the sequence.

TABLE FOR TRANSLATIONS

Use only if there are no specific instructions for subarranging translations.

.x	Cutter number of work in original language
.x13	English translation
.x14	French translation
.x15	German translation
.x16	Italian translation
.x17	Russian translation
.x18	Spanish translation

If a Bulgarian, Chinese, or Czech translation is to be inserted, the Cutter number .x12 may be used; if a Hebrew translation, .x15 or .x16; a Portuguese translation, .x16 or .x17, depending on what has already been used.

In the past, the numeral 1 was frequently omitted from the Cutter number representing the translation, e.g., .B3, original work; .B33, English translation; .B34 French translation; etc. This practice has been discontinued except in cases where the pattern has already been established in the shelflist.

OTHER VARIATIONS IN THE NOTATION

The following examples illustrate other variations in the L.C. notation:

Example 1)   A call number for a subject map:

G3824
.P6P2
1965
.P6

G	The subclass single letter meaning Geography (general)
3824	The subdivision by whole number meaning Maps of individual cities in Pennsylvania
.P6	The first Cutter number for the specific individual city, in this case Pittsburgh
P2	The subject letter-number meaning road maps
1965	Date of map situation
.P6	The second Cutter number for the main entry

This example demonstrates the apparent use of three Cutter numbers. It should be pointed out that, actually, "P2" is not a Cutter number but a subject letter-number. In the classification of maps, it is possible for the notation to appear to have three Cutter numbers because subject letter-numbers look like Cutter numbers. "P2" comes from a sequence to which arbitrary meaning has been given without the intention of cuttering. It is a subdivision of the subject table for transportation and communication as the following portion shows:

Table of Form and Subject Subdivisions
(from Class G)

P   TRANSPORTATION AND COMMUNICATION

1	General.
2	Roads.
3	Railroads.
4	Pipe lines.
5	Water transportation.
55	Ports and port facilities.
6	Air transportation. Aeronautical charts.
7	Space transportation.
8	Postal service. Postal zones. Zip codes.
9	Communications.

Example 2)   A call number with work letters:

> LD5351
> .T7gb

LD   The subclass double letters meaning an individual university, college, or school in the United States

5351   The subdivision by whole numbers meaning those individual institutions whose names are between Th-- and Tra--

.T7   The first Cutter number meaning Translyvania University in Lexington, Ky.

gb   The work letters meaning a publication about honors courses at that univerity

Example 3)   A call number for a set of maps:

> G3800
> s25
> .U5

G   The subclass single letter meaning Geography (general)

3800   The subdivision by whole numbers meaning general maps of New York State

s   The letter meaning this is a set of maps

25   The scale number meaning this set of maps has a ratio of 1:25,000. The final three digits of the ratio number are dropped

.U5   The Cutter number for the main entry

Example 4)   A call number for music containing an opus number:

> M1010
> .B41
> op. 58
> .W5

M   The subclass single letter meaning Music

1010   The subdivision by whole number meaning full scores of piano concertos

.B41   The first Cutter number for the composer, in this case Beethoven

op. 58   The opus number for this particular piano concerto, i.e., Concerto no. 4 in G

.W5   The second Cutter number for the name of publisher of this particular edition

Example 5)   A call number for music containing an opus number:

> M452
> .B42
> op. 18, no. 2
> .W5

M The subclass single letter meaning Music

452 The subdivision by whole numbers meaning individual string quartets

.B42 The first Cutter number for Beethoven

op. 18 The opus number for this particular string quartet which actually is a collection of six quartets making up opus 18

no. 2 The number of this particular quartet in opus 18

.W5 The second Cutter number for the name of publisher of this particular edition

Example 6)   A call number for music containing a thematic index number and a work letter indicating parts:

> M857
> .B4
> K.25
> .I5p

M The subclass single letter meaning Music

857 The subdivision by whole numbers meaning a wind octet

.B4 The first Cutter number for Beethoven

K.25 The Kinsky thematic index number

.I5 The second Cutter number for the publisher of this particular edition

p The letter indicating that there are separate parts for this work

In the three previous examples it should be noted that Beethoven has been given three different Cutter numbers. Each reflects the development of an individual class number in the shelflist.

DISPLAY OF THE NOTATION

In the foregoing examples, the first Cutter number was preceded by a decimal point. This is consistent with the Library of Congress practice. The use of this decimal point before the first element of the Cutter number may be traced to Cutter's own use of Cutter numbers. The remainder of the notation in the previous examples does not follow the normal Library of Congress practice. The reason for this variation is to analyze the call number graphically. The proper representation of the notation at the Library of Congress is to present the class letter or letters on one line with the integral number. Any decimal extension of the integral number would follow on a separate line to avoid the possibility of confusion should the decimal point be accidentally dropped. The next line is introduced by the decimal point for the Cutter number or numbers, which usually fill only one line even if there are two Cutter numbers. Finally, the date may be the last element on a separate line. This practice is followed at the Library of Congress for the representation of the call number on the catalog card. The representation of the call number on the spine of the book is the same except that the first line is divided into two lines with the class letter or letters on the first line and the integral number on the second. The following example demonstrates the Library of Congress representation of the call number on the catalog card and book label.

```
Z695
.1
.E3C36   Canadian Education Association.
1978          Canadian education subject headings (CanESH) : subject
          headings for the Canadian education index = Vedettes-matière
          sur l'education au Canada : vedettes-matière pour le répertoire
          canadien sur l'education / edited by Deborah C. Sawyer. — 5th
          ed. — Toronto : Canadian Education Association, 1978.

             224 p. ; 28 cm.                                    C•••
          English and French.

             1. Subject headings—Education.   I. Sawyer, Deborah C.   II. Canadian
          education index.   III. Title.   IV. Title: Vedettes matière sur l'education au
          Canada.
          Z695.1.E3C36   1978          025.3'3'37          79-341424
                                                            MARC

          Library of Congress          79
```

```
Z
695
.1
.E3C36
1978
```

Many libraries do not follow this same representation of the notation. For example, some libraries do not use the introductory decimal point for the Cutter numbers. A discussion of one library's solution to this particular problem may be found in Daniel Gore's "Further Observations on the Use of LC Classification," listed in the bibliography of this chapter.

In a MARC record, the LC call number appears in field 050. Two subfield codes are used:

$a   LC classification number

$b   Book number

For example,

Øb$aHE5623$b.E23

Øb$aHF5549.5.R44$bM35

The first indicator shows whether the book is in LC (Ø) or not in LC (1), and the second indicator is blank. If an alternative classification number is provided, it appears in the same field, separated from the first class number by subfield code $a, e.g.,

Øb$aPZ3.B554$bGat8$aPS3503.J6

BIBLIOGRAPHY

(*See also* **Bibliography to chapter 2**)

Arick, Mary Catherine. "Subclassification and Book Numbers of Documents and Official Publications," in *The Use of the Library of Congress Classification: Proceedings of the Institute on the Use of the Library of Congress Classification*, edited by Richard H. Schimmelpfeng and C. Donald Cook. Chicago: American Library Association, 1968.
Pages 135-61 present a detailed discussion with many examples of official Cutter numbers, double Cutter numbers, and expansions of Cutter numbers.

Gore, Daniel. "Further Observations on the Use of LC Classification," *Library Resources & Technical Services* 10:519-24, Fall 1966.
Gore advises the use of a lower-case "x" at the end of all locally originated L.C. call numbers to avoid any possible duplication with Library of Congress classification numbers. He also recommends the moving of the first Cutter number's decimal point from in front of the capital letter to beyond the first decimal number, e.g., "Q1M5.5x."

Holmes, Robert R. "Assignment of Author Numbers," in *The Use of the Library of Congress Classification: Proceedings of the Institute on the Use of the Library of Congress Classification*, edited by Richard H. Schimmelpfeng and C. Donald Cook. Chicago: American Library Association, 1968.
Pages 107-120 present a clear and detailed explanation of the uses and policies of the Library of Congress in regard to author or Cutter numbers.

U.S. Library of Congress. *Author Notation in the Library of Congress.* By Anna Cantrell Laws. Washington: GPO, 1937.
This is a valuable work for analyzing call numbers; however, it is dated and some of the practices described are no longer used.

NOTES

[1]*Cataloging Service Bulletin* 3:19-20 (Winter 1979).

[2]*Cataloging Service* 116:6 (Winter 1976).

[3]For tables designed for arranging places alphabetically, *see* Appendix A.

[4]*See Cataloging Service* 114:10-11 (Summer 1975).

[5]*Cataloging Service* 120:16-17 (Winter 1977); 121:19 (Spring 1977).

[6]*Cataloging Service* 112:14-15 (Winter 1975); *Cataloging Service Bulletin* 3:20-23 (Winter 1979).

4   TABLES

In order to reduce the total number of pages in individual schedules, tables representing recurring patterns of subdivision are used. A table that represents a pattern of subdivision unique to a specific subject and is applicable to a specific span of numbers only appears within the schedule either at the beginning or at the end of the span of numbers involved. These internal* tables vary in length from simple tables of two or three lines to complex tables occupying several pages. Tables that are applicable to an entire class or subclass normally appear at the end of the class or subclass immediately before the index. These are similar to the "auxiliary tables"* in other classification schemes. There are a number of tables that are used throughout the L.C. Classification system. These are sometimes called "floating tables."*

In terms of characteristics or facets of subdivision, there are six different types of tables:

1)   Form tables

2)   Geographic tables

3)   Chronological tables

4)   Subject subdivision tables

5)   Combination tables

6)   Author tables

---

*The term is not used by the Library of Congress.

All of these tables, both simple and complex, may be mastered by following the same standard pattern:

1) Determine the range of numbers in the schedule within which the subject being represented falls.
2) Choose the appropriate table to be applied to the specific range of numbers.
3) Select the number in the table which represents the subject and fit the number (normally by simple addition) into the range of numbers from the schedule.

It should be noted that the notation in the form of arabic numbers in a table indicates the order of subdivisions as they appear within a span of class numbers. To obtain the correct class number, the appropriate number from a table is *added* to a base number, and *not* attached to the class number as an additional segment. On the other hand, a Cutter number from a table, such as .U6 for United States, is *attached* to the class number as a separate segment.

The following section contains a discussion and demonstration of the use of tables in the L.C. Classification. Examples are provided for those types of tables occurring in more than one class. Details and examples of tables applicable to a specific schedule only are given in chapter 5.

FORM TABLES

A form table provides a pattern of subarrangement of materials on a particular subject by physical or bibliographic form. These tables are usually used when geographic or chronological division is not needed or has already been extensively employed. Examples of "form tables" may be found in the schedules of Class K. The following is a portion of the tables for "Form Divisions"* in schedule KF; for examples of the use of form tables, *see* discussion in chapter 5.

FORM DIVISIONS

I 20 nos.	II 10 nos.	III 5 nos.	IV 5 nos.	V 2 nos.	VI* 1 no.	
1	1	1	1.A1A-Z	1.A1A-Z	.A1A-Z	Bibliography.
.5	.5		.A2A-Z			Surveys of legal research.
(2)	(2)		(.A3)	(.A15)		Periodicals, see K1-30.
2.5						Yearbooks. Statistics.
3	2.3		.A35A-Z	.A16A-Z	.A16A-Z	Society publications.
4	.5		.A4	.A17	.A17	Congresses and conferences. By date.
						Meetings intended to result in concerted action, e.g., recommendations for law revision, new legislation, government action, etc.
						For papers and discussions devoted to the exploration of a subject, including "conferences," "institutes," workshops," etc., see Symposia, p. 274.
(5)	(3)		(.A5)	(.A2)	(.A2)	Congressional hearings and reports, see KF25 ff.
						For hearings and reports of state legislature, see Table IX(A), p. 277.

*For a complete, updated version of these tables, see Appendix C of this book.

GEOGRAPHIC TABLES

There are two types of geographic tables:

1)   Geographic division in a classified arrangement. In this type of table, geographic areas are given numbers in a classified order. An example of this type of table is the "Geographical Distribution Tables" found in Class S. A portion of these tables is given below.

GEOGRAPHICAL DISTRIBUTION TABLES

In countries to which two numbers are assigned:
(1) General.
(2) Local, A–Z.

I	II	
21		America.
22		North America.
23		United States.
24		States, A–W.
26–27	1–2	Canada.
28–29	3–4	Mexico.
30–31	5–6	Central America.
32–33	7–8	West Indies.
34	9	South America.
36–37	11–12	Argentine Republic.
38–39	13–14	Bolivia.
41–42	15–16	Brazil.
43–44	17–18	Chile.
45–46	19–20	Colombia.
47–48	21–22	Ecuador.
49–50	23–24	Guiana.
51	25–26	Paraguay.
52	27–28	Peru.
53	29–30	Uruguay.
54	31–32	Venezuela.
55	33	Europe.
57–58	35–36	Great Britain. England.
59–60	37–38	Wales.
61–62	39–40	Scotland.
63–64	41–42	Ireland.
65–66	43–44	Austria.
67–68	45–46	Belgium.
69–70	47–48	Denmark.
71–72	49–50	France.
73–74	51–52	Germany.
75–76	53–54	Greece.
77–78	55–56	Holland.
79–80	57–58	Italy.
81–82	59–60	Norway.
83–84	61–62	Portugal.
85–86	63–64	Russia.
87–88	65–66	Spain.
89–90	67–68	Sweden.
91–92	69–70	Switzerland.
93–94	71–72	Turkey.
95	73	Other countries of Europe, A–Z.

The use of this table is illustrated in the following example.

> M. Cordero del Campillo's *Semblanzas veterinarias* [a work
> about veterinary medicine in Spain]

SF	The double letter for the subclass Veterinary medicine and surgery
687	The integral number meaning a history of veterinary medicine in Spain
.C67	The Cutter number for the main entry, Cordero del Campillo

The class number 687 is arrived at by following the instruction in the schedule and the procedure outlined above for the use of tables. In the schedule, the numbers SF621-723 have been assigned to the history of veterinary medicine subdivided by country according to Table I, with the instruction to "add number in Table I to 600." In Table I reproduced above, the numbers assigned to Spain are 87-88, the first being used for a general work, meaning a work about the country as a whole. Adding 87 to the base number 600 results in the desired number 687.

The "Tables of Geographical Divisions" in Classes H and N are much more complex than the one in Class S. For examples of using these tables, *see* chapter 5.

2) Geographic division in an alphabetical arrangement. This type of table presents geographic division in an alphabetical order by means of Cutter numbers. Examples are "Regions and Countries in One Alphabet" and "Table of Cities in the United States." Some of these tables appear in more than one schedule. A number of them are applied to all classes throughout the system, although they have not been printed in all the schedules. The following is a discussion of these commonly used "floating tables" with examples. For details of the tables, *see* Appendix A.

A) **Regions and Countries in One Alphabet.** Used whenever the instruction "By country, A-Z" or "By region or country, A-Z" appears in the schedules. This table appears in Schedules C, D, E-F, H, T, U, and V. It should be noted that the Cutter numbers assigned to a particular country may vary slightly from schedule to schedule. For example, the United States is assigned .U5 in most of the schedules, but .U6 in Schedule T. These may be modified further according to what already exists in the shelflist.

> L. Bellak's *The Best Years of Your Life: A Guide to the Art and
> Science of Aging*, 1975.

HQ	The double letter for the subclass, Social groups
1064	The integral number meaning the aged
.U5	The first Cutter number (based on the Table of Countries in One Alphabet) for the United States
B35	The second Cutter number for the main entry, Bellak
1975	The date of publication

Conference Proceedings of the Midwest Regional Conference on Science, Technology, and State Government, 1970

Q	The single letter for the class, Science
127	The integral number meaning Science and state, by region or country
.U6	The first Cutter number (based on the Table of Countries in One Alphabet) for the United States
M54	The second Cutter number for the main entry, Midwest....
1970	The date of the conference

B) Table of States. Used when it is instructed: "By state, A-W," or "By region or state, A-Z." This table is included in Schedules G, H, T, U, and V.

A. H. Holmgren's *Weeds of Utah*

SB	The double letters for the subclass, Plant culture and horticulture
612	The integral number meaning weeds in the United States
.U8	The first Cutter number (based on Table of States) for Utah
H6	The second Cutter number for the main entry, Holmgren

C) Canada and Newfoundland—List of Provinces. Used when the instruction "By province, A-Z" or "By region or province, A-Z" under a class number for Canada is given. This table appears in Schedule T.

W. G. Fleming's *Ontario's Educative Society.*

LA	The double letters for the subclass, History of education
418	The integral number assigned to the provinces of Canada
.O6	The first Cutter number (cf. Canada and Newfoundland—List of Provinces) for Ontario
F55	The second Cutter number for the main entry, Fleming

CHRONOLOGICAL TABLES

Usually found under the historical division of a subject, chronological tables are simple tables of subdivision by date. These tables nearly always occur within the schedules and are usually very brief. Examples may be found in JN 5251-5299 or HJ 2391-2442 (see page 112).

JN	**CONSTITUTIONAL HISTORY – ITALY**
	Special states and regions.
	Under each:
	(1) General.
	(2) 769/843 to ca. 1268.
	(3) ca. 1268 to ca. 1495.
	(4) ca. 1495 to ca. 1793.
5251-5254	Piedmont. Savoy.
5256-5259	Liguria: Genoa.
5261-5264	Lombardy: Milan.
5266-5269	Venice.
5271-5274	Romagna. Emilia.

Venice (Republic, to 1797) *Relazioni dei Rettori Veneti in Terraferma*, 1973.

JN	The double letters for the subclass, Constitutional history
5269	The integral number assigned (based on the table above) to Venice in the period ca. 1495 to ca. 1793
.V45	The Cutter number for the main entry, Venice....
1973	The date of publication

Following is an example of a table of chronological division by means of "A" Cutter numbers.

HJ	**PUBLIC FINANCE**
	Revenue. Taxation.
	United States.
2391-2442	States individually.
	Under each:
	General works. History.
.A2	General.
	Early to 1800.
.A29	Documents.
.A3	Other.
	1801-1860.
.A39	Documents.
.A4	Other.
	1861-1865/70.
.A49	Documents.
.A5	Other.
	1865/70-1900.
.A59	Documents.
.A6	Other.

SUBJECT SUBDIVISION TABLES

The further division of a subject may also be done by the use of tables. There are relatively few tables of this type, because most of the subject or topical subdivisions are enumerated in the schedules. An example of subject subdivision tables may be found in Class L. Table I* in Class L is used for subdivisions under individual educational institutions in the United States. In the schedule, Washington State University has been assigned the numbers "LD5731.W57-66." Since the University receives a span of Cutter numbers, Table I is used. For example:

> Washington State University, Pullman. *"A Multipurpose Communication Network Prototype:" A Proposal to the Fund for Improvement of Post-Secondary Education, Department of Health, Education, and Welfare,* 1976.

LD	The double letters for the subclass Individual institutions of education
5731	The integral number assigned to certain institutions with names beginning with the letter W
.W6k	The first Cutter number within the span of numbers assigned to Washington State University, meaning a miscellaneous publication (the Cutter number .W6k corresponding to the number .x2k in Table I)
W38	The second Cutter number for the main entry, Washington....
1976	The date of publication**

COMBINATION TABLES

The most common type of auxiliary table consists of a combination of two or more of the other types of tables. Form, subject, and geographic tables are often combined. Similarly, some chronological divisions may occur in a combination table. The "Table of Arrangement of Works under Countries" in Subclass PN for journalism (see pages 114-15) may be examined as a combination table containing all of these elements.

---

*For an updated version of this table, *see* Appendix C of this book.

**The date is added in accordance with the instructions for assigning Cutter numbers and date for works entered under corporate headings. For details, *see* chapter 6.

PN   <u>Journalism. The periodical press, etc.</u>
                By region or country- Continued

TABLE FOR ARRANGEMENT OF WORKS UNDER COUNTRIES

For the United States, <u>see</u> PN4841+

20 nos.	10 nos.	
		Periodicals, <u>see</u> PN4701+
	1	Societies, conferences, collections
1		Societies
2		Conferences. Congresses
3		Collections
		History and other general works
4	2	Comprehensive
5	3	Early
	4	Recent
6		18th century
7		19th century
8		20th century
	6	Biography of editors, journalists, etc.
12	.A1-5	Collective
13	.A6-Z	Individual, A-Z
14	7	Special topics, A-Z
		.A4 Agricultural journalism
		.B55 Black press
		.B75 Broadcast journalism
		.C35 Canards
		.C4 Catholic press
		.C5 Circulation
		.C57 Commercial journalism
		.C6 Communist press
		.C63 Community newspapers
		.C67 Country newspapers. Rural
		journalism
		.C74 Crime journalism
		.E6 Employees
		.E8 Ethics of journalism
		.F4 Feuilletons
		.F45 Fiction
		.F5 Finance
		Foreign language press
		.F6 General works
		.F62 By language, A-Z
		.H4 Headlines
		.H8 Humorous periodicals
		.I8 Islamic press
		.J8 Juvenile periodicals
		.L3 Labor
		.L4 Letters to the editor.
		Readers' opinions, etc.
		.L6 Literature
		.L62 Little magazines
		.L65 Local editions
		.L8 Lutheran press

JOURNALISM   PN

Journalism. The periodical press, etc.
  By region or country

TABLE FOR ARRANGEMENT OF WORKS UNDER COUNTRIES

For the United States, see PN4841+

20 nos.	10 nos.	
14	7	Special topics, A-Z - Continued
		.M5 Military journalism
		.M68 Motion picture journalism
		Negro press, see .B55
		.P4 Periodicals. Magazines (other than newspapers
		.P58 Police
		.P6 Politics
		.P65 Prices
		.P67 Prison journalism
		.P7 Propaganda
		.R28 Race problems
		.R3 Radio journalism
		.R45 Religious journalism
		.R5 Reporters and reporting
		.R55 Reviews. Critical writing
		Rural journalism, see .C67
		.S4 Sections, columns, etc. (General)
		.S6 Social conditions
		.S63 Socialist journalism
		.S65 Sports journalism
		.T37 Technical journalism
		.T4 Television journalism
		.T43 Television program guides
		.U5 Underground literature
		.U53 Underground press
		.W25 Wages
		.W3 Wall newspapers
		.W36 War
		.W6 Women's magazines
		Local
16		By region, A-Z
17	8	By state, province, etc., A-Z
		Under each:
		.x Collections
		.x2 General works. History
19	9	By place, A-Z
		Under each, using successive Cutter numbers
		.x Collections
		.x2 General works. History
		.x3 Special newspapers, A-Z
20	10	Special magazines and other periodicals, A-Z
		For newspapers, see 19 and 9

This table should be studied carefully for the following observations: under the "20 nos." column the first four numbers, "1-4," represent a form table; the next four numbers, "5-8," are chronological dividers; numbers "12 and 13" are examples of both form and subject divisions; number "14, Special topics, A-Z," is another subject division; numbers "16-19," "Local," are geographic divisions; and number "20" is a subject division for discussion of "Special magazines and other periodicals, A-Z."

Journalism in Italy has been assigned the numbers PN5241-5250. Therefore, the ten-number table is used. An early history of journalism in Italy receives the number PN5243.

U. Bellocchi's *Storia del giornalismo italiano.*

PN	The double letters for the subclass Literature: General and universal (including journalism)
5243	The integral number meaning an early history of journalism in Italy, the last digit 3 taken from the table
.B44	The Cutter number for the main entry, Bellocchi

Internal Tables

Many of the tables within the schedules are used to subdivide further the geographic divisions of a particular subject. The tables used with AM10-100, the numbers assigned to the geographic division of the subject, description, and history of museums by country, are used below as examples. The four tables within the schedules to be used to subdivide the geographic numbers are for: three-number countries, two-number countries, one-number countries, and Cutter-number countries.

```
AM

10-100          Description and history of museums
                  By country
                    For individual museums of a general nature, see AM101
                  Under each country (Three numbers):
                    (1)  General works
                    (2)  States, provinces, etc., A-Z
                    (3)  Cities, towns, etc., A-Z
                  Under each country (Two numbers):
                    (1)  .A1A-Z  Periodicals.  Societies
                         .A2A-Z  General works
                         .A3-Z   Provinces, etc., A-Z
                    (2)          Cities, towns, etc.
                  Under each country (One number):
                    .A2A-Z  General works
                    .A3A-Z  States provinces, etc., A-Z
                    .A4-Z   Cities, towns, etc., A-Z
                  Under each country (Cutter number)
                    .x   General works
                    .x2  States, provinces, etc., A-Z
                    .x3  Cities, towns, etc., A-Z
```

Following these tables are the specific geographic divisions indicating the range of integral numbers to be used for each division.

10	**America**
11-13	United States.
21-22	British America. Canada.
23-24	Mexico.

Three-Number Countries

As shown in the table above, AM 11-13 is assigned to the United States. This means that the United States, in this case, is a three-number country. AM 11-13 is the range of numbers to be used for works on the museums in the United States. Without a table the classifier could not discern how to subdivide this range. By using the appropriate table, the classifier can easily locate the correct subdivisions. As the United States is a three-number country, the first table (for three-number countries) should be applied. The range of numbers of United States is shown below matched to the table for three-number countries.

AM 11	(1)	General works
12	(2)	States, provinces, etc., A-Z
13	(3)	Cities, towns, etc., A-Z

A general work on the museums in the United States will be assigned the first number, AM 11. For instance, the *Museums Directory of the United States and Canada* is classed as "AM 11 .M8." "AM 11" means a general work on the museums of the United States and ".M8" is the Cutter number for the main entry, which in this case is the title.

Museums Directory of the United States and Canada.

AM	The double letters for the subclass, Museums
11	The integral number meaning a general work on the museums in the United States
.M8	The Cutter number for the main entry, *Museums Directory....*

A work on the museums in one of the states of the United States would be classed in the second number in the table as applied to the range of numbers for the United States, AM 11-13. The second number is AM 12. Similarly, the third number, AM 13, would be used for a work on the museums in one of the cities in the United States (see page 118 for example).

M. J. Whittaker's *Museums of Illinois.*

AM	The double letters for the subclass, Museums
12	The integral number meaning a work on the museums in one of the states of the United States
.I3	The first Cutter number for the specific state, Illinois
W46	The second Cutter number for the main entry, Whittaker

W. H. Noble's *Philadelphia's Treasure Houses: A Guide to Museums Open to the Public.*

AM	The double letters for the subclass, Museums
13	The integral number meaning a work on the museums in a city in the United States
.P5	The first Cutter number for the city, Philadelphia
N6	The second Cutter number for the main entry, Noble

The same process as applied to the United States may be applied to any country or geographic division which has been assigned a range of three numbers on the subject of description and history of museums, AM 10-100.

Two-Number Countries

A similar process may be followed with two-number and one-number ranges. Japan has been assigned two numbers, AM 77-78. Therefore, in classifying the Japanese periodical entitled *Hakubutsukan kenykū*, the table for two-number countries is used.

Under each country (two numbers):

(1)	.A1A-Z	Periodicals. Societies
	.A2A-Z	General works
	.A3-Z	Provinces, etc., A-Z
(2)		Cities, towns, etc.

Based on this table, the call number "AM 77 .A1H653" is assigned.

Hakubutsukan kenkyū.

AM	The double letters for the subclass, Museums
77	The integral number meaning a work on the museums of Japan
.A1	The first Cutter number meaning a periodical
H653	The second Cutter number for the main entry, *Hakubutsukan....*

One-Number Countries

Norway is a one-number country to which the third table is applied.

Under each country (one number):

.A2A-Z	General works
.A3A-Z	States, provinces, etc., A-Z
.A4-Z	Cities, towns, etc., A-Z

The number for Norway is AM 63. In this case the further subdivisions make use of "A" Cutter numbers. Thus, AM 63 .A2 would be used for general works on museums in Norway.

Erling Welle-Strand's *Museums in Norway.*

AM	The double letters for the subclass, Museums
63	The integral number meaning a work on some aspect of the museums of Norway
.A2	The first Cutter number meaning a general work on the museums of Norway
W44	The second Cutter number for the main entry, Welle-Strand

Works on museums in individual cities employ the range of Cutter numbers .A4-Z. This means that instead of alphabetically subdividing from A-Z, as in other instances, the classifier cannot use .A1, .A2, or .A3, but must start the range with .A4. Any locality beginning with the letter "A" must be cuttered from .A4 — .A9. The beginner should note that this is a single alphabetical range and not two alphabetical ranges. Simply start the range with .A4 instead of .A1. Cities beginning with letters other than "A" are cuttered as usual. For instance, Oslo, Norway would be .O8, which is within the range of .A4-Z. A work on museums in Oslo would be classed "AM 63.O8."

"A directory of the museums of Oslo, Norway."

AM	The double letters for the subclass, Museums
63	The integral number meaning a work on some aspect of the museums of Norway
.O8	The first Cutter number meaning a local work on the museums of Norway, the locality being Oslo
—	The second Cutter number to be used for the main entry

Cutter-Number Countries

A final example of the use of this set of tables is the instance of Cutter-number countries. There are countries which receive only a Cutter number for their distinctive element. For example, AM 70 is for "Other European countries, A-Z." One such country is Hungary, which does not appear separately in the geographic divisions and must use AM 70.H8. The Cutter number for Hungary may be verified as ".H8." In this case, the table for a Cutter-number country is used for the remaining portion of the call number:

Under each country (Cutter number):

.x	General works
.x2	States, provinces, etc., A-Z
.x3	Cities, towns, etc., A-Z

Based on this table, a directory of museums in Hungary entitled *Magyar Muzeumok* is classed "AM 70 .H8M3."

Magyar Muzeumok [a directory of museums in Hungary].

AM	The double letters for the subclass, Museums
70	The integral number meaning a work on some aspect of the museums in the other European countries
.H8	The first Cutter number meaning the specific country, Hungary
M3	The second Cutter number for the main entry, *Magyar....*

Auxiliary Tables

The auxiliary tables used to subdivide geographic divisions for yearbooks, almanacs, directories in AY may be used as examples of tables applicable to a subclass. There are three tables at the end of Subclass AY to be used to subdivide the geographic numbers for almanacs and yearbooks of foreign countries. These tables, designed for ten-number countries, two-number countries, and one-number, or Cutter-number countries, are used only for foreign countries, as the numbers for United States yearbooks and almanacs are worked out fully in the schedules. This is often the case with subdivisions for geographic division; the United States may be given more numbers and then does not use auxiliary tables.

Ten-Number Countries

The use of the table for ten-number countries is simply a matter of carefully matching the sequence of numbers in the table with the integral numbers assigned to the geographic divisions in the schedule. For instance, the schedule for Subclass AY assigns the range AY890-899 to Italy. In order to use these ten numbers, one must apply the table for ten-number countries which is reproduced below.

TABLES OF SUBDIVISIONS UNDER COUNTRIES (AY410-1730)

I (Ten numbers, or eleven numbers modified)

	Early through 1799
(0)	Collections. By date of first volume
(1).A-Z5	Serial. By title or editor
.Z7	Other. By date
(2)	Yearbooks (without almanacs)
	Prefer classification by subject in Classes B-Z
	1800-
(3)	Collections
(4)	General. By title or editor
(5)	Newspaper, etc. By name of place, subarranged by title
(6)	Other
.A3-Z3	Literary and magazine almanacs, etc. By title or editor
.Z5	Miscellaneous. Occasional issues. By date
(7)	Almanacs in foreign languages. By language, A-Z
(8)	Special. By subject, A-Z
	For list of topics, <u>see</u> AY81
	Prefer classification by subject in Classes B-Z, e. g. Prophetic almanacs, BF1651
(9)	Local. By place, A-Z

The range of ten numbers for Italy (890-899) must be matched with the range of ten numbers in this table (0-9). As the table begins with the same last digit as the base number for Italy, there is no problem in directly matching the numbers. Thus, AY 895 would be an Italian newspaper yearbook; AY 892 would be an early Italian yearbook without almanacs; and AY 899 would be a local Italian almanac. In each case the last digits are simply matched. For example, the *Almanacco d'Italia* is classed as a general Italian almanac, "AY 894 .A58." The ".A58" is the Cutter number for the main entry, which in this case is the title, *Almanacco d'Italia*.

Almanacco d'Italia [a general Italian almanac].

AY	The double letters for the subclass, Yearbooks
894	The integral number meaning a general Italian almanac
.A58	The Cutter number for the main entry, *Almanacco d'Italia*.

Another example is a Jewish almanac published in Germany entitled *Jüdischer Almanach*. Germany's range of numbers is AY 850-860, with AY 859 for states and AY 860 for cities. Except for these last two numbers, Germany may use the table for ten-number countries even though it is really an eleven number country. The Jewish almanac is a special almanac and should receive the ninth number in the table, which is "8." (Please note that the first number in the table is "0.") The call number for this book, *Jüdischer Almanach*, is "AY 858.J4J8." "AY 858" means a special German almanac; ".J4" is the Cutter number for the special subject, Jews; and "J8" is the Cutter number for the title, *Jüdischer Almanach*.

Jüdischer Almanach [a Jewish almanac published in Germany].

AY	The double letters for the subclass, Yearbooks
858	The integral number meaning a special German almanac
.J4	The first Cutter number for the special subject, Jews
J8	The second Cutter number for the main entry, *Jüdischer Almanach*.

Two-Number Countries

The tables for two-number countries (Table II) and for one-number or Cutter-number countries (Table III) are used in a similar fashion. Table II is shown below.

II (Two numbers)

(1)	Collections and general.
(2)	Local, By place, A-Z.

For instance, New Zealand has two numbers for almanacs, yearbooks, and directories, "AY 1651" and "AY 1652." The table for two-number countries (Table II) is used to determine the individual assignment of each number. The first number, AY 1651, is used for collections and general almanacs, yearbooks, or directories of New Zealand. The second number, AY 1652, is used for local almanacs, yearbooks, or directories of New Zealand, subdivided by place, A-Z.

One-Number or Cutter-Number Countries

A one-number or Cutter-number geographic division should be used with the appropriate table for one-number or Cutter-number countries, Table III.

III (One number or Cutter number)

.A2A-Z	.x	Collections.
.A3A-Z	.x2	Serial.
.A4-Z	.x3	Local, By place, A-Z.

The subdivisions of these tables are derived through the use of successive and "A" Cutter numbers, as is usually the case when one number or a Cutter number is to have subdivisions. The use of these tables is directly parallel to the application of the table for one-number countries under AM 10-100, description and history of museums by country, which was discussed earlier in this chapter.

For example, Turkey is a one-number country, AY 1187. Therefore, *Hürriyet Ansiklopedik Yilligi*, an almanac published serially, is assigned the number "AY 1187 .A3H8."

Hürriyet Ansiklopedik Yilliği.

AY	The double letters for the subclass, Yearbooks. Almanacs. Directories.
1187	The integral number meaning Turkey
.A3	The first Cutter number for a serial publication
H8	The second Cutter number for the main entry, *Hürriyet....*

Poland is a Cutter-number country, AY 1039 .P7. Therefore, *Młoda Wieś Pisze*, an almanac published in Poland, is classed in "AY 1039 .P7M55."

Młoda Wieś Pisze: Almanach.

AY	The double letters for the subclass, Yearbooks. Almanacs. Directories.
1039	The integral number meaning "Other European" countries
.P7	The first Cutter number meaning Poland
M55	The second Cutter number for the main entry, *Młoda....*

Because this publication is cataloged as a monograph instead of a serial, the first of the successive Cutter numbers assigned to Poland, i.e., .P7, is used.

AUTHOR TABLES

Author tables are found in Class B and Class P for use with individual philosophers and literary authors for the purpose of subarranging works written by and about them. Each philosopher or author is given a span of numbers, one number, or a Cutter number. The tables are formulated according to the numbers appropriated. In Class P, there are also tables for subarranging different manifestations (e.g., editions, translations, criticism, etc.) of a particular work.

Authors with Forty-Nine Numbers

The following examples illustrate the use of author tables and tables for separate works. Robert Browning is a nineteenth century English author with a range of 49 numbers. In the appropriate schedule for Subclass PR, English literature, Browning's range of numbers is given with a list of his separate works:

4200–4248	Browning, Robert (II)
	Separate works
4205	The blot on the 'scutcheon
4206	Dramatic idyls
4207	Dramatic lyrics
4208	Dramatic romances
4209	Dramatic personae
4210	In a balcony
4211	Jocoseria
4212	King Victor and King Charles
4213	Luria
4214	Men and women
4215	Paracelsus
4216	Parleyings
4217	Pauline
4218	Pippa passes
4219	Ring and the book
4220	Sordello
4221	Strafford
4222	Other, A–Z

The more important works are each assigned a whole number, e.g., *Pippa Passes*, PR 4218. The lesser works are together assigned one number, PR 4222, Other A-Z. However, to use Browning's entire range of 49 numbers, the appropriate table must be found. Following Browning's name in the schedule is the instruction "(II)." This means that Table II, for 49 number authors, is used to class Browning's works. Following the schedule are "Tables of Subdivisions under Individual Authors." The first tables are I and II, for 98 and 49 number authors, respectively. The beginning of these tables is shown on page 125.

The appropriate column for Table II must be chosen in relation to the last two digits of the first number of an author's range of numbers. Browning's numbers begin at PR 4200. The last two digits are "00." These match with the numbers in the first column of Table II, "0." They do not match with the second column which begins at "50." In contrast, Lord Byron's range of numbers is PR 4350-4398. The last two digits of Byron's base number are "50." Hence, the second column of Table II would be used for Byron, while the first column is used for Browning.

An edition of the complete works of Browning without commentary published in 1910 is classed "PR 4200 .F10." "PR 4200" means an edition without commentary of the collected works of Browning. ".F10" is a date letter representing the year 1910. As shown in the table above, "F" equals "19" (1900-1999: F00-F99). This device retains the consistency of the notation; without it the call number would appear as "PR 4200 1910."

Robert Browning's Complete Works, 1910.

PR	The double letters for the subclass, English literature
4200	The integral number meaning an edition without commentary of the collected works of Robert Browning
.F10	The Cutter number meaning the date, "1910"

(Text continues on page 126)

TABLES OF SUBDIVISIONS UNDER INDIVIDUAL AUTHORS

May be modified in application to specific cases whenever it seems desirable

I (98 nos.)	II (49 nos.)		Authors with ninety-eight or forty-nine numbers

0	0 or 50		Collected works
			    Original editions, and reprints.
			        By date
			            To 1500: A00-A99
			            1500-1599: B00-B99
			            1600-1699: C00-C99
			            1700-1799: D00-D99
			            1800-1899: E00-E99
			            1900-1999: F00-F99

1	1	51	Editions with commentary, etc. By editor, A-Z
2	2	52	Selected works, fragments etc.
3	3	53	Selections. Anthologies. Extracts

4	4	54	Translations. By language; subarranged
			        by translator
			    .F5 French
			    .G5 German
			    .I5 Italian
			    .S5 Spanish
			    .Z5 Other

5-40	5-22	55-72	Separate works, alphabetically by title
			    Only the more important have a
			        special number or numbers assigned
			        to them; the lesser works are to
			        have Cutter numbers
			    For subdivisions where one number is
			        assigned to a work use Table X.
			        For Cutter numbers, use Table XI
			    Under each:

				0	Texts
			0	0	By date
			1	1	By editor
			2	2	Selections

			3	3	Translations (and
					            Adaptations: Drama-
					            tizations, etc.,
					            Imitations)
					        N.B. Adaptations,
					                dramatizations,
					                etc., by the
					                author of the
					                original work
					                himself to
					                precede transla-
					                tions in foreign
					                languages

			4 5-9	4	1	Criticism Special, A-Z

An edited edition of Browning's complete works, with commentary by Charlotte Porter, is classed "PR 4201 .P6." "1" is the number in Table II, column 1, for "Editions with commentary." ".P6" is the Cutter number for the editor, Charlotte Porter.

The Complete Works of Browning, edited by Charlotte Porter, 1898.

PR	The double letters for the subclass, English literature
4201	The integral number meaning an edition with commentary of the collected works of Robert Browning
.P6	The Cutter number for the author of the commentary, Porter
1898	The date of publication

In neither example is there any reason for a second Cutter number. Beginners may feel a desire to cutter for Browning or for title but either would be redundant. The range of numbers used means Browning, and the class number means his complete works.

As Table II demonstrates, the separate works or individual titles of a 49 number author are assigned as either "5-22" or "55-72." Since the first column is used with Browning's works, "5-22" is appropriate. These numbers match with the numbers assigned to Browning's separate works, as given in the schedule. For instance, Browning's *The Ring and the Book* is assigned "PR 4219." In order to complete this call number another table must be used. Table X and X^a, "Separate Works with One Number," are the appropriate tables. Table X^a is a modification of Table X for works written after 1600. *The Ring and the Book* would require the use of Table X^a, as it was written after 1600.

X (1 no.)	Xa (1 no.)	Separate works with one number Use Table Xa for works after 1600
		Texts
.A1	.A1	By date
.A11-2	.A2A-Z	By editor
	.A3	School texts
	.A35	Selections
	.A37	Adaptations, dramatizations, etc.
		Translations
.A21-39		Modern versions of medieval works
.A4-49	.A4-49	French
.A5-59	.A5-59	German
.A6-69	.A6-69	Other languages. By language
.A7-Z	.A7-Z	Criticism
.Z8	.Z8	History
.5	.5	Special parts. By date

An edition of this work without commentary published in 1868 would be classed "PR 4219 .A1 1868"; an edited version by Charlotte Porter would be "PR 4219 .A2P6," "A2" meaning an edited version and "P6" the Cutter number for the editor's name, Porter. If Charlotte Porter had written a separate monograph devoted entirely to the interpretation of *The Ring and the Book*, it would be classed "PR 4219 .P6."

Robert Browning's *The Ring and the Book*, 1868.

PR	The double letters for the subclass, English literature
4219	The integral number meaning Browning's *The Ring and the Book*
.A1	The Cutter number meaning the text without commentary
1868	The date of publication as called for by the table

Robert Browning's *The Ring and the Book*, edited by Charlotte Porter, 1897.

PR	The double letters for the subclass, English literature
4219	The integral number meaning Browning's *The Ring and the Book*
.A2	The first Cutter number meaning the text with commentary
P6	The second Cutter number for the commentator, Porter
1897	The date of publication

P. A. Cundiff's *Browning's Ring Metaphor and Truth*.

PR	The double letters for the subclass, English literature
4219	The integral number meaning Browning's *The Ring and the Book*
.C8	The Cutter number for the main entry, Cundiff

The shelf order of these three works would be:

PR	PR	PR
4219	4219	4219
.A1	.A2	.C8
1868	1897	

Criticism is given a range of Cutter numbers ".A7-Z" in Table X^a. The implications of the above operations are important. Although Browning is a 49 number author using Table II, any of his separate works requires the application of a different table—Table X or X^a for works with one number and Table XI for works with a Cutter number. The use of these tables is important in order to keep all the works about an individual work close to the individual work. The part of Table II for biography and criticism of a 49 number author follows the part of the table for the works of the author. For instance, literary dictionaries of a 49 number author use the following:

30	80	Dictionaries, indexes, etc.
		Class here general encyclopedic dictionaries only
		For special dictionaries, <u>see</u> the subject, e. g. characters, <u>see</u> 78 (Table I); 39, 89 (Table II); concordances and dictionaries, <u>see</u> 91-92 (Table I); 45, 95 (Table II)

Edward Berdoe's *The Browning Cyclopedia* is classed "PR 4230 .B4." "30" is the appropriate number within Browning's range of numbers, 4200-4248. ".B4" is the Cutter number for the author of the work, in this case Berdoe.

Edward Berdoe's *The Browning Cyclopedia*, 1892.

PR	The double letters for the subclass, English literature
4230	The integral number for a literary dictionary of Robert Browning
.B4	The first Cutter number for the main entry, Berdoe
1892	The date of publication

Browning and the Christian Faith, a monograph by Berdoe, is classed "PR 4242 .R4B4." The appropriate section in the table is:

42	92	Treatment and knowledge of special subjects
		"Other, A-Z"

"PR 4242" means Browning's treatment and knowledge of a special subject, religion. ".R4" is the Cutter number for that special subject, religion. "B4" is the Cutter number for Berdoe. In most cases the 49 number tables are simply a matter of matching the appropriate numbers with the author's range of numbers.

Edward Berdoe's *Browning and the Christian Faith*.

PR	The double letters for the subclass, English literature
4242	The integral number meaning Browning's treatment and knowledge of special subjects
.R4	The first Cutter number for the special subject, religion
B4	The second Cutter number for the main entry, Berdoe

Authors with Nine or Nineteen Numbers

The tables for authors with nine or nineteen numbers may be treated similarly to those for authors with forty-nine numbers. Table IV is for nine number authors and Table III is for nineteen number authors. Bernard Shaw is an example of a nine number author in English literature. He is assigned the range of numbers PR 5360-5368.

5360-5368	Shaw, George Bernard (IV^a).
	5360 Complete works and collected dramas.
	5361 Selections.
	5362 Translations.
	5363 Separate dramas, A-Z.

.A2,	The doctor's dilemma, etc.
.A25,	Misalliance, the dark lady of the sonnets and Fanny's first play.
.A3,	Plays pleasant and unpleasant.
.A5,	Three plays for Puritans.
.A8-Z,	Separate dramas, A-Z.

Other works.

5364	Collected.
5365	Separate, A-Z.

As Shaw is a nine number author and as "(IV^a)" appears following his name, Table IV is used in subdividing his range of nine numbers.* Table IV^a is simply a single modification of Table IV. Date letters, as used in Tables I and II, are to be used in Tables III and IV when the author is assigned III^a or IV^a. (See example on page 130.)

Table IV is used for only three of the nine numbers assigned to Shaw. If the numbers assigned to Shaw in the schedule are compared with Table IV, it should be observed that the first six numbers (5360-5365) have been assigned within the schedule for this specific author. Only numbers PR 5366, PR 5367, and PR 5368 — not described in the schedule — require use of Table IV for the assignment of subdivisions. Thus, classing is accomplished directly from the schedules as demonstrated in the following example.

The Complete Plays of Bernard Shaw, published in 1962, is classed "PR 5360 .F62." The schedule shows that "PR 5360" means the complete works or collected dramas of Bernard Shaw. ".F62" is the appropriate date letter from Table IV^a meaning "1962." Table IV is not used in this case, since the number PR 5360 is fully described in the schedules. See example on page 131.

---

*The choice of Shaw as a nine number author represents a combination of problems in using the numbers assigned within the schedules and in selecting the appropriate part of the tables for subdividing the numbers. Most of the numbers are assigned within the schedule rather than being determined from the table. Many authors have such variations where the schedule shows assigned numbers and the table is not fully utilized.

III (19 nos.)	IV (9 nos.)	Authors with nineteen or nine numbers
		˙Collected works
0	0	By date
1	1	By editor
	.5	Selected works
2	2	Selections
		For separate parts, see
		Separate works
	3	Translations
3	.A2A-Z	Modern English. By translator
4	.A3-Z	Other. By language
		Subarranged by translator
5-10	4(A-Z)	Separate works
		Under each:
		III, see Table X, or XI
		IV, see Table XI
11	5	Apocryphal, spurious works, etc.
		Biography, criticism, etc.
12.A1-5	6.A1-19	Periodicals. Societies. Serials
.A6-Z	.A2-3	Dictionaries, indexes, etc.
13.A3-39	.A31-39	Autobiography, journals, memoirs
.A4	.A4	Letters (Collections). By imprint date
.A41-49	.A41-49	Letters to and from particular individuals. By correspondent (alphabetically)
.A5-Z	.A5-Z	General works
		Criticism
14	7	General works
15		Textual. Manuscripts, etc.
		Special
16		Sources
17	8	Other, A-Z
		.A35 Aesthetics
		.A4 Ambiguity
		. . . . . .
		.W6 Women
18		Language. Grammar. Style

IIIa	IVa	Same as III and IV, but using the following date letters under "0" as in Tables I and II, p. 264
		To 1500: A00-A99
		1500-1599: B00-B99
		1600-1699: C00-C99
		1700-1799: D00-D99
		1800-1899: E00-E99
		1900-1999: F00-F99

The Complete Plays of Bernard Shaw, 1962.

PR	The double letters for the subclass, English literature
5360	The integral number meaning the collected works or collected dramas of Bernard Shaw
.F62	The Cutter number meaning the date, "1962"

Three Plays for Puritans, the text of a separate work by Shaw, is classed as "PR 5363 .A5." Again, this number is taken entirely from the schedule. For further subdivisions of this number the classifier must use Table XI, "Separate works with Cutter numbers."

Bernard Shaw's *Three Plays for Puritans*. 1901.

PR	The double letters for the subclass, English literature
5363	The integral number meaning a separate dramatic work by Shaw
.A5	The Cutter number meaning *Three Plays for Puritans*
1901	The date of publication

In the case of this title, which is the text of the separate work, *Three Plays for Puritans*, the date is the only element which needs to be added.

Frank Harris' biography of Shaw is classed in the seventh number in Table IV, which is "6." Within Shaw's range of numbers this is "PR 5366." Harris is cuttered ".H35" within the range of Cutter numbers ".A5-Z." The complete number is "PR 5366 .H35."

Frank Harris' *Bernard Shaw*, 1931.

PR	The double letters for the subclass, English literature
5366	The integral number meaning biographical works about Bernard Shaw
.H35	The Cutter number for the author of the biography, Harris
1931	The date of publication

"PR 5367 .B4" is the number assigned to Eric Bentley's critical study entitled *Bernard Shaw*. "7" is the appropriate number in Table IV for general criticism, and "PR 5367" is the corresponding number within Shaw's range of numbers. ".B4" is the Cutter number for the main entry, Bentley. See example on page 132.

Eric Bentley's *Bernard Shaw.*

PR	The double letters for the subclass, English literature
5367	The integral number meaning criticism of Bernard Shaw
.B4	The Cutter number for the author of the criticism, Bentley

Authors with One Number or a Cutter Number

Authors with only one number or a Cutter number must use a table with "A" and "Z" Cutter numbers to achieve form divisions similar to those of other authors. Tables VIII, VIII^a and VIII^b are designed for authors with one number. Tables IX, IX^a, and IX^b are for authors with only a Cutter number. Tables VIII and IX are intended for authors who wrote very few works but who have had a good deal of material written about them. Tables VIII^a and IX^a are used primarily for nineteenth and twentieth century authors. Tables VIII^b and IX^b are rarely used at all. Table IX^a may be used as an example of these tables.

PN, PR, PS, PZ   PN, PR, PS, PZ

SUBDIVISIONS UNDER INDIVIDUAL AUTHORS

VIIIa (1 no.)	IXa (Cutter no.)	Authors with one number or Cutter number
		Collected works
.A1	.x	By date
.A11-13	.xA11-13	By editor
.A14	.xA14	Uncataloged material
.A15	.xA15	Collected novels
.A16	.xA16	Essays, miscellanies, etc.
.A17	.xA17	Collected poems
.A19	.xA19	Collected plays
		Translations
.A199	.xA199	Modern versions in the same language. By date
.A2-29	.xA2-29	English. By translator
.A3-39	.xA3-39	French. By translator
.A4-49	.xA4-49	German. By translator
.A5-59	.xA5-59	Other. By language
.A6	.xA6	Selections
.A7-Z48	.xA61-Z458	Separate works
		Biography and criticism
.Z49	.xZ459	Dictionaries, indexes, etc. By date
.Z5A3-39	.xZ46-479	Autobiography, journals, memoirs
.Z5A4	.xZ48	Letters (Collections). By imprint date
.Z5A41-49	.xZ481-499	Letters to and from particular individuals. By correspondent (alphabetically)
.Z5A5-Z	.xZ5-999	General works

VIIIb (1 no.)	IXb (Cutter no.)	Authors with one number or Cutter number
		Collected works
.A1	.x	By date
.A11-14	.xA11-14	By editor
.A15	.xA15	Collected novels
.A16	.xA16	Essays, miscellanies, etc.
.A17	.xA17	Collected poems
.A19	.xA19	Collected plays
.A3-Z29	.xA3-Z29	Separate works
		Translations
.Z3-39	.xZ3-39	English
.Z4-49	.xZ4-49	French
.Z6-69	.xZ6-69	Other. By language
.Z7	.xZ7	Selections. By date
		Biography and criticism
.Z72	.xZ72	Dictionaries, indexes, etc. By date
.Z721-73	.xZ721-73	Autobiography, journals, memoirs
.Z74	.xZ74	Letters (Collections). By imprint date
.Z741-75	.xZ741-75	Letters to and from particular individuals. By correspondent (alphabetically)
.Z76-99	.xZ76-99	General works

The majority of the range of Cutter numbers, A-Z, is given to separate works, .xA61-Z458. Biography and criticism has only the range .xZ459-999. Once again it should be observed that this is a single alphabetical range of A-Z, with many "A" and "Z" Cutter numbers.

Gertrude Stein, an American author, is an example of a Cutter number author. Her number is "PS 3537 .T323." "PS" means American literature; "PS 3537" is the number within American literature for modern authors whose last name begins with "S"; and "T323" is the Cutter number for Stein based on the "-tein" part of the name, as the "S" has already been designated in the number "3537." Stein's novel, *The Making of Americans*, is classed "PS 3537.T323M3." In Table IX[a], ".T323" equals "x" and "M3" is the Cutter number for the title of the novel, "Making." This Cutter number is taken from the range of "A61-Z458" for separate works.

Gertrude Stein's *The Making of Americans*, 1926.

PS	The double letters for the subclass, American literature
3537	The integral number meaning modern American authors whose last names begin with the letter "S"
.T323	The first Cutter number for Stein
M3	The second Cutter number for the title, *Making....*
1926	The date of publication

A criticism of Stein by Donald Sutherland, *Gertrude Stein: A Biography of Her Work*, is classed "PS 3537 .T323Z83." The "Z83" represents the Cutter number for the main entry, Sutherland. "83" is chosen to place this work nearer the end of the alphabet, since "S" is nearer the end of the alphabet. Of course, "83" does not regularly mean "Su." It does only in this particular case.

Donald Sutherland's *Gertrude Stein: A Biography of Her Work.*

PS	The double letters for the subclass, American literature
3537	The integral number meaning modern American authors whose last names begin with the letter "S"
.T323	The first Cutter number for Stein
Z83	The second Cutter number meaning a biography or criticism. (*See* the preceding discussion for the full meaning of this number.)

In the following chapter, further examples illustrating the use of tables will be given in the discussion of individual classes.

BIBLIOGRAPHY

Grout, Catherine W. *Explanation of the Tables Used in the Schedules of the Library of Congress Classification, Accompanied by an Historical and Explanatory Introduction*. New York: Columbia University, School of Library Service, 1940.
This basic work is available presently in a University Microfilms edition. For a review of this *see* Andrew D. Osborn's "The L.C. Classification," *Library Journal* 66:300 (April 1, 1941).

LaMontagne, Leo E. *American Library Classification with Special Reference to the Library of Congress*. Hamden, CT: Shoe String Press, 1961.

5

INDIVIDUAL CLASSES

INTRODUCTION

This chapter introduces the reader to the individual classes of Library of Congress Classification. Each unit of this chapter begins with a synopsis of the class as found in the official *LC Classification Outline*.[1] Its inclusion is intended to orient the reader to the scope of the individual class. Next, a brief history traces the development of the schedule or schedules making up each class. The names of classifiers responsible for the planning and editing of each class or subclass are given in most cases. The sequence within each class and subclass is discussed. The order of subdivisions, i.e., order in array, is given by numerous examples. Additional tables or extensions of important schedules found only in supplements to the class schedule or in *LC Classification—Additions and Changes* are mentioned. Significant problems in the use of each class schedule are discussed: inclusiveness and exclusiveness of the scope, and problems of terminology and typography. Typical problems in the use of auxiliary and/or internal tables are presented and explained with examples of Library of Congress call numbers in the same fashion as used in chapter 4. Any unusual elements that may occur in the notation of each class are explained, e.g., the use of triple letters in Subclass KF, the use of subject letter-numbers in Class G, etc. The final section of each unit deals with the existing individual indexes to the schedules. At the end of the chapter is a complete bibliography of editions of the individual schedules and material written about them.

It is hoped that this chapter may serve to orient classifiers to individual schedules which may be unfamiliar to them. Each unit is designed to provide an introductory rather than a definitive treatment of the problems involved in using each class schedule. In each unit examples illustrate typical tables or tables that were not previously analyzed, examine an important or confusing variation in the use of notation, or clarify directions provided within the schedule or tables. Only parts of schedules or tables posing a new or a special kind of difficulty to the classifier are discussed; consequently, many subclasses are not fully analyzed. It is restated here that the reader will benefit by studying the class schedule as a whole in conjunction with the examples and tables presented in the individual units of this chapter. In addition, the reader may wish to check his/her library's shelflist for additional examples of each problem. The most effective use of this chapter can be achieved by the following steps:

1) careful reading of introductory and explanatory material in each unit

2) studying of examples provided in the text

3) consulting L.C. Classification schedules for each class

CLASS A – GENERAL WORKS

For works too general or comprehensive to be classed with any particular subject, however broad

AC		Collections. Series. Collected works
	1-195	Collections of monographs, essays, etc.
		For collections published under the auspices of learned bodies (institutions or societies), *see* AS
	801-895	Inaugural and program dissertations
	901-995	Pamphlet collections
	999	Scrapbooks
AE		Encyclopedias (General)
AG		Dictionaries and other general reference works
	1-90	Dictionaries. Minor encyclopedias
		Including popular and juvenile encyclopedias
	103-190	General works, pocketbooks, receipts, etc.
	195-196	Questions and answers
	240-243	Wonders. Curiosities
	250	Pictorial works
	305-313	Notes and queries
	500-551	Clipping bureaus. Information bureaus
AI		Indexes (General)
	21	Indexes to individual newspapers
AM		Museums (General). Collectors and collecting (General)
	10-101	Museography. Individual museums
	111-157	Museology. Museum methods, technique, etc.
	200-501	Collectors and collecting. Private collections
AN		Newspapers
		For history and description of individual newspapers, *see* PN4891-5650
AP		Periodicals (General)
	101-115	Humorous periodicals
	200-230	Juvenile periodicals
AS		Academies and learned societies (General)
	2.5-4	International associations, congresses, conferences, etc.
AY		Yearbooks. Almanacs. Directories
		For general works only
	30-1730	Almanacs
	2001	Directories
		For general works on theory, methods of compilations, etc.
AZ		History of scholarship and learning. The humanities
	999	Popular errors, delusions and superstitions

Class A—General Works is the generalia class in the L.C. Classification. The outline of the class was developed in 1906 and first published in 1911. Charles Martel was the editor of the first edition. The second edition was published in 1915 with Clarence W. Perley as the editor. The third edition, issued in 1947, was prepared for publication by L. Belle Voegelein. The fourth edition, published in 1973, was prepared under the editorial direction of Emma E. Curtis.

Class A is designed for works too general or comprehensive to be classified with any particular subject. It should not be used for works that can possibly be classed in a special subject in Classes B-Z. As may be noted in the synopsis, there are ten subclasses in Class A: AC for collections, series, and collected works which may not be classed by subject or in Subclass AS for collections published under the auspices of learned bodies; AE for general encyclopedias; AG for dictionaries and other general reference books including minor general encyclopedias, juvenile encyclopedias, question and answer books, notes and queries, and information and clipping bureaus; AI for general indexes which are not classed by subject or in Class Z; AM for museums and collectors and collecting; AN for newspapers, which is a subclass not yet fully developed in the classification scheme; AP for general periodicals which are arranged first by language and then grouped geographically—in addition, there are separate ranges of numbers for humorous periodicals and juvenile periodicals—AS for academies and learned societies of a general character; AY for general yearbooks, almanacs, annuals, and directories; and AZ for the history of scholarship and learning and the humanities. It may be observed that two common subjects for a generalia class are not included in Class A. Both bibliography and library science are located in Class Z.

The individual subclasses are arranged in an alphabetical order: AC, Collections; AE, Encyclopedias; AG, General reference works; AM, Museums, etc. The letters forming the subclasses demonstrate the use of mnemonics. This is one of the few instances in the Library of Congress Classification where mnemonics are used in the subclasses. Subclass AZ is the only subclass in Class A that does not use this mnemonic device. The most common form of division in the subclasses is geographic. Countries and other geographic areas are assigned a range of numbers, one number or a Cutter number; many simple tables may be used.

This schedule presents no major problems in use. There are a number of simple internal tables. The use of some of these tables has already been discussed in chapter 4. The following examples demonstrate the use of some of the other tables.

Tables Used with AM 101

The number AM 101 is assigned to description and history of individual museums. Each museum receives a Cutter number based on the name of the place. Two tables are provided under AM 101 for the subarrangement of material issued by or written about each individual museum.

AM

MUSEUMS. COLLECTORS AND COLLECTING

<u>Description and history of museums</u> - Continued

101   Individual museums. By place, A-Z
Under each:[1]

Table I*
Using successive cutter numbers

(0)   Collections, etc.
(1)   Acts of incorporation, statutes, bylaws,
         rules, and regulations. By date
(2)   Administration. List of officers, etc.
(2.5)   Examinations
(3)   Annual reports
(4)   Other general serials not limited to a
         subject field: periodicals, collections,
         memoirs, etc.
(4.5)   Other minor official reports. By date
(5)   Guidebooks, catalogs. By date
(5.2)   Special minor exhibits. By date
(6)   History
(6.5)   Descriptive works (official). By date
(7)   General works (nonofficial)
(9)   Miscellaneous printed matter, circulars,
         announcements. By date
e. g.   .B8-89   British Museum

Table II
Official publications
.A1-39   Serial publications
.A4-59   Monographs
.A6-Z   Other. By author, A-Z

The more complex Table I is no longer used by the Library of Congress except for museums already established in the shelflist. The following works by and/or about the British Museum illustrate the use of this table. Note that, contrary to the instruction in the schedule, the British Museum has been assigned the Cutter number .B8, based on the name rather than the place, because earlier editions of Class A required arrangement of individual museums by name.

The British Museum, A Guide to Its Public Services, 1962.

AM   The double letters meaning museums

101   The integral number meaning individual museums

.B85   The Cutter number .B8 for the British Museum and the successive Cutter number meaning guidebooks

1962   The date of publication as required in Table I

In this example, ".B8" is the Cutter number meaning the British Museum. The successive element for guidebooks, "5," is added to or rather attached to the Cutter number for the British Museum, ".B8." The resulting number is ".B85."

---

*Table I is no longer used by the Library of Congress except for museums already established; the more simplified Table II is now preferred.

A Guide to the Exhibition Galleries of the British Museum. With an introduction by E. Maunde Thompson, 1909.

AM	The double letters meaning museums
101	The integral number meaning individual museums
.B85	The Cutter number .B8 for the British Museum and the successive Cutter number meaning guidebooks
1909	The date of publication

Again in this example, ".B8" is the Cutter number meaning the British Museum. The successive element for guidebooks, "5," is again added to the Cutter number for the British Museum, resulting in the complete first Cutter number, ".B85." The date is added to complete the call number.

Statutes and Rules for the British Museum, 1932.

AM	The double letters meaning museums
101	The integral number meaning individual museums
.B81	The Cutter number .B8 for the British Museum and the successive Cutter number meaning statutes
1932	The date of publication as required in Table I

".B8" is the Cutter number meaning the British Museum. The successive element for acts of incorporation, statutes, by-laws, rules and regulations "1" is attached to this Cutter number for the British Museum, hence the number ".B81."

H. C. Shelley's *British Museum: Its History and Treasures,* 1911.

AM	The double letters meaning museums
101	The integral number meaning individual museums
.B87	The Cutter number .B8 for the British Museum and the successive Cutter number meaning nonofficial general works
S6	The second Cutter number used for the author, Shelly

".B8" is the Cutter number meaning the British Museum. The successive element for nonofficial general works, "7," is attached to this Cutter number for the British Museum, resulting in the number ".B87." Again in this case a second Cutter is available and may be used as this one is for the author of the work.

The simplified Table II is now used for museums being established in the shelflist for the first time. The following examples illustrate the use of Table II.

The Herald [a journal published by Greenfield Village & Henry Ford Museum, Dearborn, Michigan].

AM	The double letters for the subclass, Museums
101	The integral number meaning individual museums
.D36	The first Cutter number for the place, Dearborn
A24	The second Cutter number for an official serial publication

According to Table II, the official serial publications (denoted by the second Cutter number) of a museum are assigned the range of numbers ".A1-39." Within this numerical sequence, the serial publications are arranged alphabetically.

Edison Institute (Henry Ford Museum and Greenfield Village), *Selected Treasures of Greenfield Village and Henry Ford Museum.*

AM	The double letters for the subclass, Museums
101	The integral number meaning individual museums
.D36	The first Cutter number for the place, Dearborn
A45	The second Cutter number for an official monograph

Academies and Learned Societies

In Subclass AS, Academies and learned societies, three tables are provided for subarrangement of publications by and about an individual society or institution. A statement accompanying the tables indicates that Tables I and II are no longer used by the Library of Congress except for societies and institutions already established in this class.

The following is an example illustrating the use of Table III:

American Assembly, *Report.*

AS	The double letter for the subclass, Academies and learned societies
36	The integral number meaning an individual society in the United States
.A4853	The first Cutter number for the American Assembly
A3	The second Cutter number for a serial publication

A similar subarrangement is used for societies classed in subject areas in Classes B-Z. For details and examples of society publications in general, see chapter 6.

Tables in Subclass AZ

The following tables for divisions under each country are designed to be used with AZ 501-908, History of scholarship and learning by region or country:

```
AZ
                    HISTORY OF SCHOLARSHIP AND LEARNING

    501-908         By region or country
                      Under each country:
```

I	II	III	IV	
10 nos.	5 nos.	3 nos.	1 no.	
(0)	(1)	(1) .A1-3	.A1-2	Collections
(1)	(2)	.A5-Z3	.A5-Z3	General works. History
(2)				Early. Origins
(3)				Middle Ages
(4)				Modern
(6)				General special. Relations, aspects, etc.
(7)	(3)	.Z5A-Z	.Z5A-Z	Addresses, essays, lectures. Pamphlets
(8)	(4)	(2)	.Z7A-Z	States, regions, provinces, etc. Under each: (1) Collections (2) History (3) Other. Minor
⌐9⌐	⌐5⌐	⌐3⌐	⌐.Z8A-Z⌐	Cities, see DA-DU, E, F

```
                    For countries to which two numbers are assigned in the
                      schedule, use subdivisions (1) and (2) of table III;
                      for countries with four numbers, use subdivisions (1)-
                      (4) of table II
```

Many countries are assigned ten numbers, for example, Germany, "AZ 660-669." A variation is Great Britain which is assigned eight numbers, "AZ 610-617," with special numbers for its regions: England—Local, "AZ 620-623"; Scotland, "AZ 625-628"; Ireland, "AZ 630-633"; and Wales, "AZ 635-638." Table I is used for Great Britain, and Table II is used for the regions.

For example, Robert Weiss's *Humanism in England During the Fifteenth Century* is classed in "AZ 613 .W4." "613" is the fourth number assigned to Great Britain and is represented in the table by the number "3" for a history of the Middle Ages.

Robert Weiss's *Humanism in England During the Fifteenth Century*, 1967.

AZ	The double letters for the subclass, History of scholarship and learning
613	The integral number meaning a general work on scholarship and learning in Great Britain during the Middle Ages
.W4	The Cutter number for the main entry, Weiss
1967	The date of publication

Although Tables II and III specify five numbers and three numbers respectively, the actual number assigned to a country in these categories is either four or two. This creates no problem as the last number in each of the tables is optional and not used by the Library of Congress. Poland, for example, is assigned two numbers, "AZ 714-715," and therefore, Table III is used in classifying works relating to it.

S. Kot's *Five Centuries of Polish Learning.*

AZ	The double letters for the subclass, History of scholarship and learning
714	The first integral number assigned to Poland for a general work
.K6	The Cutter number for the main entry, Kot

A work on learning and scholarship of Bydgoszcz, a local subdivision of Poland, is assigned the second number.

Bydgostiana.

AZ	The double letters for the subclass, History of scholarship and learning
715	The second integral number assigned to Poland for its local subdivisions
.B9	The first Cutter number for the local subdivision, Bydgoszcz
B9	The second Cutter number for the main entry, *Bydgostiana*

Previous editions of Class A contained no index. This deficiency has been rectified in the fourth edition which includes an index for the first time.

CLASS B – PHILOSOPHY. PSYCHOLOGY. RELIGION

B		Philosophy (General)
		For general philosophical treatises, *see* BD10-41
	69-5739	History and systems
		Including individual philosophers and schools of philosophy
BC		Logic
BD		Speculative philosophy
	10-41	General philosophical works
	95-131	Metaphysics
	143-236	Epistemology. Theory of knowledge
	240-241	Methodology
	300-450	Ontology
		Including the soul, immortality
	493-708	Cosmology
		Including teleology, space and time, atomism
BF		Psychology
		For ethnic psychology, *see* GN
		For social psychology, *see* HM
	173-175	Psychoanalysis
	180-210	Experimental psychology
	231-299	Sensation
	311-499	Cognition. Perception. Intelligence
	511-593	Emotion
	608-635	Will
	636-637	Applied psychology
	660-687	Comparative psychology
	683	Motivation
	698	Personality
	699-711	Genetic psychology
		For the psychology of mental development or evolution
	712-724	Developmental psychology
	721-723	Child psychology
	795-839	Temperament. Character
	840-861	Physiognomy
	866-885	Phrenology
	889-905	Graphology
	908-940	The hand. Palmistry
	1001-1389	Parapsychology
		Including hallucinations, sleep, dreams, hypnotism, telepathy, spiritualism, mediumship, clairvoyance, telekinesis
	1405-1999	Occult sciences
		Including ghosts, demonology, witchcraft, astrology, oracles, fortunetelling
BH		Aesthetics
BJ		Ethics
	1188-1500	Religious ethics
	1545-1691	Practical and applied ethics. Conduct of life
	1801-2195	Social usages. Etiquette
		Religion
BL		Religions. Mythology. Rationalism
	175-290	Natural theology
	300-325	Mythology (General)
	425-490	Religious doctrines (General)

Religion
    Religions. Mythology. Rationalism—*continued*

BL	500-547	Eschatology
	550-619	Worship. Cultus
	660-2670	History and principles of particular religions
		Including Brahmanism, Hinduism, Jainism
	2700-2790	Rationalism
		Including agnosticism, free thought
BM		Judaism
	487-488	Dead Sea scrolls
	495-532	Sources of Jewish religion. Rabbinical literature
	600-645	Dogmatic Judaism
	650-747	Practical Judaism
	900-990	Samaritans
BP		Islam. Bahaism. Theosophy, etc.
		Islam
	100-137	Sacred books
	166	Theology (Kalam)
	174-190	The practice of Islam
	191-223	Branches, sects and modifications
	300-395	Bahaism
	500-585	Theosophy
	595-597	Anthroposophy
BQ		Buddhism
	1001-1045	Buddhist literature
	1100-3340	Tripiṭaka (Canonical literature)
	4061-4570	Doctrinal and systematic Buddhism
	4911-5720	Practice of Buddhism. Forms of worship
	7001-9800	Modifications, schools, etc.
		Christianity
BR		Christianity (General)
	45-85	Collections
		Including early Christian literature
	140-1500	Church history
	1690-1725	Biography
BS		The Bible and exegesis
BT		Doctrinal theology, Apologetics
BV		Practical theology
	5-525	Worship (Public and private)
		Including the church year, Christian symbols, liturgy, prayer, hymnology
	590-1650	Ecclesiastical theology
		Including the Church, church and state, church management, ministry, sacraments, religious societies, religious education
	2000-3705	Missions
	3750-3799	Evangelism. Revivals
	4000-4470	Pastoral theology
	4485-5099	Practical religion. The Christian life
BX		Denominations and sects
	1-9	Church unity. Ecumenical movement
	100-189	Eastern churches. Oriental churches
	200-754	Orthodox Eastern Church
	800-4795	Roman Catholic Church
	4800-9999	Protestantism

Class B—Philosophy. Psychology. Religion appears in two separately published schedules—*Part I, B-BJ Philosophy. Psychology* and *Part II, BL-BX Religion.* Edwin Wiley, under the direction of Charles Martel, edited the first edition of Part I (1910). Part II, edited by Clarence W. Perley, did not appear until 1927. L. Belle Voegelein edited the second edition of Part I which was published in 1950. The second edition of Part II, largely the work of Theodore A. Mueller, was published in 1962. In 1979, the third edition of Part I, prepared under the editorial direction of Lawrence Buzard, was published.

B-BJ Philosophy

The principal sources for the philosophy schedule were Cutter's *Expansive Classification*, Dewey's *Decimal Classification* and its revision, the *Universal Decimal Classification.* Other sources which are acknowledged are Otto Harwig's *Halle Schema*, the works of Schleiermacher, Benjamin Rand's *Bibliography of Philosophy, Psychology and Cognate Subjects*, the *Psychological Index*, and the index to *Zeitschrift für Psychologie und Physiologie der Sinnesorgane.* The inclusion of Subclass BF, Psychology, within the philosophy class demonstrates the influence of the nineteenth century point of view in the development of this schedule.

There are six subclasses in Part I, Philosophy, of Class B: Subclass B includes general philosophy serials, collections, history and systems, and the works by and about individual philosophers, except for certain editions of works by Greek and Roman philosophers;* BC is for logic; BD, for speculative philosophy, including general philosophical treatises, metaphysics, epistemology, methodology, ontology, and cosmology; BF, for psychology, parapsychology, and the occult sciences; BH, for aesthetics; BJ, for ethics, including social usages and etiquette. Geographic and language divisions are regularly employed in these subclasses.

Classification of works by individual philosophers presents a special problem, as in other classification systems. Subclass B provides numbers (B108-5739) for individual philosophers based on nationality and period; while numbers based on philosophical topics—logic, metaphysics, epistemology, ontology, cosmology, aesthetics, ethics, etc.—are provided in subclasses BC, BD, BH, BJ. This dual provision of what Perreault[2] calls national-philosophy-classes and subject classes results in typical instances of cross classification. Works by individual philosophers may be classed in Subclass B in the author numbers or in the other subclasses with the topical numbers. For example, although Lord Bertrand Russell is given a specific number in Subclass B, many of his works on specific philosophical topics are not classed there. His number is "B 1649 .R9," but his work *Human Knowledge: Its Scope and Limits* is classed in "BD 161 .R78," a number in Subclass BD meaning epistemology. This problem is even more apparent when the philosopher is also a theologian. The works of theologians, particularly modern theologians, may be scattered throughout the entire Class B.

---

*Numbers for classical philosophy exist in both B and PA schedules. The numbers in PA are used for original Greek and Latin texts, Latin translations of Greek texts, and texts with textual criticism. Translations of Greek (except translations into Latin) and Roman philosophical works, with or without original text, are classed in B.

The philosophers that are classed in Subclass B must each be carefully verified with Library of Congress practice. This can be done by checking the philosopher under his entries in the Library of Congress shelflist or catalogs.

There are five tables[3] used for subarrangement of works by and about individual philosophers in Subclass B. These tables are similar to the author tables discussed in chapter 4. They are designed for philosophers who have been assigned fifty numbers, nine numbers, four or five numbers, one number, two, three, four, or five Cutter numbers. The general pattern of subarrangement is:

1) Collected works

2) Separate works

3) Biography, criticism, etc.

Bertrand Russell's works may be used as an example of classifying a philosopher's works in Subclass B. As Russell is a Cutter number philosopher, Table 5 is used for subarranging works by and about him. The LC shelflist indicates that the following successive Cutter numbers have been developed for Russell:

		Collected works.
1)	.R9	Original texts. By date.
2)	.R91	Partial editions, selections, etc. By editor or date.
3)	.R92	Translations. By language, A−Z and date.
4)	.R93	Separate works, A−Z.
5)	.R94	General works. Biography, criticism, etc.

For instance, Russell's *Basic Writing, 1903-1959*, edited by Robert Egner, is classed as a selection or partial edition of Russell's collected works, "B 1659 .R91E38."

Russell's *Basic Writing, 1903-1959*, edited by Robert Egner.

B	The single letter for the subclass, Philosophy (general)
1649	The integral number meaning an individual British philosopher of the later nineteenth and twentieth centuries
.R91	The first Cutter number meaning the individual philosopher, Bertrand Russell (.R9), and the successive element (1) meaning a partial edition or selection of his works.
E38	The second Cutter number for the editor of the selection, Egner.

Another selection of Russell's works edited by Egner is *Bertrand Russell's Best*, which is classed "B 1649 .R91E4."

Bertrand Russell's Best, edited by Robert Egner.

B	The single letter for the subclass, Philosophy (general)
1649	The integral number meaning an individual British philosopher of the later nineteenth and twentieth centuries
.R91	The first Cutter number meaning the individual philosopher, Bertrand Russell (.R9), and the successive element (1) meaning a partial edition or selection of his works
E4	The second Cutter number for the editor of the selection, Egner
1961	The date of publication

Both of these examples are selections or partial editions of the philosopher's work, thus they use the first extension of Russell's Cutter number, ".R9." The second expansion of Russell's Cutter number is ".R92." According to Table 5 this is reserved for translations of collected works or selections. The following is a selection of Russell's works translated into Spanish.

La Filosofía en el Siglo XX y Otros Ensayos, Seguidos de Cuatro Estudios sobre la Obra de Bertrand Russell.

B	The single letter for the subclass, Philosophy (general)
1649	The integral number meaning an individual British philosopher of the later nineteenth and twentieth centuries
.R92	The first Cutter number meaning the individual philosopher, Bertrand Russell (.R9), and the successive element (2) meaning a translation of his collected or selected works
S66	The second Cutter number for the language of the translation, Spanish

Following translations of collected works or selections, the next successive Cutter number is ".R93A-Z7," to be used for separate works of the philosopher. The following are examples of the use of this number.

Bertrand Russell Speaks His Mind.

B	The single letter for the subclass, Philosophy (general)
1649	The integral number meaning an individual British philosopher of the later nineteenth and twentieth centuries
.R93	The first Cutter number meaning the individual philosopher, Bertrand Russell (.R9), and the successive element (3) meaning a separate work of Russell
B4	The second Cutter number used for the title of the separate work, *Bertrand....*

Logic and Knowledge; Essays, 1901-1950, by Bertrand Russell.

B	The single letter for the subclass, Philosophy (general)
1649	The integral number meaning an individual British philosopher of the later nineteenth and twentieth centuries
.R93	The first Cutter number meaning the individual philosopher, Bertrand Russell (.R9), and the successive element (3) meaning a separate work of Russell
L6	The second Cutter number used for the title of the separate work, *Logic....*

Bertrand Russell's *An Outline of Philosophy,* 1961.

B	The single letter for the subclass, Philosophy (general)
1649	The integral number meaning an individual British philosopher of the later nineteenth and twentieth centuries
.R93	The first Cutter number meaning the individual philosopher, Bertrand Russell (.R9), and the successive element (3) meaning a separate work of Russell
O9	The second Cutter number used for the title of the separate work, *Outline....*
1961	The date of publication

Mysticism and Logic, and Other Essays, 1932.
[originally published as *Philosophical Essays.*]

B	The single letter for the subclass, Philosophy (general)
1649	The integral number meaning an individual British philosopher of the later nineteenth and twentieth centuries
.R93	The first Cutter number meaning the individual philosopher, Bertrand Russell (.R9), and the successive element (3) meaning a separate work of Russell
P5	The second Cutter number used for the original title of the separate work, *Philosophical....*
1932	The date of publication

Frihet og Fornuft [a Norwegian translation of Bertrand Russell's *Philosophical Essays*].

B	The single letter for the subclass, Philosophy (general)
1649	The integral number meaning an individual British philosopher of the later nineteenth and twentieth centuries
.R93	The first Cutter number meaning the individual philosopher, Bertrand Russell (.R9), and the successive element (3) meaning a separate work of Russell

(Example continues on page 149)

P516	The second Cutter number used for the original title of the separate work, *Philosophical Essays* (P5), and a successive element (16) in this case meaning a translation into Norwegian

It should be noted that the translations of a separate work are cuttered immediately following the original separate work. *See* the discussion on distinguishing editions of a work in chapter 4.

Portraits from Memory, and Other Essays, by Bertrand Russell. London, 1956.

B	The single letter for the subclass, Philosophy (general)
1649	The integral number meaning an individual British philosopher of the later nineteenth and twentieth centuries
.R93	The first Cutter number meaning the individual philosopher, Bertrand Russell (.R9), and the successive element (3) meaning a separate work of Russell
P6	The second Cutter number used for the title of the separate work, *Portraits...*
1956	The date of publication

The last expansion of Russell's successive Cutter numbers is ".R94" for biography, criticism, etc., about Russell. The first works under this number are the autobiographical ones.

Bertrand Russell's *My Philosophical Development.*

B	The single letter for the subclass, Philosophy (general)
1649	The integral number meaning an individual British philosopher of the later nineteenth and twentieth centuries
.R94	The first Cutter number meaning the individual philosopher, Bertrand Russell (.R9), and the successive element (4) meaning a general work about Russell
A28	The second Cutter number used to place this autobiographical work at the beginning of the group of works about Russell

The Autobiography of Bertrand Russell. London, 1967-69.

B	The single letter for the subclass, Philosophy (general)
1649	The integral number meaning an individual British philosopher of the later nineteenth and twentieth centuries
.R94	The first Cutter number meaning the individual philosopher, Bertrand Russell (.R9), and the successive element (4) meaning a general work about Russell
A32	The second Cutter number used to place this autobiographical work at the beginning of the group of works about Russell

The first American edition (1967) of the same work is classsed "B1649.R94A33" and a Canadian edition (1968) is classed "B1649.R94A34." These examples show the use of successive Cutter numbers to distinguish editions of autobiography.

After these autobiographical works are the general works about Russell written by other authors. The following are two examples of these.

Lillian Woodworth Aiken's *Bertrand Russell's Philosophy of Morals.*

B	The single letter for the subclass, Philosophy (general)
1649	The integral number meaning an individual British philosopher of the later nineteenth and twentieth centuries
.R94	The first Cutter number meaning the individual philosopher, Bertrand Russell (.R9), and the successive element (4) meaning a general work about Russell
A47	The second Cutter number for the author of the general work about Russell, Aiken

Paul Arthur Schilpp's *The Philosophy of Bertrand Russell*, 1963.

B	The single letter for the subclass, Philosophy (general)
1649	The integral number meaning an individual British philosopher of the later nineteenth and twentieth centuries
.R94	The first Cutter number meaning the individual philosopher, Bertrand Russell (.R9), and the successive element (4) meaning a general work about Russell
S35	The second Cutter number for the author of the general work, Schilpp
1963	The date of publication

Works by Russell on specific philosophical topics are generally classed in subclasses BC-BL. For example:

Bertrand Russell's *The Conquest of Happiness.*

BJ	The double letters for the subclass, Psychology
1481	The integral number meaning a work about happiness and joy in the English language
.R75	The Cutter number for Russell

Bertrand Russell's *Atheism: Collected Essays, 1943-1949.*

BL	The double letters for the subclass, Religion
2747	The number meaning theory of rationalism
.3	The decimal extension meaning atheism
.R84	The Cutter number for Russell

Table 6, "Language Subdivisions," in Class B, Part I (page 185) presents no problem in use. It is a simple table requiring the matching of final digits.

The index to Part I includes the names of many philosophers, broad categories with many subdivisions, and many compound entries. There are very few references to other schedules.

BL-BX Religion

Class B, Part II—BL-BX Religion contains nine subclasses: BL for general works on religion, religions, mythology, and rationalism; BM for Judaism; BP for Islam, Bahaism and Theosophy; BQ for Buddhism (a new subclass developed in 1972)*; BR for Christianity in general; BS for the Bible and exegesis; BT for Christian doctrinal theology and apologetics; BV for Christian practical theology including public and private worship; and BX for Christian denominations and sects. Subclasses BS and BX are greatly enumerated and detailed.

Part II, Religion, presents certain problems in usage. This was one of the last schedules to be developed, and as a result, much material related to religion was classed in other schedules, e.g., Church and social problems in Subclass HN; Education and the church in Subclass LC; Church music in Class M; Art and architecture in Class N; Biblical languages in Subclasses PA and PJ; and Bibliography in Class Z. The other major problem occurred with Subclass BX, Denominations and sects. Before the appearance of the second edition in 1962, many libraries found this section to be incomplete. This was especially true of theological libraries. As a result there were several expansions made for individual denominations. Some of these expansions are listed in the bibliography following this chapter. In the second edition this subclass was expanded to over two hundred pages, yet it remains insufficiently developed for special theological libraries. The expanded second edition reflects the nature of Library of Congress Classification, which is intentionally devised for the collections in the Library of Congress, not for other general libraries or special libraries.

Nevertheless, one great advantage of Class B for other libraries exists in the detailed treatment of Subclass BS, Bible and exegesis. Special tables are provided for the subarrangement of the texts of the Bible and works about the Bible. An example illustrating the use of the table for the special parts of the Old Testament is shown on page 152.

---

*Previously Buddhism was classed in BL1400-1495, numbers which have now been cancelled. The new Subclass BQ was developed by Kenneth Tanaka and was published as an appendix in *LC Classification—Additions and Changes*, List 168, October-December 1972.

Table I 5 nos.	Table II 1 no.	
		Texts.[1]
1	.A1	Polyglot.
		By language.
		Under each:
		Editions. By date, translator, or editor.
		Selections. By editor.
2	.A2	Hebrew.
3	.A3	English.
.A2	.A3A2	Collections. Comparative texts.
		By editor.
4	.A4	Other early and modern European languages, A–Z.
		Modern non-European languages, *see* BS 315–355.
	.A5–Z7	Criticism, commentaries, etc.
5		Early to 1950.
		1951–
.2		Criticism.
.3		Commentaries.
.4		Sermons. Meditations. Devotions.
.5		Other.

[1] Unless otherwise provided for, facsimiles of manuscripts and works on manuscripts may be given decimal numbers or successive cutter numbers as follows:

.3	.x2 (.x=cutter no.)	General works on manuscripts.
		Individual manuscripts in facsimile.
.5	.x3	By name, A–Z.
.7	.x4	By number.

e.g. Genesis texts in Hebrew, BS 1232; General works on its Hebrew manuscripts, BS 1232.3; Individual manuscripts in facsimile, by name, BS 1232.5; by number, BS 1232.7. The Minor Prophets text in Hebrew, BS 1560.A2; General works on its Hebrew manuscripts, BS 1560.A22; Individual manuscripts in facsimile, by name, BS 1560.A23; by number, BS 1560.A24.

In the schedule, the book of *Exodus* has been assigned the numbers "BS 1241-1245.5." In classing Childs' *Exodus: A Commentary*, Table I is used.

Brevard S. Childs, *Exodus: A Critical, Theological Commentary*.

BS	The double letters for the subclass, the Bible
1245.3	The number meaning the book of Exodus (124-) and commentaries (-5.3 from Table I)
.C45	Cutter number for the main entry, Childs

There are five tables for Subclass BX, Denominations and sects. These are quite similar to those tables already discussed in this chapter and in chapter 4. In addition, there are many internal tables for subdividing ranges of numbers, single numbers, and Cutter numbers.

The index to Part II excludes names of popes and the orders of the Roman Catholic Church. There are many generic entries with many subdivisions. At times the index repeats or summarizes sections of the classification.

In addition, Class B has certain features which may be useful in reference work: the list of philosophers by nationality in Subclass B, the list of denominations in Subclass BX, and the lists of various editions of the Bible in Subclass BS. The possible reference functions of L.C. schedules in other classes and subclasses will be cited as each individual class is discussed.

(Class C begins on page 154)

CLASS C—AUXILIARY SCIENCES OF HISTORY

C		Auxiliary sciences of history (General)
CB		History of civilization
		For individual countries, *see* D-F
CC		Archaeology (General)
		For individual countries, *see* D-F, GN
	200-250	Bells. Campanology
	300-350	Crosses
	900-950	Tombs (General)
CD		Diplomatics. Archives. Seals
	921-4279	Archives
		Including works on the science of archives, guides to depositories, inventories of archival material
CE		Technical chronology. Calendar
		For historical chronology, *see* D-F
CJ		Numismatics
	4801-5450	Tokens
	5501-6661	Medals and medallions
CN		Inscriptions. Epigraphy
CR		Heraldry
	191-1020	Public and official heraldry
	1101-1131	Ecclesiastical and sacred heraldry
	1179-3395	Family heraldry
	3499-4420	Titles of honor, rank, precedence, etc.
	4501-6305	Chivalry and knighthood
		Including tournaments, duels, orders, decorations
CS		Genealogy
	2300-3090	Personal and family names
CT		Biography
		For biography associated with a particular subject, *see* that subject
	93-206	Collections (General. Universal)
	210-3150	National biography
	3200-3910	Biography of women

Class C—Auxiliary Sciences of History was first published in 1915. Clarence Perley served as editor for the schedule as well as being personally responsible for Subclasses CC, Antiquities (general), Archeology; and CT, Biography. J. D. Wolcott prepared Subclasses CB, History of civilization; CJ, Numismatics, Coins; and CR, Heraldry. Julian Leavitt also worked on Subclass CB. Subclasses CD, Archives, Diplomatics, and CE, Chronology, were prepared by Alfred Schmidt. Chief classifier, Charles Martel, and Malma A. Gilkey constructed Subclass CS, Genealogy. Subclass CN, Epigraphy, was not included in the first edition in 1915. This subclass was delayed until the completion of Subclass PA to avoid any possible duplication. Clarence Perley began the work on this subclass, which was completed for publication by L. Belle Voegelein in 1942. The second edition of Class C was published in 1948, also under Voegelein's editorship. In this edition, Class C was issued for the first time in its complete form, including

Subclass CN. The third edition, published in 1975, introduced yet another subclass—C, Auxiliary sciences of history (general)—which had not been included in the previous editions.

Class C may be considered to be the generalia and miscellania class for history. Each of the subclasses represents very precisely defined fields of study. There is little relationship among the subclasses; each subclass is a complete development within itself.

There are five tables in Class C. Tables I, II, and IIB (Class C, pp. 106-107) for National Biography require simply the matching of the final digits of the specific geographic area's range of numbers with those in the table. For example, Great Britain is a nineteen-number country, "CT 770-788." Therefore, Table I is used for national biography of Great Britain. Its range of numbers may be matched to those in Table I in the following fashion.

CT 770-788		Table I
770	0	Periodicals. Societies. Serials
771	1	Collected works (nonserial)
772	2	Early works through 1800
773	3	Dictionaries. Encyclopedias
774	4	General works, 1801-
775	5	General special
777	7	Juvenile works
.5	.5	Portraits
		By period
		Ancient, *see* D
		Medieval, *see* D
		Modern
780	10	15th-16th centuries
781	11	17th-18th centuries
782	12	19th-20th centuries
783	13	20th century
784	14	Colonies (General)
		Prefer CT278-3090
785	15	Local divisions, A-Z
		For political or historical persons, *see* D-F
		Cities, *see* D
		Rulers, *see* D-F
788	18	Individual biography, A-Z (III)
	.Z9A-Z	Persons not known by name

Leonard Alfred George Strong's *Sixteen Portraits of People Whose Houses Have Been Preserved by the National Trust* is classed as a collection of British national biography, "CT 771. S7."

L. A. G. Strong's *Sixteen Portraits of People....*

CT	The double letters for the subclass, Biography
771	The integral number meaning a collection of British national biography
.S7	The Cutter number for the author of the biography

A. L. Rowse's *The English Past* is classed as a general work of British national biography in the fifth number in Great Britain's range, "CT 774."

A. L. Rowse's *The English Past*, 1952.

CT	The double letters for the subclass, Biography
774	The integral number meaning a general work of British national biography
.R6	The Cutter number for the author of the biography
1952	The date of publication

A work classed as general special is Sir James Marchant's *If I Had My Time Again: An Anthology Contributed by Twenty Distinguished Men and Women*, "CT 775 .M3." The sixth number in Table I, hence the sixth number in Great Britain's range of numbers, is for general special works.

James Marchant's *If I Had My Time Again*, 1950.

CT	The double letters for the subclass, Biography
775	The integral number meaning a general special work of British national biography
.M3	The Cutter number for the main entry, Marchant
1950	The date of publication

Vivian de Sola Pinto's *English Biography in the Seventeenth Century* is classed in the chronological division "17th-18th centuries" as "CT 781 .P5."

V. de Sola Pinto's *English Biography in the Seventeenth Century*.

CT	The double letters for the subclass, Biography
781	The integral number meaning a work on seventeenth and eighteenth century British national biography
.P5	The Cutter number for the main entry, Pinto

Some Victorian Portraits and Others, by Hilda Martindale, is another example of a chronologically subdivided work. It is classed in the "19th-20th centuries" in number "12" as "CT 782 .M37."

Hilda Martindale's *Some Victorian Portraits....*

CT	The double letters for the subclass, Biography
782	The integral number meaning a work on nineteenth and twentieth century British national biography
.M37	The Cutter number for the main entry, Martindale
1970	The date of publication

Table III is used for the subarrangement of biography by means of Cutter numbers.* The following examples of individual American biography demonstrate the use of this table.

Forest W. McNeir's *Forest McNeir of Texas.*

CT	The double letters for the subclass, Biography
275	The integral number meaning individual American biography
.M4444	The first Cutter number for the subject of the biography, McNeir
A3	The second Cutter number from Table III meaning an autobiographical work

Catherine Gabrielson's *The Story of Gabrielle.*

CT	The double letters for the subclass, Biography
275	The integral number meaning individual American biography
.G223	The first Cutter number for the subject of the biography, Gabrielle Gabrielson
G3	The second Cutter number for the author of the biography, Gabrielson

Miriam Allen DeFord's *Up-hill All the Way: The Life of Maynard Shipley.*

CT	The double letters for the subclass, Biography
275	The integral number meaning individual American biography
.S48814	The first Cutter number for the subject of the biography, Shipley
D4	The second Cutter number for the author of the biography, DeFord

---

*This is a floating table used for subarrangement of biographical works in all classes. Details of the table are given in Appendix B in this book.

Lucie Simpson's *Contacts, Literary and Political.*

CT	The double letters for the subclass, Biography
788	The integral number meaning an individual British biography
.S536	The first Cutter number for the subject of the biography, Simpson
A3	The second Cutter number from Table III meaning an autobiographical work

In the past, certain works of national biography were classed with History in Classes D and E-F. Current policy requires that such works as dictionaries of national biography and "who's who" be classed in CT. For example,

Dictionary of American Biography.

CT	The double letters for the subclass, Biography
213	The integral number meaning an American biographical dictionary
.D7	The Cutter number for the main entry, *Dictionary...*
1974	The date of publication

Dictionary of National Biography.

CT	The double letters for the subclass, Biography
773	The integral number meaning a British biographical dictionary
.D4	The Cutter number for the main entry, *Dictionary...*

It is the policy of the Library of Congress to class biography by subject. Subclass CT, Biography, is used only for a biography for which a subject may not be readily discernible. This is true of both collective and individual biography, as the foregoing examples show. Examples in previous chapters have shown biographies of literary writers and philosophers classed with their works in Classes P and B. For further discussion and examples of classifying biography by subject, *see* chapter 6.

This schedule also contains the "Table of Countries in One Alphabet," the use of which has been discussed in chapter 4.

The index to this schedule is relatively brief, but there are some useful references to other schedules, especially for classical entries.

CLASS D—HISTORY: GENERAL AND OLD WORLD

Including geography and description of individual regions and countries

D		History (General)
	51-95	Ancient history
	111-203	Medieval history
	204-849	Modern history
	501-680	World War I
	731-838	World War II
	901-1075	Europe (General)
DA		Great Britain
	20-690	England
	700-745	Wales
	750-890	Scotland
	900-995	Ireland
DB		Austria. Czechoslovakia. Hungary
DC		France
DD		Germany
DE		The Mediterranean region. Greco-Roman world
DF		Greece
DG		Italy
DH-DJ		Netherlands. Belgium. Luxemburg
DJK		Eastern Europe
DK		Russia. Poland. Finland
DL		Northern Europe. Scandinavia
DP		Spain. Portugal
DQ		Switzerland
DR		Balkan Peninsula.
DS		Asia
DT		Africa
DU		Oceania (South Seas)
	80-398	Australia
	400-430	New Zealand
DX		Gypsies

Class D—History: General and Old World encompasses the history and topography of the world in general and of the continents and countries excluding those in the Western Hemisphere. The scheme was initially drafted by Charles Martel in 1901 and 1902. The first edition, with the title *Universal and Old World History*, was published in 1916 with Alfred Schmidt serving as editor. As in the case of Class C, the subclasses of Class D were developed by a group of experts: W. Dawson Johnston planned Subclass DA, Great Britain; DK, Russia, and DR, Turkey and the Balkan States, were the responsibility of Alexis V. Babine; DP, Spain and Portugal, and DT, Africa, were developed by Cecil K. Jones. Schmidt was primarily responsible for the remaining subclasses: D, General history; DB, Austria-Hungary; DC, France; DD, Germany; DE, Classical antiquity; DF, Greece; DG, Italy; DH-DJ, Netherlands; and DQ, Switzerland. The second edition was published in 1959 with Voegelein as editor. Prior to the publication of the second edition there were two separately published supplements for World

War I and World War II. The first supplement, for World War I, was published in 1921 with Schmidt as the editor. A second edition of this supplement was published in 1933. The supplement for World War II was published in 1946. The second edition of Class D incorporated these two supplements into the text.

Class D was the first class to use the second letter in the notation for the subclasses. This device was designed to allow individual classifiers a whole subclass to develop instead of the restriction of a specified range of numbers. The preface to the first edition of Class D is extremely helpful not only as a guide to this class but as a sound general statement on the theory of classification for history. This preface was not retained in the second edition.

Since the publication of the second edition of Class D, a new subclass, DJK, has been developed for Eastern Europe.[4] The caption for DR, originally "Eastern Europe. Balkan Peninsula," was changed to "Balkan Peninsula." Subclass DJK, developed in 1976, contains the general form divisions of Eastern Europe and local history and description of the Black Sea Region and the Carpathian Mountain Region.

The general pattern of arrangement in history subclasses and individual countries is:

1) General works
2) Description and travel
3) Antiquities. Social life and customs, etc.
4) History
5) Local history and description

The main exception to this pattern is Subclass DA, Great Britain, in which the order is 1) General works; 2) History, including antiquities, etc.; 3) Description and travel; 4) Local history and description.

The local history numbers for individual countries make use of extensive special tables within the schedules accompanied by complete directions for their use. In most cases a careful analysis of the Library of Congress practice with an individual number should show how to fit original call numbers into the previously classed material.

French local history and description in Subclass DC, French history, may be used as an example of special tables within the schedules. The local history and description of the individual regions, provinces, departments, etc., of France is classed under the number "DC 611." The following table and instructions are given in the schedule under this one number.

Under each:

(1) Periodicals. Societies.
(2) Sources and documents. Collections.
(23) Gazetteers. Directories. Dictionaries, etc.
(25) Biography (Collective).
(3) General works. Description and travel. Guidebooks.
(4) Antiquities.
(5) History (General).
By period (History and description).
(6) Early.
(7) Medieval and early modern.
(8) Modern.
(9) Special topics.

(Instructions are on page 161)

The table shows the sequence of topics when nine basic numerals are available. If eleven are indicated (23), (25), (3), etc., become (3), (4), (5), etc. If fewer are available, longer decimal or Cutter numbers may be introduced, as for example (23) and (25) above; or a number may cover more than one topic, e.g. (1) may cover (1) and (2), or (5) may cover (5) through (8). When one numeral only is indicated, .A1-9 or .A1A-Z may be used for serials.

Many of the better known localities, e.g., Alpes and Aquitaine, are fully developed in the schedules. Brittany is given a range of successive Cutter numbers, ".B841-9173." The successions are then clearly assigned in the schedule. The following is the first part of this assignment.

DC	FRANCE
611	Regions, provinces, departments, etc., A-Z.
.B841-9173	**Brittany (Bretagne).**
.B841	Periodicals. Societies.
.B842	Sources and documents. Collections.
.B843	Collected works.
.B844	Minor works. Pamphlets, etc.
.B845	Biography (Collective).
.B846	Gazetteers. Directories, etc.
.B847	General works.
.B848	Description and travel.
	Including the picturesque.
.B85	Antiquities.
.B851	Social life and customs. Civilization.
.B852	Ethnography.
	History.
.B854	General works.
.B855	General special.

For example, René Pleven's general work on Brittany entitled *Avenir de la Bretagne* is classed "DC 611 .B847P56." This book uses the assigned successive Cutter number for general works on Brittany, ".B847."

René Pleven's *Avenir de la Bretagne*.

DC	The double letters for the subclass, French history
611	The integral number meaning local history and description of an individual region, etc., of France
.B847	The first Cutter number meaning a general work on Brittany
P56	The second Cutter number used for the main entry, Pleven

A book on description and travel in Brittany is Roger Vercel's *Bretagne aux Cent Visages*. This uses the assigned successive Cutter number, ".B848." Its complete call number is "DC 611 .B848V33."

Roger Vercel's *Bretagne aux Cent Visages.*

DC	The double letters for the subclass, French history
611	The integral number meaning local history and description of an individual region, etc., of France
.B848	The first Cutter number meaning a work on description and travel in Brittany
V33	The second Cutter number used for the main entry, Vercel

A final example of the use of these assigned successive Cutter numbers is Henri Queffélec's *La Bretagne des Pardons,* a work on the religious life and customs of Brittany. This is classed under ".B851" for social life and customs.

Henri Queffélec's *La Bretagne des Pardons.*

DC	The double letters for the subclass, French history
611	The integral number meaning local history and description of an individual region, etc., of France
.B851	The first Cutter number meaning social life and customs in Brittany
Q4	The second Cutter number for the main entry, Queffélec

Similar patterns of assigned successive Cutter numbers must be verified for those localities that are not developed in the schedules. Bourbonnais is an example of this. This locality is assigned a range of five successive Cutter numbers, ".B764-768." In this case the table of nine basic subdivisions given previously must be reduced to five subdivisions. The directions following this table may be directly applied. The first two numbers may be combined and the four history numbers may be combined.

	(1)	Periodicals, Societies.
	(2)	Sources and documents. Collections.
(1)		
	(23)	Gazetteers. Directories. Dictionaries, etc.
	(25)	Biography (Collective).
(2)	(3)	General works. Description and travel. Guidebooks.
(3)	(4)	Antiquities.
	(5)	History (General).
		By period (History and description).
	(6)	Early.
(4)	(7)	Medieval and early modern.
	(8)	Modern.
(5)	(9)	Special topics.

Bourbonnais' numbers may be then tentatively assigned as:

.B764	(1)	Periodicals. Societies. Sources and documents. Collections, etc.
.B765	(2)	General works. Description and travel. Guidebooks.
.B766	(3)	Antiquities.
.B767	(4)	History.
.B768	(5)	Special topics.

The following examples of classification by the Library of Congress may be used to verify this development. A work on description and travel of Bourbonnais entitled *Visages du Bourbonnais* is classed "DC 611 .B765V5." ".B765" is the second successive Cutter number assigned to Bourbonnais and fits into the table development already worked out. The third number in the original table is now the second number, and this number includes both general works and description and travel.

Visages du Bourbonnais.

DC	The double letters for the subclass, French history
611	The integral number meaning local history and description of an individual region, etc., of France
.B765	The first Cutter number meaning a general work including description and travel of Bourbonnais
V5	The second Cutter number for the main entry, *Visages....*

André Leguai's *Histoire du Bourbonnais* is classed as a history in ".B767." This, again, is the proper number according to the previous tentative assignment.

André Leguai's *Histoire du Bourbonnais.*

DC	The double letters for the subclass, French history
611	The integral number meaning local history and description of an individual region, etc., of France
.B767	The first Cutter number meaning a history of Bourbonnais
L4	The second Cutter number for the main entry, Leguai

Another work dealing with the history of Bourbonnais, although in a more specialized sense, is Marcel Genermont's *Chateaux en Bourbonnais*. It is also classed as history, "DC 611 .B767G4."

Marcel Genermont's *Chateaux en Bourbonnais*.

DC	The double letters for the subclass, French history
611	The integral number meaning local history and description of an individual region, etc., of France
.B767	The first Cutter number meaning a history of Bourbonnais
G4	The second Cutter number for the main entry, Genermont

A specialized work dealing with the peasant life and customs of Bourbonnais is Claude Joly's *Croquis Bourbonnais*. This is classed in the number ".B768" for special topics.

Claude Joly's *Croquis Bourbonnais*.

DC	The double letters for the subclass, French history
611	The integral number meaning local history and description of an individual region, etc., of France
.B768	The first Cutter number meaning a special topic dealing with local history of Bourbonnais
J6	The second Cutter number for the main entry, Joly

These examples all verify the tentative assignment of successive Cutter numbers for Bourbonnais. This same process of tentative reduction of the table, and then verification from Library of Congress practice, should be done in all instances using unspecified successive Cutter numbers.

There are eight auxiliary tables in Class D. One is the table "List of Countries in One Alphabet," which appears in the main schedule. The other tables appear in *LC Classification—Additions and Changes*. These are included in Appendix C of this book. Tables I-III are used for subarrangement of material about countries or regions which have been assigned a single number (an integer or a number with decimal extension) or a Cutter number. Tables IV-V are used for cities with a single number or Cutter number. Tables VI and VII are used for subarranging individual biography. The divisions in these tables correspond to those found in the table for biography in general which is included in Appendix B of this book.

The following examples illustrate the use of these tables.

Mu Kaara Sani [a Nigerian periodical].

DT	The double letters for the subclass, Africa
515	The integral number meaning Nigeria
.A2	The first Cutter number (based on Table I) for a periodical
M8	The second Cutter number for the main entry, *Mu*....

Jean Paul Adrien Malval's *Essai de chronologie tchadienne, 1707-1940.*

DT	The double letters for the subclass, Africa
546.45	The decimal number (546.4) assigned to Chad and the extension (.x5 based on Table II) for a general history
.M34	The Cutter number for the main entry, Malval

Burundi. Office national du tourisme. *A la découverte du Burundi.*

DT	The double letters for the subclass, Africa
449	The integral number for Regions, cities, etc. in Tanganyika
.B82	The Cutter number (.B8) assigned to Burundi and the successive Cutter number (.x2 based on Table III) for a work of description and travel
B87	The second Cutter number for the main entry, Burundi
1975	The date of publication

Eric Rosenthal's *The Rand Rush: 1886-1911, Johannesburg's First 25 Years in Pictures.*

DT	The double letters for the subclass, Africa
944	The integral number meaning Districts, regions, cities, etc. of South Africa
.J643	The Cutter number (.J6) assigned to Johannesburg and the successive Cutter number (.x43 from Table V) for a picturesque description
R67	The second Cutter number for the main entry, Rosenthal

In Class D, the classification of Western European history is more fully developed than the history of any other area. The two single subclasses for Africa and Asia do not contain nearly as many numbers as the ten subclasses for Western Europe. As a result, the subclasses DS and DT rely a great deal on Cutter numbers for expansion.

Another characteristic of Class D is that division is generally by geographic areas rather than political areas. Similarly, geographic names are usually chosen rather than political names. The reason, no doubt, is that the former are less prone to change.

One major criticism of Class D has been that its general shape reflects the state of Europe at the time of the First World War. The stability of numbers has been offered as an explanation, as Angell, former Chief of the Subject Cataloging Division of the Library of Congress, states:

If we left Europe as it was in 1919, this would be obviously intolerable. If we attempted to change everything in accordance with that and subsequent treaties, we would be exposing ourselves and other libraries to an amount of change that they and we would find unacceptable ... it does not mean that we do not know what has happened, or that we like it; in our best judgment, we have spent our time on more important changes.[5]

Class D is another of the schedules which has potential reference uses. The local history numbers for the European countries contain comprehensive lists of counties, regions, and some cities. The index to Class D is a satisfactory reference aid.

CLASS E-F—HISTORY: AMERICA

E	11-29	America (General)
	31-46	North America
	51-99	Indians. Indians of North America
	101-135	Discovery of America and early explorations
		United States (General)
	184-185	Elements in the population
	185	Negroes
	186-199	Colonial history
	201-298	Revolution
	301-453	Revolution to the Civil War
	351-364	War of 1812
	401-415	War with Mexico
	441-453	Slavery
	456-655	Civil War
	482-489	Confederate States of America
	660-738	Late nineteenth century
	714-735	Spanish-American War
	740-	Twentieth century
F	1-975	United States local history
	1001-1140	British America. Canada
	1201-1392	Mexico
	1401-1419	Latin America (General)
	1421-1577	Central America
	1601-2183	West Indies
	2201-2239	South America (General)
	2251-2299	Colombia
	2301-2349	Venezuela
	2351-2471	Guianas. Guyana. Surinam. French Guiana
	2501-2659	Brazil
	2661-2699	Paraguay
	2701-2799	Uruguay
	2801-3021	Argentina
	3051-3285	Chile
	3301-3359	Bolivia
	3401-3619	Peru
	3701-3799	Ecuador

Class E-F, originally entitled *America: History and Geography*, was the first schedule to be published in 1901 and was prepared by the Chief Classifier at the Library of Congress, Charles Martel. The second edition appeared in 1913 and was edited by Charles A. Flagg under the supervision of Martel. The third edition, with the title **History: America,** was published in 1958 and represented the work of Willard O. Waters, Irma I. Blake, Florence B. Currie, and Kathleen F. Clifford. Voegelein served as the editor of this edition, and Dorothy Norberg prepared the index and the list of counties, departments, etc., in local history.

The order of the classes in Class E is general American history, general North American history, and general United States history; Class F completes this order with United States local history followed by our nearest neighbors, Canada and Mexico, followed by Central America and South America.

As Class E-F does not use double letters for subclasses, one major problem in using this schedule involves expansions. Many expansions are created by the use of decimal extensions, which tend to make the notation somewhat cumbersome. But basically this schedule presents no major problems to the classifier, a complete outline and a detailed index are provided.

There are nine auxiliary tables to be used with Class F. Tables I-IV are in the main volume, preceding F instead of following it as auxiliary tables usually do. Tables V-IX are in the *LC Classification—Additions and Changes.* Table I is used primarily for states with a long historical background. Tables II and III are also for states. Table IV is for metropolitan areas. As the divisions under all the individual states have been fully worked out in the schedules, these tables serve as summaries and guides to interpretation and not as is usually the case with auxiliary tables.

An example of the use of Tables I-III may be readily observed in the following comparison of the numbers assigned to the state of Wisconsin and its designated table, Table II. For example, the first of Wisconsin's 15 numbers is "F 576." This number is for "Periodicals, Societies, Collections." The first number in Table II is also for "Periodicals, Societies, Collections." The following comparison of the two tables demonstrates this point throughout:

Table II		F576-590 Wisconsin	
(1)	Periodicals. Societies. Collections.	576	Periodicals. Societies. Collections.
(3)	Museums. Exhibitions, exhibits.	578	Museums. Exhibitions, exhibits.
(4)	Gazetteers. Dictionaries. Geographic names.	579	Gazetteers. Dictionaries. Geographic names.
(4.3)	Guidebooks. Directories.	.3	Guidebooks.
(4.5)	General.		
			[State directories are no longer classified at the Library of Congress.]
(4.6)	Elite.		
(4.7)	Business.		
(5)	Biography (Collective). Genealogy (Collective).	580	Biography (Collective). Genealogy (Collective).

(5.2)	Historiography.	.2	Historiography.
	Historians, see E 175.5.		Historians, see E 175.5.
(5.5)	Study and teaching.	.5	Study and teaching.
(6)	General works. Histories.	581	General works. Histories.
(6.3)	Juvenile works.	.3	Juvenile works.
(6.5)	Minor works. Pamphlets, addresses, essays, etc.	.5	Minor works. Pamphlets, addresses, essays, etc.
(6.6)	Anecdotes, legends, pageants, etc.	.6	Anecdotes, legends, pageants, etc.
(7)	Historic monuments. Illustrative material.	582	Historic monuments. (General). Illustrative material.
(8)	Antiquities (Non-Indian).	583	Antiquities (Non-Indian).
(9)-(11)	By period.		By period.
		584	Early to 1848.
		585	1836-1848. Wisconsin Territory.
		586	1848-1950.
(11.2)	1951- .	.2	1951- .
(12)	Regions, counties, etc., A—Z.	587	Regions, counties, etc., A—Z.
(13)	Metropolis, Chief city. [Thus far, subdivision (13) has been used only for Chicago at the Library of Congress.]		
(14)	Cities, towns, etc., A—Z.	589	Cities, towns, etc., A—Z.
(15)	Elements in the population.	590	Elements in the population.

Tables V and VI are "Tables for Cities with Single Number or Cutter Number, in United States, British America and Latin America," and Tables VII-IX are "Tables for Countries, Islands, Regions with Single or Cutter Number." These tables, which were developed after the main schedule of E-F was published, are reproduced in Appendix C of this book. Tables X and XI for individual biography are identical to Tables VI and VII in Class D.

The following examples illustrate the use of these tables:

Luis Suárez's *De Tenochtitlan de Mexico.*

F	The letter for the class, United States local history and America (except United States)
1386	The integral number assigned to Mexico (City)
.3	The decimal extension taken from Table V, meaning a general history
.S8	The Cutter number for the main entry, Suárez

Rodolphe Fournier's *Lieux et monuments historiques de l'île de Montréal.*

F	The letter for the class, United States local history and America (except United States)
1054.5	The number meaning cities in Canada
.M865	The Cutter number (.M8) for Montreal and the successive Cutter number (.x65 from Table VI) meaning monuments and statues
F68	The second Cutter number for the main entry, Fournier

The extensive list of American Indians under the number "E 99" is a noteworthy reference feature of Class E. It should be noted that the names of counties in the United States are not included in the index to this schedule. The names of cities, rivers, and regions are.

The classifier should remember that subject is paramount when classing in history. Although the complete works of a literary author or a philosopher may be carefully classed together, the works of a historian are usually not classed together. The works of a historian are classed by the subject content of the individual works. For example, Thomas Carlyle's *French Revolution* is classed in Subclass DC for French history; and his *Early Kings of Norway* is classed in Subclass DL for Scandinavian history. Only if a historian wrote solely on one subject could his or her works be classed together.

CLASS G—GEOGRAPHY. ANTHROPOLOGY. RECREATION

G		Geography (General)
		For geography and description of individual countries, *see* D-F
	149-570	Voyages and travels (General)
		Including discoveries, explorations, shipwrecks, seafaring life. For travel in special continents and countries, *see* D-F
	575-890	Polar regions
		Including exploration, history, description
	905-910	Tropics (General)
	912-922	Northern and Southern Hemispheres
	1000.3-3122	Atlases
	3160-9980	Maps. Globes
GA		Mathematical geography. Cartography
		Including topographical surveys of individual countries
GB		Physical geography
		Including arrangement by country
	400-649	Geomorphology
	651-2998	Water. Hydrology
		Including ground water, rivers, lakes, glaciers
	5000-5030	Natural disasters
GC		Oceanography
	100-181	Seawater
	200-376	Dynamics of the sea
	377-399	Marine sediments
	1000-1023	Marine resources. Applied oceanography
	1080-1581	Marine pollution
GF		Human ecology. Anthropogeography
GN		Anthropology
	49-296	Physical anthropology. Somatology
	301-673	Ethnology. Social and cultural anthropology
		For descriptions of individual ethnic groups, *see* D-F
	700-875	Prehistoric archaeology
		Including arrangement by country
GR		Folklore
	72-79	Folk literature (General)
	430-940	Folklore relating to special subjects
GT		Manners and customs (General)
		For works limited to special countries, *see* D-F
	170-474	Houses. Dwellings
	500-2370	Costume. Dress. Fashion
	2400-5090	Custom relative to private and public life
		Including love, marriage, eating, smoking, treatment of the dead, town life, customs of chivalry, festivals and holidays
	5320-6720	Customs relative to special classes, by birth, occupation, etc.
GV		Recreation
	191.2-200.5	Outdoor life. Outdoor recreation
		Including camping for individuals or small groups, organized camps, trailer camping, hiking, mountaineering
	201-555	Physical training
	561-1198.995	Sports
	1199-1570	Games and amusements
	1580-1799	Dancing
	1800-1860	Circuses, spectacles, etc.
		Including rodeos, waxworks, amusement parks, etc.

The first edition of **Class G,** with the title, *Geography, Anthropology, Sports and Games,* was published in 1910 under the editorship of Clarence Perley. The preliminary work on the schedule was prepared by W. Dawson Johnston, C. K. Jones, and J. Christian Bay, under the direction of Martel in 1904 and 1905. They were responsible for Subclasses G, Geography (General); GA, Mathematical and astronomical geography;* GB, Physical geography; GC, Oceanology and oceanography; GF, Anthropogeography; and GN, Anthropology. S. C. Stuntz prepared Subclass GV, Sports and games. Subclasses GR, Folklore, and GT, Manners and customs, were omitted in the first edition. These two subclasses were first published separately in 1915. The second edition of Class G appeared in 1928 and included a provisional scheme for atlases (G 1001-3035). In 1945 C. W. Buffum of the Map Division of the Library of Congress prepared a preliminary draft for a classification of maps using the numbers G 3160-9999 from Subclass G. This material was incorporated into the third edition of Class G issued in 1954 under the editorship of Voegelein. The fourth edition, with the title, *Geography, Maps, Anthropology, Recreation,* was published in 1976. In this edition, extensive revision was made in the atlas and map section of Subclass G. Many jurisdictions were realigned in order to reflect the current political situation. A new feature is the inclusion of many illustrative maps to show these alignments.

Class G may be seen as a connective schedule between the history classes on one side and the remaining social sciences on the other. Five of the subclasses are related directly to geography; nevertheless, much geographical material, especially the topography and description of individual continents and countries, is placed in the history schedules, D-F.

Tables for Maps and Atlases

The main topic to be discussed in this section is the use of the detailed tables for atlases and maps at the end of Subclass G. The other tables in this schedule are similar to previously discussed tables and should present no major problems in use.

"Special Instructions and Tables of Subdivisions for Atlases and Maps" appear on pages 206-223 of the schedule. Subclass G for atlases and maps is essentially a form class, in that all atlases and maps, regardless of subject matter, are classed here. Subdivisions are provided for individual areas and jurisdictions which are further subdivided, when necessary, by subject. In other words, in this subclass, the citation order is form-place-subject. Furthermore, the date of map situation or the date of publication often constitutes a part of the class number. Table III, "Area Subdivisions," provides subarrangement of atlases and maps of a particular area. A major area is the general geographic area to which a specific range of integral numbers is assigned in the schedule. For instance, the range of numbers "G 3700-3702" is assigned in the schedule to maps of the United States, and the range of numbers "G 3800-3804" is assigned to New York (State).

---

*This and the following captions of subclasses have been revised in later editions. *See* outline.

Therefore, both the United States and New York (State) are considered major areas. A sub-area is a specific geographic area within the major area. A sub-area may be a region or a natural feature of the major area, a major political division of the major area (e.g., province, county, etc.), or a city or town in the major area.

There are five subdivisions in Table III:

AREA SUBDIVISIONS (abridged)

(1)	0 or 5	General
(2)	1 or 6	By subject
(3)	2 or 7	By region, natural feature, etc., when not assigned individual numbers, A-Z
(4)	3 or 8	By major political division (Counties, states, provinces, etc.) when not assigned individual numbers, A-Z
(5)	4 or 9	By city or town, A-Z

Major Areas

The first two numbers in Table III are used for major areas only. The first number, "0 or 5," matching the last digit of the number assigned to the area in the schedule, is used for general maps and atlases of the major area which have no special subject interest. The second number, "1 or 6," is used for maps and atlases of the major area which have special subject interest. This second number is further subarranged by Table IV which will be discussed in the section on subject letter-numbers below.

For example, New York State has a specific range of numbers assigned for maps, "G 3800-3804," which makes New York State a major area. The first number of this range, "G 3800," is used for general maps of the state which have no special subject interest. The second number of this range, "G 3801," is used for maps of the major area which have special subject interest, such as a railroad map of New York State. The first page of Table III (*Class G*, p. 208) demonstrates the use of these numbers for both maps and atlases.

Sub-areas

The other three numbers of Table III are used for sub-areas. The three types of sub-areas are: regions or natural features of the major area, major political divisions of the major area, and cities or towns in the major area.

When the states or provinces of a country are given their own ranges of numbers, they are treated as major areas, instead of as sub-areas of the particular country, as in the case of the states of the United States. In such cases, the country is given a span of only three numbers, without the last two numbers corresponding to the fourth and fifth numbers in Table III.

The third number of Table III, "2 or 7," is used for maps and atlases covering only a region or natural feature of the major area. A map of the Adirondack Mountains of New York State will be classed in the third number of the range of numbers for New York State, "G 3802 .A2." ".A2" is the Cutter number for the specific region, Adirondack Mountains, in the major area, New York State. The Adirondack Mountains are, in this case, a sub-area of New York State.

The fourth number of Table III, "3 or 8," is used for maps and atlases covering only a major political division (such as a county) of the major area. A map of Monroe County, New York, will be classed in the fourth number of the range of numbers for New York State, "G 3803 .M6." ".M6" is the Cutter number for the specific major political division, in this case, Monroe County. Monroe County is thus a sub-area of New York State.

The fourth edition of Class G introduces the use of the colon, a new feature in the L.C. Classification, to indicate further subdivisions of a sub-area. For example, under the fourth number in Table III, a colon (:) following the Cutter number for the political division and followed by the number 3 indicates an administrative subdivision. This is followed by a second Cutter number for the subordinate division. For example, the number "G 3823.A4:3A5" represents Pennsylvania, Allegheny County, Aleppo Township.[6]

The fifth number of Table III, "4 or 9," is used for maps and atlases covering only a city or town of the major area. A map of Rochester, New York, will be classed in the fifth number of the range of numbers for New York State, "G 3804.R6." ".R6" is the Cutter number for the specific city or town, in this case, Rochester. Rochester is thus a sub-area of New York State. All sub-areas are subarranged alphabetically by means of Cutter numbers.

Under the number assigned to a particular city, a colon (:) followed by the number 2 is used for further geographic subdivision, and a colon (:) followed by the number 3 is used for further political subdivision. For example, the number "G3804.N4:3Q4" represents New York City, Queens, and the number "G3804.N4:2C4" means New York City, Central Park.

Subject Letter-Numbers

The directions for the use of Table IV, "Subject Subdivisions," explain that it is used for maps and atlases with specific subject interest. It is not used with general maps and atlases or maps covering several subjects or topics.

This table consists of seventeen form and subject divisions which are represented by capital letters; subtopics are designated by arabic numerals. These symbols are called "subject letter-numbers." Although they resemble Cutter numbers in appearance, they are not Cutter numbers and have no alphabetical significance. These subject letter-numbers are treated as decimals. The summary of the seventeen categories of form and subject divisions is shown on the top of page 175.

A typical development of subject letter-numbers is illustrated by the division Q, shown on the bottom of page 175.

Summary of Form and Subject Subdivisions

A Special category maps and atlases
B Mathematical geography
C Physical sciences
D Biogeography
E Human and cultural geography. Anthropogeography.
    Human ecology
F Political geography
G Economic geography
H Mines and mineral resources
J Agriculture
K Forests and forestry
L Aquatic biological resources
M Manufacturing and processing. Service industries
N Technology. Engineering. Public works
P Transportation and communication
Q Commerce and trade. Finance
R Military and naval geography
S Historical geography

Q   Commerce <u>and</u> <u>Trade</u>. <u>Finance</u>

.Q1   General
.Q2   Business statistics
.Q3   Movement of commodities
        Class here works on trade routes, caravan routes,
          etc.
        Cf. .Q5, Tariffs and other trade barriers
        For maps and atlases which emphasize the carrier
          and show specific routes, <u>see</u> .P
.Q4   Marketing
.Q42   Trade centers and trading areas
.Q44   Shopping centers. Shopping malls
.Q46   Retail sales outlets
.Q48   Fairs, exhibitions, etc.
        Class individual fairs and exhibitions as
          regions, e. g. New York Worlds Fair, and
          Transpo '72
.Q5   Tariffs and other trade barriers
.Q8   Finance
        Class here works on coins and currencies, foreign
          exchange credit, special types of financial
          institutions, individual financial firms, etc.

Examples of the Use of Tables III and IV

The following examples supplement those shown in Tables III and IV for maps and atlases.

General Maps and Atlases

The complete call number for an area atlas without specific subject interest consists of three parts:

Area number
Cutter number(s)
Date of atlas publication

Major-area Atlas

Richards' Atlas of New York State, 1959.

G1250	First (based on Table III) of the numbers assigned to the atlases of New York State (area number)
.R5	The Cutter number for the authority responsible for the atlas, Richards....
1959	Date of publication

Sub-area Atlas

Richard Horwood's *Plan of the Cities of London and Westminster*, 1799.

G1819	The fifth number (based on Table III) assigned to the atlases of England for subdivision by city or town
.L7H65	The sub-area Cutter number (.L7) for London plus the Cutter number (H65) for Horwood
1799	Date of atlas publication

Major-area Maps

The complete call number for a major-area map consists of three parts:

Area number
Date of map situation
Cutter number for authority responsible for the map

Superior Map of New York, 1954, by George F. Cram Co.

G3800	The first number (based on Table III) assigned to the maps of New York State
1954	Date of map situation
.C7	Cutter number for Cram

Sub-area Maps

The complete call number for a sub-area map consists of four parts:

Area number
Sub-area Cutter number
Date of map situation
Cutter number for authority responsible for the map

Department of Highways Map of Livingston County, New York, 1954.

G3803	The fourth number (based on Table III) assigned to New York State, representing a major political division
.L5	The Cutter number for the sub-area, Livingston County
1954	Date of map situation
.L5	Cutter number for authority responsible for the map, Livingston County....

Subject Maps and Atlases

Major-area Subject Atlas

The complete call number of a major-area atlas with special subject interest consists of three parts:

> Subject-area number
> Subject letter-number plus Cutter number for the authority responsible for the atlas
> Date of publication

Charles G. Huntington's *The Cyclist's Road-Book of Connecticut*, 1888.

G1241	Subject-area number (second number based on Table III) for Connecticut
.P2H8	Subject letter-number (from Table IV) meaning roads plus Cutter number for Huntington
1888	Date of publication

Sub-area Subject Atlas

The complete call number for a sub-area subject atlas consists of three parts:

> Area number
> Sub-area Cutter number plus subject letter-number plus Cutter number for the authority responsible for the atlas
> Date of publication

George Washington Bromley's *Atlas of the City of Philadelphia, 35th Ward, from Actual Survey and Official Plans*, 1927.

G1264	The fifth number (based on Table III) assigned to atlases of Pennsylvania for subdivision by city or town
.P5G46B77	The sub-area Cutter number (.P5) for Philadelphia plus the subject letter-number (G46 from Table IV) meaning cadastral maps and the Cutter number (B77) for the main entry, Bromley
1927	Date of publication

Major-area Subject Map

The complete call number for a major-area subject map consists of four parts:

> Subject-area number
> Subject letter-number
> Date of map situation
> Cutter number for the authority responsible for the map

U.S. Geological Survey, *Geologic Map Index of New York*, 1952.

G3801	The second number (based on Table III) assigned to the maps of New York State to be subdivided by subject
.C5	The subject letter-number from Table IV meaning geology
1952	Date of map situation
.U5	Cutter number for the source of the map, U.S....

Sub-area Subject Map

The complete call number for a sub-area subject map consists of four parts:

> Area number
> Sub-area Cutter number plus subject letter-number
> Date of map situation
> Cutter number for the authority responsible for the map

Port of New York Authority's *New York Harbor Terminals*, 1956- .

G3804	The fifth number (based on Table III) assigned to the maps of New York State for subdivision by city or town
.N4P55	The sub-area Cutter number (.N4) for New York City plus the subject letter-number (P55 from Table IV) meaning ports and port facilities
year	Date of map situation
.P6	Cutter number for Port of New York Authority

In the case of sets of maps, the letter "s" in the lower case is added to the main number and the date in the call number is replaced by the denominator of the "representative fraction" scale, minus the last three digits. For example:

United States. Aeronautical Chart and Information Service. *AAF United States Plotting Chart[s]*, 1943-
(scale: 1:1,000,000).

G3701s	The second number (based on Table III) assigned to United States meaning a subject map, and the letter "s" indicating a set of maps
.A1	The subject letter-number meaning outline and base maps
1,000	The scale minus the last three digits
.U5	Cutter number for United States....

Other Auxiliary Tables in Class G

There are three tables of geographical subdivisions at the end of the schedule. These present no serious problems in use. The first of these tables provides a list of decimal extensions to be added to any subject number in order to further subdivide geographically. The following is a part of this table:

.69	Asia
.7	China
.71	India
.77	Japan
.78	Iran

This type of decimal extension may be seen as a development from Charles Ammi Cutter's "Local List" in his *Expansive Classification*, rather than from Melvil Dewey's *Decimal Classification*. An example of the use of this table is the number "GV 863.77.A1O26" assigned to Robert Obojski's *The Rise of Japanese Baseball Power*. The first Cutter number ".A1" is an "A" Cutter number for general works (*see* discussion on pages 88-89).

A number of topics, such as folklore, social customs, and manners, classed in Class G also appear in other classes. Detailed instructions with regard to placement of specific topics or materials and cross references are provided at the begining of the subclasses and under individual numbers.

The comprehensive index to the third edition of Class G, which included a large number of entries under geographic names (names of countries, provinces, states, counties, and many cities), has been pruned down considerably in the index to the fourth edition, in which geographic names are limited to those for the states, provinces, constituent countries, and larger regions in the United States, Canada, and Great Britain, and to the names of countries and larger or international regions for the rest of the world.

CLASS H – SOCIAL SCIENCES

H		Social sciences (General)
HA		Statistics
		Including collections of general and census statistics of special countries. For mathematical statistics, *see* QA
		Economics
HB		Economic theory
		Including value, price, wealth, capital, interest, profit, consumption
	848-875	Population
	879-3700	Demography. Vital statistics
	3711-3840	Crises. Business cycles
HC		Economic history and conditions. National production
HD		Land. Agriculture. Industry
	1-91	Production. Industrial management
	101-1395	Land
		Including public lands, real estate, land tenure
	1401-2210	Agricultural economics
		Including agricultural laborers
	2321-9999	Industry
	2709-2930	Corporations. Trusts, Cartels
	2951-3570	Industrial cooperation
	3611-4730	The state and industrial organization
		Including state industries, public works, municipal industries
	4801-8942	Labor
		Including wages, strikes, unemployment, labor unions, industrial relations, social security, professions, state labor. For civil service, *see* J
	9000-9999	Special industries and trades
HE		Transportation and communication
	331-380	Traffic engineering. Roads and highways
	381-971	Water transportation
	1001-5600	Rail transportation
	5601-5720	Automotive transportation
	6000-7500	Postal service. Stamp collecting
	7601-8688	Telecommunication. Telegraph
	8689-8700	Radio and television
	8701-9715	Telephone
	9761-9900	Air transportation
HF		Commerce
	294-343	Boards of trade. Chambers of commerce
	1701-2701	Tariff policy
	5001-5780	Business. Business administration
	5549	Personnel management
	5601-5689	Accounting
	5801-6191	Advertising
HG		Finance
	201-1496	Money
	1501-3542	Banking
	3701-3781	Credit
	3810-4000	Foreign exchange
	4001-4495	Corporation finance
	4501-6270	Stocks, investment, speculation
	8111-9970	Insurance

(Class H continues on page 181)

		Economics—*continued*
HJ		Public finance
	2005-2199	Income and expenditure. The budget
	2240-5957	Revenue. Taxation
	6041-7384	Customs. Tariff
	8003-8963	Public credit. Debts. Loans
	9000-9698	Local finance
	9701-9995	Public accounting
		Sociology
HM		Sociology (General and theoretical)
	251-291	Social psychology
HN		Social history. Social problems. Social reform
	30-39	The church and social problems
		Social groups
HQ		The family. Marriage. Woman
	12-449	Sexual life
	450-471	Erotica
	503-1064	The family. Marriage
		Including child study, eugenics, desertion, adultery, divorce, polygamy, the aged
	1101-2030	Woman. Feminism. Women's clubs
HS		Societies: Secret, benevolent, etc. Clubs
		Including Freemasons, religious societies, ethnic societies, political societies, Boy Scouts
HT		Communities. Classes. Races
	101-384	Urban sociology. Cities and towns
		Including the social and economic aspects of city planning and urban renewal. For architectural aspects, *see* NA9000-9425
	390-395	Regional planning
	401-485	Rural sociology
	601-1445	Social classes
		Including middle class, serfdom, slavery
	1501-1595	Races
		For works on the race as a social group and race relations in general
HV		Social pathology. Social and public welfare. Criminology
	40-696	Charities
	697-4959	Protection, assistance, and relief
		Arranged by special classes of persons, as determined by age, defects, occupation, race, economic status, etc.
		Including protection of animals
	5001-5720	Alcoholism. Intemperance. Temperance reform
	5725-5770	Tobacco habit
	5800-5840	Drug habits. Drug abuse
	6001-9920	Criminology
	6251-7220	Crimes and offenses
	7231-9920	Penology
		Including police, prisons, punishment and reform, juvenile delinquency
HX		Socialism. Communism. Anarchism
	806-811	Utopias

Class H—Social Sciences includes only the generalia class for the social sciences and two individual social science disciplines, economics and sociology. The remaining individual disciplines may be found in Classes C, D, E-F for history, G for geography and anthropology, and the following Classes, J for political science, K for law, and L for education.

Roland R. Falkner and Charles Martel worked together in developing the original pattern of schedules H—J—L. They were assisted by W. Dawson Johnston, Luis Perez, and Edwin Wiley. George M. Churchill prepared Subclasses HS, Associations, and HT, Communities. The first edition of Class H was published in 1910 without Subclass HT, which was published separately in 1915. A second edition of Class H including Subclass HT was issued in 1920. The third edition of Class H appeared in 1950 under the editorship of Voegelein. Classifiers in charge of Class H from 1920 to 1950 were C. K. Jones, Leo LaMontagne, and Philip Krichbaum.

There are sixteen subclasses in Class H. The first two subclasses form the generalia section for the social sciences: Subclass H for general works in the social sciences and Subclass HA for general statistics. Seven subclasses form the economics section: HB for economic theory, HC and HD for economic history and conditions, including national production and economic conditions of individual countries in HC, and land, agriculture, and industry in HD; HE for transportation and communication; HF for commerce; HG for finance, including money, banking, and insurance; and HJ for public finance. The remaining seven subclasses make up the section for sociology: HM for general works and theory of sociology; HN for social history, social problems, and social reform; HQ, HS, and HT for social groups, with HQ including the family, marriage, and woman, HS including societies, and HT including communities, classes, and races; HV for social pathology, social and public welfare, and criminology; and HX for socialism, communism, anarchism, and utopia works and theories. The position of this last subclass creates an interesting collocation to the following Class J, for political science. The most common form of detailed enumeration in Class H is by geographic area.

Complex Tables of Geographical Divisions

Some of the most typographically complex auxiliary tables in the L.C. Classification are the "Tables of Geographical Divisions" in Class H. Ten tables make use of a single column of geographical locations.[7] The reader should carefully follow the examples given below with the classification schedule in order to become acquainted with the typographical features of these tables. The use of these tables is further complicated by the fact that the subject subdivisions are represented by tables within the schedules. For instance, works dealing with labor in geographic areas other than the United States must be classed within the range of HD 8101-8942 using Table VIII. Following this statement of the range of numbers in the schedule is the table for subject subdivisions for twenty-number countries, ten-number countries, five-number countries, one-number countries, and Cutter number countries. A condensed form of this particular table is shown below.

B   Labor.   HD 8101-8942

Cutter no.	1 no.	20 nos.	10 nos.	5 nos.	
					Documents.
.x	.A1-4	(1)	(1)	(1)	General.
		(2)	(1.5)	(1.5)	State.
.x2A-Z	.A5A-Z	(3)	(2)	(2)	Associations and periodicals.
		(4)			Conferences.
		(5)	(3)		Annuals.
		(6)			Directories.
		(7)			Statistics.
.x3A-Z	.A6-Z7	(8)	(4)	(3)	History (General).
					General works and history.
					By period.
		(9)	(5)		Early to 1848.
		(10)	(6)		Later, 1849-1945.
		(11)	(6.5)	(3.5)	1945- .
		(13)	(7)	(3.7)	Biography.
					.A1A-Z Collective.
					.A2-Z Individual.
			(8)		Labor in politics.
		(15)			General works.
		(16)			Chartist movement (Gt. Britain).
		(17)			Local, A-Z.
		(18)	(8.5)		Immigrant labor, by race, A-Z.
.x4A-Z	.Z8A-Z	(19)	(9)	(4)	By state, A-Z.
		(20)	(10)	(5)	By city, A-Z.

Twenty-Number Countries

Before using Table VIII, however, the classifier must determine the range of geographic numbers available to the geographic area in question. For instance, in Table VIII, Great Britain has a range of numbers from 281 to 300. Great Britain is thus a twenty-number country. These twenty numbers are to be applied to the subject subdivisions for a twenty-number geographic division. For example, a general historical work on British labor entitled *Essays in Labour History* by Asa Briggs is classed in the following fashion. As Great Britain is a twenty-number country in Table VIII, the twenty-number column of the table for HD 8101-8942 is used. A general historical work will use the eighth number in the table, hence the eighth number in Great Britain's range of 281 through 300. The eighth number in that range is 288. This number is then added to the base number for labor in areas other than the United States. A footnote instructs the classifier to add the country number directly to 8100. This gives the number HD 8388. Cuttering for the main entry, Briggs, gives ".B7." The completed number is "HD 8388.B7."

Asa Briggs' *Essays in Labour History* (i.e., British labor history).

HD		The double letters for the subclass, Economic history
	8100	The base number for foreign labor as given in the footnote
	288	The adjusted country number meaning a general historical work on labor in Great Britain
	———	
	8388	
8388		The integral number meaning a general historical work on labor in Great Britain
.B7		The Cutter number for the main entry, Briggs

Another example of this may be seen in Arthur Redford's *Labour Migration in England, 1800-1850*, which is classed "HD 8389 .R4." This is an "early to 1848" general work and history, thus it uses the ninth number in the subject table. The ninth number in Great Britain's range is 289. When 289 is added to 8100, the base number for labor in areas other than the United States, the result is 8389. This is the correct class number for this work, "HD 8389." ".R4" is simply cuttering for the main entry.

Arthur Redford's *Labour Migration in England, 1800-1850*.

HD		The double letters for the subclass, Economic history
	8100	The base number for foreign labor as given in the footnote
	289	The adjusted country number meaning work on early British labor history
	———	
	8389	
8389		The integral number meaning a work on early British labor history
.R4		The Cutter number for the main entry, Redford

Another example is the classification of *The Age of Chartists, 1832-1854*, by John Lawrence Le Breton Hammond. This work is classed "HD 8396.H3." The sixteenth number in this case is for the Chartist movement in the subject table and the sixteenth number in Great Britain's range is 296. The 296 added to 8100 gives HD 8396.

John Hammond's *The Age of Chartists, 1832-1854*.

HD		The double letters for the subclass, Economic history
	8100	The base number for foreign labor as given in the footnote
	296	The adjusted country number meaning the Chartist movement in Great Britain
	———	
	8396	
8396		The integral number meaning a work on the Chartist movement in Great Britain
.H3		The Cutter number for the main entry, Hammond

Ten-Number Countries

An example of a ten-number geographic area is Europe. In Table VIII, Europe has a range of 271 to 280. A work on labor in relation to the Common Market by Val Schur, entitled *Labour in Britain and the Six*, is classed "HD 8376.5 .S35." This would be a current work on labor and would use the "6.5" number in the table for ten-number countries. This number adjusted to Europe's range of numbers is 276.5. 276.5 added to 8100, as directed by the foot-note, gives 8376.5. Again the Cutter number for the author is ".S35." The completed number is "HD8376.5.S35."

Val Schur's *Labour in Britain and the Six.*

HD		The double letters for the subclass, Economic history
	8100	The base number for foreign labor as given in the footnote
	276.5	The adjusted country number meaning a work on current labor in Europe
	8376.5	
8376.5		The integral number meaning a work on current labor in Europe
.S35		The Cutter number for the main entry, Schur

The tables in Class H present no great problems in use provided these steps are followed. First, the appropriate position in the schedule must be located. Second, the correct geographical table must be used. Third, the range of numbers within that table for a specific geographic area must be discerned. Fourth, that range of numbers must be applied to the appropriate table of subject subdivisions. Fifth, the adjusted geographic number must be added to the designated base number. This base number is usually given in a footnote. The classifier must always be careful to avoid simple errors in addition.

Perhaps the greatest single problem in the use of Class H and the other social science classes is where to class material dealing with more than one of the disciplines in the social sciences. The safest solution to this problem is to establish a precedent within Library of Congress practice for a particular type of material.

The index to Class H includes many summaries of small sections of the classification, i.e., the undistributed as well as distributed relatives may be found as subdivisions. There are very few geographic entries in the index, since much of the geographic subdivision is accomplished by auxiliary tables.

Special reference uses of this schedule include the list of industries and trades under HD 8039 and HD 9999 and the businesses and activities under HF 5686.

CLASS J — POLITICAL SCIENCE

J		Official documents
		General serial documents only. For documents limited to special subjects, *see* the subject in B-Z
	1-9	Official gazettes
		United States documents
		For congressional hearings, reports, etc., *see* KF
	80-85	Presidents' messages and other executive documents
	86-87	State documents
	100-981	Other countries
		For documents issued by local governments, *see* JS
JA		Collections and general works
JC		Political theory. Theory of the state
	311-323	Nationalism. Minorities. Geopolitics
	325-341	Nature, entity, concept of the state
	345-347	Symbolism, emblems of the state: Arms, flag, seal, etc.
	348-497	Forms of the state
		Including imperialism, the world state, monarchy, aristocracy, democracy, fascism, dictatorships
	501-628	Purpose, functions, and relations of the state
	571-628	The state and the individual. Individual rights. Liberty
JF		Constitutional history and administration
		General works. Comparative works
	201-723	Organs and function of government
		Including executive branch, cabinet and ministerial government, legislative bodies
	800-1191	Political rights and guaranties
		Including citizenship, suffrage, electoral systems, representation, the ballot
	1321-2112	Government. Administration
	1411-1674	Civil service
	2011-2112	Political parties
		Special countries
JK		United States
JL		British America. Latin America
JN		Europe
JQ		Asia. Africa. Australia. Oceania
JS		Local government
	3-27	Serial documents (General)
	141-231	Municipal government
	241-285	Local government other than municipal
JV		Colonies and colonization. Emigration and immigration
JX		International law. International relations
	63-1195	Collections. Documents. Cases
	101-115	Diplomatic relations (Universal collections)
	120-191	Treaties (Universal collections)
	1305-1598	International relations. Foreign relations
		For international questions treated as sources of or contributions to the theory of international law. For histories of events, diplomatic histories, etc., *see* D-F
	1625-1896	Diplomacy. The diplomatic service
		Political science
JX	1901-1995	International arbitration. World peace. International organization
		Including peace movements, League of Nations, United Nations, arbitration treaties, international courts
	2001-5810	International law (Treatises and monographs)

Class J — Political Science was first published in 1910 under the editorship of Edwin Wiley. Subclasses JA, General works; JC, Political science, Theory of the state; and JK, United States Constitutional history and administration, were constructed by W. Dawson Johnston. Subclass JX, International law, was prepared by Philip D. Phair. The second edition, issued in 1924, was prepared by George M. Churchill and C. K. Jones. No new edition of this class has yet been published, although one is currently in preparation. In 1966 the second edition was reprinted with supplementary pages of additions and changes as of October 1965.

Eleven subclasses make up Class J: Subclass J for general serial official government documents; JA for collections and general works on political science; JC for political theory on the origin, nature, symbolism, functions, relations of the state, including a detailed enumeration of the works of Thomas Paine; JF for general and comparative works on constitutional history and administration; JK for United States constitutional history and administration; JL for the constitutional history and administration of other countries in the western hemisphere; JN for European constitutional history and administration; JQ for the constitutional history and administration of Asia, Africa, Australia, and Oceania; JS for local government subdivided geographically; JV for colonies and colonization and for emigration and immigration; and JX for international law, including international relations, diplomacy, international arbitration, and the documents of the League of Nations and the United Nations. The location of this subclass places international law immediately before the developing Class K for law.

W. C. Berwick Sayers described this class as the most revolutionary notion used in the entire system: "It is no less than the application of the 'national' method of grouping (familiar in the treatment of literature), conjoined with a chronological development, in complete contrast to the 'topical' method so familiar to users of the Decimal scheme."[8] This method of inserting the geographical divisions between the topical or subject divisions of a subject may be seen in the scheme for Constitutional history and administration. Subclass JF is for General works, but Subclasses JK, JL, JN, and JQ are all for geographic areas: the United States; British America, Latin America; Europe; and Asia, Africa, Australia, and the Pacific Islands. This device allows the furthur subdivisions under geographic areas to be designed directly in relation to an individual area's constitutional history. Obviously, the United States has a different pattern of development for its constitutional history than France or Germany. For example, there are eleven numbers allotted to suffrage for women in the United States, JK 1880-1911, while the similar topic in French constitutional history has only one number, JN 2954, for women's suffrage; similarly, Germany has only one number for this topic, JN 3825. Another example is political parties: over one hundred numbers are assigned for political parties in the United States, JK 2251-2391; France has only three numbers, JN 2997, JN 2999, and JN 3007; and Germany has six numbers, JN 3925, JN 3931, JN 3933, JN 3934, JN 3941, and JN 3946. In each case the appropriate range of numbers was assigned in relation to the amount of material at the Library of Congress.

There are thirteen tables in Class J which are similar to the tables already discussed in chapter 4. There are five auxiliary tables to be used for local government in Subclass JS. Table 1 is for states or cities with ninety-nine numbers; Table 2 is for states or cities with twenty numbers; Table 3 is for states or cities with nine numbers; Table 4 is for states or cities with one number; and Table 5 is for cities with a Cutter number.

Twenty-Number States or Cities

Chicago is a city which is assigned twenty numbers in the schedule, "JS 701-720." Chicago thus uses Table 2 for its subdivisions. The following is an abridgment of Table 2.

1		Periodicals, societies, etc.
		Manuals, registers, etc., by date.
2	.A1-2	Administrative, judicial, etc., districts.
	.A3	Registers, etc.
3		Separate documents, charters, etc., by date.
4*		Laws, ordinances, codes, digests, etc.
		History and description.
5	.A2	Collections: statistics, etc.
	.A5-Z	General.
6		Early history (Medieval, etc.)
7		19th century to 1880.
8		Recent history.
10		Reform literature, etc.
		Special.
11		Local government and the state.
12		Other special, A-Z.
13		Local government other than municipal.
		Executive: Mayor, etc. Administration.
14	.A1	General.
	.A13	Special offices, departments, commissions, etc., A-Z.
	.A15	Special subjects, A-Z.
		Civil service.
	.A2	Report.
	.A3	Rules.
	.A4	Other, by date.
15		Legislative: Alderman, Council, etc.
16		Judiciary: Municipal courts.
17	.A2	Citizenship.
		Suffrage.
	.A3	General.
	.A4	Board of election commissioners. Annual report,etc.
	.A5	Lists of voters, etc.
		Election practice and systems.
18		Election law.
	.A2*	Codes, manuals, by date.
	.A5*	Separate, by date.
	.A7-Z	Other, A-Z.
19		Political corruption.
20		Local, by city, borough, parish, district, ward, etc., A-Z.

---

*Note that the law numbers in this table and those in the other tables and elsewhere in Class J are no longer used by the Library of Congress. Legal materials are now classed in Class K with the exception of certain areas within international law which remain in Subclass JX. *See* the discussion of Class K.

For example, a recent history of the governments of Chicago by H. M. Karlen is classed in "JS708.K3."

H. M. Karlen's *The Governments of Chicago.*

JS	The double letters for the subclass, Local government
708	The integral number for a recent history of Chicago
.K3	The Cutter number for the main entry, Karlen

A work about elections in Chicago is classed in "JS718."

H. F. Gosnell's *Getting Out the Vote.*

JS	The double letters for the subclass, Local government
718	The integral number meaning election practice and systems
.G6	The Cutter number for the main entry, Gosnell

An example which illustrates the use of an "A" Cutter number under number "14" in the table is given below:

C. S. Westerhof's *The Executive Connection: Mayors and Press Secretaries, the New York Experience.*

JS	The double letters for the subclass Local government
1234	The fourteenth number (in the range 1221-1240) assigned to New York City, meaning "Executive: Mayor, etc."
.A15	The "A" Cutter number for "special subjects, A-Z"
P688	The second Cutter number for the special subject, the press

In general, Class J does not create any unusual problems. However, it should be noted that political and diplomatic history is often classed in the appropriate history class in "D" or "E-F," and not in "J."

The index for Class J contains many summaries of the classification and appears to be not as complete and detailed as many of the other indexes.

The enumerations for government documents, international documents, and the works of Thomas Paine should have reference uses.

CLASS K — LAW

Completed: Subclasses K, KD, KE, and KF.

K		Law (General)
	237-487	Jurisprudence. Philosophy and theory of law
	540-5570	Comparative law. International uniform law
	7051-7720	Conflict of laws
		Law of the United Kingdom and Ireland
KD		Law of England and Wales
	8850-9312	Local laws of England
	9320-9355	Local laws of Wales
	9400-9500	Law of Wales
KDC		Law of Scotland
KDE		Law of Northern Ireland
KDG		Law of Isle of Man and the Channel Islands
KDK		Law of Ireland (Eire)
		Law of Canada
KE		Federal law. Common and collective provincial law
KEA-KEY		Law of individual provinces and territories
KEO		e.g. Ontario
KEQ		Quebec
KEZ		Law of individual cities, A-Z
		Law of the United States
KF		Federal law. Common and collective state law
KFA-KFW		Law of individual states
KFA	0-599	e.g. Alabama
	1200-1799	Alaska
KFW	0-599	Washington
KFX		Law of individual cities, A-Z
KFZ		Law of individual territories

The schedules for **Class K — Law** represent the latest development in the Library of Congress Classification. Although Class K was included in the original outline for the classification, little work was done at the beginning on developing a classification schedule for law at the Library of Congress. There were several reasons for this. First, much of the material to be classed in K was already assigned by subject in Martel's seven points: school law in Class L for education, library law in Class Z for Library science, etc. Second, as the Library of Congress maintains a separate Law Library, which utilized the traditional form arrangement of law libraries, a subject classification was not deemed vital.

In 1948 a scheme constructed by Elizabeth Benyon for the Law Library of the University of Chicago was published by the Library of Congress but was not adopted by the Library. In 1949, a joint meeting of the Library of Congress Committee on a Classification for Law and the Committee on Cooperation with the Library of Congress of the American Association of Law Libraries began work on developing Class K. The content of Class K was projected and a tentative outline and notation were developed. Between 1953 and 1960 nine working papers were prepared at the Library and distributed to librarians and scholars. The papers covered the following topics: 1) German law; 2) Roman law; 3) History of German law; 4) Canon law; 5) Chinese law; 6) English law; 7) Law of Japan; 8) Classification of American law (A Survey); and 9) Law of the United States. Subclass KF is the result of Working Paper No. 9.

The subclasses of Class K are shown in the outline above. To date, four of the schedules in Class K have been published. These will be discussed below.

Subclass K

Class K, Subclass K—Law [General], developed by John Fischer with the assistance of Jan Wawrzkow, was published in 1977. This subclass contains the philosophy and theory of law, comparative law, international uniform law, and conflict of laws. As pointed out in the preface to the schedule, public international law as a discipline remains in Subclass JX. Treaties or multilateral agreements on topics previously classed elsewhere in Class K will now be classed in Subclass K as part of international uniform law. International conventions concerning political relations. international arbitration, the seas and outer space, and war and peace will be classed in Subclass JX. The schedule includes four form tables and a detailed index, containing many distributed relatives.

OUTLINE

K

1-36	Periodicals
37-44	Bibliography
46	Monographic series
48	Encyclopedias
50-54	Dictionaries. Words and phrases
58	Maxims. Quotations
64	Yearbooks·
68-70	Directories
85-88	Legal research
94	Legal composition and draftsmanship
100-103	Legal education
110	Law societies. International bar associations
115-129	The legal profession
133	Legal aid. Legal aid societies
140-165	History of law
170	Biography
175	Congresses
176-177	Collected works (nonserial)
179	Addresses, essays, lectures
181-184	Miscellany
190-195	Primitive law. Ethnological jurisprudence
237-487	Jurisprudence. Philosophy and theory of law
540-5570	Comparative law. International uniform law
7051-7690	Conflict of laws

Subclass KD

Class K, Subclass KD — Law of the United Kingdom and Ireland, prepared by John Fischer, was published in 1973. Werner B. Ellinger's Working Paper No. 6 (English law), used originally as the basis for arrangement of the subject matter, was substantially modified in order to conform, as far as possible, to the systematic order established in Schedule KF, Law of the United States.

SYNOPSIS

KD	LAW OF ENGLAND AND WALES
KDC	LAW OF SCOTLAND
KDE	LAW OF NORTHERN IRELAND
KDG	LAW OF ISLE OF MAN. CHANNEL ISLANDS
KDK	LAW OF IRELAND (EIRE)

KD includes the law of the United Kingdom as a whole and the common law system (Anglo-American law) in general. There are five form tables. Also included are the "Table of Regnal Years of English Sovereigns" and a list of "Greater London Boroughs." The index provides detailed topical entries and a small number of geographic name entries.

Subclass KE

Class K, Subclass KE — Law of Canada, published in 1976, represents a joint effort between the Library of Congress and the National Library of Canada. Ann Rae of the National Library of Canada was responsible for the development of the subclass, with the exception of the section on the law of Quebec which was developed by Guy Tanguay.

In general, the schedule for KE follows the pattern of Subclass KF, Law of the United States, except where Subclass KD, Law of the United Kingdom, provides a better model because of the structure of Canadian law.

The arrangement of the subclasses is shown in the following synopsis.

SYNOPSIS

KE	LAW OF CANADA
KEO	LAW OF CANADA - ONTARIO
KEQ	LAW OF CANADA - QUEBEC
KEA-KEY	CANADA - PROVINCES AND TERRITORIES
KEZ	CANADA - CITIES, TOWNS, ETC.

The notation follows closely that of Subclass KF. Law of provinces is represented by triple capital letters, the third letter being a mnemonic based on the name of the province. Law of cities, towns, etc., is classed in KEZ with integral numbers apportioned to individual cities and towns in an alphabetical sequence. Similar types of auxiliary form tables and internal tables as found in KF are used. A detailed index includes topical entries and a small number of geographic name entries.

Subclass KF

Class K, Subclass KF—Law of the United States, prepared by Werner B. Ellinger with the assistance of John Fischer and the consultations of Miles O. Price and Carleton W. Kenyon, was issued in a preliminary edition in 1969. This is the first of the schedules of Class K to appear. It introduced a new feature to the Library of Congress notation—triple capital letters. Law of individual states is classed in KFA-KFW. The third letter is mnemonic, based on the initial letter of the name of the state, e.g., KFA for law of Alabama, Alaska, Arizona, and Arkansas; KFL for law of Louisiana, etc.

The general arrangement of the subclass begins with KF, Federal law, followed by the law of individual states in KFA-KFW. Each state is assigned six hundred numbers, e.g., KFA 0-599, Alabama; KFO 2400-2999, Oregon; etc., with the exception of California and New York each of which is assigned twelve hundred numbers: KFC 0-1199, California; and KFN 5000-6199, New York. The subdivisions of the law of California and New York are individually developed. For the other states, a uniform "Table of Subject Divisions for the Law of the States and Territories of the United States" containing six hundred integral numbers (some with decimal extensions), is provided. The law of individual states is followed by the law of cities, KFX 0-9999. The numbers are apportioned to all cities in the United States in an alphabetical sequence, e.g.,

KFX

1097	Austin, Texas
1098	Austin to Baltimore
1101-1119	Baltimore, Maryland
1121	Baltimore to Bangor

Each city is assigned twenty numbers, one number, or a Cutter number, based on literary warrant. The only exception is the city of New York which is assigned the numbers KFX 2001-2099, with specially developed subject divisions. Three tables—twenty-number, one-number, and Cutter-number—are provided for subject divisions of the law of individual cities. Following KFX, the law of cities, is KFZ, the law of territories of the United States and the law of Confederate States of America.

There are nine auxiliary form division tables*: Table I, twenty-number subjects; Table II, ten-number subjects; Tables III and IV, five-number subjects; Table V, two-number subjects; Table VI, one-number subjects; Table VII, Cutter number subjects; Table VIII, single-number captions for general works; and Table IX, modified form divisions for state law. The index is very detailed, displaying many useful distributed relatives.

---

*For an updated version of these tables, *see* Appendix C of this book.

Examples of Classification of Law

D. C. Joseph's *Send Me Up a Blanket: A Lawyer's Recollection.*

KF	The double letters for the subclass, Law of the United States
373	The third integral number meaning an individual biography (see internal table in the schedule) in a range of numbers, 371-374, assigned to the recent history of U.S. Law
.J66	The first Cutter number for the biographee, Joseph
A3	The second Cutter number (based on the Biography Table)* for an autobiography.

Indiana General Corporation Law, as amended 1969, 1969.

KFI	The triple letters for the subclass, Law of states of the United States with names beginning with "I"
3213	The integral number meaning general works on business corporations derived from the following procedure: KFI 3000-3599 Numbers assigned to Indiana 213 Number from the Table of Subject Divisions for the Law of the States, with the caption: Business corporations General (VI)
.A333	The first Cutter number meaning a particular act. The number is based on Table IX. Although the instruction in the schedule calls for Table VI, a footnote in Table VI refers to Table IX for Modified Form Divisions for State Law.
A2	The second Cutter number (also from Table IX) meaning an unannotated monographic text
1969	The date of publication

Constitution of the State of Florida, as amended in 1968, 1969.

KFF	The triple letters for the subclass, Law of states of the United States with names beginning with "F"
401	The integral number (based on the Table of Subject Divisions for the Law of the States and fitted into the range of numbers 000-599 assigned to Florida) meaning particular constitutions, arranged by date of constitution
1885	The date of constitution
.A333	The Cutter number meaning an official edition of the text of the constitution

---

*See Appendix B.

The Revised Ordinances of Honolulu, 1969, 1971- .

KFX	The triple letters for the subclass, Law of cities of the United States
1511	The integral number assigned to cities Holyoke to Houston
.H59	The first Cutter number for Honolulu
A35	The second Cutter number (based on Table C, Divisions under Cities Represented by Cutter Numbers) meaning codes of ordinances
1971	The date of publication

CLASS L—EDUCATION

L		Education (General)
		For periodicals, congresses, directories, etc.
LA		History of education
LB		Theory and practice of education
	51-885	Systems of individual educators and writers
	1025-1050	Teaching (Principles and practice)
		Including programmed instruction, remedial teaching, nongraded schools, audiovisual education, methods of study, reading (General)
	1051-1091	Educational psychology
	1101-1139	Child study. Psychical development
	1140	Preschool education
	1141-1489	Kindergarten
	1501-1547	Primary education
	1555-1602	Elementary or public school education
	1603-1695	Secondary education. High schools
	1705-2286	Education and training of teachers
	2300-2430	Higher education
	2801-3095	School administration and organization
	3201-3325	School architecture and equipment
	3401-3499	School hygiene
	3525-3640	Special days. School life. Student customs
LC		Special aspects of education
	8-63	Forms of education
		Including self, home, and private school education
	65-245	Social aspects of education
		Including education and the state, religious instruction in public schools, compulsory education, illiteracy, educational sociology, community and the school, endowments
	251-951	Moral and religious education. Education under church control
	1001-1091	Types of education
		Including humanistic, vocational, and professional education
	1390-5158	Education of special classes of persons
		Including women, Blacks, gifted and handicapped children, orphans, middle class
	5201-6691	Adult education. Education extension
		Individual institutions: universities, colleges, and schools
LD		United States
LE		America, except United States
LF		Europe
LG		Asia. Africa. Oceania
LH		College and school magazines and papers
LJ		Student fraternities and societies, United States
		For other countries, *see* LA, LE-LG
LT		Textbooks
		For textbooks covering several subjects. For textbooks on particular subjects, *see* those subjects in B-Z

Class L—Education was first published in 1911. J. C. Bay and W. D. Johnston developed Subclasses L, General works; LA, History of education; LB, Theory and practice of education; LC, Special forms, relations and applications; LD, Universities and colleges of the United States; LE, Other American universities and colleges; and LG, Universities and colleges of Europe. A. F. Schmidt revised the work of Bay and Johnston and completed the schedule with the exception of Subclasses LC, Special forms; LJ, College fraternities and their publications; and LT, Textbooks. These three subclasses were completed by J. D. Wolcott. In 1928 the second edition of Class L was issued. G. M. Churchill and C. K. Jones were responsible for the revisions in the second edition. The third edition, published in 1951, represented the successive work of C. K. Jones, Leo LaMontagne, R. O. Sutter, Philip Krichbaum, and Leonard Ellinwood. Voegelein served as the editor of this edition of Class L.

Class L contains eleven subclasses: Subclass L for general works on education, including official documents and reports; LA for general, national, and local history of education; LB for theory and practice of education; LC for special aspects of education; LD-LG for individual universities, colleges, and schools, with LD for the United States, LE for America except the United States, LF for Europe, and LG for Asia, Africa, and Oceania; LH for college and school magazines and papers which are not classed with the specific institution in LD-LG; LJ for student fraternities and societies in the United States; and LT for general textbooks.

This class presents no serious problems to the classifier. There are eleven tables in this class,* all relatively easy to use. The most complex tables are for the subdivisions for individual institutions in Subclasses LD and LE. However, these tables are similar to the tables already discussed and should create no problem in application. The only difference is in the use of Table I, which is used for all institutions without a particular designated table. Table I is designed to establish a constant successive Cutter number sequence to use with a designated range of Cutter numbers. Although such a device may appear confusing to the beginner, it is clearly illustrated in two examples included in Table I. The other tables in this class do not contain such elements.

Trinity College, Hartford, Connecticut, is assigned a range of Cutter numbers, ".T37-46," under the integral number "LD 5361." As Trinity College is not designated to use Tables II-V, it uses Table I. The directions to use Table I call for substituting for "x1, x2" of Table I, the initial and first digit or digits of the assigned Cutter numbers. In the case of Trinity College, "T3" is substituted for "x1" and "T4" is substituted for "x2."

"Degrees and honors" are represented in Table I by "x2j," therefore a work by Trinity College entitled *Prizes and Prizemen, 1849-1907* is classed "LD 5361 .T4j 1907." This is an example of the use of workmarks on Cutter numbers that Table I uses extensively.

Prizes and Prizemen, 1849-1907, of Trinity College, 1907.

LD	The double letters for the subclass, Colleges and universities in the United States
5361	The integral number meaning an individual institution whose initial letters are "Tri-"
.T4j	The first Cutter number meaning a work on degrees and honors at Trinity College, Hartford, CT
1907	The date of publication

---

*See Appendix C for an updated version of Tables I-V which have undergone certain changes since the publication of the main schedule.

Alumni directories use the number "21a" in Table I. The Trinity College *Alumni Directory* is classed "LD 5361 .T41a." Again, "T4" has been substituted for "x2" in the table number "x21a."

Alumni Directory, Trinity College. 1946.

LD	The double letters for the subclass, Colleges and universities of the United States
5361	The integral number meaning an individual institution whose initial letters are "Tri-"
.T41a	The Cutter number meaning an alumni directory of Trinity College, Hartford, CT
1946	The date of publication

The number in Table I for a general history is "x22." A history of Trinity College is classed "LD 5361 .T42." "T4" has been substituted for "x2" in the table number "x22."

T. D. Lockwood's *Trinity College: 150 Years of Quality Education.*

LD	The double letters for the subclass, Colleges and universities in the United States
5361	The integral number meaning an individual institution whose initial letters are "Tri-"
.T42	The first Cutter number meaning a general history of Trinity College, Hartford, CT
L62	The second Cutter number for the main entry, Lockwood

In the table, "x249" carries the caption "Other special days and events. By date." To represent a convocation held at the Trinity College, the Cutter number ".T449" is used.

New World Ahead: 1960 Convocation, sponsored by Trinity College and the Trinity College Associates, Hartford, CT, Apr. 9, 1960.

LD	The double letters for the subclass, Colleges and universities in the United States
5361	The integral number meaning an individual institution whose initial letters are "Tri-"
.T449	The Cutter number (based on the notation x249 in Table I) meaning a special day or event
1960	The date of the convocation

Textbooks

Subclass LT for textbooks is designed only for those textbooks covering several subjects; textbooks on a particular subject are classed with that subject in Classes B-K and M-Z. If a library wishes to collect all textbooks, as in a curriculum library, it is possible to affix a locational label "LT" to the spine of the book in addition to its subject call number. Without using such a device, however, it would be impossible to collocate all textbooks in one place.

Works on Teaching Methods in Special Subjects

LB 1572-1599 provide for works on teaching methods in special subjects. Works of this type at the elementary level as well as those at both the elementary and secondary levels combined are classed in these numbers. Works of this type dealing with subjects not included in LB 1572-1599 are classed with the subjects in Classes B-K and M-Z. For example, a work on science instruction for elementary and secondary school teachers should be classed in LB 1585-1585.5; instruction in the field of astronomy, however, is classed in QB61 because there is no provision for astronomy in Class LB. Works on teaching methods in special subjects at the secondary level alone are classed with the subjects in the various schedules, except English (LB1631-1632) and ethics (LB1694).

The index to Class L is similar to the index to Class J. There are many summaries of the classification in the index.

CLASS M—MUSIC

M	Music
5-1459	Instrumental music
6-175	One instrument without accompaniment
177-986	Two or more solo instruments
	Including chamber music not orchestral
1000-1356	Orchestral music
1495-2199	Vocal music
1497-1998	Secular vocal music
1500-1527	Dramatic music
1530-1610	Choral music, part songs, etc.
1611-1626	Songs for one voice
1627-1985	Songs (Part and solo)
1627-1853	National music
	Including primitive, folk, traditional, patriotic, political, and typical music, with or without accompaniment, and with or without words
1999-2199	Sacred vocal music
2000-2017	Oratorios, masses, services, etc.
2018-2101	Cantatas, anthems, part songs
2102-2114	Songs for one voice
2115-2146	Hymn, psalm, and choral books
2147-2188	Liturgy and ritual
2198-2199	Temperance, revival, rescue, and gospel songs
ML	Literature of music
48-54	Librettos (Texts for music)
111-158	Bibliography
155.3-158	Phonorecords
159-3795	History and criticism
	Including biographies of individual composers
460-1354	Instruments and instrumental music
1100-1354	Chamber and orchestral music. Band (Military music)
1400-3275	Vocal music
1500-1554	Choral music (Sacred and secular)
1600-2862	Secular vocal music
	Including dramatic music, cantatas, songs (Part and solo)
2900-3197	Sacred vocal music
	Including church music, oratorios, cantatas
3400-3465	Dance music
3545-3776	National music
3800-3923	Philosophy and physics of music
	Including physiology, psychology, color and music, aesthetics, ethics, therapeutics
3930	Juvenile literature
MT	Music instruction and study
40-67	Composition
	Including rhythm, scales, melody, harmony, modulation, counterpoint
68	Improvisation
70-86	Orchestra and orchestration, conducting, etc.
90-145	Analytical guides, etc. (Hermeneutics)
	How to listen to and how to understand special musical compositions. For historical, biographical, critical, or aesthetic works, *see* ML410 under the composer
170-810	Instrumental technics
820-949	Singing and voice culture
955-960	Production of operas. Music in theaters

Oscar G. Sonneck, Chief of the Division of Music of the Library of Congress, developed **Class M — Music** in 1902, and the first edition was published in 1904. A revised edition was issued in 1917. The third edition, representing the editorial efforts of Siegrun H. Folter, was published in 1978.

In the prefatory note to the first edition, Sonneck described the development of this class:

> As a matter of course the scheme, at least so far as it concerns music proper, took a form leaning toward the classified catalogues of publishers, and somewhat different from the schemes adopted by the notable American and European libraries. But care was taken to profit by the experience of these. In its present form the scheme embodies many valuable suggestions of the Chief Classifier of the Library, Mr. Charles Martel, besides such modifications as he considered necessary in conformity with the arrangement of other classes of books in the Library.

This schedule differs in several ways from the other schedules, which were prepared entirely by classifiers. There are only three subclasses: M, Music; ML, Literature of music; and MT, Musical instruction and study. Subclass M has a section devoted to definitions of musical terms and special rules. In fact, the actual classification in this schedule tends to be a scheme based on physical form rather than subject classification. Not all of the works by and about a composer will be found in one place. In Subclass M, separate numbers are given to different musical forms, i.e., M 452 for string quartets, M 1001 for symphonies, M 1500 for operas, etc. For example, Beethoven's Third Symphony is classed "M 1001 .B4 op. 55." In this case "M 1001" means the musical form, the symphony; ".B4" is the Cutter number for the composer, Beethoven; and "op. 55" is the opus number for Beethoven's Third Symphony. It should be noted that opus numbers rather than symphony numbers are used.

Beethoven's *Symphony No. 3.*

M	The single letter for the subclass, Music
1001	The integral number meaning the musical form, a symphony
.B4	The Cutter number for the main entry, Beethoven
op. 55	The designation of the particular symphony, No. 3, by opus number

Beethoven's First Symphony, opus 21, is classed "M 1001 .B4 op. 21."

Beethoven's *Symphony No. 1.*

M	The single letter for the subclass, Music
1001	The integral number meaning the musical form, the symphony
.B4	The Cutter number for the main entry, Beethoven
op. 21	The designation of the particular symphony, No. 1, by opus number

The opus number is the distinctive element in the notation. The symphony number does not appear in the notation. A score of Beethoven's First Symphony containing a piano arrangement by Anis Fuleihan is classed "M 1001 .B4 op. 21 .F8.

> Beethoven's *Symphony No. 1*, with a piano arrangement by Anis Fuleihan.

M	The single letter for the subclass, Music
1001	The integral number meaning the musical form, the symphony
.B4	The first Cutter number for the main entry, Beethoven
op. 21	The designation of the particular symphony, No. 1, by opus number
.F8	The second Cutter number for the arranger, Fuleihan

A Eulenburg miniature score edition of Beethoven's Second Symphony is classed "M 1001 .B4 op. 36 .E8."

> Beethoven's *Symphony No. 2*, Eulenburg miniature score.

M	The single letter for the subclass, Music
1001	The integral number meaning the musical form, the symphony
.B4	The first Cutter number for the main entry, Beethoven
op. 36	The designation of the particular symphony, No. 2, by opus number
.E8	The second Cutter number for the edition of the score, Eulenburg

There are other unique additions to the notation that occur in Class M. These are explained in the schedule, and examples are often provided. A special number in Subclass ML is "ML 410" for all biographies of musicians, including a complete expansion for the German composer Richard Wagner. For instance, Anton Felix Schindler's *Biographie von Ludwig van Beethoven*, published in 1949, is classed "ML 410 .B4S333 1949."

> A. F. Schindler's *Biographie von Ludwig van Beethoven*, 1949.

ML	The double letters for the subclass, Literature of music
410	The integral number meaning biographies of musicians
.B4	The first Cutter number for the subject of the biography, Beethoven
S333	The second Cutter number for the author of the biography, Schindler
1949	The date of publication

It should also be noted that the range of numbers ML 111-158 is provided for bibliography of music. This is one of the few instances in L.C. Classification where bibliography is classed with the subject rather than separately in Class Z.

Another difference which may be found in this schedule is the use of many "divide like" notes instead of auxiliary tables. For instance, instrumental music for the harmonium is classed in Subclass M in the following fashion:

M   Harmonium (Reed organ)

15	Miscellaneous collections.
	Original compositions.
16	Collections.
17	Separate works.
	Arrangements.
18	Collections.
19	Separate works.

However, instrumental music for other instruments is simply given a range of five numbers to be subarranged like M15-19. Such devices are commonly used in Class M.

60-64	Flute
65-69	Oboe
70-74	Clarinet

Arrangement of Class M by physical form rather than by subject raises some criticism. However, it must be remembered that the author catalog will assemble all the works by a composer in one place, and in this case, the classification provides another access to the material. Such an arrangement of material is in all probability easier for the musician to use than the musicologist.

Catalogs of Sound Recordings

Catalogs of sound recordings, including those on nonmusical topics, are classed in ML156-158.

Supplementary Numbers for Music[9]

The Library of Congress maintains a classed catalog of its holdings of music scores (Class M). It not only files entries under the assigned class number but, when warranted, it also files additional copies of the entry under 1) other numbers in the schedule that represent additional aspects and 2) numbers not part of the regular schedule that are assigned to represent subjects or musical forms that are of interest but would not be used for shelf arrangement. These latter numbers are called "supplementary numbers."

In response to the interest expressed by a number of music libraries in the idea of subject and form control for music by means of a classed catalog, the Library of Congress provides on its cataloging records, in addition to the regular call number for works classed in M, the numbers assigned to secondary subject or form entries in its classed catalog. When such secondary numbers are part of the regular schedule they are enclosed in brackets. Numbers that are part of the series of special supplementary numbers are indicated by the use of parentheses within brackets, as in the example below.

> **Stravinskii, Igor Fedorovich**, 1882-
> [Le chant du rossignol. Marche chinoise ; arr.]
>
> Marche chinoise, from Le chant du rossignol, for piano
> solo by Igor Stravinsky. [Arr. by Frederick Block] New
> York, E. B. Marks Music Corp. [1941]
>
> 10 p. 31 cm. (Kaleidoscope edition, no. 11502)
>
> Cover title.
> 1 excerpt from the symphonic poem.
>
> 1. Marches (Piano). 2. Symphonic poems—Excerpts, Arranged.
> I. Title.
>
> M35.5.S
> [M28] [(M35.582)] ◀——

This work is shelved in M35.5 because it is an arrangement of an excerpt from an orchestral work and a record is filed in the classed catalog under this number. A record is also filed under M28 because the work is a march. M28 is a number that may be used for shelving, and it appears in the regular classification schedule. Another record is filed under M35.582 because the work is an excerpt from a symphonic poem. This number is not in the regular classification schedule but is one of the special series of supplementary numbers. It is, therefore, printed within parentheses as well as brackets.

The two-card entry shown on page 205 is another example of providing supplementary numbers. A list of the supplementary music classification numbers appears on pages 149-151 of the M schedule.

The index to Class M is very detailed and displays many distributed relatives. In addition to the lists of musical instruments and forms in Subclass M, the list of separate Latin liturgical texts and the Special Scheme for Richard Wagner have reference uses.

Händel, Georg Friedrich, 1685–1759.
₍Concerto grosso, op. 3, no. 2, Bb major. Minuet; arr.₎
Minuet : from Concerto grosso, op. 3, no. 2, for descant, treble, and tenor recorders, or four violins, and continuo (with bass recorder/cello) / George Frideric Handel ; edited by Freda Dinn. — London : Schott ; New York : Schott Music Corp., ₍c1972₎

score (4 p.) and   parts ; 30 cm. — (Recorders and strings series ; no. 44)

"This menuet was originally scored for two oboes, two solo violins, cello, and harpsichord ... ₍with₎ string orchestra and harpsichord."

    (Continued on next card)

Händel, Georg Friedrich, 1685–1759.
₍Concerto grosso, op. 3, no. 2, Bb major. Minuet; arr.₎
Minuet ... ₍c1972₎   (Card 2)

Figured bass realized for keyboard instrument; includes part for bass recorder or violoncello.

1. Minuets (Recorders (4), continuo) 2. Minuets (Violins (4), continuo) 3. Concerti grossi—To 1800—Excerpts, Arranged.   I. Dinn, Freda.

M519.H   76–770310
[(M519.63)] [(M619.63)] [(M624.63)] [(M514.63)] [(M614.63)]

CLASS N — FINE ARTS

For the arts in general, *see* NX

N		Visual arts (General)
		For photography, *see* TR
	400-4040	Art museums, galleries, etc.
		Arranged by country, subarrangement by city
	4390-5098	Exhibitions
	5198-5299	Private collections and collectors
	5300-7418	History of art
	7430-7433	Technique, composition, style, etc.
	7475-7483	Art criticism
	7575-7624	Portraits
	7790-8199	Religious art
	8555-8585	Examination and conservation of works of art
	8600-8675	Economics of art
	8700-9165	Art and the state. Public art
NA		Architecture
	190-1613	History. Historical monuments
	2699-2790	Architectural design and drawing
	2835-4050	Architectural details, motives, decoration, etc.
	4100-8480	Special classes of buildings
	9000-9425	Aesthetics of cities. City planning and beautification
NB		Sculpture
NC		Drawing. Design. Illustration
	997-1003	Commercial art. Advertising art
	1300-1766	Caricature. Pictorial humor and satire
	1800-1855	Posters
ND		Painting
	1290-1460	Special subjects
		Including human figure, landscapes, animals, still life, flowers
	1700-2495	Watercolor painting
	2550-2888	Mural painting
	2890-3416	Illuminating of manuscripts and books
NE		Print media
	1-978	Printmaking and engraving
	1000-1352	Wood engraving. Woodcuts. Xylography
	1400-1879	Metal engraving. Copper, steel, etc.
		Including color prints
	1940-2230	Etching and aquatint
	2236-2239	Serigraphy
	2250-2570	Lithography
	2800-2890	Printing of engravings
NK		Decorative arts. Applied arts. Decoration and ornament
		Including antiques in general
	1135-1149	Arts and crafts movement
	1700-3505	Interior decoration. House decoration
	3600-9955	Other arts and art industries
	3700-4695	Ceramics. Pottery. Porcelain
	4700-4890	Costume and its accessories
	4997-6050	Enamel. Glass. Glyptic arts
		Including gems, jade, ivory, bone
	6400-8459	Metalwork
		Including armor, jewelry, plate, brasses, pewter
	8800-9505	Textile arts and art needlework
	9600-9955	Woodwork
		Including carvings, fretwork, inlaying
NX		Arts in general
		Including works dealing with two or more of the fine arts media, i.e. literature, performing arts, and the visual arts. For works on any one of these subjects, *see* the subject, i.e. GV, M, N, P, TR
	654-694	Religious arts
	700-750	Patronage of the arts
	798-820	Special arts centers

Class N—Fine Arts was prepared under the direction and supervision of Charles Martel. The first edition was published in 1910 and a second edition appeared in 1917. The third edition was issued under the direction of Clarence W. Perley in 1922. This schedule was influenced by the fine arts sections of both the *Dewey Decimal Classification* and Cutter's *Expansive Classification*. In addition, the catalog of the Library of the Kunstgewerke-Museum of Berlin was used for special features; The Library of the Art Institute of Chicago recommended ideas from its modifications of the *Decimal Classification*.

The close relationship of this schedule to the other two classification schemes may be observed in the use of subclasses for different artistic forms or media: NA, Architecture; NB, Sculpture; NC, Graphic arts in general; ND, Painting; NE, Engraving. Because of this division, the pattern in the fine arts differs from the patterns in literature and philosophy. Not all of the works by and about an individual artist will be classed in the same place.

In 1970 a thoroughly revised fourth edition was published. William B. Walker of the Library of the National Collection of Fine Arts and the National Portrait Gallery (a branch of the Smithsonian Institution Libraries) made the basic proposals for changes in the new edition. Additional recommendations were made by Anna Smislova. The schedule was prepared for publication by Emma E. Curtis, Editor of the Classification Schedules.

Eight subclasses make up Class N: Subclass N for the visual arts in general; NA for architecture; NB for sculpture; NC for drawing, design, and illustration; ND for painting, including illuminated manuscripts and books; NE for print media, including printmaking and engraving; NK for the decorative arts, the applied arts, decoration and ornament; and NX for the arts in general, including only "works dealing with two or more of the fine arts media, i.e., literature, performing arts (dance, motion pictures, music, opera, theater) and the visual arts."

In the Preface to the fourth edition, Charles C. Bead states the basic approach and scope of the new version:

> Perhaps the most striking innovations of this revision are the regrouping of numbers for similar types of publications which had heretofore been dispersed in several places (e.g. works on art collectors and patrons have been brought closer to material on private collections) and the combining in the same numerical sequence of works on the history of art in a particular medium with books of reproductions of works in the same medium. There has also been some relocation in order to provide a more logical collocation of general works and works on the techniques and materials of various art forms. In all cases where class numbers are no longer used by the Library of Congress they have been parenthesized for the continued use of other libraries which may not wish to adopt these changes, and appropriate references have been made. Extensive additions have been made to update the schedules or to increase their comprehensiveness. A new subclass NX has been added, dealing with the arts in general including literature and the performing arts as well as the visual arts. An attempt has been made throughout to indicate more clearly than in the past the principles of priority governing the classification of material which is

characterized by two or more facets, each of which has a classification site provided. Lastly, the geographic tables which can be applied throughout the schedule have been updated to reflect the current jurisdictional situation.

Order of Preference

Art materials, particularly reproductions of works of art, which can be classed in several numbers manifesting different aspects treated in the works, are classified according to the following order of preference:

1)   Individual artists under the country number

2)   Genre by nationality or period (e.g., Italian sculpture; Medieval caricature)

3)   Genre (General) (e.g., Sculpture)

4)   Special topics (e.g., Roses in art)

Examples:

1)   A collection of the paintings of one artist all on the theme of roses should be classed with the individual artist.

2)   A collection of paintings by Italian artists using roses as a theme should be classed with Italian painting.

Exception:

There exist in various locations of the N schedule certain written directions which contradict the above statement (e.g., NC101-376). In such cases, observe the written directions in the schedules.

The following example illustrates the order of preference.

L. Küppers' *Die Gottesmutter: Marienbild in Rheinland u. in Westfalen.*

N   The single letter for the subclass, general visual arts

6879   The integral number meaning art in Rhine provinces, Germany (base number 6500 + 379 from Table IV)

.K78   The Cutter number for the main entry, Küppers

This work is classed in the number for art in Rhine provinces rather than in the number for the special topic, Virgin Mary in art.

Tables

There are five auxiliary tables at the end of Class N.* The first four of these (I, II, III, and III-A) are relatively simple tables of geographic subdivisions. Table IV is a table of geographic subdivisions with special added elements such as collective and individual biography of artists. The following is an excerpt from the first page of this table.

Table IV

01	America.
02	Latin America.
03	North America.
	United States.
05	General works.
07	Colonial period; 18th (and early 19th) century.
10	19th century.
12	20th century.
15	New England.
17	Middle Atlantic States.
20	South.
22	Central.
25	West.
26	Northwestern states.
28	Pacific states.
30	States, A-W.
35	Cities, A-Z.
36	Collective biography.
37	Special artists, A-Z.
38	Special races and ethnic groups, A-Z.
	Canada
40	General works.
	[etc.]

The range of numbers for Modern art, "N 6501-7413" uses Table IV. This is indicated in the schedule by the Roman numeral "IV" which follows the listing of this range of numbers:

N	Fine Art
	Modern Art.
6501-7413	Special Countries (Table IV).

A general work on modern art in the United States is Henri Dorra's *The American Muse*. It is classed as "N6505.D65." The first two digits of Table IV and the first number in the subject range match. "N6501" is for modern art in all the Americas, as "01" is the table number for the geographic area "America." Similarly, in the above example the "05" from the table, meaning the geographic area of the United States, fits into the range of numbers "N 6501-7413" as the number "N 6505." In short, the classifier finds that the table number, in this case, is added to a base number, "N 6500."

---

*See Appendix C of this book for an updated version of these tables.

Henri Dorra's *The American Muse.*

N	The single letter for the subclass, General fine arts
6505	The integral number meaning a work on modern art in the United States
.D65	The Cutter number for the main entry, Dorra

A typical semantic problem may be observed in this example. The adjective "American" is used to mean the geographic area the United States. This usage also may be seen in Lloyd Goodrich's *Pioneers of Modern Art in America.* This work is classed as a work on modern art in the United States during the twentieth century. The appropriate table number for the twentieth century of the United States is "12." The appropriate subject number is then "N 6512," or "12" added to "N 6500." The complete call number is "N 6512 .G62."

Lloyd Goodrich's *Pioneers of Modern Art in America.*

N	The single letter for the subclass, General fine arts
6512	The integral number meaning twentieth century modern art in the United States
.G62	The Cutter number for the main entry, Goodrich

The following example illustrates the use of the number "28" in Table IV, meaning the Pacific states.

M. Kingsbury's *Art of the Thirties: The Pacific Northwest.*

N	The single letter for the subclass, General fine arts
6528	The integral number meaning art in the Pacific states
.K5	The Cutter number for the main entry, Kingsbury

A work on an individual state in the United States makes use of the number "30" in Table IV. A work about art in Iowa is therefore classed in "N6530.I8."

J. M. Drake's *Brief Information Concerning Iowa Artists.*

N	The single letter for the subclass, General fine arts
6530	The integral number meaning art in one of the states in the United States
.I8	The first Cutter number for Iowa
D7	The second Cutter number for the main entry, Drake

Similarly, the number "35" in Table IV is used for art in a particular city in the United States. A work about art in Philadelphia is therefore classed in "N6535.P5."

E. Longstreth's *The Art Guide to Philadelphia*.

N	The single letter for the subclass, General fine arts
6535	The integral number meaning art in an individual city in the United States
.P5	The first Cutter number for the city, Philadelphia
L6	The second Cutter number for the main entry, Longstreth

The number "37" in Table IV is used for individual artists, arranged alphabetically by means of Cutter numbers. Works about the artist Andy Warhol are therefore classed in "N6537.W28."

J. Coplans' *Andy Warhol*.

N	The single letter for the subclass, General fine arts
6537	The integral number meaning individual artists in the United States
.W28	The first Cutter number for the artist, Warhol
C6	The second Cutter number for the main entry, Coplan

The following example illustrates the use of number "38" from Table IV, meaning special races and ethnic groups.

J. Rashell's *Jewish Artists in America*.

N	The single letter for the subclass, General fine arts
6538	The integral number meaning modern art in the United States covering a special race and/or ethnic group
.J4	The first Cutter number for the special ethnic group, Jews
R3	The second Cutter number for the main entry, Rashell

In previous editions, at the end of this table was a list of "art cities," which was used in conjunction with the range of numbers, "N 6501-7413." In this edition those art cities have been incorporated into Table IV at their appropriate geographic entries. For example, Rome is an art city listed in this table as "420." An exhibition catalog of modern art in Rome from 1930 to 1945 by Giorgio Castelfranco and Dario Durbé, entitled *La Scuola Romana dal 1930 al 1945*, is classed in "N 6920 .C33." When "420" is added to the base number "N 6500," the result is "N 6920."

La Scuola Romana dal 1930 al 1945, by Giorgio Castelfranco and Dario Durbé.

N	The single letter for the subclass, General fine arts
6920	The integral number meaning modern art in Rome
.C33	The Cutter number for the main entry, Castelfranco

There are other special tables within the schedules, including some which use a prescribed range of successive numbers. "NA 4410-4510," the architecture of government buildings is an example of this.

NA	Architecture.
	Special classes of buildings.
	Classed by use.
4410-4417	Capitols.
4410	General works.
4411	United States.
4412	States, A-W.
4413	Cities, A-Z.
4415	Other countries, A-Z.
	Under each:
	(1) General.
	(2) Local, A-Z.
	e.g., .G7 Great Britain.
	.G72L6 London.
4420-4427	Government offices and bureaus. Prefectures, etc.*
4430-4437	City halls. Town halls.*

---

*Divided like NA4410-4417.

For example, a work dealing with the architecture of German city halls is classed in "NA4435.G3." The range of numbers for city halls "NA4430-4437" is divided like "NA4410-4417." Therefore, "NA4435," like "NA4415," is used for foreign countries, subarranged alphabetically by country, with two successive numbers, one for general works and the other for local works.

Walter Kiewert's *Deutsche Rathäuser.*

NA	The double letters for the subclass, Architecture
4435	The integral number for architecture of city halls in foreign countries
.G3	The first successive Cutter number meaning a general work on German city halls
K5	The second Cutter number for the main entry, Kiewert

Examples illustrating the use of most of these tables are included in the subclass schedules. None of the tables in Class N creates any major difficulties. There are many extensive directions and notes in the fourth edition. Problems arise more frequently in the selection of material to be assigned to Class N; a work may appear to fit into more than one category. Comparison of the work to be classed in "N" with similar books already cataloged will provide guidance to the best choice and will maintain consistency within established practice. For instance, material on aesthetics may be classed in Subclass N or NX, or it may be classed in Subclass BH if the work deals with the theory and philosophy of aesthetics and the arts in general. Works on photoengraving may be classed in Subclass NE, Engraving, or in Subclass TR, Photography. The improved index in the fourth edition solves many of these problems. A work on alphabets such as E. Lebner's *Alphabets and Ornaments* is classed "NK 3600 .L36," while J. Bouuaert's *Historie de l'alphabet* is classed in "P 211 .B68." Both numbers are valid locations for material on alphabets—one from an artistic viewpoint and the other from a philological one.

(Class P begins on page 214)

CLASS P – LANGUAGE AND LITERATURE

P		Philology and linguistics (General)
	87-96	Communication. Mass media
	101-409	Language (General)
	101-115	Philosophy, psychology, origin, etc. of language
	121-141	Science of language. Linguistics
	201-297	Comparative grammar
		Including origin of the alphabet, phonetics, morphology, parts of speech, syntax
	301	Style. Composition. Rhetoric
	306-310	Translating and interpreting
	311	Prosody. Metrics. Rhythmics
	327-365	Lexicography
	375-381	Linguistic geography
	501-769	Indo-European philology
	901-1081	Extinct (Ancient or Medieval) Asian and European languages
PA		Classical languages and literature
	227-1179	Greek philology and language
	2001-2915	Latin philology and language
		Greek literature
	3051-4500	Ancient (Classic) to ca. 600 A.D.
	5000-5660	Byzantine and modern
		Latin literature
	6001-6971	Ancient Roman
	8001-8595	Medieval and modern
		Modern European languages
PB	1-431	General works
		Celtic languages and literatures
	1201-1449	Irish
	1501-1709	Gaelic. Scottish Gaelic
	1801-1888	Manx
	2001-3029	Brythonic group
		Including Welsh, Cornish, Breton, Gallic
PC		Romance languages
	601-872	Romanian language and literature
	1001-1977	Italian
	2001-3761	French. Provençal
	3801-3976	Catalan language and literature
	4001-4977	Spanish
	5001-5498	Portuguese
PD		Germanic languages
	1001-1350	Old Germanic dialects
		Including Gothic, Vandal, Burgundian, Langobardian
	1501-5929	Scandinavian. North Germanic
	2201-2392	Old Norse. Old Icelandic and Norwegian
	2401-2489	Icelandic
	2571-2999	Norwegian
	3001-3929	Danish
	5001-5929	Swedish
PE		English
PF		West Germanic
	1-979	Dutch
	1001-1184	Flemish
	1401-1558	Friesian language and literature
	3001-5999	German

		Language and literature
		Modern European language—*continued*
PG		Slavic. Baltic, Albanian languages and literatures
	1-7925	Slavic
	615-716	Church Slavic
	801-1164	Bulgarian. Macedonian
	1201-1696	Serbo-Croatian
	1801-1962	Slovenian
	2001-3987	Russian. White Russian. Ukrainian
	4001-5546	Czech. Slovak
	5631-7446	Polish. Sorbian
	8001-9146	Baltic
	8501-8772	Lithuanian
	8801-9146	Latvian
	9501-9678	Albanian
PH		Finno-Ugrian, Basque languages and literatures
	101-1109	Finnish
	101-405	Finnish (Proper)
	601-671	Estonian
	701-735	Lappish
	801-836	Cheremissian
	1201-3445	Ugrian. Hungarian
	5001-5490	Basque
		Oriental languages and literatures
PJ	1-995	General works
	1001-2199	Egyptian. Coptic
	2301-2551	Hamitic
	2353-2367	Libyan group
	2369-2399	Berber
	2401-2539	Cushitic
	3001-9293	Semitic
	3101-4083	Assyrian. Sumerian
	4501-5192	Hebrew
	5201-5329	Aramaic
	5403-5809	Syriac
	6001-8517	Arabic
	8991-9293	Ethiopian
PK	1-6996	Indo-Iranian
		Including Vedic, Sanskrit, Pali, Assamese, Bengali, Hindi, Urdu, Hindustani, Sinhalese, Persian
	8001-8958	Armenian
	9001-9201	Caucasian. Georgian
PL		Languages and literatures of Eastern Asia, Africa, Oceania
	501-889	Japanese language and literature
	901-998	Korean language and literature
	1001-3207	Chinese language and literature
	5001-7511	Oceanic languages and literatures
	8000-8844	African languages and literatures
PM	101-7356	American Indian languages
	8001-9021	Artificial languages
		Literature
PN		Literary history and collections (General)
	80-99	Criticism
	101-245	Authorship
	441-1009	Literary history
		Including folk literature, fables, prose romances
	1010-1551	Poetry
	1560-1590	The performing arts. Show business

		Language and literature
		Literature
		Literary history and collections (General)—*continued*
PN	1600-3299	The drama
	1660-1692	Dramatic composition
	1865-1999	Special types of drama
		Including tragedy, comedy, vaudeville, puppet plays, pantomimes, ballet, radio and television broadcasts, motion pictures
	2000-3299	Dramatic representation. The theater
		Including management, the stage and accessories, amateur theatricals, tableaux and pageants
	3311-3503	Prose. Prose fiction
	4001-4355	Oratory. Elocution, recitations, etc.
	4400	Letters
	4500	Essays
	4699-5650	Journalism. The periodical press, etc.
	6011-6790	Collections of general literature
	6080-6095	Quotations
	6099-6110	Poetry
	6110.5-6120	Drama
	6121-6129	Orations
	6130-6140	Letters
	6141-6145	Essays
	6147-6231	Wit and humor. Satire
	6249-6790	Miscellaneous
		Including anecdotes, aphorisms, maxims, mottoes, toasts, riddles, proverbs, comic books, comic strips
PQ		Romance literatures
PR		English literature
PS		American literature
PT		Germanic literatures
PZ		Fiction and juvenile belles lettres
	1-4	Fiction in English
		Including English translations of foreign authors
	5-90	Juvenile belles lettres
		In English and foreign languages

Class P—Language and Literature took over forty years to construct. Much of the work was done by Walter F. Koenig, who began the work in 1909. Class P was completed in 1948 with the publication of Subclass PG (in part), Russian literature. Class P, which contains over one-third of the pages of the entire classification, is made up of eleven different schedules: 1) Subclass P-PA, General Philology and Linguistics, Classical Languages and Literatures; 2) a supplement to Subclass PA for Byzantine and Modern Greek Literature, Medieval and Modern Latin Literature; 3) Subclasses PB-PH, Modern European Languages; 4) Subclass PG (in part), Russian Literature; 5) Subclasses PJ-PM, Languages and Literatures of Asia, Africa, Oceania, American Indian Languages, Artificial Languages; 6) an Index to Languages and Dialects in P-PM; 7) Subclasses PN, PR, PS, PZ, General Literature, English and American Literature, Fiction in English, Juvenile belles lettres; 8) Subclass PQ, part 1, French Literature; 9) Subclass PQ, part 2, Italian, Spanish, and Portuguese Literatures; 10) Subclass PT, part 1, German Literature; and 11) Subclass PT, part 2, Dutch and Scandinavian Literatures. Of these eleven schedules only the Index to Languages and Dialects and the schedule for Subclasses PN, PR, PS, PZ are in a second edition.

Classification of Literature

Before the individual schedules in Class P are examined, certain characteristics of classifying literature by the Library of Congress should be considered first.

Classification of Belles Lettres[10]

All works of belles lettres are now being classed in P regardless of any previous provisions for belles lettres found in other schedules. For example, DC203.8 provides for works discussing Napoleon in literature. Such numbers are no longer valid and are being converted to *see* references to P.* For example,

	[The Revolution, 1775-1783]
E (295)	Illustrative materials
	Poetry, ballads, songs. Drama, pageants, *see* PQ-PT

	[Life of Christ]
BT (309)	Fictional lives of Christ
	Stories of the life of Christ, *see* P-PZ

	[Literature of music]
ML (3925)	Fiction, *see* PA-PZ

Pattern of Subarrangement

For each national literature, a recurring plan or pattern for subarrangement of materials is used:

1) History and criticism

2) Collections or anthologies of more than one author

3) Individual authors

4) Non-national literature if appropriate

Literary Collections[11]

The determining factor in the classification of literary collections consisting of two or more independent works by different authors is the treatment given the publication in accordance with *AACR 2*.

---

*These changes are printed in newly revised schedules or *LC Classification—Additions and Changes*.

Publications with Collective Titles. These are classed as a collection, regardless of the number of individual works included in the publication and in spite of the fact that author-title added entries have been made for the individual works. Such works are cuttered under the title.

Publications without Collective Titles. These are classed as a collection, regardless of the number of individual works included. The Cutter number is based on the name of the compiler or editor, if an added entry has been made under his or her name. Otherwise the Cutter number is taken from the main entry heading. However, if the first named work is the essential, most important aspect of the volume and the remaining works are intended to be supplementary, the work is classed as a single work of the first-named author and title.

Individual Authors

The third element in the pattern of subarrangement given above, individual authors, is a most important characteristic of the Library of Congress Classification. Works written in a particular language by a literary author and works about the author are arranged in a single group regardless of literary form. Subdivision by literary form, common in the *Dewey Decimal Classification*, does not occur under individual authors in the Library of Congress Classification, with the exception of Elizabethan drama in Subclass PR, English literature, which is treated as a separate form.

Because many authors have written in more than one language or have been citizens of more than one country, the same author may be assigned numbers in different national literatures. The following statement[12] issued by the Library of Congress explains the placement of literary authors:

> Provision is made for classifying works by and about individual literary authors in Class P by means of individual literary author numbers. The principal factors to be considered in determining the location of these numbers are the language in which the author wrote, the author's nationality, and, if required, the time period during which the author was productive. The simplest situation encountered in establishing an author's number is the author who wrote in one language only and was a citizen of only one country. For such an author a number would be provided under the literature of the language in which the author wrote, with the possibility of further subarrangement by country and period. Authors living in the country most commonly associated with a particular language are classed with the general literature area for that language. For example, George Sand is classed under general French literature, specifically, 19th century in PQ2393 + .

> Authors of a country other than the one most commonly associated with the language in which they write may be classed by country in the area developed for that literature in other countries. For example, a number for the Canadian novelist Lucy Maud Montgomery (PR9199.3.M6) is provided in the subclass for English literature in the area for English literature in Canada. Many literatures, however, have no geographic development, and may be only

partially expanded (such as literature of former colonies), or may have special locations for collections but not for individual authors. The literature of the United States is the exception to the standard arrangement of keeping the literature of a particular language together in the same subclass. No special section for United States literature exists in subclass PR, English Literature. Instead, subclass PS has been reserved for literature in English of the United States.

Authors Writing in More Than One Language. If an author writes in more than one language, a number for the author is provided under the literature of each language; no effort is made to keep all the works of the author together. (For example, Vladimir Nabokov wrote works in both Russian and English; his Russian language works are classed with Russian literature in PG3476.N3 and his English language works are classed with American literature in PS3527.A15.) Translations and critical studies of individual works in each case are classed with the original works. A collective criticism of several works is classed according to the general emphasis of the group of works studied, e.g., a criticism of Nabokov's English works should be classed in his subclass PS number. General criticism and all bibliographical works, however, are classed in one predetermined number that best represents the total literary output of the author, e.g., for Nabokov, the Russian literature number is used.

Authors Associated with More Than One Country. After determining with which particular literature an author should be classed, the particular country of that literature under which the author's number should be established may need to be determined. Under any particular literature an author may be classed under one country. The author is classed with the country of citizenship, if this can be determined. If the author was a citizen of several countries, the preferred classification is under the country in which the author's most productive years were spent or under the country usually associated with the author by scholars in the field. If no preference can be determined, an arbitrary selection is made. Once a decision has been made to class a living author with a particular country, however, this number will usually continue to be used regardless of subsequent changes of residence by the author; an author is moved from one place to another in the schedule only when absolutely necessary.

For living authors whose works are being cataloged for the first time and about whom there is little information (citizenship is not known), the selection of the country is based on available information, such as (in order of importance) birthplace, parentage, residences, place of publication of the work(s) being cataloged. If this information does not justify the choice of one country over another, an arbitrary decision is made. Once the literary author number has been established under a country, only if new information becomes available demonstrating conclusively that the original decision was faulty is the originally assigned number cancelled and a new number established in a more appropriate location.

Individual authors are grouped by period under each national literature. Under each period, they have been assigned individual numbers in an alphabetical sequence. Authors prior to the twentieth century are assigned ranges of numbers according to the amount of material by and about them. Major authors, such as Shakespeare (PR2750-3112) and Goethe (PT1891-2239), have been assigned over three hundred numbers each. Other important authors, such as Robert Browning and Friedrich von Schiller, receive up to fifty numbers each. Most of the authors receive one number or a Cutter number.

All twentieth century authors are assigned a Cutter number each, regardless of the amount of material. For example, William Faulkner has been assigned the number PS3511.A86. It must be carefully noted that the Cutter number for the author is based on the second letter of the author's last name. This is necessary because the cardinal number refers to the first letter of the author's last name. In other words, PS3511 is used for twentieth century American authors whose names begin with the letter F.

Regardless of the range of numbers assigned to an author, works written by and about the author are subarranged according to a recurring pattern:

1) Collected works

2) Selected works

3) Translations

4) Separate works, alphabetically by title

5) Biography and criticism

In some cases, the second and third items appear in reverse order. Numerous author tables, based on the range of numbers, are included in the schedules for subarrangement of works written by and about an author according to the pattern above. Special tables are also included for individual works (which have appeared in numerous texts and translations) and works about them. Examples of using the author tables and tables for individual works appear in chapter 4 and further examples will be presented later.

In most cases, there are special provisions for translations of an author's works and biographies in the author tables. These specific provisions or instructions take precedence over the floating tables for translations and biography.

Exhibitions on Individual Literary Authors

Previously, exhibitions focusing on individual literary authors and their writings were classed in Z under "Personal bibliography." Now they are classed under the individual author numbers of the P schedules.

Texts in Little Known Languages[13]

A work that is in an exotic or little-known language and for which no one on the Library of Congress staff possesses the linguistic competence for ascertaining the nature of the contents is classified in Subclasses PB-PM with the specific language under the special number for texts, e.g., PM3696.Z66, Cocopa texts.

Subclasses PN, PR, PS, PZ

The schedule for Subclasses PN, PR, PS, PZ was the first of the Class P schedules issued. This schedule, under the editorship of Edwin Wiley, was published in 1915. The four subclasses included in this schedule are: PN, world literature; PR, English literature (i.e., literature written originally in English in all countries except the United States); PS, American literature; and PZ, fiction in English, and juvenile belles lettres.

A second edition of this schedule was published in 1978. Basically, it is a cumulative edition with updated terminology rather than a revised edition. Two features of the first edition were removed.[14] The index to the second edition no longer includes entries for personal names, because it was felt that a list of personal names would be a replication of the schedule. Secondly, many author Cutter numbers which appeared in the 1964 reissue of the first edition have been left out of the second edition. The reason given was that the author Cutter numbers had never been incorporated into the official schedules in the Subject Cataloging Division of the Library of Congress, from which the second edition was prepared. As a result, classifiers who found these features of the first edition useful should retain it for reference purposes.

Outline of PN

PN

LITERATURE: GENERAL AND UNIVERSAL
LITERARY HISTORY.   COLLECTIONS

1-9	Periodicals
20-30	Societies
45-57	Theory. Philosophy. Esthetics
59-72	Study and teaching
80-99	Criticism
101-245	Authorship
172-239	Technique. Literary composition. Rhetoric
241	Translating as a literary pursuit
441-1009	Literary history
451-492	Biography
500-519	Collections
599-605	Special relations, movements, and currents of literature
610-769	By period
611-649	Ancient
661-694	Medieval (to 1500)
684-687	Legends
688-691	Poetry
692-693	Prose. Prose fiction
695-779	Modern
715-749	Renaissance (1500-1700)
801-820	Romance literatures
821-840	Germanic literatures
851-883	Comparative literature
905-1008	Folk literature
980-994	Fables
1010-1525	Poetry
1031-1049	Theory, philosophy, relations, etc.
1065-1085	Relations to, and treatment of, special subjects
1105-1279	History and criticism
1301-1333	Epic poetry
1341-1347	Folk poetry
1351-1389	Lyric poetry
1530	The monologue
1551	The dialogue
1560-1590	The performing arts. Show business
1585-1589	Centers for the performing arts
1600-3299	Drama
1635-1650	Relations to, and treatment of, special subjects
1660-1692	Technique of dramatic composition
1720-1861	History
1865-1988	Special types
1990-1992.9	Broadcasting
1991-1991.9	Radio broadcasts
1992-1992.9	Television broadcasts
1993-1999	Motion pictures
1997-1997.85	Plays, scenarios, etc.
2000-3299	Dramatic representation. The theater
2061-2071	Art of acting
2085-2091	The stage and accessories
2131-2193	By period
2131-2145	Ancient
2152-2160	Medieval
2171-2179	Renaissance
2181-2193	Modern

PN

LITERATURE: GENERAL AND UNIVERSAL
LITERARY HISTORY. COLLECTIONS

	Drama
	Dramatic representation. The
	theater – Continued
2220-3030	Special regions or countries
3035	The Jewish theater
3151-3171	Amateur theatricals
3175-3191	College and school theatricals
3203-3299	Tableaux, pageants, "Happenings," etc.
3311-3503	Prose. Prose fiction
3329-3352	Philosophy, theory, etc.
3355-3383	Technique
3428-3448	Special kinds of fiction
4001-4355	Oratory. Elocution, etc.
4071-4095	Study and teaching
4177-4191	Debating
4199-4321	Recitations (in English)
4331-4355	Recitations in foreign languages
4699-5650	Journalism. The periodical press, etc.
4735-4748	Relation to the state. Law, regulation
	and control
4775-4784	Technique. Practical journalism
4825-4830	Amateur journalism
4840-5645	By region or country
6010-6790	Collections of general literature
6066-6069	Special classes of authors
6080-6095	Quotations
6081-6084	English
6086-6089	French
6090-6093	German
6099-6110	Poetry
6110.5-6120	Drama
6121-6129	Orations
6130-6140	Letters
6141-6145	Essays
6147-6231	Wit and humor. Satire
6157-6222	By region or country
6233-6238	Anacreontic literature
6244-6246	Literary extracts. Commonplace books, etc.
6249-6258	Ana
6259-6268	Anecdotes. Table talk
6269-6278	Aphorisms. Apothegms
6279-6288	Epigrams
6288.5-6298	Epitaphs
6299-6308	Maxims
6309-6318	Mottoes
6319-6328	Sayings, bon mots, etc.
6329-6338	Thoughts
6340-6348	Toasts
6349-6358	Emblems, devices
6361	Paradoxes
6366-6377	Riddles, acrostics, charades, conundrums, etc.
6400-6525	Proverbs
6700-6790	Comic books, strips, etc.

Outline of PR

PR   ENGLISH LITERATURE

1-56	Literary history and criticism
57-78	Criticism
111-116	Women authors
125-138	Relations to other literatures and countries
161-479	By period
171-236	Anglo-Saxon (beginnings through 1066)
251-369	Medieval. Middle English (1066-1500)
401-479	Modern
421-429	Elizabethan era (1550-1640)
431-439	17th century
441-449	18th century
451-469	19th century
471-479	20th century
500-618	Poetry
521-611	By period
621-739	Drama
641-739	By period
751-888	Prose
821-888	Prose fiction. The novel
901-907	Oratory
908	Diaries
911-917	Letters
921-927	Essays
931-937	Wit and humor
951-978	Folk literature
1098-1369	Collections of English literature
1110	Special classes of authors
1119-1150	By period
1170-1226	Poetry
1241-1273	Drama
1281-1309	Prose (General)
1321-1329	Oratory
1330	Diaries
1341-1349	Letters
1361-1369	Essays
1490-1799	Anglo-Saxon literature
1803-2165	Anglo-Norman period. Early English. Middle English
2199-3195	English renaissance (1500-1640)
3291-3785	17th and 18th centuries (1640-1770)
3991-5990	19th century, 1770/1800-1890/1900
6000-6049	1900-1960
6050-6076	1961-
9080-9680	English literature outside of Great Britain

Outline of PS

PS   AMERICAN LITERATURE

126-138	Biography, memoirs, letters, etc.
147-152	Women authors
185-228	By period
185-195	17th-18th centuries
201-217	19th century
221-228	20th century
241-286	Special regions, states, etc.
241-255	North
261-267	South
271-285	West and Central

PS   AMERICAN LITERATURE

301–325	Poetry
330–351	Drama
360–379	Prose
400–408	Oratory
409	Diaries
410–418	Letters
420–428	Essays
430–438	Wit and humor. Satire
451–478	Folk literature
501–688	Collections of American literature
530–536.2	By period
537–574	By region
538–549	North
551–559	South
561–572	West and Central
580–619	Poetry
593	By form
601–615	By period
623–635	Drama
642–659.5	Prose (General)
651–659	By period
660–668	Oratory
666–668	By period
669	Diaries
670–678	Letters
680–688	Essays
700–3576	Individual authors
700–893	Colonial period (17th and 18th centuries)
991–3390	19th century
3500–3549	1900–1960
3550–3576	1961–
(8001–8599)	CANADIAN LITERATURE

Auxiliary Tables in PN, PR, PS, PZ

There are more than twenty tables for use with the individual authors and their separate works in Subclasses PR, English literature, and PS, American literature. Only in a few cases are the subdivisions worked out within the schedules — e.g., William Shakespeare or Geoffrey Chaucer. Each author is assigned a range of numbers appropriate to the amount of material written by and about him/her. There are tables for authors assigned ninety-eight numbers (although none yet exist), forty-nine numbers, nineteen numbers, nine numbers, five numbers, four numbers, one number, or only a Cutter number. Separate works with nine, five, two, one, and Cutter numbers have separate tables, as do anonymous literary works.

Thomas Carlyle is a nineteenth century English author with a range of nineteen numbers, "PR 4420-4438." Carlyle's entry in the schedule includes the following elements:

PR English Literature.
  4420-4438   **Carlyle, Thomas (III[a]).**
        Separate works.
         Chartism, *see* DA.
         Choice of books, *see* Z 1003.
         Cromwell's letters and speeches, *see* DA.
         Early kings of Norway, etc., *see* DL 460.
     4425 Essays.
        .A2,   Collected. By date.
        .A3,   Minor collections. By date.
        A5-Z,   Separate essays and minor collections.
             By title.
         Frederick the Great, *see* DD.
         French revolution, *see* DC.
     4426 Heroes and hero worship.
         Inaugural address, University of Edinburgh, 1866;
          Choice of books, *see* Z 1003.
         Latter day pamphlets, *see* HN 388.
         Past and present, *see* HN 388.
     4429 Sartor resartus.
         Schiller, Friedrich, *see* PT.
         Sterling, John, *see* PR 5473.S8.
         Translations from the German, *see* PT.
     4430 Other works, A-Z.

Carlyle's more important literary works are assigned a whole number each, e.g., *Heroes and Hero Worship*, "PR 4426." The lesser literary works together are assigned one number, "PR 4430, A-Z." Carlyle's non-literary works are classed by subject rather than in literature as the above section demonstrates, e.g., *Early Kings of Norway, see* "DL 460." However, to use Carlyle's entire range of nineteen numbers, the appropriate auxiliary table must be identified. Following Carlyle's name in the schedule is "(III[a])." This means that Table III[a], for nineteen number authors, is used to class Carlyle's works. Following the schedule are auxiliary tables called "Tables of Subdivisions under Individual Authors." Tables I and II are for ninety-eight and forty-nine number authors, respectively. The use of Table II is discussed in chapter 4. Tables III and IV are the next tables. Table III is to be used for nineteen number authors. Date letters are to be used in Table III and Table IV when the author is assigned III[a] or IV[a]. The nineteen numbers assigned to Carlyle are matched with the numbers in Table III in the following manner:

PR 4420-4438		**Table III**
		Collected works.
4420	0	By date.
4421	1	By editor.
4422	2	Selections.
		Translations.
(4423)	3	Modern English. By translator.
4424	4	Other, by language. Subarranged by translator.

(Continued on next page)

			Translations (cont'd)
4425-4430	5-10		Separate works.
			see Table X or XI.
4431	11		Apocryphal, spurious works, etc.
			Biography, criticism, etc.
4432	.A1-5	12 .A1-5	Periodicals. Societies. Serials.
	.A6-Z	.A6-Z	Dictionaries, indexes, etc.
4433		13 .A3-39	Autobiography, journals, memoirs
		.A4	Letters (Collections). By imprint date.
		.A41-49	Letters to and from particular individuals. By correspondent (alphabetically).
		.A5-Z	General works.
			Criticism.
4434	14		General works.
4435	15		Textual. Manuscripts, etc.
			Special.
4436	16		Sources.
4437	17		Other, A-Z.

.A35	Aesthetics.
.A4	Ambiguity.
.A6	Allegory.
* * * *	
.V4	Versification.
.W6	Women.

4438	18		Language. Grammar. Style.

Table III^a

Same as III, using the following date letter:

To 1500:	A00-A99
1500-1599	B00-B99
1600-1699	C00-C99
1700-1799	D00-D99
1800-1899	E00-E99
1900-1999	F00-F99

In the date letters, the first two digits of a date are replaced by a letter. This particular device may be traced to Cutter's use of Biscoe Date-Letters. Perhaps the greatest advantage of this table is that it provides a figure that resembles a Cutter number in the book's call number.

Carlyle's *Complete Works* published in 1885 is classed "PR 4420 .E85." "PR 4420" means an edition without commentary of the collected works of Thomas Carlyle. ".E85" is the appropriate date letter from Table III^a meaning "1885."

Thomas Carlyle's *Complete Works*, 1885.

PR	The double letters for the subclass, English literature
4420	The integral number meaning the collected works without commentary of Thomas Carlyle
.E85	The date letter meaning the date of publication, 1885

An edition with commentary of Carlyle's collected works would be classed in the second number of his range, according to Table III. *Selections* from Carlyle with an introduction and notes by A. M. D. Hughes is classed in the third number, "PR 4422."

Selections, of Carlyle.

PR	The double letters for the subclass, English literature
4422	The integral number meaning a selection of the works of Thomas Carlyle
.H8	The Cutter number for the editor of the selection, Hughes

The fourth number in Table III, "3," for translations into modern English, is not used for Carlyle, as Carlyle wrote in modern English. A German edition of Carlyle's works translated by Friedrich Bremer uses the fifth number in Table III. The call number for this work is "PR 4424 .G4B7." The first Cutter number is used for the languages of the translation, in this case German, and the second for the name of the translator, Bremer.

Thomas Carlyle's *Werke*. Translated by F. Bremer.

PR	The double letters for the subclass, English literature
4424	The integral number meaning a translation of collected works of Thomas Carlyle
.G4	The first Cutter number for the language of the translation, German
B7	The second Cutter number for the name of the translator, Bremer

Carlyle's separate works or individual titles are classed according to the assigned numbers in the schedule. For further subdivisions of these numbers use Table X^a, "Separate Works with One Number," and Table XI, "Separate Works with Cutter Numbers." Under Carlyle's separate works both his major literary and his non-literary works are listed alphabetically. His non-literary works are classed with the appropriate subjects. An example is his *Early Kings of Norway* which is classed in Class D under Norwegian history.

Thomas Carlyle's *Early Kings of Norway*.

DL	The double letters for the subclass, Scandinavian history
460	The integral number meaning general works on early and medieval Norway
.C3	The Cutter number for the author, Carlyle

In the example above, the Cutter number is for Carlyle. It would be incorrect to use a Cutter number for Carlyle within the range of literature numbers assigned to him as this range of numbers means Carlyle. The classifier must always take care not to be redundant when he is classing in literature.

The first of Carlyle's literary works listed, his essays, is assigned special subdivisions in the schedule.

PR

4425   Essays.

      .A2   Collected. By date.

      .A3   Minor collections. By date.

      .A5-Z   Separate essays and minor collections. By title.

For instance, his *Critical and Miscellaneous Essays: Collected and Republished*, 1847, is classed "PR 4425 .A2 1847."

Thomas Carlyle's *Critical and Miscellaneous Essays*, 1847.

PR	The double letters for the subclass, English literature
4425	The integral number meaning literary essays of Thomas Carlyle
.A2	The Cutter number meaning collected essays
1847	The date of publication as required by the schedule

"PR 4426" is the second number for Carlyle's separate literary works. This number is for *Heroes and Hero Worship*. As no subdivisions for this number are given in the schedule, Table X[a] (page 230) must be used.

Table X^a

	Texts.
.A1	By date.
.A2A-Z	By editor.
.A3	School texts.
.A35	Selections.
.A37	Adaptations, dramatizations, etc.
	Translations.
.A4-49	French.
.A5-59	German.
:A6-69	Other languages. By language.
.A7-Z	Criticism.
.Z8	History.
.5	Special parts. By date.

An edition of *Heroes and Hero Worship* published in 1841 is classed in "PR 4426 .A1 1841." ".A1" means an edition without commentary of the text of the work.

On Heroes and Hero Worship and the Heroic in History, 1841.

PR	The double letters for the subclass, English literature
4426	The integral number meaning Carlyle's *Heroes and Hero Worship*
.A1	The Cutter number for an edition without commentary of the text of the work
1841	The date of publication as required by Table X^a

A German translation of this work entitled *Helden und Heldenverehrung*, translated by Ernst Wicklein, is classed "PR 4426 .A58." ".A5-59" is the range of Cutter numbers for German translations according to Table X^a. ".A58" is a Cutter number within that range, with ".A5" meaning a German translation and "8" a translator whose name is near the end of the alphabet, such as Wicklein.

Helden und Heldenverehrung, translated by Ernst Wicklein.

PR	The double letters for the subclass, English literature
4426	The integral number meaning Carlyle's *Heroes and Hero Worship*
.A58	The Cutter number meaning a German translation of the above work translated by a person whose last name is near the end of the alphabet

A Russian translation of this same work translated by Valentin Ivanovich Îakovenko is classed in "PR 4426 .A64I3." In this case ".A6-69" are used for languages other than French and German. ".A6" means a translation in a language other than the original English or French or German; the decimal extension "4" in this case means Russian. The second Cutter number is used for the translator.

Geroi i Geroischeskoe v Istorii, translated by Valentin Ivanovich Îakovenko.

PR	The double letters for the subclass, English literature
4426	The integral number meaning Carlyle's *Heroes and Hero Worship*
.A64	The Cutter number meaning a Russian translation of the above work
I3	The second Cutter number for the translator, Îakovenko

A Spanish translation of *Heroes and Hero Worship* issued in 1932 is classed in "PR 4426 .A65 1932." In this case the decimal extension "5" means Spanish.

Los Héroes, 1932.

PR	The double letters for the subclass, English literature
4426	The integral number meaning Carlyle's *Heroes and Hero Worship*
.A65	The Cutter number meaning a Spanish translation of the above work
1932	The date of publication

Carlyle's biographical works are classed with the subject of the biography and not with Carlyle's literary works. The following example demonstrates this.

Thomas Carlyle's *The Life of Friedrich Schiller*, 1869.

PT	The double letters for the subclass, Germanic literatures
2482	The integral number meaning a general biography of the individual author in German literature, Friedrich Schiller
.C3	The Cutter number for the author of the biography, Carlyle
1869	The date of publication

Carlyle's lesser works are classed under the one number, "PR 4430" and arranged alphabetically by Cutter number. For instance, a text of Carlyle's *Reminiscences* issued in 1881 is classed "PR 4430 .R4 1881."

Thomas Carlyle's *Reminiscences*, 1881.

PR	The double letters for the subclass, English literature
4430	The integral number meaning a lesser work of Carlyle
.R4	The Cutter number for the title of the lesser work, meaning that this is a text of the work
1881	The date of publication as required by Table XI

To class biographical and critical material about Carlyle, Table III is used to locate the specific numbers "13-18" (PR 4433-4438). James Lorimer Halliday's *Mr. Carlyle My Patient, a Psychosomatic Biography* is also classed in this general biographical number, "PR 4433 .H27."

J. L. Halliday's *Mr. Carlyle My Patient, a Psychosomatic Biography*.

PR	The double letters for the subclass, English literature
4433	The integral number meaning a general biographical work about Thomas Carlyle
.H27	The Cutter number for the author of the biography, Halliday

Charles Frederick Harrold's general criticism, *Carlyle and German Thought*, published in 1963, is classed "PR 4434 .H3 1963."

C. F. Harrold's *Carlyle and German Thought*, 1963.

PR	The double letters for the subclass, English literature
4434	The integral number meaning a general criticism of Carlyle
.H3	The Cutter number for the author of the criticism, Harrold
1963	The date of publication

Finally, a specialized criticism on religion in Carlyle's works, *Teleologisches geschichtsbild und theokratische Staatsauffassung im Werke Thomas Carlyle* by Jürgen Kedenburg, published in 1960, is classed "PR 4437 .R4K4 1960." "PR 4437" is a specialized criticism of Thomas Carlyle. ".R4" is the Cutter number for the special subject, religion.

Jürgen Kedenburg's *Teleologisches geschichtsbild und theokratische Staatsauffassung im Werke Thomas Carlyle*, 1960.

PR	The double letters for the subclass, English literature
4437	The integral number meaning a specialized criticism of Carlyle
.R4	The first Cutter number for the special subject, religion
K4	The second Cutter number for the author of the criticism, Kedenburg
1960	The date of publication

Chapter 3 contains a discussion and demonstration of shelflisting different manifestations (editions, translations, etc.) of a particular work. For literary works, special tables are used. Chapter 4 provides examples of using Table X in Subclasses PN, PR, PS, PZ for separate works with one number. The following examples show the use of Table XI for "Separate works with Cutter numbers."

XI (Cutter no.)	Separate works with Cutter numbers

(1).x date
.xA-Z
	Texts
	Translations. By language
	   .A3-39 Modern versions in same language
	   .A4-Z Other languages

(3).xA-Z	Criticism
	   Note: In Table XI, (1), (2), and (3), .x
	       represents successive Cutter num-
	       bers, as , for example: .F6, .F7,
	       .F8 or .F66, .F67, .F68
	   In the case of works where division (2)
	    is inapplicable the numbers may be
	    modified by using two Cutter numbers
	    only, as .F4, .F5 or .F4, .F41

In the note to this table it should be pointed out that ".F" represents a Cutter number for the title of a work beginning with "F." In the case of ".F66," ".F67," and ".F68," the ".F" represents a Cutter number standing for the title of a work probably having the initial letters "Fo," as for example "Fourscore." This table cannot be applied without first establishing the Cutter number sequence being used for an individual work at the Library of Congress.

Herman Melville's novel *Moby Dick* may be used as an example.

The Limited Edition Club publication of *Moby Dick*, 1943.

PS	The double letters meaning American literature
2384	The integral number for individual works of the author, Herman Melville
.M6	The Cutter number for *Moby Dick*. The lack of any successive Cutter number indicating that this is the text of the work.
1943	The date of publication as required in the table

".M6" is the Cutter number for the title of Melville's novel *Moby Dick*. It may be assumed at this point that the variation of the "1-2-3" being used is "0-1-2"; however, this is only an assumption and must be proved by further establishment of the sequence. This further establishment may be done by verifying other elements involved in Table XI, i.e., translations and criticism.

A translation of *Moby Dick* in Hebrew.

PS	The double letters meaning American literature
2384	The integral number for individual works of the author, Herman Melville
.M6	The first Cutter number for *Moby Dick*. The lack of any successive Cutter number indicating that this is one form of the text of the work
H4	The second Cutter number used for the language of the translation, Hebrew

This example is consistent with the assumption that the variation of the sequence is "0-1-2."

William Gleim's *The Meaning of Moby Dick*, 1962.

PS	The double letters meaning American literature
2384	The integral number for individual works of the author, Herman Melville
.M62	M6 is the *first* Cutter number for *Moby Dick*. 2 is the successive Cutter number meaning criticism.
G5	The second Cutter number used for the author of the criticism, Gleim.

This example proves the original assumption that the variation of the sequence being used is "0-1-2." If the text of *Moby Dick* is ".M6" and criticism of *Moby Dick* is ".M62," then obviously the text is really cuttered ".M60," with the "0" dropped as the meaningless last element of a decimal extension. This method should be employed in any instance when similar successive Cutter numbers are used.

Some of the tables in Class P have two or three versions, e.g., X, Xa; VIII, VIIIa, VIIIb. Normally, the second version, e.g., Xa, VIIIa, etc., is used for works after 1600. The third version, e.g., VIIIb, is used only when specific instruction is given in the schedules or when the pattern is already established in the shelflist under the particular class number.

Outline of PZ

FICTION AND JUVENILE BELLES LETTRES

<u>Fiction in English</u>

	Collections of novels, short stories, etc. Including Tales from Blackwood's
1.A1	Periodicals. Serials
.A2-Z	General collections
	Individual authors
3	1750 through 1950
4	1951-

<u>Juvenile Belles Lettres</u>

5-10.3	American and English
10.72-.78	Arabic
.82-.88	Chinese
11-18	Dutch. Afrikaans
21-28	French
31-38	German
41-48	Italian
49.2-.8	Japanese
50.52-.58	Korean
	Scandinavian
51-54.3	Danish
54.4-.9	Norwegian
55-56	Icelandic
57-60.3	Swedish
	Slavic
61-68	Russian
69	Polish
70	Other, A-Z
71-78	Spanish
81-88	Portuguese
90	Other languages, A-Z

This subclass was first developed in 1906. At that time PZ consisted of two numbers only—PZ 1 and PZ 3. PZ 1 was used for collections of fiction in English—e.g., anthologies or short stories. PZ 3 was used for individual or separate works of individual authors. Recently, PZ 3 has been qualified to include individual authors to 1950, and restricted to the period 1750-1950. PZ 4 has been developed for individual authors after 1950. Subdivision within each of these numbers is made alphabetically by modified three-figure Cutter numbers.

Until July 1, 1980, all works of fiction in English, including translations into English, were classed in PZ at the Library of Congress. The only exceptions were made for works assigned to the Rare Book Division, in which case the work is classed with the regular literature subclasses of the P schedule. Even though many special class numbers exist under literary authors for individual novels in English, these numbers were used only for books assigned to the Rare Book Division and for discussions about the English translation.

The value of classing fiction in English in PZ has often been questioned. The practice separated British and American fiction from the rest of British and American literature. Furthermore, critical works about an author's fiction were separated from the author's fiction. For instance, W. Somerset Maugham's novels were classed in PZ 3, while all his plays and biographical works about him as well as criticism of his fiction were classed in PR. The use of the PZ numbers also separated English translations of foreign fiction from the original version and from all other translations.

In view of these disadvantages, the Library of Congress has announced a change of policy with regard to the treatment of Fiction in English.[15] Beginning July 1, 1980, American fiction is to be classed in PS, English fiction in PR, and translations into English with the original national literature.

Previously, juvenile non-fiction was also classed in PZ. This has been changed. Now all juvenile non-fiction is classed with the topic in the appropriate subject classes, except in rare cases of amorphous children's works which do not lend themselves to subject classification.

For examples of classifying juvenile belles lettres, *see* chapter 6.

Subclass P-PA

Subclass P-PA, Philology, Linguistics, Classical Philology, Classical Literature, was prepared by Walter F. Koenig. The first edition was published in 1928. The supplement to this schedule for PA, Byzantine and Modern Greek literature and Medieval and Modern Latin literature, was completed by Clarence Perley in 1933 and first published in 1942. This schedule represents one of the finest works of scholarship in all classification systems. Koenig provided a detailed introduction to the schedule with directions for the use of the schedule. In addition, he provided many valuable footnotes throughout the schedule. The Appendix includes a list of subjects in other classes in Library of Congress Classification that are related to classical philology, auxiliary tables with complete explanations and examples, and a list of authorities used in the preparation of this schedule. Further, as Koenig writes in his prefatory note, the sections of the schedules for Greek and Roman authors contain,

> an extensive list of authors, designed to aid the classifier in distinguishing homonymous writers and in the occasionally difficult arrangement of names. The inclusion of many more or less obscure names may seem unnecessary; it is justified, nevertheless, because it enables the classifier to avoid cumbersome and injudicious notation. Inasmuch as the classical literature practically

presents a closed *fond*, the extent of possibilities may be very nearly indicated, whereas with modern literature this is obviously impracticable.

It should be pointed out that these lists of names of Greek and Latin authors are valuable reference sources. Both the Greek and the Roman names are given in the traditional Latin form. In addition, in the prefatory note Koenig observes a method for abridging this schedule:

> The minute classification devised for some parts of the scheme may create the impression that it is intended for the use of large university libraries only; but an examination of the scheme will prove that any college library or any library desirous of owning a representative collection of classical literature may make use of this scheme by ignoring the minor subdivisions—in other words, by using the condensed schedules as represented in Synopsis III and IV.

Synopsis III is the outline for Greek authors and Synopsis IV is the outline for Roman authors. The original Greek titles, with Latin translations, and the original Latin titles are provided for these authors' works, although no English translations are given. The application of this schedule demands a certain amount of specialized knowledge, but the technical aspects of the schedule should create no unusual difficulty in classifying.

The index does not include the names of individual authors.

Topical Greek and Roman Classics[16]

Original texts of topical Greek and Roman classics are, in general, classed in Subclass PA, as are translations into all languages except English. English translations are classed with the appropriate discipline in Classes B through Z.

An exception is made for works in the field of philosophy. Translations, including those accompanied by the original text, are classed in Class B, unless they contain textual criticism or are translations into Latin, both of which are classed in Subclass PA.

The following examples of Aristotle's works demonstrate the classification of topical Greek and Roman classics.

Aristotle

Politika. 1939.
PA3893.P8 1939

Politics & Poetics. Translated by B. Jowett and S. H. Butcher. 1964.
JC71.A41J6 1964

Die Metaphysik des Aristoteles.
[A German translation with original text; translated by Albert Schwegler. 1960 reprint of 1847 edition]
B434.A7S35 1847a

Aristotelis Naturalis auscultationis libri VIII.
[Text in Greek and Latin; commentary in Latin. 1964 reprint of
1596 edition]
PA3893.P3 1596a

Subclasses PB-PH

The schedule for Subclasses PB-PH, Modern European Languages, was published in 1933. Koenig was also chiefly responsible for the preparation of this schedule under the supervision of Charles Martel. Subclass PB includes general works on modern European languages and specifically Celtic languages and literatures. Romance languages are contained in Subclass PC, and Scandinavian languages in Subclass PD. The English language is contained in Subclass PE. German, Dutch, and other Germanic languages are classed in PF. Subclass PG is designed for Slavic languages and literatures, and PH is for Finno-Ugrian and Basque languages and literatures.

There are 31 auxiliary tables in the schedule. These tables are similar to those discussed in chapter 4 of this guide. The classifier should be aware when using these auxiliary tables that special modifications must be made, as directed, for each language. Tables I-V, for language subdivisions, are eight pages long. Middle English, with a range of numbers "PE 501-685," is assigned to use Table III. This table consists of two hundred language subdivisions. Grammatical works on Middle English use the range of numbers for grammar in Table III.

	I	II	III	IV	V
Grammar—					
Comparative (two or more languages)	99	59	29	18	
Historical	101	61	31	19	
Treatises			33	21	11
To 1800	103	63			
Later	105	64			
General special (Terminology, etc.)	107	65	34	22	12
Text-books			35	23	13
Early to 1870	109	66			
Later, 1871-	111	67			
Readers—					
Series	113	68	36	24	
Primers. Primary grade readers	115	69	37	25	
Intermediate and advanced	117	71			
Outlines, Syllabi, Tables, etc.	118				
Examination questions, etc.	119				
Manuals for special classes of students, A-Z	120	72	38	26	
e. g., Commercial, Cf. HF.					

Karl Brunner's *An Outline of Middle English Grammar* is classed as an historical grammar using the number "31" in Table III. The thirty-first number in the range of numbers "PE 501-685" is "PE 531."

Karl Brunner's *An Outline of Middle English Grammar.*

PE	The double letters for the subclass, English language
531	The integral number meaning a historical Middle English grammar
.B713	The Cutter number (.B7) for the main entry, Brunner and the successive element (13) for an English translation

A Handbook of Middle English by Fernando Mossé is classed as a textbook under grammar using the number "35" in Table III. The thirty-fifth number in the range of numbers "PE 501-685" is "PE 535."

Fernando Mossé's *A Handbook of Middle English.*

PE	The double letters for the subclass, English language
535	The integral number meaning a textbook on Middle English grammar
.M62	The Cutter number for the main entry, Mossé

There is no index to this schedule.

Subclasses PJ-PM

The schedule for Subclasses PJ-PM, Languages and Literatures of Asia, Africa, Oceania, American Indian Languages, Artificial Languages, was first published in 1935, the work of Walter F. Koenig. This schedule contains the less common languages and literatures. The four subclasses in this schedule include PJ-PM, Oriental (including Egyptian, Coptic, Hamitic, Semitic, Indo-Iranian, Armenian, Caucasian, and Georgian) languages and literatures; PL, Languages and literatures of Eastern Asia (Japanese, Korean, and Chinese), Africa, and Oceania; and PM, American Indian languages and Artificial languages. It should be noted that the sections for Chinese and Japanese literatures have been expanded considerably since the publication of the main schedule.*

This schedule contains auxiliary tables similar to those in Subclasses PB-PH, Modern European languages. There is no index in this schedule. However, an index to the languages and dialects covered in Subclasses P-PM, prepared by L. Belle Voegelein, has been published separately (2nd ed., 1957).

---

*Cf. *LC Classification—Additions and Changes.*

Subclasses PQ and PT

Subclass PQ, part 1, French literature, was developed and used at the Library of Congress as early as 1913. The schedule remained in manuscript form until the first publication in 1936. Koenig prepared the original scheme for this part as well as for part 2. Subclass PQ, part 2, Italian, Spanish, and Portuguese literature, was also used in manuscript form for some time. The first edition was published in 1937. C. K. Jones developed many of the details in these schedules, particularly the Spanish and Portuguese names. One deterrent in the use of these two schedules is the lack of an index. There is, however, a very detailed outline at the beginning of each schedule which may be used in place of an index. Both of these schedules contain valuable lists of names according to main entry form, including birth and death dates. Auxiliary tables similar to those used for English or American literature are used with these schedules.

Subclass PT, part 1, German literature, also developed by Koenig, was not published until 1938. Clarence Perley revised and prepared this schedule for printing. Subclass PT, part 2, Dutch and Scandinavian literatures, was not published until 1942. Clarence Perley prepared the sections on Dutch, Flemish, and Afrikaans literature, and he revised the section on Scandinavian literature, which was originally prepared by Jules Dieserud in 1915 and 1916. These schedules are similar to those making up Subclass PQ. Neither part 1 nor part 2 of PT has an index, although long outlines do appear. The lists of names in both schedules are quite useful.

Subclass PG, In Part

Subclass PG (in part), Russian literature, completes the eleven schedules making up Class P. Developed by Voegelein and published in 1948, this schedule covers the range of numbers 2900-3560 in Subclass PG. This scheme was begun by Clarence Perley in the 1930s to serve as a system to class translations of Russian literature. The prefatory note to the schedule states:

> The discontinuance of the Slavic Division and incorporation of the Library's Russian collections, of which the Yudin Collection was the nucleus, into the general collections made it necessary to develop a scheme to cover Russian literature in the original as well as in translation. The Yudin Collection had in part been classified according to a scheme devised by Alexis V. Babine, which could not be applied to the combined collection, since it took no account of translations and did not follow the notation used in other sections of the Library of Congress classification.

Voegelein developed the present schedule. This schedule lacks both an index and a detailed outline. The lists of Russian names are transliterated in accordance with the Library of Congress system of transliteration. These lists contain full names and dates and many syndetic devices. There are auxiliary tables for one number and Cutter number authors and anonymous works.

CLASS Q – SCIENCE

Q		Science (General)
	300-385	Cybernetics. Information theory
QA		Mathematics
	9-10	Mathematical logic
	76	Computer science. Electronic data processing
	101-141	Elementary mathematics. Arithmetic
	150-271	Algebra
		Including machine theory, game theory
	273-274	Probabilities
	276-280	Mathematical statistics
	297-299	Numerical analysis
	299.8-433	Analysis
		Including analytical methods connected with physical problems
	440-699	Geometry
	611-614	Topology
	801-939	Analytic mechanics
		For non-theoretical mechanics, *see* QC120+
QB		Astronomy
	140-237	Practical and spherical astronomy
	275-343	Geodesy
	349-421	Theoretical astronomy and celestial mechanics
		Including perturbations, tides
	460-465	Astrophysics
	468-479	Non-optical methods of astronomy
	500-991	Descriptive astronomy
		Including stellar spectroscopy, cosmogony
QC		Physics
	81-114	Weights and measures
	120-168	Descriptive and experimental mechanics
	170-197	Atomic physics. Constitution and properties of matter
		Including quantum theory, solid-state physics
	220-246	Acoustics. Sound
	251-338	Heat
	350-467	Optics. Light
		Including spectroscopy
	474-496	Radiation physics (General)
	501-766	Electricity and magnetism
	770-798	Nuclear and particle physics. Atomic energy. Radioactivity
	801-809	Geophysics. Cosmic physics
	811-849	Geomagnetism
	851-999	Meteorology. Climatology
QD		Chemistry
	23.3-26	Alchemy
	71-142	Analytical chemistry
	146-197	Inorganic chemistry
	241-441	Organic chemistry
	450-731	Physical and theoretical chemistry
		Including quantum chemistry, stereochemistry, chemical reactions, surface chemistry, thermochemistry, solution chemistry, electrochemistry, radiochemistry, radiation chemistry, photochemistry
	901-999	Crystallography

(Schedule continues on page 242)

		Science—*continued*
QE		Geology
	351-399	Mineralogy
	420-499	Petrology
	500-625	Dynamic and structural geology
	640-699	Stratigraphic geology
	701-996	Paleontology
		Including paleozoology and paleobotany
QH		Natural history (General)
	75-77	Nature conservation. Landscape protection
	201-278	Microscopy
	301-705	General biology
	426-470	Genetics
	471-489	Reproduction
	501-531	Life
	540-549	Ecology
		Including general and animal ecology. For human ecology, *see* GF; for plant ecology, *see* QK
	573-671	Cytology
QK		Botany
	641-673	Plant anatomy
	710-899	Plant physiology
	901-938	Plant ecology
QL		Zoology
	750-795	Animal behavior and psychology
	801-950	Anatomy
	951-991	Embryology
QM		Human anatomy
	601-691	Human embryology
QP		Physiology
	351-495	Neurophysiology. Neuropsychology
	501-801	Animal biochemistry
	901-981	Experimental pharmacology
QR		Microbiology
	75-99	Bacteria
	180-189	Immunology
	355-484	Virology

The first edition of **Class Q—Science** was published in 1905. James David Thompson was responsible for Subclass Q, Sciences (general); QA, Mathematics; QB, Astronomy; QC, Physics; QD, Chemistry; and QE, Geology. F. B. Weeks worked with Thompson on Subclass QE. Subclass QK, Botany, was developed by S. C. Stuntz. J. Christian Bay prepared the remaining Subclasses QH, Natural history; QL, Zoology; QM, Human anatomy; QP, Physiology; and QR, Bacteriology. Thompson served as editor for the entire class in the first edition. The second edition appeared in 1913 with Clarence Perley as editor. Perley also served as editor of the third edition, which was issued in 1921. The fourth edition was published in 1948 with Voegelein as the editor; she also served as editor of the fifth edition, published in 1950. The sixth edition was published in 1973. This is a thoroughly revised edition which, in addition to incorporating additions and changes occurring since the previous edition, also includes expansion and rearrangement of topics in many areas. The terminology has also been updated.

Internal Tables

There are very few problems in the use of this schedule. There are no auxiliary tables and the application of the internal tables is obvious. An example of this is the geology of individual states of the United States. Each is assigned two numbers with the direction, "The second number assigned to each state is used for special localities (i.e., counties or physiographic divisions) arranged alphabetically." California is assigned the numbers "QE 89-90." The first of these is to be used for works on geology of the state in general and the second for particular regions. *Geology of California* by Norris is classed in "QE89.N67."

R. M. Norris' *Geology of California.*

QE	The double letters for the subclass, Geology
89	The integral number meaning a general work on the geology of California
.N67	The Cutter number for the main entry, Norris

John Maxson's *Death Valley: Origin and Scenery* is classed in the second number for specific regions of California as "QE 90 .D35M3." In this case the first Cutter number is used for the specific region, Death Valley.

John Maxson's *Death Valley: Origin and Scenery.*

QE	The double letters for the subclass, Geology
90	The integral number meaning a regional or local work on the geology of California
.D35	The first Cutter number for the region, Death Valley
M3	The second Cutter number for the main entry, Maxson

Book Numbers

One unusual classification device used in Class Q is the "book numbers." One use of these numbers is shown under "QB 543-544" for Solar eclipses.

QB ASTRONOMY

	Solar eclipses
541	General works, treatises, and textbooks
542	Through 1799
543	1800-1899*
544	1900-1999*

---

*Book number = last two figures of the year, followed by author number, e.g., QB 544.47U6 U.S. National Almanac Office, Total eclipse of the sun, May 20, 1947.

"Book numbers" are decimal extensions of integral numbers indicating a particular decade and year of a predetermined century. An example of the use of "book numbers" to subdivide an integral number chronologically by year is the U.S. Nautical Almanac Office's *Total Eclipse of the Sun, June 30, 1954*, classed in "QB 544 .54 U6." ".54" is the "book number" which refers to the year of the particular eclipse in the century "1900-1999"; or, ".54" means 1954.

Total Eclipse of the Sun, June 30, 1954.

QB	The double letters for the subclass, Astronomy
544	The integral number meaning a twentieth century solar eclipse
.54	The "book number" meaning 1954, the date of the eclipse
U6	The Cutter number for the main entry, U.S. Nautical...

The use of book numbers precludes the use of the first decimal point for the first Cutter number. *Astronomical Data for the Solar Eclipse, 15 February 1961*, by A. Kranjc, published in 1960, is similarly classed "QB 544 .61 K7." The book number is taken from the date of the eclipse, not the date of publication of the individual book.

Astronomical Data for the Solar Eclipse, 15 February 1961, by A. Kranjc.

QB	The double letters for the subclass, Astronomy
544	The integral number meaning a twentieth century solar eclipse
.61	The "book number" meaning 1961, the date of the eclipse
K7	The Cutter number for the main entry, Kranjc

It should be noted that Cutter numbers are often used for subject subdivisions in Class Q. For instance, "QD 181," the number in chemistry for special elements, uses Cutter numbers from the symbols of the Periodic Table for further subdivisions.

.A2	Ac	Actinium
.A3	Ag	Silver (Argentum)
.A4	Al	Aluminum
.A5	Am	Americium
.A6	Ar	Argon
.A7	As	Arsenic
.A8	At	Astatine (Alabamine)
.A9	Au	Gold (Aurum)

This device is also used under QE516, Geochemistry.

The index to Class Q is detailed and specific. Many distributed relatives are displayed.

The exhaustive lists of the various taxa in Subclasses QK, Botany, and QL, Zoology, are useful as a reference source.

CLASS R—MEDICINE

R		Medicine (General)
	131-684	History of medicine
	735-847	Medical education
	895	Medical physics. Electronics. Radiology, radioisotopes, etc.
RA		Public aspects of medicine
	5-418	Medicine and the state
		Including medical statistics, medical economics, provisions for medical care, medical sociology
	421-790	Public health. Hygiene. Preventive medicine
		Including environmental health, disposal of the dead, transmission of disease, epidemics, quarantine, personal hygiene
	791-954	Medical geography. Medical climatology and meteorology
	960-998	Medical centers. Hospitals. Clinics
	1001-1171	Forensic medicine
	1190-1270	Toxicology
RB		Pathology
RC		Internal medicine. Practice of medicine
		Including diagnosis, individual diseases and special types of diseases, diseases of systems or organs
	86-88	First aid in illness and injury
	321-576	Neurology and psychiatry
	952-954	Geriatrics
	955-962	Arctic and tropical medicine
	963-969	Industrial medicine
	970-1015	Military medicine
	1030-1097	Transportation medicine
		Including automotive, aviation and space medicine
	1200-1245	Sports medicine
RD		Surgery
	92-96	Wounds and injuries
	701-796	Orthopedics
RE		Ophthalmology
RF		Otorhinolaryngology
RG		Gynecology and obstetrics
RJ		Pediatrics
RK		Dentistry
RL		Dermatology
RM		Therapeutics. Pharmacology
	214-258	Diet therapy. Diet and dietetics in disease
	270-282	Serum therapy. Immunotherapy
	283-298	Endocrinotherapy
	300-666	Drugs and their action
	695-890	Physical medicine. Physical therapy
	845-862	Medical radiology
RS		Pharmacy and materia medica
RT		Nursing
RV		Botanic, Thomsonian, and eclectic medicine
RX		Homeopathy
RZ		Other systems of medicine
	201-265	Chiropractic
	301-397	Osteopathy
	400-408	Mental healing

Class R—Medicine was developed by J. Christian Bay in 1904. The first edition of Class R was not published until 1910, at which time Clarence Perley prepared the schedule for the printer. The second edition was issued in 1921 under Perley's editorship, and in 1953 the third edition was published. A fourth edition, representing a cumulation of the third edition and the changes made since 1953, is scheduled for publication in 1980.

There are seventeen subclasses in this schedule: Subclass R for general works on medicine; RA for public aspects of medicine; RB for pathology; RC for internal medicine and the practice of medicine; RD for surgery; RE for ophthalmology; RF for otorhinolaryngology; RG for gynecology and obstetrics; RJ for pediatrics; RK for dentistry; RL for dermatology; RM for therapeutics and pharmacology; RS for pharmacy and materia medica; RT for nursing; RV for botanic, Thomsonian, and eclectic medicine; RX for homeopathy; and RZ for other systems of medicine.

There are no major auxiliary tables for this class, although there are many internal tables which employ both double Cutter numbers and successive Cutter numbers.

Class R was developed to classify medical literature within a general library, not in a medical library. There are specialized classifications for medical libraries that are superior to Class R. One of these schemes which is directly related to the Library of Congress Classification is that of another federal library, the National Library of Medicine. This library was formerly the U.S. Army Medical Library. In the early 1940s a survey showed the need for a special classification for the Army Library. In 1948 a preliminary edition of this classification was prepared by Mary Louise Marshall. This edition was modified and revised by Dr. Frank B. Rogers in 1950 and issued as the first edition of the *Army Medical Library Classification* in 1951. The second edition was published in 1956 as the *National Library of Medicine Classification*. The third edition appeared in 1964 and the fourth edition in 1978.

The *National Library of Medicine Classification* makes use of the vacant Class W and Subclasses QS-QZ which have been permanently excluded from the Library of Congress Classification. Class W is used for Medicine and related subjects and Classes QS-QZ for Preclinical sciences. By adopting the L.C. notation, the National Library of Medicine can use the remainder of the L.C. Classification for its nonmedical books, with the exception of Class R (Medicine) and Subclasses QM (Anatomy) and QR (Microbiology).

The following is a synopsis of the *National Library of Medicine Classification*.

PRECLINICAL SCIENCES

QS	Human Anatomy	QW	Bacteriology and Immunology
QT	Physiology	QX	Parasitology
QU	Biochemistry	QY	Clinical Pathology
QV	Pharmacology	QZ	Pathology

MEDICINE AND RELATED SUBJECTS

W	Medical Profession	WD500	Plant Poisoning
WA	Public Health	WD600	Diseases Caused by Physical Agents
WB	Practice of Medicine	WD700	Aviation and Space Medicine
WC	Infectious Diseases	WE	Musculoskeletal System
WD100	Deficiency Diseases	WF	Respiratory System
WD200	Metabolic Diseases	WG	Cardiovascular System

MEDICINE AND RELATED SUBJECTS (cont'd)

WD300	Diseases of Allergy	WH	Hemic and Lymphatic Systems
WD400	Animal Poisoning	WR	Dermatology
WI	Gastrointestinal System	WS	Pediatrics
WJ	Urogenital System	WT	Geriatrics. Chronic Disease
WK	Endocrine System	WU	Denistry. Oral Surgery
WL	Nervous System	WV	Otorhinolaryngology
WM	Psychiatry	WW	Ophthalmology
WN	Radiology	WX	Hospitals
WO	Surgery	WY	Nursing
WP	Gynecology	WZ	History of Medicine
WQ	Obstetrics		

Class W employs many original features for a classification scheme. For instance, serials are not classified but rather are separated by form in one of six broad categories. Books printed prior to the nineteenth century are arranged alphabetically by author within the century. Nineteenth century materials (1801-1913) are divided into 80 broad subject classes. Only twentieth century material is classed in the scheme developed in Class W. Cutter numbers are not used widely for subject subdivisions but usually only for authors. The *Cutter-Sanborn Three-Figure Author Table* is used. There are brief outlines at the beginning of each class. Bibliography in medicine is prefaced by the letter Z, followed by the class number for the particular subject of the bibliography. For example, the American Medical Association's bibliographic work entitled *Health Publications* is classed "ZWB 120 A512h." "Z" means the work is bibliographic in nature; "WB 120" is the class number for "Popular medicine (general)"; "A512" is the author number for the American Medical Association; and "h" is the workmark for the title.

There is only one auxiliary table, Table G for geographic subdivisions. It is used mainly with serial publications of governments and hospital publications.

Most of the major medical libraries in this country use the *National Library of Medicine Classification*. The advantages of using this scheme are the currency of the arrangement of material and use of terminology; its compatibility with the *Medical Subject Headings List*; and the availability of the call numbers appearing on the printed cards of the National Library of Medicine and in the *National Library of Medicine, Current Catalog*. Furthermore, all shared cataloging of medical literature prepared by the National Library of Medicine for the Library of Congress show both Class R and Class W numbers. Class W is well worth the serious study of any student of classification and is an example of a truly current classification scheme. The examples on page 248 illustrate the provision of alternative numbers based on the NLM scheme on Library of Congress cataloging records.

Sandritter, Walter.
    Makropathologie : Lehrbuch u. Atlas f. Studierende u. Ärzte
/ von W. Sandritter u. C. Thomas. Mit 14 Tab. — 3., verb. u. erw.
Aufl. — Stuttgart ; New York : Schattauer, 1975.
    xii, 364 p. : 680 ill. (some col.) ; 27 cm.   GFR75-A
    Bibliography: p. 342-351.
    Includes index.
    ISBN 3-7945-0436-4 : DM98.00

    1. Anatomy, Pathological.   I. Thomas, Carlos, joint author.   II. Title.
    ᵣDNLM: 1. Pathology—Atlases.   QZ17 S219c 1975ᵣ

ᵣRB25.S26 1975ᵣ   616.07   75-596087
                                                        MARC

Passman, Jerome.
    The EKG—basic techniques for interpretation : a practical
guide for interpreting and analyzing the electrocardiogram /
Jerome Passman, Constance D. Drummond ; foreword by Alvin
H. Freiman. — New York : McGraw-Hill, ᵣ1976ᵣ
    xv, 316 p. : ill. ; 23 cm.
    "A Blakiston Publication."
    Bibliography: p. 306.
    Includes index.
    ISBN 0-07-048715-4

    1. Electrocardiography.   I. Drummond, Constance D., joint author.   II.
Title.
    ᵣDNLM: 1. Electrocardiography.   WG140 P288eᵣ
    RC683.5.E5P34   616.1'2'0754   75-16068
                                                        MARC

CLASS S — AGRICULTURE

S		Agriculture (General)
	560-575	Farm management. Farm economics
	583-589	Agricultural chemistry and physics
	590-599	Soils
	605-621	Reclamation and irrigation of farm land
		Including organic farming
	622-627	Soil conservation
	631-667	Fertilizers and soil improvement
	671-760	Farm machinery and engineering
	900-972	Conservation of natural resources
		For wildlife conservation, *see* QL; for marine resources conservation, *see* SH; for mineral resources conservation, *see* TN
	950-954	Land conservation
	970-972	Recreational resources conservation
SB		Plant culture
	110-112	Methods for special areas
		Including dry-land and tropical agriculture, irrigation farming
	114-118	Seeds
	119-125	Propagation
	183-317	Field crops
	318-450	Horticulture
	320-353	Vegetables
	354-402	Fruit culture and orchard care
	403-450	Flowers. Ornamental plants
	449-450	Flower arrangement and decoration
	451-466	Gardens and gardening
	469-479	Landscape gardening
	481-485	Parks and public reservations
	599-999	Diseases and pests
		Including treatment and control
SD		Forestry
	391-409	Sylviculture
	411-428	Conservation and protection
		Including forest reserves
	430-557	Exploitation and utilization
		Including timber trees, logging, transportation, valuation
	561-668	Forest policy and administration
SF		Animal culture
	91-92	Housing and environmental control
	95-99	Feeds and feeding. Animal nutrition
	105-109	Breeds and breeding
		Including artificial insemination, stock farms
	114-121	Exhibitions. Judging. Stock shows
	191-275	Cattle
	221-275	Dairying. Dairy products
	277-359	Horses
		Including horsemanship, racing
	371-379	Sheep. Wool
	381-386	Goats
	391-397	Swine
	402-405	Fur-bearing animals
	405.5-407	Laboratory animals
	411-459	Pets
	461-513	Birds
		Including cage birds, pigeons, poultry, game birds
	521-561	Insects
		Including bees, silkworm, cochineal
	600-1100	Veterinary medicine
SH		Aquaculture. Fisheries. Angling
		Including shellfish, lobsters, crabs, sealing, whaling
	401-691	Angling
SK		Hunting
	351-579	Wildlife management. Game protection

S. C. Stuntz of the United States Department of Agriculture developed **Class S — Agriculture — Plant and Animal Industry** on a plan outlined by the Chief Classifier, Charles Martel. Stuntz used existing bibliographies and classification schemes to formulate the details of the subclasses. One subclass, SD, Forestry, was based on "corresponding sections of the systematic catalog of the K. Sachsische Forstakademie (more recently known as the Forstliche Hochschule) at Tarandt" (Preface to the third edition).

The first edition of Class S was published in 1911. George M. Churchill prepared this edition for the printer. The second edition was issued in 1928 under the editorship of Clarence Perley. L. Belle Voegelein prepared the third edition of this class, which was published in 1948. This edition was reprinted with additions and changes in 1965.

Six main classes make up Class S: Subclass S for agriculture in general; SB for plant culture; SD for forestry; SF for animal culture; SH for aquaculture, fisheries, and angling; and SK for hunting.

There are no major problems in the use of this schedule. There are only two auxiliary tables. These geographical distribution tables were used as examples of auxiliary tables in chapter 4. For a discussion and examples of using these tables, *see* pages 109-110.

Hunting and Fishing

The sports of hunting and fishing are included in the schedules for Subclasses SH, Fish culture and fisheries; and SK, Hunting. This is probably a far more useful location for this material than classing hunting and fishing with other sports in Subclass GV.

The index for Class S is detailed and specific; it does, however, contain some summaries of the classification.

CLASS T – TECHNOLOGY

T		Technology (General)
	54-55	Industrial safety
	55.4-60	Industrial engineering
		Including operations research, systems analysis, management information systems, production efficiency, human engineering in industry, work measurement, methods engineering
	201-339	Patents. Trademarks
	351-385	Engineering graphics. Mechanical drawing
	391-995	Exhibitions. World's fairs
TA		Engineering (General). Civil engineering (General)
	166-167	Human engineering
	168	Systems engineering
	177.4-185	Engineering economy
	349-360	Mechanics of engineering. Applied mechanics
	401-492	Materials of engineering and construction
		Including strength of materials, testing and properties of materials
	501-625	Surveying
	630-695	Structural engineering (General)
	705-710	Engineering geology. Rock mechanics. Soil mechanics
	715-787	Earthwork. Foundations
	800-820	Tunneling. Tunnels
	1001-1280	Transportation engineering (General)
	1501-1820	Applied optics. Lasers
		Including applied holography, optical data processing
	2001-2030	Plasma engineering. Applied plasma dynamics
TC		Hydraulic engineering
		Including harbors and coast protective works, water-supply engineering, dams, canals, irrigation projects, drainage, ocean engineering
TD		Environmental technology. Sanitary engineering
	159-167	Municipal engineering
	172-195	Environmental pollution
	201-500	Water supply for domestic and industrial purposes
		Including water quality and pollution, treatment, saline water conversion, distribution systems
	511-780	Sewage collection and disposal systems. Sewerage
	785-812	Municipal refuse. Solid wastes
	813-870	Street cleaning. Litter and its removal
	877.5-893	Special types of pollution
		Including soil, air, noise pollution
	895-899	Industrial sanitation. Industrial wastes
TE		Highway engineering. Roads and pavements
TF		Railroad engineering and operation
		Including street railways and subways
TG		Bridge engineering
TH		Building construction
	845-895	Architectural engineering. Structural engineering of buildings
	1000-1725	Systems of building construction
		Including fireproof, wood, masonry, concrete and steel construction

(Outline continues on page 252)

Technology

Building construction—*continued*

TH	2031-3000	Details
		Including foundations, walls, chimneys, roofs, floors
	4021-4970	Buildings: Construction with reference to use
		Including public buildings, factories, dwellings, farm buildings
	5011-5701	Construction by phase of work (Building trades)
		Including masonry, carpentry, metalworking
	6014-7975	Environmental engineering
		Including plumbing, heating, ventilation, lighting
	9025-9745	Protection of buildings
		Including protection from dampness, fire prevention and extinction, protection from burglary
TJ		Mechanical engineering and machinery
	212-225	Control engineering
	268-740	Steam engineering
		Including boilers, engines, locomotives
	1125-1345	Machine shops and machine-shop practice
		Including machine and hand tools
	1480-1496	Agricultural machinery
TK		Electrical engineering. Electronics. Nuclear engineering
	1001-1841	Production of electric energy. Powerplants
	2000-2891	Dynamoelectric machinery
		Including generators, motors, transformers
	3001-3521	Distribution or transmission of electric power. The electric power circuit
	4125-4399	Electric lighting
	5101-6720	Telecommunication
	7800-8360	Electronics
	7885-7895	Computer engineering
	9001-9401	Nuclear engineering. Atomic power
TL		Motor vehicles. Aeronautics. Astronautics
	1-390	Motor vehicles
	500-777	Aeronautics
	780-785	Rockets
	787-4050	Astronautics
TN		Mining engineering. Metallurgy
		Including the mineral industries
TP		Chemical technology
	155-156	Chemical engineering
	200-248	Manufacture and use of chemicals
	315-360	Fuel
	368-456	Food processing and manufacture
	480-498	Low temperature engineering. Refrigeration
	500-659	Fermentation industries. Beverages
	690-692	Petroleum refining and products
	700-762	Gas industry
	785-888	Clay industries. Ceramics. Glass. Cement industries
	890-933	Textile dyeing and printing
	934-944	Paints, pigments, varnishes, etc.
	1080-1185	Polymers, plastics and their manufacture
TR		Photography
TS		Manufactures
	155-193	Production management
		Including quality control, production control, inventory control, product engineering, process engineering, plant engineering

		Technology
		Manufactures—*continued*
TS	195-198	Packaging
	200-770	Metal manufactures. Metalworking
		Including forging, casting, stamping, instrument making, firearms, clocks, metal finishing, jewelry
	800-937	Wood technology
		Including lumber, furniture, chemical processing of wood
	940-1070	Leather industries. Tanning
	1080-1268	Paper manufacture. Woodpulp industry
	1300-1865	Textile industries
	1870-1935	Rubber industry
	1950-1982	Animal products
	2120-2159	Cereals and flour. Milling industry
	2220-2283	Tobacco industry
TT		Handicrafts. Arts and crafts
	161-170	Manual training. Industrial arts. School shops
	180-200	Woodworking. Furniture making. Upholstering
	205-267	Metalworking
	300-385	Painting. Industrial painting
	387-410	Soft home furnishings
	490-695	Clothing manufacture. Dressmaking. Tailoring
	697-924	Needlework. Decorative crafts
	950-979	Hairdressing. Barbers' work
	980-999	Laundry work
TX		Home economics
	301-339	The house
		Including arrangement, care, pests, finance, servants
	341-641	Nutrition. Foods and food supply
	645-840	Cookery
	901-953	Hotels, restaurants, taverns. Food service
	955-985	Building operation and maintenance
	1100-1107	Mobile home living

The original schedules for **Class T—Technology** were first the responsibility of Clarence Perley; he developed the schedules for Subclasses T through TT in 1903. S. C. Stuntz completed the schedules with the development of Subclass TX, Domestic science. In 1905 H. H. B. Meyer restructured the schedules into four main classes: the Engineering and Building group, the Mechanical group, the Chemical group, and the Composite group. Subclasses TH, Building construction, and TK, Electrical engineering and industries, and the part of TA relating to structures and materials, "Engineering (General). Civil engineering" were developed by A. Lau Voge in 1907. At this point Perley again became the editor for the schedule and prepared it for the printer. The first edition of Class T appeared in 1910; the second edition was issued in 1922. In 1937 the third edition was published and the fourth edition appeared in 1948. The fifth edition, with updated terminology and spot developments, prepared under the direction of Eugene T. Frosio, was published in 1971.

Auxiliary Tables

The auxiliary tables create no serious problems in use and are often used as an introduction to the use of auxiliary tables in L.C. Classification. The following portion of Table I, "History and Country Divisions," demonstrates this.

TABLE I

HISTORY AND COUNTRY DIVISIONS

```
                     History
      15                 General works
      16                 Ancient
      17                 Medieval
      18                 Modern
      19                 19th century
      20                 20th century
                     Special countries
                         Under each country with two numbers:
                             (1)  General works
                             (2)  Local or special, A-Z
                         The numbers for "Cities or other special," "Local or
                         special," "Provinces or special" may be used in some
                         cases for the local subdivision, in other cases for
                         special canals, rivers, harbors, railroads, or bridges,
                         as specified in the particular scheme to which this table
                         is applied
                         Under both general and local subdivisions arrange as
                             follows:
                             .A1-5  Official documents
                             .A6-Z  Nonofficial.  By author, A-Z
                         e. g. TD257.A5, 1966, Gt. Brit.  Water Resources Board.
                             Water supplies in South East England
                             TD264.T5P6, 1967, Port of London Authority.  The
                             cleaner Thames.
                             TD224.C3A53, 1963, California.  Dept of Water
                             Resources.  Alameda County investigation

      21             America
      22               North America
      23                 United States
       .1                  Eastern states.  Atlantic coast
       .15                 New England
       .2                  Appalachian region
       .3                  Great Lakes region
       .4                  Midwest.  Mississippi Valley
       .5                  South.  Gulf states
       .6                  West
       .7                  Northwest
       .8                  Pacific coast
       .9                  Southwest
      24                   States, A-W
                             e. g.   .A4  Alaska
                                     .H3  Hawaii
      25                   Cities (or other special), A-Z
      26                 Canada
      27                   Provinces (or other special), A-Z
       .5               Latin America
      28-29             Mexico
      30                Central America
      31                  Special countries, A-Z
```

This table is used, for instance, to classify works about study and teaching of home economics. In the schedule, the following numbers are designated for this subject:

TX   Home Economics

	Study and teaching
165.A1A-Z	Periodicals, societies, etc.
.A3-Z	General works
167	Textbooks
170	Examinations, questions, etc.
171-274	Special countries. Table I
	(Add 150 to numbers in the table.)

For example, the U.S. Office of Education, Division of Vocational Education's *Homemaking Education in Secondary Schools of the United States* is classed in "TX173.A5 1947." "23" is the number in Table I for the United States. "23" added to "150" gives the number "TX173" for study and teaching of home economics in the United States. ".A5" is the use of an official Cutter number.

U.S. Office of Education. Division of Vocational Education. *Homemaking Education in Secondary Schools of the United States.*

TX	The double letters for the subclass, Home economics
150	The designated base number in the schedule
23	The number from Table I for the United States
173	
173	The integral number meaning study and teaching of home economics in the United States
.A5	The "A" Cutter number for an official publication (*See* instruction in Table I)
1947	The date of publication

Mary Stewart Lyle's *Educational Needs of Three Socio-economic Groups of Rural Homemakers in Iowa* is an example of study and teaching of home economics in an individual state of the United States. "24" is the number in Table I for individual states of the United States. When this number is added to the base number "150," the result is "TX174." The complete call number is "TX174.I8L9."

M. S. Lyle's *Educational Needs of Three Socio-economic Groups of Rural Homemakers in Iowa.*

TX	The double letters for the subclass, Home economics
150	The designated base number in the schedule
24	The number from Table I for individual states of the United States
174	
174	The integral number meaning study and teaching of home economics in an individual state of the United States
.I8	The first Cutter number for the individual state, Iowa
L9	The second Cutter number for the main entry, Lyle

Another aspect of using this schedule is the distinction to be made between pure and applied science. Class Q, Science, is normally used for pure science; applied science is classed in Class T, Technology. However, the additional science schedules create further distinctions. For example, Werner Von Bergen's *American Wool Handbook* is classed in "TS 1631 .V6" in the technology subclass for manufactures; however, Archer Butler Gilfillan's *Sheep Culture* is properly classed in "SF 375 .G5," the correct number in the agricultural subclass for animal culture.

The index to this schedule is also detailed and specific.

CLASS U — MILITARY SCIENCE

For military history, *see* D-F

U		Military science (General)
	750-773	Military life, manners and customs
	800-897	History of arms and armor
UA		Armies: Organization, description, facilities, etc.
		Including the military situation, policy, defenses of individual countries
UB		Military administration
UC		Maintenance and transportation
UD		Infantry
UE		Cavalry. Armored and mechanized cavalry
UF		Artillery
UG		Military engineering
		Including fortification, chemical warfare, signaling
	622-1425	Air forces. Air warfare
UH		Other services
		Including medical and sanitary service, public relations, social welfare services, recreation

CLASS V — NAVAL SCIENCE

For naval history, *see* D-F

V		Naval science (General)
	720-743	Naval life, manners and customs
	750-995	War vessels: Construction, armament, etc.
	990-995	Fleet ballistic missile systems
VA		Navies: Organization, description, facilities, etc.
		Including the naval situation and policy of individual countries
VB		Naval administration
VC		Naval maintenance
VD		Naval seamen
VE		Marines
VF		Naval ordnance
VG		Minor services of navies
		Including communications, bands, air service, medical service, public relations, social work, recreation
VK		Navigation. Merchant marine
	588-597	Marine hydrography. Hydrographic surveying
	600-794	Tide and current tables
	798-997	Pilot guides. Sailing directions
	1000-1249	Lighthouse service
	1250-1299	Shipwrecks and fires
	1300-1491	Saving of life and property
	1500-1661	Pilots and pilotage
VM		Naval architecture. Shipbuilding. Marine engineering
	975-989	Diving

Class U — Military Science was originally developed by Charles Martel in 1903 and was first issued in 1910. "The extensive additions incident to the military developments of the First World War made it necessary to issue a second edition in 1928" (Preface). The third edition was published in 1952 under the editorship of L. Belle Voegelein. The fourth edition, published in 1974, incorporates additions and changes made from 1952 through June 1973. The major change in this edition is the revision and expansion of Subclass UG to provide for material on aerial warfare and the air forces of the world.

Class V — Naval Science was first planned in 1904 by S. C. Stuntz under the direction of Charles Martel. In 1905 Clarence Perley took charge of this schedule and served as the editor of the first edition in 1910. The second edition was issued in 1953 under Voegelein's editorship. The third edition was published in 1974. No major rearrangement occurred in this edition.

The *Classification and Index* of the Military Information Division of the Adjutant-General's Office of U.S. War Department served as the basis for Class U, as well as for most of Class V. Subclass VK, Navigation, was based on the order of the publications of the British Hydrographic Office.

There are nine subclasses in Class U: Subclass U for general military science; UA for armies; UB for military administration; UC for maintenance and transportation; UD for infantry; UE for cavalry and armored and mechanized cavalry; UF for artillery; UG for military engineering and air forces and air warfare; and UH for other services.

There are ten subclasses in Class V: Subclass V for general naval science; VA for navies; VB for naval administration; VC for naval maintenance; VD for naval seamen; VE for marines; VF for naval ordnance; VG for minor services of navies; VK for navigation and the Merchant Marine; and VM for naval architecture, shipbuilding, and marine engineering.

Neither of these two short schedules is difficult to use. Each contains three tables of subdivisions: Region and Country Subdivisions, Countries in One Alphabet, and States of the United States. "Divide like" notes occur frequently in these schedules; for example, numbers for the National Guard of any state are arranged like the numbers for the first listed state, Alabama, "UA 50-59."

One very detailed internal table using Cutter numbers is for material concerning West Point. The following is a portion of that development of Cutter numbers.

U MILITARY SCIENCE (GENERAL)

	United States. Military Academy, West Point
410(.A1)	Act of incorporation, *see* KF7313
	Administration
.C3	Regulations
.C4	General orders
.C5	Conduct grades
.C7	Circulars
.C8	Memoranda
.E1	Annual report of Superintendent
.E3	Annual report of Inspectors
.E4	Annual report of Board of Visitors
.E45	Special reports, hearings, etc., of Board of Visitors
.E5	General congressional documents. By date
.E9	Documents relating to hazing. By date
.F3	Commencement orations
.F5	Miscellaneous addresses and speeches
.F7	Other documents, reports, etc.
	Including semiofficial material

U   MILITARY SCIENCE (GENERAL) (cont'd)

	United States. Military Academy, West Point (cont'd)
.F8	Special days and events. By date
.G3	Information for graduates
	* * * * * * *
.L1	General works on the academy. Histories
	.A1-5 Official works
.L3	Illustrated works. Views
	Biography
	Cf. U410.H3-8, Registers
.M1A1-5	Collective
.M1A6-Z	Individual, A-Z

For example, an official history entitled *Building Leaders: The Story of West Point*, issued in 1949, uses the Cutter number ".L1." The complete call number is "U410.L1A4 1949." "A4" is used to indicate that this is an official work.

> U.S. Military Academy, West Point. *Building Leaders: The Story of West Point*, 1949.

U	The single letter for the subclass, Military science (general)
410	The integral number meaning the U.S. Military Academy, West Point
.L1	The first Cutter number meaning a history
A4	The second Cutter number meaning this is an official work
1949	The date of publication

A history of West Point that is not an official work, such as Sidney Forman's *West Point: A History of the United States Military Academy* is classed in "U410.L1F6."

> Sidney Forman's *West Point: A History of the United States Military Academy*.

U	The single letter for the subclass, Military science (general)
410	The integral number meaning the U.S. Military Academy, West Point
.L1	The first Cutter number meaning a history
F6	The second Cutter number for the main entry, Forman

In the case of a collective biography both Cutter numbers are taken from the schedule.

R. E. Dupuy's *Men of West Point*.

U	The single letter for the subclass, Military science (general)
410	The integral number meaning the U.S. Military Academy, West Point
.M1	The first Cutter number for biography
A3	The second Cutter number meaning a collective biography

An autobiographical work by Marty Maher, *Bringing Up the Brass: My 55 Years at West Point*, is classed in "U410.M1M3."

Marty Maher's *Bringing Up the Brass: My 55 Years at West Point*.

U	The single letter for the subclass, Military science (general)
410	The integral number meaning the U.S. Military Academy, West Point
.M1	The first Cutter number for biography
M3	The second Cutter number for the subject and author of the biography, Maher

One interesting device used in Subclass UF, Artillery, under the number "565" is the possibility of a Cutter number with double workmarks. Under the heading for Ordnance material the following is listed:

565		Other countries, A-Z.
	e.g.	Great Britain gun handbooks.
		.G7 By inches.
		.G72 By pounds.

Further subdivision is made by adding the following letters as needed:

B.L.	Breech loading.
M.L.	Muzzle loading.
Q.F.	Quick firing.
H.	Hotchkiss.
N.	Nordenfelt.

Guns of different marks have the numbers added in parentheses; thus, for marks II to IV add (2-4).

Arrange different editions by date.

Obviously, these directions could cause unusual original notations to result depending on the particular foreign gun handbook.

The indexes to both these schedules are adequate. Their form is similar to the other indexes in the sciences.

CLASS Z—BIBLIOGRAPHY. LIBRARY SCIENCE

Z		
		Books in general
	4-8	History of books and bookmaking
	40-115	Writing
	41-42	Autographs. Signatures
	43-45	Calligraphy. Penmanship
	48	Copying processes
	49-51	Typewriting
	53-102	Shorthand
	103-104	Cryptography
	105-115	Paleography
		Book industries and trade
	116-265	Printing
	266-276	Bookbinding
	278-549	Bookselling and publishing
	662-1000	Libraries and library science
	679-680	Architecture and planning of the library
	687-718	The collections. The books
		Including acquisition, cataloging, classification, shelflisting, information storage and retrieval systems, reference work, circulation
	719-876	Libraries
		Including histories, reports, statistics of individual libraries
	881-980	Library catalogs and bulletins
	987-997	Private libraries. Book collecting
	998-1000	Booksellers' catalogs. Book prices
	1001-8999	Bibliography
	1041-1107	Anonyms and pseudonyms
	1201-4980	National bibliography
	5051-7999	Subject bibliography
	8001-8999	Personal bibliography

Class Z—Bibliography and Library Science was the first schedule of L.C. Classification to be prepared. It was completed in 1898 and published in 1902. Charles Martel developed the original schedules for this class. The second edition was issued in 1910 and the third edition in 1926. The fourth and present edition was published in 1959. A fifth edition, representing a cumulation of the previous edition and the changes made since 1959, is scheduled for publication in 1981.

Class Z is designed to contain all bibliographies classed in Library of Congress Classification. A discussion of the historical development of this schedule is contained in the first chapter of this book. There are separate ranges of numbers for National Bibliography (Z 1201-4941), Subject Bibliography (Z 5051-7999), and Personal Bibliography (Z 8001-8999).

It should be noted that Class M, Music, and Class K, Law, contain numbers for bibliographies on these subjects. The Library of Congress uses these numbers instead of those in Class Z.

National Bibliography

There are six auxiliary tables to be used with Class Z: Tables I, II, and III for National Bibliography, and Tables IV, V, and VI to be used with Subject Bibliography. The basic use of all six of these tables as illustrated by Table I is usually direct numerical transfer or matching of final digits. The following is an abridgment of Table I.

Table I

(1)	General bibliography.
(2)	Bibliography of early works.
(3)	Publishers' catalogs.
(5)	Periodicals.
(6)	Societies.
(7)	Collections.
(9)	Government publications.
(10)	Biobibliography.
(11)	Literature (General).
	By period.
(12)	Early to 1800.
(13)	1801-1950.
(13.3)	1951- .
(14)	Special topics, A-Z.
(15)	Philology.
(16)	History and description (General).
	By period.
(17)	To 1500.
(17.5)	16th century.
(18)	17th-18th centuries.
(19)	19th century.
(20)	Early 20th century.
(20.3)	1945- .
(21)	Special topics not in (17)-(20), A-Z.
	Local.
(23)	General.
(24)	Special, A-Z.
(27)	Special topics not otherwise provided for, A-Z.
(29)	Catalogs.

In the schedules, Great Britain is assigned a range of numbers "Z 2001-2029" for national bibliography. The classifier is instructed in the schedules to use Table I with this range of numbers. The *British National Bibliography Cumulated Subject Catalogue* is classed in "Z2001.B752." In this case the first number in Table I for general bibliography is applied to the first number in Great Britain's range.

British National Bibliography Cumulated Subject Catalogue.

Z	The single letter for the class, Bibliography and library science
2001	The integral number meaning a general British national bibliography
.B752	The Cutter number for the main entry, *British....*

Pollard and Redgrave's *Short Title Catalogue* is classed as a bibliography of early works, the second number in Table I. Great Britain's second number is "Z 2002." The complete call number is "Z 2002 .P77 1976."

Pollard and Redgrave's *Short Title Catalogue*, 1976.

Z	The single letter for the class, Bibliography and library science
2002	The integral number meaning British national bibliography of early works
.P77	The Cutter number for the main entry, Pollard
1976	The date of publication

Literature, philology, and history are all treated as subdivisions of Table I for national bibliography. This material, if of a national scope, is then treated by the Library of Congress as national bibliography and not subject bibliography. The eleventh number of Table I is for general national bibliography of literature. "Z 2011" is the eleventh number in Great Britain's range. George Watson's *The Concise Cambridge Bibliography of English Literature, 600-1950* is classed in "Z 2011 .W3."

George Watson's *The Concise Cambridge Bibliography of English Literature.*

Z	The single letter for the class, Bibliography and library science
2011	The integral number meaning a general bibliography of British literature
.W3	The Cutter number for the main entry, Watson

The Royal Historical Society's *Writings on British History, 1901-1933* is classed in a general national bibliography of history using the sixteenth number in Table I. Great Britain's sixteenth number is "Z 2016."

Writings on British History, 1901-1933.

Z	The single letter for the class, Bibliography and library science
2016	The integral number meaning a general bibliography of British history
.W74	The Cutter number for the main entry, *Writings....*

Finally, William Matthew's *British Autobiographies: An Annotated Bibliography* uses the twenty-seventh number for "special topics not otherwise provided for, A-Z." It is classed in "Z 2027 .A9M3." ".A9" in this case is the Cutter number for the subject of the special topic, autobiography.

William Matthew's *British Autobiographies: An Annotated Bibliography*.

Z	The single letter for the class, Bibliography and library science
2027	The integral number for British bibliographies of special topics not provided for otherwise
.A9	The first Cutter number for the special topic, autobiography
M3	The second Cutter number for the compiler, Matthew

Class Z has received many criticisms, mainly because of its collocation by form — bibliography — rather than by subject. The fact that all subject bibliographies are classed together in Class Z and separate from the subject classes is considered by many to be a weakness. However, where all bibliographies are shelved in a reference collection, a separate class for them is most useful.

Recognizing the need of many libraries to collocate subject bibliographies with their appropriate subjects, the Library of Congress now provides alternative class numbers for certain bibliographical materials. Alternative subject class numbers appear in brackets immediately following the LC call numbers on LC cataloging records.

The alternative class numbers are provided for all bibliographies, indexes, and book catalogs, with LC call numbers falling within the following ranges of numbers:

Z1201-4990, National bibliography (except in the case of bibliographies having no topical focus)

Z5001-7999, Subject bibliography

Z8001-8999, Personal bibliography

The following are examples of alternative numbers for bibliographies:

J. A. Baird's *Northern California Art: An Interpretive Bibliography to 1915*.

Z5961.C2B34	LC call number
[N6530.C2]	Alternative number in Class N, Fine Arts

The alternative number is given even if the Z number itself is an alternative number, as in the case of an analytic of a collected monographic series.

T. A. Beehr's *Empirical Research on Job Stress and Employee Health: A Selected Bibliography* (Exchange Bibliography — Council of Planning Librarians, 1515).

Z5942.C68 no. 1515	LC call number for the series
[Z6663.S83]	Alternative number for the analytic entry
[QP82.2.S8]	Alternative number in Subclass QP, Physiology

Normally, the "General works" number under the appropriate subject is selected as the alternative number, since there is generally no form subdivision for bibliographies in the subject classes. The numbers for special forms, e.g., periodicals, directories, pictorial works, etc., are not used for this purpose. In the case where General works in a discipline are represented by a span of numbers, the most general number (often with the caption "Treatises" or a variation thereof) is selected.

As a rule, the alternative number does not include the book number since it is not a valid LC call number.

Alternative numbers for special types of bibliographies are selected according to the following table:

Special Materials	Assign as the Alternative No.:
National bibliography without topical focus, e.g. imprints of individual countries	No number.
Subject bibliography, including topical works classed in National bibliography	Corresponding number for topic in regular classes, A-Z1121. If topic at level of interest has a span of numbers, assign the number for General works.
Personal bibliography	Corresponding biography number of the regular classes. If the person has a span of numbers, assign the General works number.
Belles lettres	The General works number under History and criticism in Class P, as appropriate for the language, form and period discussed.
Children's literature	PN1009, and appropriate numbers for special forms in P subclasses.
Government publications (i.e. comprehensive bibliographies of individual countries)	The appropriate number in J, e.g. J83, U.S. agencies collectively. For bibliographies of individual agencies, see the topic, A-Z1121.
Dissertations of general institutions	General collections from a single institution: AS11+. Comprehensive collections from many institutions of a country: assign no number.
Newspapers	PN4700+

LC Publications

A special *Classification Scheme for Library of Congress Publications* appears at the end of the Z schedule. It is a detailed development of the class number Z663. This is to be used for complete sets of all Library of Congress publications. Libraries that do not possess an extensive collection of LC publications may wish to class them by subject in Classes B-Z. When an LC publication is assigned this special number, an alternative subject class number is also provided on the LC cataloging record.

The index to Class Z is fairly complete and specific and contains many useful references.

BIBLIOGRAPHY

Class A

U.S. Library of Congress. Classification Division. *Classification. Class A: General Works, Polygraphy.* Washington: GPO, 1911.

U.S. Library of Congress. Classification Division. *Classification. Class A: General Works, Polygraphy. Adopted 1911. As in force June 1915.* Washington: GPO, 1915.

U.S. Library of Congress. Subject Cataloging Division. *Classification. Class A: General Works, Polygraphy.* 3rd ed. Washington: GPO, 1947, reprinted with supplementary pages, 1963.

U.S. Library of Congress. Subject Cataloging Division. *Classification. Class A: General Works.* 4th ed. Washington: Library of Congress, 1973.

Class B

U.S. Library of Congress. Classification Division. *Classification. Class B, Part I, B−BJ: Philosophy.* Printed as manuscript. Washington: GPO, 1910.

U.S. Library of Congress. Subject Cataloging Division. *Classification. Class B, Part I, B−BJ: Philosophy.* 2nd ed. Washington: GPO, 1950, reprinted with supplementary pages, 1968.

U.S. Library of Congress. Subject Cataloging Division. *Classification. Class B, Subclasses B−BJ: Philosophy. Psychology.* 3rd ed. Washington: Library of Congress, 1979.

U.S. Library of Congress. Classification Division. *Classification. Class B, Part II, BL−BX: Religion.* Printed as manuscript. Washington: GPO, 1927.

U.S. Library of Congress. Subject Cataloging Division. *Classification. Class B, Part II, BL−BX: Religion.* 2nd ed. Washington: GPO, 1962.

Class B: Readings

Butz, Helen S. "Princeton Theological Seminary Library and the Library of Congress Classification for·Church History." Unpublished master's thesis, Drexel Institute of Technology, 1955.

Davis, N. E. "Modification and Expansions of the Library of Congress Classification Schedule at the University of Chicago," *Proceedings of the Seventh Annual Conference, American Theological Library Association, Evanston, Illinois, June 11-12, 1953*. Dayton, OH: Bonebrake Theological Seminary, 1953. pp. 23-24.

Headicar, B. M. "Library of Congress Classification: Classes B, N, R, and Z," *Library Association Record* 12:515-16, 1910.

Mueller, Theodore A. "Workshop on the Library of Congress Classification and Its New BL – BX Schedules," *Summary of Proceedings, Fifteenth Annual Conference, American Theological Library Association, Wesley Theological Seminary, Washington, D.C., June 13-15, 1961*. Austin, TX: Episcopal Theological Seminary of the Southwest, 1961. pp. 68-83.
This is a detailed discussion on the classification of religion with many invaluable statements by the principal developer of the second edition of Subclasses BL – BX.

Satory, M. Max. "Class B – Philosophy and Religion of the Library of Congress Classification Schedules," *Library Journal* 62:450-53, June 1, 1937.

Stouffer, M. I. "Princeton and the Library of Congress Schedule," *Summary of Proceedings, Seventh Annual Conference, American Theological Library Association, Evanston, Illinois, June 11-12, 1953*. Dayton, OH: Bonebrake Theological Seminary, 1953. pp. 21-23.

Stouffer, M. I. "Round Table on Library of Congress Classification," *Summary of Proceedings, Ninth Annual Conference, American Theological Library Association (Union Theological Seminary), New York, New York, June 15-17, 1955*. Maywood, IL: Chicago Lutheran Theological Seminary, 1955. pp. 46-47.

Turner, D. "Report of Round Table on Library of Congress Classification," *Summary of Proceedings, Third Annual Conference, American Theological Library Association (Chicago Theological Seminary), Chicago, Illinois, June 20-21, 1949*. Evanston, IL: Garrett Biblical Institute, 1949. p. 47.

Uhrich, H. B. "Abridgement of the LC Schedule in Religion," *Summary of Proceedings, Seventh Annual Conference, American Theological Library Association, Evanston, Illinois, June 11-12, 1953*. Dayton, OH: Bonebrake Theological Seminary, 1953. pp. 24-27.

Class B: Modifications of BL – BX

Jacobsen, Karl Theodor. *Library of Congress Classification Schedules for the Lutheran Church, Modified and Expanded, Together with an Alphabetical List of Lutheran Synodical Organizations*. Monograph series, Vol. 2, No. 4. Minneapolis: Board of Christian Education, Evangelical Lutheran Church, 1953.

Lynn, Jeannette Murphy. *An Alternate Classification for Catholic Books: Ecclesiastical Literature, Theology, Canon Law, Church History. For Use with the Dewey Decimal, Classification Decimale, Library of Congress Classifications.* 2nd ed., rev. by Gilbert C. Peterson. Washington: Catholic University of America Press, 1954. (1965 supplement by Thomas G. Pater.)

Markley, Lucy W. *A Methodist Book Classification.* 2nd ed., rev. by Delbert E. Hollenberg. Evanston, IL: The Library, Garrett Theological Seminary, 1964.

Peterson, K. G. "Further Expansion of Library of Congress Classification Schedules for the Lutheran Church Based upon the Modification and Expansion as Compiled by Karl T. Jacobsen." Berkeley, CA: Pacific Lutheran Theological Seminary, n.d.

Class C

U.S. Library of Congress. Classification Division. *Classification. Class C: Auxiliary Sciences of History.* Printed as manuscript. Washington: GPO, 1915.

U.S. Library of Congress. Subject Cataloging Division. *Classification. Class C: Auxiliary Sciences of History. Subclass CN: Epigraphy.* Washington: GPO, 1942.

U.S. Library of Congress. Subject Cataloging Division. *Classification. Class C: Auxiliary Sciences of History.* 2nd ed. Washington: GPO, 1948, reprinted with supplementary pages, 1967.

U.S. Library of Congress. Subject Cataloging Division. *Classification. Class C: Auxiliary Sciences of History.* 3rd ed. Washington: Library of Congress, 1975.

Class D

U.S. Library of Congress. Classification Division. *Classification. Class D: Universal and Old World History.* Printed as manuscript. Washington: GPO, 1916.

U.S. Library of Congress. Classification Division. *Classification. Universal and Old World History. European War, D501-659.* Printed as manuscript. Washington: GPO, 1921.

U.S. Library of Congress. Subject Cataloging Division. *Classification. Universal and Old World History. European War, D501-725.* 2nd ed. as in force August 1933. Washington: GPO, 1933, reprinted with supplementary pages, 1954.

U.S. Library of Congress. Subject Cataloging Division. *Classification. Class D, Supplement 2, Second World War.* Preliminary edition as of June 1946. Washington: GPO, 1947.

U.S. Library of Congress. Subject Cataloging Division. *Classification. History: Class D, General and Old World.* 2nd ed. Washington: GPO, 1959, reprinted with supplementary pages, 1966.

Class D: Readings

Veryha, Wasyl. "Library of Congress Classification and Subject Headings Relating to Slavic and Eastern Europe," *Library Resources & Technical Services* 16:470-87, Fall 1972.

Comment by E. J. Blume, *Library Resources & Technical Services* 17: 268, Spring 1973.

Veryha, Wasyl. "Problems in Classification of Slavic Books with Library of Congress Classification Schedules and Subject Headings," *College and Research Libraries* 28:277-83, July 1967.

Veryha, Wasyl. "Proposal for the Revision of the Library of Congress Classification Schedule in History for Eastern Europe," *Library Resources & Technical Services* 21:354-67, Fall 1977.

Class E — F

U.S. Library of Congress. Classification Division. *America: History and Geography*. Preliminary and Provisional Scheme of Classification, January 1901. Washington: GPO, 1901.

U.S. Library of Congress. Classification Division. *Classification. Class E—F: America*. 2nd ed. Printed as manuscript. Washington: GPO, 1913.

U.S. Library of Congress. Subject Cataloging Division. *Classification. History: Class E—F, America*. 3rd ed. Washington: GPO, 1958, reprinted with supplementary pages, 1965.

Class E — F: Readings

Yeh, Thomas Yen-Ran. "The Treatment of the American Indian in the Library of Congress E-F Schedule," *Library Resources & Technical Services* 15: 122-28, Spring 1971.

Comment by Eugene T. Frosio, pp. 128-31.

Class G

U.S. Library of Congress. Classification Division. *Classification. Class G: Geography, Anthropology, Sports and Games*. Printed as manuscript. Washington: GPO, 1910.

U.S. Library of Congress. Classification Division. *Classification GR: Folk-lore, GT: Manners and Customs. Completing Class G: Geography, Anthropology, Sports and Games*. Printed as manuscript. Washington: GPO, 1915.

U.S. Library of Congress. Classification Division. *Classification. Class G: Geography, Anthropology, Folklore, Manners and Customs, Sports and Games*. 2nd ed. Washington: GPO, 1928.

U.S. Library of Congress. Subject Cataloging Division. *Classification. Class G: Maps, G3160-9999*. Preliminary draft. Washington: GPO, 1946.

U.S. Library of Congress. Subject Cataloging Division. *Classification. Class G: Geography, Anthropology, Folklore, Manners and Customs, Recreation.* 3rd ed. Washington: GPO, 1954, reprinted with supplementary pages, 1966.

U.S. Library of Congress. Subject Cataloging Division. *Classification. Class G: Geography, Maps, Anthropology, Recreation.* 4th ed. Washington: Library of Congress, 1976.

Class G: Readings

Allen, F. P. "Anthropology: Its Library Classification Problems," *Special Libraries* 24:90-93, May 1933.

Class H

U.S. Library of Congress. Classification Division. *Classification. Class H: Social Sciences*. Printed as manuscript. Washington: GPO, 1910.

U.S. Library of Congress. Catalog Division. *Classification HT. Social Groups: Communities, Classes, Races. Completing Class H: Social Sciences.* Printed as manuscript. Washington: GPO, 1915.

U.S. Library of Congress. Classification Division. *Classification. Class H: Social Sciences*. 2nd ed. Printed as manuscript. Washington: GPO, 1920.

U.S. Library of Congress. Subject Cataloging Division. *Classification. Class H: Social Sciences*. 3rd ed. Washington: GPO, 1950, reprinted with supplementary pages, 1965.

Class H: Readings

Arick, Mary Catherine. "Subclassification and Book Numbers of Documents and Official Publications," *The Use of the Library of Congress Classification*, edited by Richard H. Schimmelpfeng and C. Donald Cook. Chicago: American Library Association, 1968. pp. 135-61.

Bogardus, Janet. "Classification Schemes for Business and Financial Libraries," *Special Libraries* 43:409-410, December 1952.

Hagedorn, Ralph. "Random Thoughts on L.C. Classification," *Special Libraries* 52:256-57, May 1961.

Hedlesky, Nicholas. "Special Problems in Social and Political Sciences," *The Use of the Library of Congress Classification*, edited by Richard H. Schimmelpfeng and C. Donald Cook. Chicago: American Library Association, 1968. pp. 33-61.

"Library of Congress: Class H, Social Sciences," *American Journal of Sociology* 17:418, November 1911.

Class J

U.S. Library of Congress. Classification Division. *Classification. Class J: Political Science.* Printed as manuscript, subject to revision. Washington: GPO, 1910.

U.S. Library of Congress. Subject Cataloging Division. *Classification. Class J: Political Science.* 2nd ed. Washington: GPO, 1924, reprinted with supplementary pages, 1966.

Class J: Readings

Duhrsen, Lowell R. "Classification of United Nations Documents Using the JX Schedule and Document Numbers," *Library Resources & Technical Services* 14:84-91, Winter 1970.

Pease, Mina. "Plain 'J': A Documents Classification Scheme," *Library Resources & Technical Services* 16:315-25, Summer 1972.
This paper presents a modification of Class J for the classification of documents.

Class K

U.S. Library of Congress. Subject Cataloging Division. *Classification. Class K, Subclass K: Law [General].* Washington: Library of Congress, 1977.

U.S. Library of Congress. Subject Cataloging Division. *Classification. Class K, Subclass KD: Law of the United Kingdom and Ireland.* Washington: Library of Congress, 1973.

U.S. Library of Congress. Subject Cataloging Division. *Classification. Class K, Subclass KE: Law of Canada.* Washington: Library of Congress, 1976.

U.S. Library of Congress. Subject Cataloging Division. *Classification. Class K, Subclass KF: Law of the United States.* Preliminary ed. Washington: Library of Congress, 1969.

Class K: Variants

Benyon, Elizabeth V. *Classification. Class K. Law.* Printed as manuscript. Washington: Library of Congress, 1948.

Canada. Parliament Library. *Class K, Law, Based on Law Library of Congress Classification Scheme.* Ottawa: Parliamentary Library, 1956.

Los Angeles County Law Library. *Classification: Class K: Law.* Rev. ed. Los Angeles: Los Angeles County Law Library, 1965.

U.S. Department of Justice. Library. "Tentative Law Classification Scheme with Annotations." Washington: GPO, June 1940.

Class K: Readings

Angell, Richard S. "Development of Class K at the Library of Congress," *Law Library Journal* 57:352-76, November 1964.

Benyon, Elizabeth V. "Classification of Law Books," *Law Library Journal* 50:542-65, 1947.

Charpentier, A. A., and others. "Library of Congress Classification Schedule for Anglo-American Law (panel with discussion)," *Law Library Journal* 57: 352-76, November 1964.

Ellinger, Werner B. "Progress of Class K," *Law Library Journal* 50:542-65, 1947.

Hess, E. B. "Study of the Classification of Legal Materials in the Law Libraries of the Library of Congress, the Los Angeles County Law Library, and the University of Chicago," *Law Library Journal* 69:33-40, February 1976.

Kwan, C. H. "Classification Policies in Law Libraries Using Subclass KF: The Results of a Questionnaire," *Law Library Journal* 66:34-36, February 1973.

Moys, E. M. "Library of Congress Classification: Class KF: A Review Article," *Law Librarian* 1:24-27, August 1970.

Piper, Patricia Luster, and Cecilia Hing-Ling Kwan. *A Manual on KF: The Library of Congress Classification Schedule for Law of the United States.* South Hackensack, NJ: Published for American Association of Law Libraries by F. B. Rothman & Co., 1972. (AALL Publications Series, no. 11).

Tipler, Suzanne. "Classifying Law Materials Using the Library of Congress Classification," *Library Resources & Technical Services* 19:60-63, Winter 1975.

Class L

U.S. Library of Congress. Classification Division. *Classification. Class L: Education.* Washington: GPO, 1911.

U.S. Library of Congress. Classification Division. *Classification. Class L: Education.* 2nd ed. Washington: GPO, 1929.

U.S. Library of Congress. Subject Cataloging Division. *Classification. Class L: Education.* 3rd ed. Washington: GPO, 1951, reprinted with supplementary pages, 1966.

Class M

U.S. Library of Congress. Division of Music. *Classification. Class M, Music; Class ML, Literature of Music; Class MT, Musical Instruction.* Adopted December 1902; as in force April 1904. Washington: GPO, 1904.

U.S. Library of Congress. Subject Cataloging Division. *Classification. Class M: Music and Books on Music.* 2nd ed. Washington: GPO, 1917, reprinted with supplementary pages, 1968.

U.S. Library of Congress. Subject Cataloging Division. *Classification. Class M: Music and Books on Music.* 3rd ed. Washington: Library of Congress, 1978.

Class M: Readings

Bryant, Eric Thomas. *Music Librarianship: A Practical Guide.* London: J. Clarke; New York: Hafner, 1959.
Pages 154-61 cover a discussion of the possible uses of Class M in a music library. A comparison with the *Decimal Classification* is made.

Cunningham, Virginia. "The Library of Congress Classed Catalog for Music," *Library Resources & Technical Services* 8:285-88, Summer 1964.
This article discusses the classed catalog of the Music Division of the Library of Congress, including its use of mnemonic "imaginary numbers" (decimal extensions to numbers used in the classed catalog but not used in the classification numbers of books).

Mullally, G. "Some Remarks on the Library of Congress Classification Schedule for Music," *Fontis Artis Musicae* 23:60-61, April 1976.

U.S. Library of Congress. *The Music Division in the Library of Congress.* Washington: GPO, 1960.

Class N

U.S. Library of Congress. Classification Division. *Classification. Class N: Fine Arts.* Printed as manuscript. Washington: GPO, 1910.

U.S. Library of Congress. Classification Division. *Classification. Class N: Fine Arts.* Adopted 1909. As in force April 1917. Washington: GPO, 1917.

U.S. Library of Congress. Subject Cataloging Division. *Classification. Class N: Fine Arts.* 3rd ed. Washington: GPO, 1922, reprinted with supplementary pages, 1962.

U.S. Library of Congress. Subject Cataloging Division. *Classification. Class N: Fine Arts.* 4th ed. Washington: GPO, 1970.

Class N: Readings

Headicar, B. M. "Library of Congress Classification: Classes B, N, R, and Z," *Library Association Record* 12:515-16, 1910.

Class P

U.S. Library of Congress. Subject Cataloging Division. *Classification. Class P, P–PA: Philology, Linguistics, Classical Philology, Classical Literature.* Washington: GPO, 1928, reprinted with supplementary pages, 1968.

U.S. Library of Congress. Subject Cataloging Division. *Class P, Subclass PA Supplement: Byzantine and Modern Greek Literature, Medieval and Modern Latin Literature.* Washington: GPO, 1942, reprinted with supplementary pages, 1968.

U.S. Library of Congress. Subject Cataloging Division. *Classification. Class P, Subclasses PB—PH: Modern European Languages.* Washington: GPO, 1933, reprinted with supplementary pages, 1966.

U.S. Library of Congress. Subject Cataloging Division. *Classification. Class P, Subclass PG, in part: Russian Literature.* Washington: GPO, 1948, reprinted with supplementary pages, 1965.

U.S. Library of Congress. Subject Cataloging Division. *Classification. Class P, Subclasses PJ—PM: Languages and Literatures of Asia, Africa, Oceania, America, Mixed Languages, Artificial Languages.* Washington: GPO, 1935, reprinted with supplementary pages, 1965.

U.S. Library of Congress. Classification Division. *Classification. Philology. Index to Languages and Dialects in the Volumes P—PA, PB—PH, PJ—PM.* Printed as manuscript. Washington: GPO, 1936.

U.S. Library of Congress. Subject Cataloging Division. *Classification. Class P, Subclasses P—PM Supplement: Index to Languages and Dialects.* 2nd ed. Washington: GPO, 1957, reprinted with supplementary pages, 1965.

U.S. Library of Congress. Subject Cataloging Division. *Classification. Class P, Subclasses PN, PR, PS, PZ: Literature (General), English and American Literatures, Fiction in English, Juvenile Literature.* Washington: GPO, 1915, reprinted with supplementary pages, 1964.

U.S. Library of Congress. Subject Cataloging Division. *Classification. Class P, Subclasses PN, PR, PS, PZ: General Literature, English and American Literature, Fiction in English, Juvenile Belles Lettres.* 2nd ed. Washington: Library of Congress, 1978.

U.S. Library of Congress. Subject Cataloging Division. *Classification. Class P, Subclass PQ, part 1: French Literature.* Washington: GPO, 1936, reprinted with supplementary pages, 1966.

U.S. Library of Congress. Subject Cataloging Division. *Classification. Class P, Subclass PQ, part 2: Italian, Spanish and Portuguese Literatures.* Washington: GPO, 1937, reprinted with supplementary pages, 1965.

U.S. Library of Congress. Subject Cataloging Division. *Classification. Class P, Subclass PT, part 1: German Literature.* Washington: GPO, 1938, reprinted with supplementary pages, 1966.

U.S. Library of Congress. Subject Cataloging Division. *Classification. Class P, Subclass PT, part 2: Dutch and Scandinavian Literatures.* Washington: GPO, 1942, reprinted with supplementary pages, 1965.

Class P: Readings

Amaeshi, B. "Classification of Modern African Literature," *Libri* 25:40-47, March 1975.

Hines, Patricia S. "Special Problems in Literature (Class P)," in *The Use of the Library of Congress Classification*, edited by Richard H. Schimmelpfeng and C. Donald Cook. Chicago: American Library Association, 1968. pp. 62-79.

Hughes, S. F. D. "Notes on the Author Notations and Tables Used in Library of Congress Schedule for Icelandic Literature—Some Further Considerations," *Library Resources & Technical Services* 21:375-80, Fall 1977.

Immroth, Phillip. "To PZ or not to PZ," *Colorado Academic Library* 3:17-19, Winter 1966.

Jones, Gerda, Annemarie Jones, and Elizabeth H. Weeks. "Expansion of Library of Congress Classes PT2600-2688," *Library Resources & Technical Services* 17:32-34, Winter 1973.

Lockwood, Elizabeth. "Subclassification and Book Numbers in Language and Literature," in *The Use of the Library of Congress Classification*, edited by Richard H. Schimmelpfeng and C. Donald Cook. Chicago: American Library Association, 1968. pp. 121-34.

Mowery, Robert L. "The Classification of African Literature by the Library of Congress," *Library Resources & Technical Services* 17:340-52, Summer 1973.

Noe, A. C. von. "The New Classification of Languages and Literatures by the Library of Congress." Bibliographical Society of America, *Papers* 6:59-65, 1911.

Pincherle, Alberto. "La Literatura y la Historia Italiana a Traves de las Clasificaciones Dewey y del Congress," *Fenix. Revista de la Biblioteca Nacional* 3: 459-84, 1945.

Rothschild, N. P., and J. A. Moorman. "Classification of Fiction into the Library of Congress Literature Schedule," *North Carolina Libraries* 32: 23-26, Winter 1974.

Zirny, L. M. [Review of PQ, part 2], *Casopis Ceskoslovenskych Knihovniku* 17: 56, 1938.

Class Q

U.S. Library of Congress. Classification Division. *Classification. Class Q: Science.* Preliminary, July 1, 1905. Washington: GPO, 1905.

U.S. Library of Congress. Classification Division. *Classification. Class Q: Science.* Adopted 1905. As in force November 1912. Washington: GPO, 1913.

U.S. Library of Congress. Classification Division. *Classification. Class Q: Science.* 3rd ed. Washington: GPO, 1921.

U.S. Library of Congress. Subject Cataloging Division. *Classification. Class Q: Science.* 4th ed. Washington: GPO, 1948.

U.S. Library of Congress. Subject Cataloging Division. *Classification. Class Q: Science.* 5th ed. Washington: GPO, 1950, reprinted with supplementary pages, 1967.

U.S. Library of Congress. Subject Cataloging Division. *Classification. Class Q: Science.* 6th ed. Washington: Library of Congress, 1973.

Class Q: Readings

Allen, F. P. "Pure Science: L.C. vs. D.C.," *Library Journal* 58:124-27, February 1, 1933.

Bartle, Robert G. "One Mathematician Looks at the Classification of Mathematics," *The Role of Classification in the Modern American Library. Papers Presented at an Institute Conducted by the University of Illinois Graduate School of Library Science, November 1-4, 1959.* Champaign, IL: Illini Union Bookstore, 1959. pp. 93-102.

Blume, Edward J. "Special Problems in Science and Technology (Classes Q– V)," in *The Use of the Library of Congress Classification*, edited by Richard H. Schimmelpfeng and C. Donald Cook. Chicago: American Library Association, 1968. pp. 80-106.

Class R

U.S. Library of Congress. Classification Division. *Classification. Class R: Medicine.* Printed as manuscript. Washington: GPO, 1910.

U.S. Library of Congress. Classification Division. *Classification. Class R: Medicine.* 2nd ed. Washington: GPO, 1921.

U.S. Library of Congress. Subject Cataloging Division. *Classification. Class R: Medicine.* 3rd ed. Washington: GPO, 1952, reprinted with supplementary pages, 1966.

Class R: Readings

Hallam, B. B., and Mrs. O. K. Goodman. "Library of Congress Classification with Emphasis on Edition 3, 1952 of Class R: Medicine," *Medical Library Association Bulletin* 41:353-56, October 1953.

Haykin, David J. "The Classification of Medical Literature in the Library of Congress," *Libri* 3:104-106, 1954.

Class S

U.S. Library of Congress. Classification Division. *Classification. Class S: Agriculture—Plant and Animal Industry.* Printed as manuscript. Washington: GPO, 1911.

U.S. Library of Congress. Classification Division. *Classification. Class S: Agriculture, Plant and Animal Industry, Fish Culture and Fisheries, Hunting and Sports.* 2nd ed. Washington: GPO, 1928.

U.S. Library of Congress. Subject Cataloging Division. *Classification. Class S: Agriculture, Plant and Animal Industry, Fish Culture and Fisheries, Hunting Sports.* 3rd ed. Washington: GPO, 1948, reprinted with supplementary pages, 1965.

Class T

U.S. Library of Congress. Classification Division. *Classification. Class T: Technology.* Printed as manuscript. Washington: GPO, 1910.

U.S. Library of Congress. Classification Division. *Classification. Class T: Technology.* 2nd ed. Washington: GPO, 1922.

U.S. Library of Congress. Classification Division. *Classification. Class T: Technology.* 3rd ed. Washington: GPO, 1937.

U.S. Library of Congress. Subject Cataloging Division. *Classification. Class T: Technology.* 4th ed. Washington: GPO, 1948, reprinted, 1953.

U.S. Library of Congress. Subject Cataloging Division. *Classification. Class T: Technology.* 5th ed. Washington: Library of Congress, 1971.

Class U

U.S. Library of Congress. Classification Division. *Classification. Class U: Military Science.* Printed as manuscript. Washington: GPO, 1910.

U.S. Library of Congress. Classification Division. *Classification. Class U: Military Science.* 2nd ed. Washington: GPO, 1928.

U.S. Library of Congress. Subject Cataloging Division. *Classification. Class U: Military Science.* 3rd ed. Washington: GPO, 1952, reprinted with supplementary pages, 1966.

U.S. Library of Congress. Subject Cataloging Division. *Classification. Class U: Military Science.* 4th ed. Washington: Library of Congress, 1974.

Class V

U.S. Library of Congress. Classification Division. *Classification. Class V: Naval Science.* Printed as manuscript. Washington: GPO, 1910.

U.S. Library of Congress. Subject Cataloging Division. *Classification. Class V: Naval Science.* 2nd ed. Washington: GPO, 1953, reprinted with supplementary pages, 1966.

U.S. Library of Congress. Subject Cataloging Division. *Classification. Class V: Naval Science.* 3rd ed. Washington: Library of Congress, 1974.

Class W

U.S. Army Medical Library. "Classification: Medicine." Preliminary ed. Washington: [GPO], 1948. (Mimeographed).

U.S. Army Medical Library. *Army Medical Library Classification: Medicine. Preclinical Sciences: QS–QZ, Medicine and Related Subjects: W.* 1st ed. Washington: GPO, 1951.

U.S. National Library of Medicine. *National Library of Medicine Classification. A Scheme for the Shelf Arrangement of Books in the Field of Medicine and Its Related Sciences.* 2nd ed. Washington: GPO, 1956.

U.S. National Library of Medicine. *National Library of Medicine Classification: A Scheme for the Shelf Arrangement of Books in the Field of Medicine and Its Related Sciences.* 3rd ed. Public Health Service Publication No. 1108. Bethesda, MD: U.S. Department of Health, Education, and Welfare, Public Health Service, National Library of Medicine, 1964.

U.S. National Library of Medicine. *National Library of Medicine Classification: A Scheme for the Shelf Arrangement of Books in the Field of Medicine and Its Related Sciences.* 4th ed. DHEW Publication No. (NIH) 78-1535. Bethesda, MD: U.S. Department of Health, Education, and Welfare, Public Health Service, National Institutes of Health, National Library of Medicine, 1978.

Class W: Readings

The National Medical Library: Report of a Survey of the Army Medical Library. Financed by the Rockefeller Foundation and made under the auspices of the American Library Association, by Keyes D. Metcalfe, Janet Doe, Thomas P. Fleming, Mary Louise Marshall, L. Quincy Mumford, and Andrew D. Osborn. Chicago: American Library Association, 1944.

Class Z

U.S. Library of Congress. Classification Division. *Classification. Class Z: Bibliography and Library Science.* Adopted 1898. As in force January 1, 1902. Washington: GPO, 1902.

U.S. Library of Congress. Classification Division. *Classification. Class Z: Bibliography and Library Science.* Adopted 1898. As in force January 1910. Washington: GPO, 1910.

U.S. Library of Congress. Subject Cataloging Division. *Classification. Class Z: Bibliography and Library Science.* 3rd ed. January 1926. Washington: GPO, 1927.

U.S. Library of Congress. Subject Cataloging Division. *Classification. Class Z: Bibliography and Library Science.* 4th ed. Washington: GPO, 1959, reprinted with supplementary pages, 1965.

Class Z: Readings

Rodríguez, Robert D. "Use of Alternative Class Numbers for Bibliography in the Library of Congress Classification System," *Library Resources & Technical Services* 23:147-55, Spring 1979.

The Outline of the Classes

U.S. Library of Congress. Classification Division. *Classification. Outline Scheme of Classes.* Washington: GPO, 1903.

U.S. Library of Congress. Classification Division. *Classification. Outline Scheme of Classes.* Washington: GPO, 1904.

U.S. Library of Congress. Classification Division. *Classification. Outline Scheme of Classes.* Washington: GPO, 1906.

U.S. Library of Congress. Classification Division. *Classification. Outline Scheme of Classes.* Washington: GPO, 1907.

U.S. Library of Congress. Classification Division. *Classification. Outline Scheme of Classes.* Preliminary, December 1909. Washington: GPO, 1910.

U.S. Library of Congress. Classification Division. *Classification. Outline Scheme of Classes.* Preliminary. Rev. to January 1914. Washington: GPO, 1914.

U.S. Library of Congress. Classification Division. *Classification. Outline Scheme of Classes.* Rev. to February 1917. Washington: GPO, 1917.

U.S. Library of Congress. Classification Division. *Classification. Outline Scheme of Classes.* Rev. to August 1920. Washington: GPO, 1920.

U.S. Library of Congress. Subject Cataloging Division. *Outline of the Library of Congress Classification.* Revised and enlarged edition of "Outline Scheme of Classes." Washington: GPO, 1942, reprinted, 1965.

U.S. Library of Congress. Subject Cataloging Division. *Outline of the Library of Congress Classification.* 2nd ed. Washington: GPO, 1970.

U.S. Library of Congress. Subject Cataloging Division. *LC Classification Outline.* 3rd ed. Washington: Library of Congress, 1975.

U.S. Library of Congress. Subject Cataloging Division. *LC Classification Outline.* 4th ed. Washington: Library of Congress, 1978.

Additions and Changes

U.S. Library of Congress. Subject Cataloging Division. *LC Classification: Additions and Changes.* List 1- . 1928- . Washington: Library of Congress. Issued quarterly.

U.S. Library of Congress. Subject Cataloging Division. *Library of Congress Classification Schedules: A Cumulation of Additions & Changes.* Detroit: Gale Research Company, 1974- .
Separate volumes for individual classes.

NOTES

[1]Fourth edition, 1978.

[2]Jean M. Perreault, "The Classification of Philosophy," *Libri* 14:32-39 (1964).

[3]*See* pages 105-109 in the schedule for Subclasses B-BJ (3rd ed.).

[4]*See LC Classification—Additions and Changes*, List 181 (January-March 1976), pp. 12-14.

[5]*The Use of the Library of Congress Classification: Proceedings of the Institute on the Use of the Library of Congress Classification*, edited by Richard H. Schimmelpfeng and C. Donald Cook (Chicago: American Library Association, 1968), p. 60.

[6]*Cataloging Service* 106:5 (May 1973).

[7]The tables printed in the main schedule of Class H have been updated in *LC Classification—Additions and Changes*, Lists 186 (April-June 1977), 190 (April-June 1978), and 191 (July-September 1978). The updated version is included in Appendix C of this book.

[8]W. C. Berwick Sayers, *A Manual of Classification for Librarians and Bibliographers*. Rev. 3rd ed. (London: Grafton, 1955), p. 160.

[9]*Cataloging Service* 90:1-2 (Sept. 1970).

[10]*Cataloging Service* 124:28 (Winter 1978).

[11]*Cataloging Service* 117:14 (Spring 1976).

[12]*Cataloging Service Bulletin* 3:16-18 (Winter 1979).

[13]*Cataloging Service* 114:11 (Summer 1975).

[14]*Cataloging Service Bulletin* 2:45 (Fall 1978).

[15]"Cataloging Change Announced," *Library of Congress Information Bulletin* 38:335 (Aug. 24, 1979). Prior to this change, from 1968 to 1980, the Library of Congress assigned alternate class numbers in addition to the PZ numbers to fiction in English as a service to libraries that prefer to class such works in the regular literature numbers.

[16]*Cataloging Service* 121:19 (Spring 1977).

6 CLASSIFICATION OF SPECIAL TYPES OF LIBRARY MATERIALS

Chapter 5 presents a discussion of individual classes in the Library of Congress Classification system. Certain types of library materials which occur in more than one subject area require special treatment because of their unique characteristics. These are discussed below. This discussion is based on current practice at the Library of Congress. It should be noted that practices have varied over the years and that older LC cataloging records may reflect obsolete practices.

SERIAL PUBLICATIONS

Serial publications not limited to a particular subject are classed in the appropriate subclasses in Class A, General Works. Serial publications on specific subjects are classed in Classes B-Z. Normally they are classified in one of three ways: 1) in special form numbers under the appropriate subject; 2) by means of "A" Cutter numbers; and 3) in "General Works" numbers.

Special Form Numbers for Serials

In the schedules, at the head of each important topic, there is normally a class number or a group of class numbers designated for serial publications on that topic, generally with the caption "Periodicals. Societies. Serials." Unless there are specific provisions to the contrary, this number is used for all serial publications, including periodicals, yearbooks, numbered monographic series, and serial society publications. This number is normally not used for congresses or nonserial collections or collected works (unless specifically provided for in the caption).

The following is an example of specially assigned form numbers.

TR PHOTOGRAPHY

1	Periodicals. Societies. Almanacs. Yearbooks
5	Congresses
6	Exhibitions. Museums

Petersen's Photographic Magazine.

TR	The double letters for the subclass, Photography
1	The integral number assigned to periodicals, societies, almanacs, and yearbooks
.P46	The Cutter number for the main entry, *Petersen's....*

"A" Cutter Numbers for Periodicals or Serial Publications[1]

In the past, LC shelflisters were instructed to assign "A" Cutter numbers to periodicals or serial publications if the schedule for the topic did not provide individual classification numbers for them. These "A" Cutter numbers were not generally recorded in the printed schedules, however, but only in the LC shelflist. The practice of assigning unpublished "A" Cutter numbers was discontinued some years ago. Only those "A" Cutter numbers printed in the schedules are being used now.

An example of an "A" Cutter number for periodicals which is printed in the schedule is shown below.

TS MANUFACTURES

	Quality control.
156.A1A-Z	Periodicals, societies, etc.
.A2-Z	General works

Quality Assurance [a journal].

TS	The double letters for the subclass, Manufactures
156	The integral number meaning quality control
.A1	The "A" Cutter number for periodicals, societies, etc.
Q328	The second Cutter number for the main entry, *Quality....*

"General Works" Numbers Used for Periodicals

At the Library of Congress, periodicals are classed in "General works" numbers and cuttered by author or title in the manner of monographs, as long as 1) the topic is represented in the schedule by a few numbers only; 2) no provision for special forms, including periodicals, has been provided; and 3) the topic is fairly inactive. On the other hand, if the file appears to be an active one and the assumption can be made that numerous periodicals on the topic will be received by the Library, a special class number for periodicals will be established at the time a new periodical is received for cataloging.

Since unpublished "A" Cutter numbers still existing in the LC shelflist are no longer valid, subject catalogers at the Library of Congress are instructed either to cancel them when cataloging new serials (using in their place the "General works" number or establishing a separate class number) or, if more than several serials are involved, to establish the "A" Cutter number for inclusion in the appropriate schedule.

An example of a periodical classed in a "General works" number is:

QB   ASTRONOMY

History

15	General works
16	Ancient
17	Chinese
18	Hindu

Journal for the History of Astronomy.

QB	The double letters for the subclass, Astronomy
15	The integral number meaning a general work on the history of astronomy
.J68	The Cutter number for the main entry, *Journal....*

Certain types of serial publications are given special treatment. These are discussed below.

Yearbooks

A yearbook is defined as a publication that appears annually, each volume of which summarizes the accomplishments or events of that year within the particular discipline or area of endeavor. The term "Yearbooks" is extended to include also those publications appearing biennially or triennially that otherwise conform to the definition given above.

Under major subjects, separate numbers for yearbooks are often provided. These numbers are used only for yearbooks conforming to the definition above. Annual publications which are not yearbooks are classed under periodicals.

If, under a particular subject, there is no special number for yearbooks, the number assigned to periodicals is used for yearbooks. If there is no separate number for periodicals either, the "General works" number is used.

Serial Continuations

When the title of a serial publication, the corporate body, or the name of the corporate body under which the serial publication is entered, undergoes a change, a new cataloging record is created according to *AACR 2.* The Library of

Congress normally assigns the same call number to the new record if the volume or issue numbering continues after the change, in order to keep the entire serial together on the shelves.

The Library of Congress advises that "either the continuation being processed must be classified with the number originally assigned or, if a different number is to be assigned, the volumes of the serial previously cataloged must be reclassified. As a practical matter, the Subject Cataloging Division urges catalogers to make every effort to assign the original class number of the serial to its continuation, even if in so doing a number is used which no longer represents wholly the subject contents of the serial. On the other hand, if the original number is totally incorrect and cannot be used under any circumstances, the cataloger should reclassify all of the original volumes to the new number."[2]

If the new entry supersedes (i.e., begins a new sequence of numbering) the previous one, it is treated as an entirely new publication and a different call number is assigned.

For discussions and examples of serial publications issued by corporate bodies, see later sections in this chapter entitled "Society Publications" and "Government Publications," pages 295-97.

Examples of serial continuations are shown below.

From the State librarian's desk. no. 1–34; Dec. 1951–Dec. 1962. Sacramento ₁California State Library₁

no. 28 cm. Irregular

Continued by: From the California State librarian.

1. Libraries—California—Periodicals.   I. California.   State Library. Sacramento.

Z732.C2F76   027'.0794   79–640298
                                                        MARC-S

Library of Congress   79

From the California State librarian. no. 35–
Aug. 1963–
Sacramento ₍California State Library₎

no. 28 cm. irregular.

Continues : From the State librarian's desk.
Continued by : From the State librarian's desk.

1. Libraries—California—Periodicals.   I. California.   State Library, Sacramento.

Z732.C2F76   027′.0794   79–640297
                                                                   MARC-S

Library of Congress   79

MONOGRAPHIC SERIES, NONSERIAL COLLECTIONS, COLLECTED SETS, AND COLLECTED WORKS

Classification

The works in a monographic series or a set may be cataloged as separate monographs or as a collected item. When cataloged as separate items, each item is assigned the class number appropriate to the content of that item. When cataloged as a collected item, a class number appropriate for the entire series or set is assigned. When classifying a collected item from one volume, the classifier should be careful not to assign a number which is appropriate for that volume only (i.e., a number appropriate for the analytic rather than the entire set).

Monographic Series

For a monographic series classified as a collected item with analytics, the number designated for periodicals, if available, is used. For example:

Bulletin of the British Museum (Natural History).
  Zoology.

QL	The double letters for the subclass, Zoology
1	The integral number meaning periodicals, societies, congresses, serial collections, yearbooks
.B75	The Cutter number for the main entry, British Museum

Nonserial Collections or Collected Works

The numbers with the caption, "Collected works (Nonserial)" found at the head of major topics in the schedules are used with the following types of publications:

1)   Multivolume sets of monographic works by more than one author. This category refers to groups of monographs issued in the form of collected sets, such as the *Harvard Classics*. It includes multivolume monographs which the Library of Congress has classed as a set with full analytics. Multivolume monographs which are not analyzed are classed with "General works."

2)   Collected works of one author, e.g., the complete works of one author, including monographs, essays, etc.

3)   Selected works of one author on one topic. A collection of miscellaneous papers on one topic by one author is classed with the number designated for "Addresses, essays, lectures" (see below).

When there is no special number provided for nonserial collections or collected works, the "General works" number is used. The class number designated for periodicals is not used for the collected works of one author or multivolume sets of more than one author, for single volumes of miscellaneous works by one or more authors, or for anthologies, unless the caption of the number specifically provides for these types of works.

Selected Works

The selected works of an author which are of a monographic nature are classed with the "Collected works" number. If the selected works are papers or essays but represent collectively the author's total output at least in the one field in question (although the author may have made contributions in other fields that are not present in the work being cataloged), they are also classed with the "Collected works" number. On the other hand, a collection of selected papers or essays by one author on a topic which represents a fraction of the author's previously published output on that one topic in question is classed with the "Addresses, essays, lectures" number. The "Collected works" number and the "Addresses, essays, lectures" numbers normally correspond to the subdivisions "Collected works" and "Addresses, essays, lectures" in the subject headings assigned to the work.

Analysis of Monographic Series and Sets

Since 1972, the Library of Congress[3] has analyzed all analyzable monographic series currently being acquired and cataloged by the Library, except for those that are documents, technical reports, or reprints from journals, and those requiring page analysis.

When a monographic series or set is classed as a "collect" item, alternative class numbers for individual issues are provided on LC cataloging records. In addition to the call number for the collected item, a bracketed monographic class number is supplied, based on the content of the monograph represented by the analytic entry.

The alternative numbers are supplied in brackets on the LC cataloging records and the author Cutter numbers are generally omitted, since they do not represent valid LC call numbers. The alternative number is carried out as far as needed to cover topical elements. For example,

---

Harmon, Robert Bartlett, 1932-
    Indexes as sources of information in political science / Robert B. Harmon. — Monticello, Ill. : Council of Planning Librarians, 1978.

    9 p. ; 28 cm. — (Exchange bibliography - Council of Planning Librarians ; 1546)

    Cover title.
    $1.50

    1. Bibliography—Bibliography—Political science. 2. Bibliography—Bibliography—Social sciences. 3. Political science—Indexes—Bibliography. 4. Social sciences—Indexes—Bibliography. I. Title. II. Series: Council of Planning Librarians. Exchange bibliography ; 1546.

Z5942.C68 no. 1546   016.3092 s   78-105264
[Z7161.A1]   [016.01632]   MARC
[JA71]

Library of Congress   79

Glass, John B
    The Boturini collection and the Council of the Indies, 1780-1800 / John B. Glass. — Lincoln Center, Mass. : Conemex Associates, 1976.

    56 p. ; 28 cm. — (His The Indian museum of Lorenzo Boturini ; v. 1, chapters 9, 10) (Contributions to the ethnohistory of Mexico ; no. 4)
    Bibliography: p. 56.

    1. Boturini Benaducci, Lorenzo, 1702-1751—Manuscripts—Catalogs. 2. Indians of Mexico—History—Sources—Bibliography—Catalogs. 3. Indians of Mexico—History—Manuscripts—Catalogs. 4. Indians of Mexico—History—Sources. I. Title. II. Series: Contributions to the ethnohistory of Mexico ; no. 4.

Z6616.B666G57   vol. 1, chap. 9, 10   78-103857
               016.972'004'97

[F1225.B67]   MARC

Library of Congress   79

On LC cataloging records, when the series is classed as a "collect" item, and an analytic of the series represents a subseries, each piece of which is unanalyzed, a bracketed alternative monographic number is assigned to the subseries. If the individual pieces of the subseries are analyzed, an alternative number is assigned to each piece and no alternate number is assigned to the subseries.

> E. J. Brandl's *Australian Aboriginal Paintings in Western and Central Arnheim Land.* (Australian Aboriginal Studies, no. 52; Prehistory and Material Culture Series, no. 9).
>
> LC call number: DU120.A8 no. 52 (for the main series)
> Alternative class number: [ND1101] (for the individual issue)
> No alternative number is assigned to the subseries.

Alternative monographic class numbers are also provided for occasional numbers of periodicals or other series for which analytic records are provided.

ABSTRACTS[4]

Background

For classification purposes, a collection of abstracts may be regarded as a collection of miscellaneous works. Abstracts, therefore, should normally be classed with a "Collected works" number under the topic in the topical classes, unless a specific number for abstracts has been provided. On the other hand, annotated bibliographies, which also list publications with comments about them, should be classed in Z. The difference is that abstracts summarize works in such a way as to include substantive information on the topic, whereas annotated bibliographies offer only descriptive comments about the works.

Procedures

1) Class abstracts with the subject in the topical classes and not in Z.

2) Class abstracts in the appropriate number designated for abstracts if the schedule provides specifically for them; however, such numbers are rare.

3) If no special number exists, a) class abstracts with "Collected works (nonserial)" if such a number or its equivalent exists. (Exception: If the work being cataloged is a serial, class it with the number for serials); b) the Library of Congress will normally establish a number for "collected works (nonserial)" or for periodicals, as required, if the topic in the schedule already provides for several special forms, such as dictionaries, congresses, addresses, essays, lectures, etc.; c) if no special form captions are provided and if it is unlikely that form captions will be necessary in the future, class the

abstracts with "General works." (Note: At the Library ofCongress, form captions are initiated under a topic only if there are at least five titles in the form already classed in the general works number under that topic in the shelflist. For serials, the minimum number is two.)

INDEXES[5]

The following summarizes the treatment of indexes by the Library of Congress:

1) Indexes to individual publications (including serials): Classify with the work indexed. This is accomplished by one of the following methods:

    A) Adding "Suppl." to the call number assigned to the main work,* e.g.,

        AP2.H32   *Harper's Weekly*

        AP2.H32 Suppl.   *Harper's Weekly. Index.*

    B) Using successive Cutter numbers.** The successive Cutter number .x2 is generally used for an index, unless there is a conflict in the shelflist. If the call number of the main work contains one Cutter number only, a second Cutter number based on the main entry of the index is added, e.g., .W552J67 (where .W55 is the Cutter number for the main work). If the call number of the main work already contains two Cutter numbers, a successive element is added to the second Cutter number in order to avoid using triple Cutter numbers, e.g., .N48W5524 (where .N48W55 are the Cutter numbers for the main work).

2) Indexes to the publications of an individual author: Classify with biography and criticism of that author, or use a more specific number under the author if so provided in the schedule.

3) Indexes to the publications of an individual society, etc.: Classify in Z 1201-7999 with bibliographies on the topic in which the organization specializes.

---

*The practice of adding the term "Index" has been discontinued.

**This method is also used for shelflisting a commentary on individual work. The successive Cutter number used in this case is .x3 unless there is a conflict in the shelflist.

4) Comprehensive indexes to lists of books or serials on a topic: Classify as bibliography on the topic in Z 1201-7999, e.g.,

---

Canadian business periodicals index.

Toronto, Information Access.

v. 29 cm. annual.

1. Business—Periodicals—Indexes. 2. Canada—Economic conditions—1945-   —Periodicals—Indexes. 3. Canada—Commerce—Periodicals—Indexes.

Z7164.C81C24   016.3309′71′0644   78–643116
                                                          MARC–S

Library of Congress   78

Chicorel index to reading and learning disabilities, an annotated guide: Books.
[New York] Chicorel Library Pub. Corp.

v. 27 cm. annual. (Chicorel index series)

1. Reading disability—Indexes. 2. Learning disabilities—Indexes. I. Title.

Z5818.L3C55   016.3719   78–641516
[LB1050.5]   MARC–S

Library of Congress   78

SUPPLEMENTS

A separately cataloged supplement to an individual work is classified with the main work. The call number for the main work with the addition of the term "Suppl." is assigned to the supplement.

Bibliography of society, ethics, and the life sciences. Supplement.
Hastings-on-the-Hudson, N. Y., Institute of Society, Ethics, and the Life Sciences.
    v. 28 cm.
    Key title: Bibliography of society, ethics, and the life sciences. Supplement, ISSN 0191-4081.
    1. Bioethics—Bibliography—Periodicals. 2. Medical ethics—Bibliography—Periodicals. 3. Medical research—Moral and religious aspects—Bibliography—Periodicals. I. Institute of Society, Ethics, and the Life Sciences.

Z5322.B5B52 Suppl.   016.174'2   79–642704
[QH332]   MARC-S

Library of Congress   79

University Microfilms International.
    1979 supplement to author, title, and subject guides to books on demand. — Ann Arbor, Mich. : University Microfilms International, 1978.
    viii, 119 p. ; 28 cm.
    Includes index.
    ISBN 0-8357-0337-1

    1. Books on microfilm—Bibliography—Catalogs. 2. Bibliography—Photomechanical editions—Catalogs. 3. Out-of-print books—Bibliography—Catalogs. I. Title.

Z1033.M5U53 1977 Suppl.   78–112624
                    011
                                           MARC

Library of Congress   79

(Card examples continue on page 292)

Haycock, Ken.
  Sears list of subject headings : Canadian companion / compiled by Ken Haycock and Lynne Isberg. — New York : H. W. Wilson Co., 1978.

  vii, 50 p. ; 26 cm.

  "To be used with the 11th edition of Sears list of subject headings, published in 1977."
  ISBN 0-8242-0629-0 : $5.50

  1. Subject headings.   I. Isberg, Lynne.   II. Sears, Minnie Earl, 1873-1933. List of subject headings for small libraries.   III. List of subject headings.   IV. Title.

  Z695.S43   1977 Suppl.   025.3'3   78-13687
                                                       MARC

  Library of Congress   78

MATERIALS CATALOGED UNDER CORPORATE HEADINGS

Shelflisting Procedures[6]

The following direction to LC shelflisters provides the procedures and techniques which have been applied at the Library of Congress since May 1973 for shelflisting monographs and serials cataloged under a corporate heading. However, these procedures do not apply to Library of Congress publications classified in Z663-Z663.99, which are cuttered by title.

Upon receipt of a publication cataloged under a corporate heading already represented in the particular class to which the publication has been assigned, the shelflister disregards all previously assigned author Cutter numbers for that heading and formulates a new number for the heading that will shelve immediately after all existing ones used for the body.

1)   **Cutter numbers.** All publications cataloged under a corporate heading and classified under the same number are assigned the same Cutter number. In formulating a Cutter number for a corporate heading, the cataloger should disregard all subheadings. For example, the same Cutter number is used to shelflist publications cataloged under the following headings:

  American Library Association
  American Library Association. Library Administration
    Division.
  American Library Association. Reference Services
    Division.

However, any word or phrase at the end of a corporate heading which distinguishes between two bodies having the same name or similar names is considered. For example, different Cutter numbers are assigned to the following headings:

> Loyola University, Chicago.
> Loyola University, New Orleans.

When the entire class number is for the official documents of a specific country, the Cutter numbers are based on the name of the particular agency. If the name of the country appears at the beginning of the entry it is disregarded. As stated in the preceding paragraph, subheadings that appear in the heading are disregarded. For example, the same ".C" Cutter number is used to shelflist all publications cataloged under the following headings:

> United States. Congress. House.
> United States. Congress. House. Select Committee on
>   Government Organization.
> United States. Congress. Joint Committee on the
>   Library.
> United States. Congress. Senate.

2)   **Monographs.** To formulate a distinctive call number for a monograph cataloged under a corporate heading, the date of imprint is added to the call number. If the date of imprint covers more than one year, the earliest date of imprint is used. The earliest available imprint date, not necessarily that of the first volume or of the volume in hand, is used for multivolume monographs and looseleaf materials. Publications with identical dates of imprint are distinguished by adding successive work letters to the date in the call number. No attempt is made to relate the editions, reprint editions, translations, facsimiles, photocopies, etc., of a work.

3)   **Serials.** To formulate a distinctive call number for serials (e.g., periodicals and collected series) cataloged under a corporate heading, successive work letters, beginning with "a" for the first serial, are added to the Cutter number for the heading in the order of receipt of the publications.

The following are examples of call numbers for monographs and serials cataloged under corporate headings:

> xxxx   Auburn University. Agriculture Experiment Station.
> .A8   [Monographic title] 1953.
> 1953

> xxxx   Auburn University.
> .A8   [Multivolume monographic title] 1953-1958.
> 1953a

> xxxx   Auburn University. Labor Institute.
> .A8   [Open entry multivolume monographic title] 1957-
> 1957

xxxx .F3 1966	Farmacopee-Commissie. [Monographic title] 1966.
xxxx .F3 1966a	Farmacopee-Commissie. [Monographic title] 1966.
xxxx .F3a	Farmacopee-Commissie. [Open entry serial title] 1969-
xxxx .F3b	Farmacopee-Commissie. [Closed entry serial title] 1956-1968.
xxxx .N28 1949	National Research Council. [Monographic title] 1949.
xxxx .N32 1954	National Research Council (Canada). [Monographic title] 1954.
xxxx .U3 1958	United States. Army. General Staff. [Monographic title] 1958.
xxxx .U3 1963	United States. Army. [Multivolume monographic title] 1963-1964.
xxxx .U3 1963a	United States. Army. Far East Command. [Monographic title] 1963.

Cutter Numbers for Specific Institutions: Captions with Single Element (Either by Name, A-Z; or by Place, A-Z)

Most schedules of the LC system make use of single class numbers under which individual institutions (in particular, museums, libraries, schools, laboratories) are arranged alphabetically by Cutter numbers. The Cutter numbers are either taken from the names of the institutions, or from the cities or places in which the institutions are located. Recently revised or added numbers carry captions that clearly state which of the two elements, name or place, is to be employed in any individual situation. Examples:

GN39	Museums. By place, A-Z
Z733	Individual libraries. By name, A-Z

However, in the past, various forms of captions have been used. The following table is a display of the captions currently in use:

By name	By place
By name, A-Z	By place, A-Z
By place (or name), A-Z	By name or place, A-Z
By name or place, A-Z	Prefer classification by place
By place or name, A-Z	By city, A-Z
By name (generally name of place), A-Z	By place (unless nonurban), A-Z
By place (except where the institution has a well known name), A-Z	
By institution, A-Z	

"By name" in all cases is understood to mean the author heading for the institution in whatever form represented in the Catalog. For example, "New York (City). Museum of Modern Art" is the complete official heading for a particular museum, the first word of which happens to be the name of a city. The Cutter number is taken therefore from "New York...."

"By place" means that the name of the city will be used for shelflisting purposes, regardless of the catalog entry for the official name of the institution in question. When an individual institution is found to exist outside of any local jurisdiction—but only in such cases—it may be cuttered under its name alone, rather than under a place name.

Society Publications[7]

Form captions at the head of each major discipline in the classification schedules normally provide both for serials, including periodicals, and for societies. Most often the caption line places both forms together, e.g., "Periodicals. Societies. Serials," or some variation thereof. Sometimes, however, these forms are on two separate lines, each with its own class number:

> Periodicals, etc.
> Societies

Separate Class Numbers for Societies

Unless there are explicit provisions to the contrary, separate class numbers for societies should be reserved for works *about* particular societies, including official business publications, membership lists, constitutions, histories, reports of business meetings, etc. Publications issued by a society on topics of interest to the society, or on both topical matters and matters about the society itself, should be classed in numbers appropriate to the particular topic and form of the publication. For example, if an American medical society issues an official series on the topic of general medicine, it should be classed with medical periodicals (serials), not with the number for medical societies.

The individual societies under a separate number for societies are arranged alphabetically. The basic Cutter number for the name of a society is determined in accordance with the normal procedures for assigning Cutter numbers (see pages 292-94 above). Subarrangement under each society is by three successive Cutter numbers as follows:

1) Official serials;
2) Official monographs;
3) Nonofficial publications. By author, A-Z.

Although not all official publications are entered under the name of the society, any publication which is so entered should be considered an official publication. Since unofficial publications are invariably nonserials, they are normally assigned double Cutter numbers, the second Cutter number corresponding to the main entry heading. *But*, when the society number is already on a second Cutter number (e.g., Q80, Societies. Other regions or countries, A-Z), a successive Cutter element for the author is used to avoid the use of triple Cutter numbers.

Numbers for Serials and Societies Together

The situation is more complicated when both serials and societies are grouped together in one caption. The same Cutter arrangement is used not only for works about a society, but also for topical works when they are entered under the name of the society.

1) **Topical Serials.** All serials classed in such numbers, including serials published by a society, are cuttered according to the main entry heading. Therefore, serial society publications entered under title are not kept together with works about the society, but are dispersed throughout the entire span of Cutter numbers under the class number. On the other hand, serial society publications entered under the name of the society are cuttered for the name of the society, making use of the three successive Cutter subarrangement above. Since these serials with entry under the name of the society would always be official works, they would be assigned the first of the three successive Cutter numbers.

2) **Other Topical Publications.** The serials caption in a few schedules also includes other forms, such as congresses, e.g., QA1, "Periodicals, societies, congresses, serial collections, yearbooks." These works make use of the subarrangement above, if entered under the name of the society. For example, congress proceedings issued as a monograph and entered under the name of the society (hence an official publication) would be assigned the second Cutter number.

3) **Works about the Society.** All works about a society, unofficial or official, are cuttered by the name of the society, not by the main entry heading. Subarrangement is according to the three successive Cutter numbers above. In this manner all works about the society are kept together in one place.

Examples (theoretical authors and titles used)

QA1	Periodicals, societies, congresses, serial collections, yearbooks
.C6	Congress of Mathematical ...
.M3	Mathematical update; official journal of the ... Society
.N315	National Mathematical Society. Journal
.N316	Math business: reports of the official business meetings of the National Mathematical Society
.N325	National Mathematical Society. Members of the organization
.N327	National Mathematical Society. Report of a meeting to discuss the status of mathematics
.N33J6	Jones, T. History of the National Mathematical Society

Government Documents[8]

The section dealing with shelflisting works entered under corporate headings notes that government documents would no longer be handled as a distinct category of material unless the schedule in which the document is classed contains a separate provision for documents. Below is an indication of which publications are to be classed as documents when the schedule expressly provides for documents.

1)   **Monographs.** Do not class monographic documents by document numbers unless the schedule also includes separate numbers for monographs. Unless monographs are explicitly mentioned, it is assumed that the provision is only for serial documents and monographic documents are to be classed as any other monographic publication.

2)   **Corporate Entries.** Do not class documents by document numbers unless the corporate main entry heading consists of a jurisdictional name with the agency name as a subheading, e.g., "New South Wales. Dept. of Railways." If the main entry heading has been established in any other manner, including headings for government bodies entered under their own names, e.g., "Naval Research Laboratory," treat the work as a non-document publication.

Congressional and State Legislative Hearings and Reports

U.S. congressional hearings and reports of U.S. state legislatures are classed in Subclass KF without exception. Committee prints are classed with the pertinent topic in Classes B-Z. They are not regarded automatically as legal publications. Publications of other countries which are the equivalent of U.S. congressional hearings and reports are classed with the appropriate topics in Classes B-Z, or in J if general.

Congresses, Conferences, etc.

Classifying Congresses, Conferences, etc.

At the head of many topics in the L.C. Classification schedules, there is a special form number for congresses. This number is used for collected papers delivered at, or published on the occasion of, individual named or unnamed congresses, conferences, etc. It is also assigned to reports of the proceedings and discussions, lists of delegates, etc., or combinations of these. Such a publication may have as its main entry heading the name of a congress, the name of a corporate body, or a title.

Following is a set of guidelines[9] provided by the Library of Congress for classifying congresses.

General Procedures

1)   If a congress number exists under the topic, class all congresses, including serial congresses, in this special congress number. Do not class congresses with periodicals unless congresses are explicitly stated in the periodicals caption, e.g., Class Q.

2)   If a congress number does not exist under the topic and there are not enough previously classified works in this form to justify establishing a separate number, class congresses in the general works number. Do not class serial congresses with periodicals unless congresses are explicitly stated in the periodicals caption.

3)   If a separate number for the form under the topic does not exist, the Library of Congress will normally establish the required number if one of the following criteria has been met: There are at least five congresses already classed in the general works number; or, one or more standard form captions already exist under the particular topic, although less than five congresses have been classed in the general works number. Only the one word, *Congresses*, will be used in the caption unless it is a standard feature of the schedule to use other wording, e.g., Class Q.

Special Procedures

1)   Monographic works:

   a)   Class each monographic congress solely on the basis of its individual contents. If a separate cataloging record is prepared for each meeting, do not attempt to keep the various meetings of a particular named congress together. Class according to the subject of each.

   b)   If by chance different publications of the same named congress are classed in the same number, the same Cutter number will be assigned to each publication. However, identical Cutter numbers are not possible for congresses with entry under corporate body or title.

   c)   If the name of the congress changes, make no attempt to keep the works issued under the various names together on the shelves, even if the same class number is involved. A different Cutter number is assigned for each name.

2)   Congresses cataloged as serials:

   a)   Class all open entry congresses, including serial congresses, in the congress number, following the provisions and exceptions noted in "General Procedures."

   b)   Name Changes. If a new record is prepared for the new serial and it is treated as a continuation of the old, the old and the new serials are kept together on the shelves by using the same call number for both. If there is no continuation statement, make no effort to keep the old and new entries together.

3)   Class works about an individual congress in the same number assigned to the congress itself (or the number that would be assigned if the library had a copy of the actual proceedings, etc.).

4)   Do not class publications of business meetings of societies in congress numbers if they contain no substantive information about the topic of interest to the society, but only cover business matters relating to the society. Treat such works as discussions about the society, classing them with the number for the society. (*See* discussion of society publications on pages 295-97.)

Shelflisting Congresses, Conferences, etc.[10]

The following shelflisting procedures are applied by the Library of Congress to all publications newly cataloged or recataloged under headings for conferences, congresses, meetings, etc., regardless of the treatment applied to previously shelflisted materials. Shelf arrangements that are published in the Library of Congress classification schedules for these materials take precedence over any of the guidelines outlined below.

1)   Main entry under name of congress, conference, etc.

   a)   Monographs classed in a congress, general works, or society number.

      Cutter number. Assign a Cutter number based on the name of the congress, plus the date of the congress, e.g.,

      TE5   International Road Congress, 8th, Hague,
      .I6   1938.
      1938

      TE5   International Road Congress, 10th, Istanbul,
      .I6   1955
      1955

If the congress meets at various intervals without change of name, and its publications are classed in the same number, the same Cutter number is used for each publication.

Date. Add the year in which the congress met. If the congress met for more than one year, assign only the latest year, e.g.,

QH51   Conference on Undergraduate Curricula in
.C77   Biological Sciences, Washington, D.C.,
1957   1956 and Chapel Hill, N.C., 1957.

Work letters. In order to formulate unique call numbers, consecutive work letters — i.e., a, b, c, etc. — are added to the date, e.g.,

GN50	GN50	GN50	
.M21	.M21	.M21	etc.
1950	1950a	1950b	

The work letter "z" is not used for these publications (see p. 301). If all single work letters have been used, assign double letters — i.e., aa, ab, ac, ad, etc. Facsimiles, reprints, translations, etc. will not stand next to the original or related publication.

    The same procedure applies to a congress which was held two or more times within one year. This represents a change in practice. Previous practice required that successive Cutter numbers and date be assigned to later congresses in the same year.

b)   Serials classed in a congress, general works, or society number.

Cutter number. A Cutter number based on the main entry is assigned.

Work letters. Successive work letters are added to the Cutter number in order to formulate distinctive call numbers, e.g.,

GN50	GN50	GN50	
.T26	.T26a	.T26b	etc.

The work letters, beginning with letter "a" are assigned in order of receipt of the publications.

Date. No date is assigned.

2)   Main entry under name of corporate body (both monographs and serials).

a)   In a congress number. Assign a Cutter number based on the name of the corporate body, including its subheadings (if any).* The date is not added. Example:

GN3   Institut international d'anthropologie.
.I35   IIe ... session ... 1924.

*Note that for other society publications, the subheadings are disregarded.

b)   In a general works number. Assign a Cutter number according to the procedures for other publications entered under corporate headings (*see* pages 292-94). Ignore the fact that the publication is from a congress.

    If, in applying the procedures for shelflisting works entered under corporate headings, a date with work letter must be assigned to create a distinct call number, use the *imprint* date instead of the meeting date.

c)   In a society number. *See* "Shelflisting Congresses Classed in Society Numbers" below (*see* pages 302-303).

3)   Main entry under title (both monographs and serials).

a)   In a Congress number. Formulate a Cutter number based on the title, and do not add the date, e.g.,

GV4   Work and leisure... Based on papers presented...
.W58   1973.

b)   In a general works number. Same as (a) above.

c)   In a society number. Same as (a) above as long as the publication contains substantive information. If it contains only business matters relating to the society, follow the procedures outlined under "Shelflisting Congresses Classed in Society Numbers" (*see* pages 302-303).

Shelflisting Works about Congresses, Conferences, etc.

1)   Works discussing a named congress classed in a congress, general works, or society number.

a)   The congress being discussed is treated as being monographic.

    i) If the work discusses a particular congress, the Cutter number for the original congress, plus the year in which the congress met, plus a work letter, z, or za, zb, zc, etc. (in order of receipt), is used.

    ii) If the work discusses a named congress in general (no specific year given), double Cutter numbers—first Cutter number for the congress (using the third successive number in accordance with normal shelflisting procedures for works of an individual author in a single number; *see* page 296), and the second Cutter number for the main entry of the work—are used.

b)   The congress being discussed is treated as a serial. Follow the same procedure outlined in (ii) above.

2)   Works discussing a congress with main entry under corporate headings (both monographs and serials).

    a)   In a congress number. Double Cutter numbers—first for the author and title of the congress (using third successive number in accordance with normal shelflisting procedures) and second for the main entry—are used.

    b)   In a general works number. Follow the procedures for shelflisting "Materials Cataloged Under Corporate Headings" (pages 292-94).

    c)   In a society number. Use the society table in the following section entitled "Shelflisting Congresses Classed in Society Numbers" (*see* page 303).

3)   Works discussing a congress with main entry under title (both monographs and serials).

    Regardless of the kind of class number (i.e., congress, general works, or society number) used, assign double Cutter numbers—first Cutter number for the title of the congress (using the third successive number in accordance with normal shelflisting procedures; *see* page 296) and the second Cutter number for the main entry of the work.

4)   Works discussing collectively various congresses on a topic.

    Regardless of the kind of class number involved, assign a single Cutter number for the main entry. The date is not used.

Shelflisting Congresses Classed in Society Numbers

In the classification schedules, there are a few numbers which are designated for both congresses and societies, e.g.,

        QA1   Periodicals, societies, congresses,
                        serial collections, yearbooks

Shelflisting congresses in these numbers will sometimes require different procedures from the above when the special provisions for societies and congresses clash. In such cases, the provisions for societies will prevail over those for congresses.

Procedures

1)   Follow normal procedures for congresses when shelflisting an individual congress in a society number as long as the main entry of the congress is not a corporate heading. However, if the publication of a congress with main entry under title contains only business matters relating to a corporate body with

no substantive information about the subject, it is treated as a publication *about* the corporate body rather than as a publication issued by the congress.

2) If the main entry or the first subject heading assigned is the heading for the corporate body, the publication is treated as a society publication and assigned a successive Cutter number according to the society table below:

1) Official serials
2) Official monographs
3) Nonofficial publication. By author, A-Z.

Official serials and monographs are those publications resulting from a congress or conference with main entry under the heading of the corporate body. Official reports of the business meetings of a society (without substantive information), entered under title or corporate heading, are also considered official serials or monographs as the case may be. The Cutter number is assigned in accordance with the procedures for shelflisting materials cataloged under corporate headings (*see* pages 292-94), disregarding subheadings. However, in this case, the imprint date or work letters are not added. Distinctive call numbers are formulated by using successive Cutter numbers in the case of official publications and double Cutter numbers in the case of unofficial publications.

The table on page 304 summarizes the provisions outlined above. The primary terms used in this table should be defined as follows:

Normal Shelflisting—using normal rules for successive Cutters, arranging works in the same manner as works by and about an individual author in a single class number.

Double Cutter—using third successive number in accordance with normal shelflisting procedures such as for works by and about an individual author in a single class number to bring out criticism. Assign a second Cutter for the author of work in hand.

Combined Society Number—a single class number which explicitly provides for both congresses and societies (and perhaps other publication forms as well). *See* page 302 for an example. Note: In normal society numbers, the society table above prevails in all cases.

Corporate Body Shelflisting—procedures outlined in section entitled "Materials Cataloged Under Corporate Headings" (pages 292-94).

TABLE SHOWING CUTTERING ARRANGEMENTS FOR CONGRESSES

Kind of Main Entry of the Congress	Congress Number	General Works Number	Combined Society Number
Monographs			
Name of Congress	Cutter + Date (& work letter if needed)	Cutter + Date (& work letter if needed)	Cutter + Date (& work letter if needed)
Corporate Body Entry	Normal Shelflisting	Corporate body shelf-listing	Society table
Title Entry	Normal Shelflisting	Normal Shelflisting	Normal Shelflisting or Society table
Serials			
Name of Congress	Cutter + work letter	Cutter + work letter	Cutter + work letter
Corporate Body Entry	Normal Shelflisting	Corporate body shelf-listing	Society table
Title Entry	Normal Shelflisting	Normal Shelflisting	Normal Shelflisting or Society table
Works About Congresses*			
Monographs			
Name of Congress	Cutter + Date z (& work letter if needed)	Cutter + Date z (& work letter if needed)	Cutter + Date z (& work letter if needed)
Corporate Body Entry	Double Cutter	Corporate body shelf-listing	Society table
Title Entry	Double Cutter	Double Cutter	Double Cutter
Serials			
Name of Congress	Double Cutter	Double Cutter	Double Cutter
Corporate Body	Double Cutter	Corporate body shelf-listing	Society table
Title Entry	Double Cutter	Double Cutter	Double Cutter

*In this section the "Kind of Main Entry" refers to the main entry of the congress discussed.

Following are examples of classifying and shelflisting congresses, conferences, etc.

A monograph classed in a *Congress number* with main entry under the conference.

International Conference of Printing Research Institutes, 14th, Marbella, Spain (Málaga), 1977.
　　Advances in printing science and technology : proceedings of the 14th International Conference of Printing Research Institutes, Marbella, Spain, June, 1977 / edited by W. H. Banks for the International Association of Research Institutes for the Graphic Arts Industry. — London : Pentech Press, 1979.

　　455 p. : ill. ; 23 cm.　　　　　　　　　　　　　　　　　GB***

　　Conference organized by the Association [sic] de Investigacion de la Industria Grafica.
　　Includes bibliographies.

(Continued on next card)

79-307398
MARC

79

International Conference of Printing Research Institutes, 14th, Marbella, Spain (Málaga), 1977. — Advances in printing science and technology ... 1979. (Card 2)

　　ISBN 0-7273-0106-3 : £18.00

　　1. Printing　Congresses.　　I. Banks, William H.　　II. International Association of Research Institutes for the Graphic Arts Industry.　　III. Asociación de Investigación de la Industria Gráfica.　　IV. Title.

Z120.5.I57　1977　　　　　　686.2　　　　　　79-307398
MARC

Library of Congress　　　　　　79

A monograph classed in a *General works number* with
main entry under the conference.

**International Symposium on Finite Element Methods in Flow
Problems, 2d, Santa Margherita Ligure, Italy, 1976.**
Second International Symposium on Finite Element Methods
in Flow Problems, S. Margherita Liguer (Italy), June 14-18,
1976 : preprints. — Genova : Stampa Microlito, [1978?]
iv, 796 p. : ill. ; 24 cm. — (Conference series - International Centre for
Computer Aided Design ; no. 2/76)   It78-July
At head of title: ICCAD, International Centre for Computer Aided Design.
Includes bibliographical references.

1. Fluid dynamics—Congresses. 2. Finite element method—Congresses.
I. International Centre for Computer Aided Design. II. Title. III. Series: International Centre for Computer Aided Design. Conference series - Intern-
tional centre for Computer Aided Design ; no. 2/76.
TA357.I58   1976   620.1'064   78-322211
                                                    MARC

Library of Congress   *78

A monograph classed in a *combined* (congress and society) *number*
with main entry under the conference.

**Clinic on Library Applications of Data Processing, University of
Illinois, 1977.**
Negotiating for computer services / J. L. Divilbiss, editor. —
Urbana-Champaign : University of Illinois, Graduate School of
Library Science, c1978.

117 p. ; 24 cm. — (Proceedings of the 1977 Clinic on Library Applications
of Data Processing)

Title on spine: Library applications of data processing.
"Papers presented at the 1977 Clinic on Library Applications of Data Proc-
essing, April 24-27, 1977.
Includes index.
ISBN 0-87845-048-3

(Continued on next card)
                                           78-13693
                                            MARC
78

((Card 2 of this example is shown at the top of page 307)

Card 2.

Clinic on Library Applications of Data Processing, University of Illinois, 1977. — Negotiating for computer services ... c1978. (Card 2)

    1. Libraries—Automation—Congresses.   I. Divilbiss, J. L. II. Title. III. Title: Library applications of data processing. IV. Series: Clinic on Library Applications of Data processing. Proceedings ; 1977.

Z678.9.A1C5 1977   021'.0028'54 s   78-13693
                        ɾ025.1'828'54ɹ   MARC

Library of Congress   78

Monographs classed in a *General works number* with main entry under a corporate body.
(Note that in assigning the Cutter number for the corporate body, the subheading is ignored).

Library Association.
    Proceedings ɾofɹ the Library Association Centenary Conference. — London : The Association, ɾ1977ɹ

    96 p. ; 30 cm.   GB78-06616

    Held in London, 1977.
    Errata slip inserted.
    Includes bibliographies.
    ISBN 0-85365-820-X : £2.50

    1. Library conferences. 2. Libraries—Great Britain—Addresses, essays, lectures.

Z673.L74L5 1977   020'.941   78-318128
                                      MARC

Library of Congress   78

(The second card of this example is shown on the top of page 308)

Card 2.

Library Association. London and Home Counties Branch.
　　Librarianship 1999 : papers read at the one-day Conference of
the London and Home Counties Branch of the Library Association held at the Library Association, 11th May 1977 under the
chairmanship of M. J. Saich / edited by Vaughan Whibley. —
Orpington : Library Association, London and Home Counties
Branch, 1977.

　　48, ₍1₎ p. ; 19 cm.　　　　　　　　　　　　　　　　GB78-15974

　　ISBN 0-902119-21-4 : £2.50

　　1. Library science—Great Britain—Congresses.　2. Libraries—Great Britain
　Addresses, essays, lectures.　　I. Whibley, Vaughan.　　II. Title.

Z673.L74L53　　1977　　　　　021'.00941　　　　　　79-303722
　　　　　　　　　　　　　　　　　　　　　　　　　　　　　MARC

Library of Congress　　　　　　　79

**Monograph classed in a *Congress number* with
main entry under the title.**

The Public library : circumstance and prospects : proceedings of
the thirty-ninth conference of the Graduate Library School,
April 10-11, 1978 / edited by W. Boyd Rayward. — Chicago :
University of Chicago Press, 1978.

　　162 p. ; 24 cm. — (University of Chicago studies in library science)

　　"The papers in this volume were published originally in the Library Quarterly,
October 1978."
　　Includes bibliographical references.
　　ISBN 0-226-70585-4 : $9.00

　　1. Public libraries—Congresses.　　I. Rayward, W. Boyd, 1939-　　　. II.
Chicago.　University.　Graduate School.　III. Series: Chicago.　University.
University of Chicago studies in library science.

Z672.5.P84　　　　　　　027.4　　　　　　　　　78-19604
　　　　　　　　　　　　　　　　　　　　　　　　　　　　　MARC

Library of Congress　　　　　　　78

**Monograph classed in a *General works number* with
main entry under the title.**

The Information worker : identity, image and potential : proceedings of a one day joint Aslib-Institute of Information Scientists
conference held at the Geological Society of London on 22nd
November 1976 / edited by Margaret R. Raffin, Rona Passmore.
— London : Aslib : Institute of Information Scientists, 1977.

[3], 58 p. : ill. ; 30 cm.   GB78-00013

Includes bibliographies.
ISBN 0-85142-099-0 : £3.25

1. Information scientists— Addresses, essays, lectures.   I. Raffin, Margaret
R. II. Passmore, Rona.   III. Aslib.   IV. Institute of Information Scientists.

Z674.4.I55   029'.023   78-313356
                                                           MARC

Library of Congress   78

JUVENILE MATERIALS

Full Library of Congress call numbers are supplied for all juvenile titles added to the Library's classified collection. Alternative class numbers for juvenile fiction in English classed in PZ7 are not supplied.[11]

In general, materials intended for children and young adults ranging in age
from preschool through sixteen are treated as juvenile materials. Thus, works
designated by the publishers as "10 up," "14+," or "suitable for senior high
school students" are juvenile, since the lower end of the designated span includes
at least one year of the 0 through 16 range. Generally, works with the notation
"for all ages" may also be considered juvenile.

Juvenile Belles Lettres

Belles lettres for children are classed in PZ5-90. For works written in the
English language classed in PZ5-8, unique Cutter numbers are assigned to individual authors and work letters are used to distinguish different works by the
same author. The work letters, based on the title (disregarding initial articles),
consist of a capital letter followed by one or more letters in lower case. Variant
editions of the same work are differentiated by adding an arabic number (1, 2, 3,
etc. in the order of receipt of the publications) to the work letters.

N. Borisoff's *Bird Seed & Lightning*.

PZ	The double letters for the subclass, Fiction in English and juvenile belles lettres
7	The integral number meaning American and English juvenile belles lettres, 1870-
.B648455	The Cutter number for Borisoff
Bi	The work letters based on the title, *Bird....*

V. C. Renshaw's *Thalassine*.

PZ	The double letters for the subclass, Fiction in English and juvenile belles lettres
7	The integral number meaning American and English juvenile belles lettres, 1870-
.R293	The Cutter number for Renshaw
Th3	The work letters (Th) based on the title, *Thalassine*, and the arabic number (3) indicating a variant edition

Paul Annixter's *The Best Nature Stories*.

PZ	The double letters for the subclass, Fiction in English and juvenile belles lettres
10.3	The number meaning animal stories
.A59	The Cutter number for the main entry, Annixter
Be	The work letters based on the title, disregarding the initial article

For works with main entry under the title, the Cutter number is based on the title, and the work letters are then unnecessary.

Sleep, Baby, Sleep: An Old Cradle Song.

PZ	The double letters for the subclass, Fiction in English and juvenile belles lettres
8.3	The number meaning verses for children
.S632	The Cutter number for the main entry, *Sleep....*

Work letters are not used with juvenile belles lettres in languages other than English.

E. Libenzi's *Il Pianeta dei matti,* 1971.

PZ	The double letters for the subclass, Fiction in English and juvenile belles lettres
43	The number meaning general juvenile belles lettres in the Italian language
.L5	The Cutter number for Libenzi

L. Escobio's *Evocación de la madre marinera: [teatro juvenil].*

PZ	The double letters for the subclass, Fiction in English and juvenile belles lettres
77	The number meaning juvenile drama in the Spanish language
.E75	The Cutter number for Escobio

Picture Books for Children

A work intended by its publisher to be a picture story book for young children with little or no accompanying text is classed with juvenile belles lettres in the PZ juvenile area. Even when the work is entered under the artist, it is not regarded as a work of art to be classed in N. It is treated as a story book. For example,

R. Stewart's *The Daddy Book.*

PZ	The double letters for the subclass, Fiction in English and juvenile belles lettres
7	The integral number meaning American and English juvenile belles lettres, 1870-
.S8498	The Cutter number for the author, Stewart
Dad	The work letters for the title *Daddy....*

Bedtime Stories, illustrated by Tibor Gergely.

PZ	The double letters for the subclass, Fiction in English and juvenile belles lettres
8	The integral number meaning fairy tales
.B389	The Cutter number for the main entry, *Bedtime....*

E. Miller's *Mousekin's ABC.*

PZ	The double letters for the subclass, Fiction in English and juvenile belles lettres
8.3	The number with decimal extension meaning verses for children and stories in rhyme
.M6133	The Cutter number for the author, Miller
Mo	The work letters for the title, *Mousekin's....*

Topical Juvenile Materials

The former practice of classing certain topical juvenile materials in PZ9-10, 15-16, etc., has been discontinued. All topical juvenile materials are now classed with the subjects in the regular subject classes. The number designated for "Juvenile works" under the appropriate subject is chosen, for example,

G. Laycock's *Air Pollution.*

TD	The double letters for the subclass, Environmental technology
883.13	The number meaning a juvenile work on air pollution and its control
.L38	The Cutter number for the main entry, Laycock

If no "Juvenile works" number is available under the particular topic, the "General works" number is used, e.g.,

Peter Muccini's *Discovering Italy.*

DG	The double letters for the subclass, History of Italy
417	The integral number for a general work on medieval and modern Italy
.M8	The Cutter number for the main entry, Muccini

School Textbooks

School textbooks for children up through the age of sixteen are classed with the subject in the regular subject classes. Under the topic in question, the class number for textbooks is assigned, e.g.,

George Howard Bruce's *High School Chemistry.*

QD	The double letters for the subclass, Chemistry
33	The integral number meaning an elementary textbook
.B88	The Cutter number for the main entry, Bruce

If such a number is not provided in the schedules, the number for "Juvenile works" is used. If neither number is available, a school textbook is classed with the "General works" class number. A school textbook should never be classed under the "Study and teaching" number. Textbooks intended for students older than sixteen are either classed in special form numbers for textbooks, if available, or in the "General works" numbers.

NONBOOK MATERIALS

Audiovisual Media

The Library of Congress does not use class numbers for shelving audiovisual media and special instructional materials. However, as a service to other libraries, bracketed class numbers have been provided on LC cataloging records for films and filmstrips, sound recordings, and slide sets. The value of this service is being reassessed by the Library of Congress in order to determine whether to continue supplying these numbers.[12]

In general, the same principles and policies with regard to classifying books apply to the classification of nonbook materials. Treatment of juvenile belles lettres and topical juvenile materials has been discussed earlier in the chapter.

The following are examples of LC cataloging records for nonbook materials with bracketed class numbers.

The Age of space transportation. [Motion picture] / United States National Aeronautics and Space Administration. — Washington : The Administration : distributed by National Audiovisual Center, 1976.

1 reel, 20 min. : sd., col. ; 16 mm.

SUMMARY: Discusses technological advances in the area of transportation and considers the space shuttle as a potential mode of travel.

1. Reusable space vehicles. I. United States. National Aeronautics and Space Administration.

[TL795.5]   629.04   77-700798
                                                        MARC

National Audiovisual
Center
for Library of Congress   77   F

(Text continues on page 316)

Bizet, Georges, 1838–1875.
  ₁Carmen. Selections₁ ₁Sound recording₁
  Carmen (fragments of Acts one & two).   Unique Opera
Records UORC 262. ₁197–?₁
  on side 2 of 1 disc. 33⅓ rpm. mono. 12 in.

  With : Verdi, G. Aïda. Selections.
  "Private record, not for sale."
  Opera excerpts ; Bruna Castagna in the title role ; Suzanne
Fisher as Micaela ; René Maison as Don José ; John Brownlee as
Escamillo ; other soloists, chorus, and orchestra ; Gennaro Papi, con-
ductor ; sung in French.
  Recorded in 1938.

  1. Operas—Excerpts.   I. Castagna, Bruna.   II. Fisher, Suzanne.
III. Maison, René.   IV. Brownlee, John, 1900–1967.   V. Papi, Gennaro.   VI. Title.

[M1505]   ◯   76–760175
Library of Congress   76   R

Frost, David.
  The Frost report on Britain. ₁Sound recording₁ Written by David Frost and John Cleese.   Starline MRS 5084.
p1966.
  1 disc. 33⅓ rpm. mono. 12 in.

  Title on container : Report on Britain.
  Comedy sketches.
  David Frost, narrator, with John Cleese, Tim Brooks-Taylor, and
others.
  CONTENTS : Matter of taste. — Schoolmaster. — Just four just
men.—Internal combustion.—Deck of cards.—Top of the form.—
Unknown soldier.—Scrapbook.—Adventure. — Numbers. — Bulletin. —
Hilton.—Zookeeper.

  1. English wit and humor.   I. Cleese, John.   II. Title : Report on
Britain. ₁Sound   recording₁

[PN6175]   ◯   76–740150
Library of Congress   76   MN

A Man's reach should exceed his grasp. ₍Videorecording₎ / United States National Aeronautics and Space Administration. — Washington : The Administration ; distributed by National Audiovisual Center, 1972.

1 cassette, 24 min. : sd., col. ; 3/4 in.

U standard.
CREDITS: Narrator, Burgess Meredith.
SUMMARY: Presents the history of flight and of man's reach for a new freedom through aviation and the exploration of space, recounting developments from the Wright Brothers' flight to the landing on the Moon and plans for future missions to other planets. Emphasizes the creative role of research and cites statements by scientists, writers, poets, and philosophers which document man's

(Continued on next card)

77-706031
MARC
77   F

A Man's reach should exceed his grasp. ₍Videorecording₎ / ...
(Card 2)

search for knowledge.

1. Aeronautics—History.   2. Astronautics—History.   I. United States. National Aeronautics and Space Administration.

₍TL515₎   629.13   77-706031
MARC

National Audiovisual
Center
for Library of Congress   77   F

An Inquiry into the future of mankind: designing tomorrow today.
[Slide set]   Center for Humanities, 1974.

160 slides.   color.   2 x 2 in.   and 2 phonodiscs (2 s. each), 12 in., 33 1/3
rpm., 29 min.

Also issued with phonotape in cassette.
With teacher's guide.
SUMMARY: Explores man's continuing fascination with how and why and
where he is going. Stresses man's real ability to act in facing the challenges of
the future.

1. Civilization, Modern—1950-   2. Forecasting.   I. Center for
Humanities.

[CB161]   301   74-732528
                                                               MARC

Center for Humanities
for Library of Congress   74   F

Catalogs of Nonbook Materials

Catalogs of sound recordings, even those on nonmusical topics, are classed
in ML, e.g.,

> A. O. Maleady's *Record and Tape Reviews Index*
> ML156.9.M28

Catalogs of motion pictures are classed with the pertinent subject. General
catalogs of films are classed in PN1998, and general catalogs of films as
audiovisual aids in LB1044.Z9, e.g.,

> J. A. Kislia's *"Let's See It Again": Free Films for Elementary Schools*
> LB1044.Z9K57

> National Information Center for Educational Media.
> *Index to Educational Audio Tapes*, 1974
> LB1044.4.Z9N3 1974

MICROFILMS

At the Library of Congress, microfilms are arranged by accession numbers
called "control numbers." The call number for a microfilm consists of three
elements:

> Microfilm
> [control number]   (a sequential number)
> [class letter(s)]   (based on the class or subclass)

For example, *The Anglo-American Times: An International, Commercial, and General Newspaper** is assigned the following call number:

Microfilm
02381
AP

For libraries that wish to arrange microfilms by class numbers, bracketed class numbers are provided on LC cataloging records. The bracketed number is carried out as far as needed to cover topical elements, often including a topical Cutter number, but not the Cutter number indicating form or author. Alternative class numbers, if applicable, are also enclosed in brackets. For example,

---

British Library. Reference Division.
₍Official publications in the British Library Reference Division. — London : The Library, 1976₎

13 reels ; 16 mm.

Title from publisher's brochure.
Includes index.

1. Government publications—Bibliography—Catalogs. I. Title.

Microfilm 69003 Z   78–335013
[Z7164.G7]   [J9.5]

Library of Congress   78

MICROFICHE

In the Library of Congress, the call number for a microfiche consists of the term "Microfiche" followed by the class number (including the topical Cutter number(s) but not the Cutter number indicating form or author). For example,

---

*The call number for the original is AP4.A52.

Singerman, Robert.
    Index of Western States Jewish history in the American Israelite (Cincinnati), 1854–1900 / Robert Singerman, compiler. — ₁Cincinnati?₁ : Singerman, c1976.

    7 sheets ; 11 x 15 cm.

    Title from heading area.

    1. Jews in the West—Bibliography. 2. American Israelite—Indexes. 3. The West—Bibliography.   I. American Israelite. II. Title: Index of Western States Jewish history ...

Microfiche Z6373.U5   77–398036
[F591]

Library of Congress   78

Xerox University Microfilms.
    Out-of-print book catalog : authors. — ₁Ann Arbor, Mich.₁ : Xerox University Microfilms, 1974.

    16 sheets (1222 p.) : 11 x 15 cm.

    Microfiche.
    Title from heading area.
    Title on jacket: Catalog of out-of-print books.

    1. Out-of-print books—Bibliography—Catalogs. 2. Books on microfilm—Catalogs.   I. Title. II. Title: Catalog of out-of-print books.

Microfiche Z1000.5   75–567152

Library of Congress   75

INCUNABULA

    At the Library of Congress, incunabula, i.e., books printed before 1501, are housed in the Rare Book Division, except those assigned to special collections such as the Law Library. Materials assigned to the incunabula collection in the Rare Book Division receive one of two broad classifications: "Incun. [date]"

(used for entries which have definite imprint dates) or "Incun. X" (used when the precise date of publication is uncertain). For example,

Imprint shows	Call number
1492	Incun. 1492
[1494]	Incun. 1494
1490-1495	Incun. 1490
3 Mar. 1483/84	Incun. 1484
[1486?]	Incun. X
[not after 1479]	Incun. X
[after 16 June 1486]	Incun. X
[between 1472-1474]	Incun. X
[ca. 1490]	Incun. X
[ca. 1490-1495]	Incun. X
[149-]	Incun. X

A Cutter number based on the main entry is added to complete the call number, e.g.,

Incun. 1492 .P7	Incun. 1492 .P72	Incun. 1494 .A5
Incun. X .D895	Incun. X .M3533	

Bracketed Alternative Class Numbers for Incunabula

For libraries that wish to classify incunabula in the regular manner, bracketed numbers are provided on LC cataloging records. The bracketed number is carried out as far as needed to cover topical elements, including the Cutter number for specific localities, persons, institutions, etc., but does not include the Cutter number indicating form or author.

Facsimiles of Individual Incunabula

At the Library of Congress, facsimiles of individual incunabula or excerpts from such facsimiles are treated as normal works and classed by subject. The class number Z241 is assigned only when it is clear that the publisher intends the work to serve as a specimen of early printing.

TRANSLATIONS

In many places in the schedules, special numbers are assigned to translations. If, under a particular discipline or topic, such a number does not exist, a translation is assigned the same call number as the original edition, with a successive Cutter element attached to the book number.* The successive Cutter element is based on the language of the translation. The general pattern for subarranging translations in different languages is presented in the Table for Translations on page 100. For example,

P. Delsol's *Horoscopes chinois*
BF1714.C5D4
BF1714.C5D413   An English translation with the title
Chinese Astrology

J. G. Heineccius' *Elementa juris naturae et gentium*
JX2314.E3
JX2314.E318   A Spanish translation with the title
Elementos del derecho natural y de gentes

Parallel Texts[13]

As a general rule, a publication which contains an original text, as well as a translation of the text, is treated as a translation, because users of this type of publication are normally most interested in the translation and the critical matter that is in the language of the translation. Such a work is assigned the translation number rather than treated as an edition of the original work. This is especially true if the title page and/or the introductory material and notes are in the language of the translation.

Ludwig Wittgenstein's *Über Gewissheit*
B3376.W563U3

B3376.W563U313 1969b   *On Certainty*, an English translation
with German and English on opposite
pages.

---

*For a discussion of Cutter numbers for translations, *see* chapter 3, pages 100-101.

"BOUND-WITH" BOOKS[14]

As a general rule, a volume of two or more bibliographically independent works bound together after publication is classed with the first work of the volume. A book bound in the "upside-down" manner is classed with the topic listed first in the classification scheme. For example, if one work belongs in PS, and the other in PR, the volume is classed in PR. An exception is made for a bound-with volume containing two works, one of which is overwhelmingly larger than the other. In such a case, the class number appropriate to the larger work is chosen for the volume.

The same call number is assigned to the cataloging record of each work in the volume. In addition, a bracketed alternative class number is assigned to each additional record, unless it is the same as the class number for the entire volume.

Rossignol, Louis, 1694-1739.
 Nouveau livre d'écriture d'après les meilleures exemples de Rossignol. Gravé par Le Parmentier. Paris, Daumont [ca. 1770?]

 20 l. 34 cm.

 L.C. copy imperfect: leaf [3] wanting.
 Bound with Royllet, Sébastien. Les fidèles tableaux de l'art d'écrire ... Paris, 1764.

 1. Calligraphy. I. Le Parmentier,. II. Title.

 Z243.A2R68 1770   78-371769
                                                        MARC

 Library of Congress   78

Royllet, Sébastien, 1700-1767.
 Les fidèles tableaux de l'art d'écrire par colonnes de démonstrations, par lesquelles les principes sont développés. Paris, Chez la veuve David, libraire; Regnard, libraire & imprimeur, 1764.

 9 p., 29 plates. 34 cm.

 Bound with Rossignol, Louis. Nouveau livre d'écriture ... Paris [ca. 1770?]
 Several of the plates signed: Baisiez sculp.

 1. Calligraphy. I. Baisiez,. II. Title.

 Z243.A2R68 1770   78-371770
                                                        MARC

 Library of Congress   78

PICTORIAL BOOKS*

Many books contain important pictorial material in addition to the literary text. Such works may be the result of collaboration of an artist and an author. In other cases, the pictorial material may be present in order to illustrate an individual work; or, in reverse situations, the text may only represent a minor element of the publication. Unless there are special directions to the contrary in the schedules, the main entry is used as the determining factor in the selection of the class number. If the main entry is under the artist, the work is classed in N, TR, etc. If the main entry is under the writer of the text, the work is classed in P, BS, etc.

BIOGRAPHY

It is a characteristic of the Library of Congress Classification system that biographies of persons associated with particular fields are classed with the subjects represented in the various schedules. The Subclass CT is restricted to general biography of persons not associated with any particular field (*see* discussion and examples in chapter 5).

Different types of biographical writings about a person, such as autobiography, letters, speeches, biography and criticism, are assigned the same class number (usually containing a Cutter number based on the name of the biographee) and differentiated by means of successive Cutter numbers. A table (*see* Appendix B) has been devised for this purpose and is used for subarranging biographical works about individuals in all classes except Class N and Class P which have their own special tables.

The following examples demonstrate the classification of individual biography with the subject classes:

H. Myers' *Vincent Lombardi: Young Football Coach.*

GV	The double letters for the subclass, Recreation and leisure
939	The integral number meaning biography in the field of football
.L6	The first Cutter number for the biographee, Lombardi
M9	The second Cutter number for the main entry, Myers

F. Stenzel's *Cleveland Rockwell: Scientist and Artist, 1837-1907.*

TA	The double letters for the subclass, Engineering
533	The integral number meaning an individual biography in the field of surveying
.R63	The first Cutter number for the biographee, Rockwell
S83	The second Cutter number for the main entry, Stenzel

---

*For pictorial books for children, *see* pages 311-12.

M. Flückiger's *Albert Einstein in Bern*.

QC	The double letters for the subclass, Physics
16	The integral number meaning an individual biography
.E5	The first Cutter number for the biographee, Einstein
F56	The second Cutter number for the main entry, Flückiger

Biographies of chiefs of state, statesmen, politicians, other public figures, and persons identified with specific historical events or movements are classed in the history classes, D and E-F. Normally, the local history number is chosen unless the person was more prominent on the national than on the local level, in which case the number for "Biography and memoirs" under a particular monarch's reign, a particular president's administration, etc. is chosen. If the person was more prominent on the local level and the locality is further subdivided by periods, the number for the appropriate period is used.

A double Cutter number—i.e., the first for the biographee and the second for the author—is used even when the class number is not designated specifically for biography.

S. H. Young's *Alaska Days with John Muir*, 1972.

F	The single letter for the class, United States local history
908	The integral number meaning history of Alaska, 1867-1896
.M96	The first Cutter number for the biographee, Muir
Y6	The second Cutter number for the main entry, Young
1972	The date of publication

A. Passeron's *De Gaulle, 1958-1969*.

DC	The double letter for the subclass, History of France
373	The integral number meaning twentieth century individual biography
.G3	The first Cutter number for the biographee, Gaulle
P37	The second Cutter number for the main entry, Passeron

Michael A. Lofaro's *The Life and Adventures of Daniel Boone*.

F	The single letter for the class, United States local history
454	The integral number meaning early history of Kentucky
.B66	The first Cutter number for the biographee, Boone
L63	The second Cutter number for the main entry, Lofaro

Viscount J. M. Morley's *The Life of William Ewart Gladstone.* *

DA	The double letters for the subclass, History of Great Britain
563	The integral number assigned to Gladstone
.4	The decimal extension for a biography
.M8	The Cutter number for the main entry, Morley
1968	The date of publication

Under a number for an individual reign or administration which includes the life of the ruler or chief of state, only one Cutter number, for the author of the work, is assigned, e.g.,

M. M. Luke's *Gloriana: The Years of Elizabeth I*, 1974.

DA	The double letters for the subclass, History of Great Britain
355	The integral number meaning general works on life and reign of Elizabeth I
.L84	The Cutter number for the author, Luke
1974	The date of publication

G. Brook-Shepherd's *The Last Habsburg*, 1969.

DB	The double letters for the subclass, History of Austria
92	The integral number meaning general works on life and reign of Karl I
.B76	The Cutter number for the author, Brook-Shepherd
1969	The date of publication

T. W. Handford's *The Life and Sayings of Theodore Roosevelt: The Twenty-sixth President of the United States.*

E	The single letter for the class, History of the United States
757	The integral number meaning a biography of Theodore Roosevelt
.H23	The Cutter number for the author, Handford

Memoirs of persons associated with particular companies are classed with the numbers for the companies in H or T, if possible, or with the activity in which the companies are engaged. Collective biographies of persons associated with particular subject fields are classed in a similar manner as individual biographies. Under many topics, special numbers are provided for collective biography which normally precede those assigned to individual biography. Obituaries are classed with collective biography, e.g.,

---

*Only a single Cutter number for the author is used here because the class number means a biography of Gladstone.

Virginia. State Library, Richmond. *Index to Obituary Notices in the Richmond Enquirer from May 9, 1804, through 1828, and the Richmond Whig from January, 1824, through 1838,* 1974.

F	The single letter for the class, United States local history
225	The integral number meaning a collective biography of persons from Virginia
.V83	The Cutter number for the main entry, Virginia
1974	The date of publication

NOTES

[1]*Cataloging Service* 116:7 (Winter 1976).

[2]*Cataloging Service* 116:8 (Winter 1976).

[3]*Cataloging Service* 104:6 (May 1972).

[4]*Cataloging Service* 124:26-27 (Winter 1978).

[5]*Cataloging Service* 116:7 (Winter 1976).

[6]*Cataloging Service* 110:6-8 (Summer 1974).

[7]*Cataloging Service* 124:27-28 (Winter 1978).

[8]*Cataloging Service* 121:19 (Spring 1977).

[9]*Cataloging Service Bulletin* 3:18-19 (Winter 1978).

[10]Cf. *Cataloging Service* 112:15-16 (Winter 1975). Note that some of the procedures outlined in this issue of *Cataloging Service* have been revised since 1975.

[11]*Cataloging Service* 86:2 (January 1969).

[12]*Cataloging Service Bulletin* 2:45 (Fall 1978).

[13]*Cataloging Service* 114:11 (Summer 1975).

[14]*Cataloging Service Bulletin* 1:21 (Summer 1978).

APPENDIX A
TABLES OF GENERAL APPLICATION

REGIONS AND COUNTRIES IN ONE ALPHABET

The numbers in this list are intended to be used as a guide for the best distribution of numbers and not necessarily as a fixed standard. Considerable latitude may be used in cases where the countries are arranged in continental groups.

Abyssinia, *see* .E8	
Afghanistan	.A3
Africa, South	.A35
Algeria	.A4
Arabia, Saudi, *see* .S33	
Argentine Republic	.A7
Australia	.A8
Austria	.A9
Bangladesh	.B3
Belgium	.B4
Bolivia	.B5
Borneo	.B54
Botswana	.B57
Brazil	.B6
British Guiana, *see* .G95	(.B7)
British Honduras	.B8
Bulgaria	.B9
Cambodia	.C16
Cameroon	.C17
Canada	.C2
Central Africa	.C42
Ceylon, *see* .S73	
Chile	.C5
China	.C6
Colombia	.C7
Congo (Brazzaville)	.C75
Costa Rica	.C8
Cuba	.C9
Czechoslovak Republic	.C95

Denmark	.D4
Dutch East Indies, *see* .I5	
Dutch Guiana, *see* .S75	(.D8)
East Africa	.E18
Ecuador	.E2
Egypt	.E3
Ethiopia	.E8
Formosa, *see* .T28	
France	.F8
French Guiana	.F9
French-speaking Equatorial Africa	.F82
French-speaking West Africa	.F83
Gabon	.G23
Germany. Federal Republic	.G3
Democratic Republic	.G35
Ghana (Gold Coast)	.G4
Great Britain	.G7
Greece	.G8
Greenland	.G83
Guatemala	.G9
Guinea	.G92
Guyana	.G95
Haiti	.H2
Holland, *see* .N4	(.H7)
Honduras	.H8
Hong Kong	.H85
Iceland	.I2
India	.I4
Indonesia	.I5
Iran	.I7
Israel	.I75
Italy	.I8
Japan	.J3
Jordan	.J6
Korea	.K8
Korea, North	.K83
Kuwait	.K85
Laos	.L28
Lebanon	.L4
Lesotho	.L45
Liberia	.L7
Libya	.L74
Luxemburg	.L9

Macao	.M2
Madagascar	.M28
Malawi	.M3
Malaya	.M318
Malta	.M33
Mauritania	.M39
Mauritius	.M4
Mekong River Valley	.M45
Mexico	.M6
Morocco	.M8
Mozambique	.M85
Netherlands	.N4
Nicaragua	.N5
Nile River Valley	.N6
North Sea	.N67
Northern Rhodesia, *see* .Z3	
Norway	.N8
Nyasaland, *see* .M3	
Pakistan	.P18
Palestine, *see* .I75	
Panama	.P2
Paraguay	.P3
Persia, *see* .I7	(.P4)
Peru	.P5
Philippine Islands	.P6
Poland	.P7
Portugal	.P8
Romania	.R6
Russia	.R9
Rwanda	.R93
Sahel	.S18
Salvador	.S2
Santo Domingo	.S3
Saudi Arabia	.S33
Senegal	.S38
Siam, *see* .T5	(.S5)
Singapore	.S53
Somalia	.S59
South Africa, *see* .A35	
Spain	.S7
Sri Lanka	.S73
Sudan	.S74
Surinam	.S75
Swaziland	.S79
Sweden	.S8
Switzerland	.S9
Syria	.S94

Taiwan	.T28
Tanzania	.T35
Thailand	.T5
Togo	.T64
Trucial States, *see* .U54	
Tunisia	.T8
Turkey	.T9
Uganda	.U4
United Arab Emirates	.U54
United States	.U6
Upper Volta	.U66
Uruguay	.U8
Venezuela	.V4
Vietnam (Democratic Republic)	.V53
Yugoslavia	.Y8
Zambia	.Z3

UNITED STATES

Alabama	.A2
Alaska	.A4
Arizona	.A6
Arkansas	.A8
California	.C2
Colorado	.C6
Connecticut	.C8
Dakota (Territory)	.D2
Delaware	.D3
District of Columbia	.D6
Florida	.F6
Georgia	.G4
Hawaii	.H3
Idaho	.I2
Illinois	.I3
Indian Territory	.I4
Indiana	.I6
Iowa	.I8
Kansas	.K2
Kentucky	.K4
Louisiana	.L8
Maine	.M2
Maryland	.M3
Massachusetts	.M4
Michigan	.M5
Minnesota	.M6
Mississippi	.M7

Missouri	.M8
Montana	.M9
Nebraska	.N2
Nevada	.N3
New Hampshire	.N4
New Jersey	.N5
New Mexico	.N6
New York	.N7
North Carolina	.N8
North Dakota	.N9
Ohio	.O3
Oklahoma	.O5
Oregon	.O7
Pennsylvania	.P4
Rhode Island	.R4
South Carolina	.S6
South Dakota	.S8
Tennessee	.T2
Texas	.T4
Utah	.U8
Vermont	.V5
Virginia	.V8
Washington	.W2
West Virginia	.W4
Wisconsin	.W6
Wyoming	.W8

CANADA AND NEWFOUNDLAND — LIST OF PROVINCES

Alberta	.A3
Assiniboia	.A6
Athabasca	.A8
British Columbia	.B8
Franklin	.F8
Keewatin	.K3
Labrador	.L2
Mackenzie	.M2
Manitoba	.M3
New Brunswick	.N5
Newfoundland	.N6
Northwest Territories	.N7
Nova Scotia	.N8
Ontario	.O6
Prince Edward Island	.P8
Quebec	.Q3
Saskatchewan	.S2
Ungava	.U6
Yukon	.Y8

APPENDIX B
CUTTER NUMBERS FOR
INDIVIDUAL BIOGRAPHY[1]

The following table is used as a guide in formulating Cutter numbers for autobiography, individual biography, etc., in all classes except N (Fine Arts) and P (Language and Literature). *See* page 396 of this book for tables for Class N and consult the appropriate schedules for tables for Class P.

Autobiography, individual biography, etc. Table

.x	Cutter number for individual
.xA2	Collected works. By date of imprint
.xA25	Selected works. Quotations. By date of imprint
.xA3-39	Autobiography, diaries, etc.
.xA4	Letters. By date of imprint
.xA42-49	Letters to an individual. By correspondent, A-Z
.xA5-59	Speeches, etc.
.xA6-Z	Biography and criticism

---

[1]This table is a revised and updated version of the one published in *Cataloging Service* 107:5-6 (December 1973).

APPENDIX C
TABLES USED WITH INDIVIDUAL CLASSES

This appendix contains tables from individual classes or subclasses which have undergone considerable revision or changes since the publication of the latest edition of the main schedules of those classes. The tables printed here incorporate revisions and changes published in *LC Classification—Additions and Changes* (through List 194, April-June 1979). Tables in recently revised editions which are readily available from the main schedules of the individual classes are excluded.

Class B: BL-BX

BQ

BUDDHISM

TABLES OF SUBDIVISIONS

TRIPITAKA AND OTHER EARLY TEXTS

Tables			
I	II	III	
0	0	.x	Original texts (Pāli, Sanskrit, Tibetan, Chinese, etc.).
			Subarranged by editor or date of imprint.
1	.1	.x1	Partial editions, selections, etc.
			Subarranged by editor or date of imprint.
			For selections sacred to a particular sect, see Table IV, 8, etc.
			Translations and adaptations (with or without original text).
			Subarranged by translator or adaptor.
2.A1A-Z	.2.A1A-Z	.x2	Polyglot.
.A2-Z	.2.A2-Z	.x22	Western languages, A-Z.
3	.3	.x3	Oriental and other languages, A-Z.
			Commentaries.
5	.5	.x5	Early works to 1800.
7	.7	.x7	1801-
			Including modern criticism, interpretation, etc.
8	.8	.x8	Sermons.
9	.9	.x9	Dictionaries. Indexes. Concordances.
			Bibliography, see Z7862-7862.9.

Class B: BL-BX

BQ

BUDDHISM

TABLES OF SUBDIVISIONS

TRIPITAKA AND OTHER EARLY TEXTS

Tables		
IV	V	
0	0	Periodicals. Yearbooks.
	1	Societies, councils, associations, clubs, etc.
		For societies, associations, etc. in local areas, see 2.
1		General works. History.
.2		International associations, A-Z.
.4		Young Buddhist associations.
.6		Young men's associations.
.8		Women's associations.
2	2	By region or country, A-Z.
		Under each country:
		.x General works. History.
		.x2 Local, A-Z.
		.x3 Individual, A-Z.
		Financial institutions. Trusts.
3	3	General works.
4	4	Individual, A-Z.
	5	Congresses. Conferences.
5		General.
.5		Special. By date.
6	6	Directories.
7	7	Museums. Exhibitions. By city, A-Z.
8	8	Collections. Collected works.
		Including selections sacred to a particular sect.
9	9	Encyclopedias. Dictionaries.
.5		Terminology.
		Religious education.
10	10	General works. History.
11		By region or country, A-Z.
		Under each country:
		.x General works. History.
		.x2 Local, A-Z.
.2	11	Religious education of the young. Sunday schools, etc.
.4		Religious education in the home.

Class B: BL-BX

BQ

BUDDHISM

TABLES OF SUBDIVISIONS

SPECIAL MODIFICATIONS, SECTS, ETC.

Tables		
IV	V	
	12	History.
12		Collections. Collected works. Sources. Chronological tables.
		General works.
.2		Early works through 1800.
.3		1801-
.4		Historiography.
		By period.
.5		Early to ca. 1200 A.D.
.6		1201-1850.
.7		1851-1945.
.8		1945-
.9		By region or country, A-Z.
		Under each country:
		.x General works. History.
		.x2 Local, A-Z.
	13	Persecutions.
13		General works. History.
.5		By region or country, A-Z.
		Under each country:
		.x General works. History.
		.x2 Local, A-Z.
	14	Literature.
		Including juvenile works.
14		Collections.
.2		History and criticism.
.4		By region or country, A-Z.
		Under each country:
		.x Collections.
		.x2 History and criticism.
	15	General works.
15		Early works through 1800.
.2		1801-1945.
.4		1946-

Class B: BL-BX

BQ

BUDDHISM

TABLES OF SUBDIVISIONS

SPECIAL MODIFICATIONS, SECTS, ETC.

Tables		
IV	V	
15.6		Popular works. Pictorial works.
.7		Juvenile works.
.8		General special.
		e.g. Introduction to the sacred books of the sect, etc.
.9		Essence, genius, and nature.
16	16	Addresses, essays, lectures, etc.
17	17	Questions and answers. Maxims.
	18	Doctrine.
		General works.
18		Early works through 1800.
.2		1801-1945.
.3		1946-
.4		History.
.5		Introductions.
.6		General special.
.7		Addresses, essays, lectures, etc.
.8		Creeds and catechism.
.9		Systemization of teachings based on the sect.
19	19	Controversial works against the sect. Polemics.
.2		Apologetic works.
.4		Relations to other religious and philosophical systems, A-Z.
		.C35 Catholic Church.
		.C5 Christianity.
		.C65 Confucianism.
		Shinto, see BL2222.23
		.T3 Taoism.
.6		Relations to other branches of Buddhism, A-Z.
		Prefer classification with smaller or less-known sect.
20	20	Religious practice. Forms of worship.
.2		Ceremonies and rites. Ceremonial rules.
		Service books.
.4		For priests, etc.
.6		For the laity.
21	21	Special ceremonies and rites, A-Z.
		.C66 Confirmation.
		.F8 Funeral service. Wakes. Burial service. Cremation.
		.I57 Installation.
		.M4 Memorial services for the dead.

Class B— BL-BX

BQ

BUDDHISM

TABLES OF SUBDIVISIONS

SPECIAL MODIFICATIONS, SECTS, ETC.

Tables		
IV	V	
		Religious practice. Forms of worship - Continued
		Hymns. Chants. Recitations.
22	22	Collections of hymns.
.5		By region or country, A-Z.
		Under each country:
		.x General.
		.x2 Local, A-Z.
		History and criticism.
23	23	General works.
.5		By region or country, A-Z.
		Under each country:
		.x General works.
		.x2 Local, A-Z.
24	24	Individual texts. By author or title.
.5		Liturgical objects. Vestments, etc.
25	25	Temple organization. Membership. Finance.
26	26	Ministry. Organization. Government.
27	27	Handbooks. Manuals.
28	28	Election, selection, succession, appointment, etc. Ordination.
29	29	Hierarchical offices.
30	30	Heresy trials. By date.
31	31	Education and training of the ordained ministry.
32	32	Special ministries, A-Z.
		Prefer classification in BQ5305, unless unique to the sect.
		Preaching.
33	33	General works.
.5		Practical preaching.
		Sermons.
		Prefer classification with specific subject or canonical text.
34	34	Several authors.
35	35	Individual authors. By author and title, A-Z.

Class B— BL-BX

BQ

BUDDHISM

TABLES OF SUBDIVISIONS

SPECIAL MODIFICATIONS, SECTS, ETC.

Tables		
IV	V	
		Religious practice. Forms of worship - Continued
		Religious life.
36	36	General works.
.2		Popular works, stories, etc.
		Including exempla.
.4		Religious duties, etc. of the laity.
	37	Devotional literature.
37		History and criticism.
		Collections. Collected works.
.2		Early works through 1800.
.4		1801-
.6		Selections for daily reading. Devotional
		calendars.
38	38	Devotion. Meditation. Prayer. Spiritual
		life. Mysticism. Enlightenment.
	39	Devotions. Meditations. Prayers.
		General works.
39		Early works through 1800.
.5		1801-
		Festivals. Days and seasons.
40	40	General works. History.
.2		By region or country, A-Z.
		Under each country:
		.x General works.
		.x2 Local, A-Z.
.4		Special, A-Z.
		Prefer classification in BQ5720, unless
		unique to the sect, e.g. .F6 Founder's
		Day.
	41	Folklore.
41		Collections. General works.
.2		History and criticism.
.4		By region or country, A-Z.
		Under each:
		.x Collections.
		.x2 History and criticism.

Class B: BL-BX

BQ

BUDDHISM

TABLES OF SUBDIVISIONS

SPECIAL MODIFICATIONS, SECTS, ETC.

Tables		
IV	V	
	42	Benevolent work. Social work. Welfare work, etc.
42		Periodicals. Societies. Associations.
.2		Directories. Yearbooks.
.3		History.
.4		General works.
.6		Biography (Collective).
		By region or country, see BQ5899.
	43	Missionary work.
43		Museums. Exhibitions.
.2		History.
.4		General works. Treatises.
.6		By region or country, A-Z.
		Under each country:
		.x General works.
		.x2 Local, A-Z.
	44	Monasticism and monastic life.
44		History.
.2		General works.
.4		By region or country, A-Z.
		Under each country:
		.x General works.
		.x2 Local, A-Z.
	45	Monastic life. Vows. Discipline. Rules.
		General works.
45		Early works through 1800.
.5		1801-
	46	Monasteries. Temples. Shrines. Sites.
46		History.
.5		General works.
		By region or country, see BQ6330-6388.

Class B: BL-BX

BQ

BUDDHISM

TABLES OF SUBDIVISIONS

SPECIAL MODIFICATIONS, SECTS, ETC.

Tables '		
IV	V	

48	48	Biography.
		  Collective.
		  Founders and other important leaders, A-Z.

49	49	Including local founders.
		      Subarranged by Table VIII.
		  Other individuals, see BQ940-999.

VI	VII	
0	.x	Periodicals. Societies. Congresses. Directories. Collections.
1	.x1	Religious education.
2	.x2	History. General works.
3	.x3	Literature. Folklore, etc.
4	.x4	Doctrine. Forms of worship.
5	.x5	Organization. Government.
6	.x6	Religious life. Devotional literature.
7	.x7	Benevolent work. Social work. Missionary work.
8	.x8	Monasticism. Temples.
		Biography.
9.A2A-Z	.x9	Collective.

.A3-Z	.x92	Founders and other important leaders, A-Z.
		    Including local founders.
		      Entries using Table VI are subarranged by
		        Table VIII.
		  Other individuals, see BQ940-999.

Class B— BL-BX

BQ   BUDDHISM

TABLES OF SUBDIVISIONS

INDIVIDUAL BIOGRAPHY

Table
VIII

.x   Collected works.
                 Subarranged by date.
.x2   Partial editions. Selections. Quotations, etc.
                 Subarranged by date.
.x3   Translations. By language, A-Z, and date.
.x4   Individual works. By title, A-Z.
.x5   Periodicals. Societies. Congresses. Exhibitions.
.x6   Dictionaries. Indexes. Concordances.
.x7   Biography and criticism.
.x9   Sermons about the founder, etc.

Class D

TABLES FOR COUNTRIES AND REGIONS WITH SINGLE NUMBER OR
CUTTER NUMBER

I[1]	II[2]	III[3]	
.A2A–Z	.x.A2A–Z	.xA2–29	Periodicals. Societies.
.A3A–Z	.x.A3A–Z	.xA3–39	Sources and documents. Collections.
.A5–Z	.x.A5–Z	.xA5–Z	General works.
.2	.x2	.x2	Description and travel. Guidebooks. Gazetteers.
.3	.x3	.x3	Antiquities.
.4	.x4	.x4	Social life and customs. Civilization.
.42	.x42	.x42	Ethnography. Races.
			History
.5	.x5	.x5	General works.
.6	.x6	.x6	Biography and memoirs (Collective).
			Political and diplomatic history. Foreign and general relations. Nationalism.
.62	.x62	.x62	General works.
			By period, <u>see</u> the specific period.
.63	.x63	.x63	Relations with individual countries, A–Z.
			For list of countries, <u>see</u> pp. 605–606.
			By period.
			Early.
.65	.x65	.x65	General works.
.66	.x66	.x66	Biography and memoirs.
			.A2A–Z Collective.
			.A3–Z Individual, A–Z.
			Colonial.
.7	.x7	.x7	General works.
.72	.x72	.x72	Biography and memoirs.
			.A2A–Z Collective.
			.A3–Z Individual, A–Z.
			20th Century.
.75	.x75	.x75	General works.
.76	.x76	.x76	Biography and memoirs.
			.A2A–Z Collective.
			.A3–Z Individual, A–Z.
			Independent.
.8	.x8	.x8	General works.
.82	.x82	.x82	Biography and memoirs.
			.A2A–Z Collective.
			.A3–Z Individual, A–Z.
.9	.x9	.x9	Local, A–Z.

See footnotes on page 343.

Class D

TABLES FOR CITIES WITH SINGLE NUMBER OR CUTTER NUMBER

To be used only where indicated in schedules.

IV[4]	V[5]	
.A2	.x	Periodicals. Societies. Collections.
.A3	.x2	Museums. Exhibitions, exhibits.
.A4	.x3	Guidebooks. Gazetteers. Directories.
.A5-Z	.x4	General works. Description.
.1	.x43	Monumental and picturesque.
.13	.x45	Minor works. Pamphlets, addresses, essays.
.15	.x47	Antiquities.
.2	.x5	Social life and customs. Intellectual life. History.
.23	.x53	Biography.[6]
.25	.x55	Historiography. Study and teaching.
.3	.x57	General works.
.4	.x6	Sections, districts, etc.[6]
.5	.x65	Monuments. Statues.[6]
.6	.x7	Parks. Squares. Circles.[6]
.7	.x75	Streets.[6]
.8	.x8	Buildings.[6]
.9	.x9	Elements in the population.[6]

---

[1]e.g. Nigeria: DT515.A2-515.9.

[2]e.g. Gabon: DT546.1.A2-546.19. { (.x in Table II is decimal part of class number)

[3]e.g. Upper Volta: DT553.U7-79 { (.x in Table III is Cutter number for country)

[4]e.g. Melbourne: DU228.A2-228.9.

[5]e.g. Johannesburg: DT944.J6-69. { (.x in Table V is Cutter number for city)

[6]Subdivided as follows:
   Table IV
      .A1-19 Documents.
      .A2A-Z General. Collective.
      .A3-Z   Individual.

   Table V
      .A1-19 Documents
      .A2-29 General. Collective.
      .A3-Z   Individual.

Class D

INDIVIDUAL BIOGRAPHY

Use the tables below to subarrange numbers and cutters for individual
persons under each class number of the D schedule providing for
biography and memoirs, e.g. DA566.9.C5, Churchill, Sir Winston
Leonard Spencer. Exception: for class numbers designating individual reigns, including the life of the ruler, e.g. DA539, General
works on life and reign of William IV, cutter only for the author
of the work without further subarrangement.

VI One no.	VII Cutter no.	
.A2	.xA2	Collected works. By date.[7]
.A25	.xA25	Selected works. By date.[7]
.A3–39	.xA3–39	Autobiography, diaries, etc. Al- phabetically by title.
.A4	.xA4	Letters (Collections). By imprint date.
.A41–49	.xA41–49	Letters to an individual. Al- phabetically by correspondent.
.A5–59	.xA5–59	Speeches (Collective and individ- ual), etc. Alphabetically by title.
.A6–Z	.xA6–Z	Biography and criticism.

[7]Class here collected or selected works by the individual
on general historical or political topics pertaining to the
period during which he lived. For his collected or selected
works on a special topic, see the topic.

Class F

TABLES FOR CITIES WITH SINGLE NUMBER OR CUTTER NUMBER,
IN UNITED STATES, BRITISH AMERICA AND LATIN AMERICA*

To be used only where indicated in schedules.

V[1]	VI[2]	
.A2	.x	Periodicals. Societies. Collections.
.A3	.x2	Museums. Exhibitions, exhibits.
.A4	.x3	Guidebooks. Gazetteers. Directories.
.A5-Z	.x4	General works. Description.
.1	.x43	Monumental and picturesque.
.13	.x45	Minor works. Pamphlets, addresses, essays.
.15	.x47	Antiquities.
.2	.x5	Social life and customs. Intellectual life.
		History.
.23	.x53	Biography.[3]
.25	.x55	Historiography. Study and teaching.
.3	.x57	General works.
.4	.x6	Sections. Districts, etc.[3]
.5	.x65	Monuments. Statues.[3]
.6	.x7	Parks. Squares. Circles.[3]
.7	.x75	Streets.[3]
.8	.x8	Buildings.[3]
		Elements in the population.
.9.A2A-Z	.x9A2-29	General. Collective.
.9.A3-Z	.9A3-Z	Individual, A-Z.
		For lists of Cutters, see
		E184, United States; F1035,
		Canada; F1392, Mexico;
		F1477, Guatemala; etc.

---

[1]e.g. Buenos Aires: F3001.A2-3001.9.

[2]e.g. São Paulo: F2651.S2-29. $\{$(.x in Table VI is Cutter number for city)

[3]Subdivided as follows:
   Table V

      .A2A-Z General. Collective.
      .A3-Z   Individual.

   Table VI

      .A2-29 General. Collective.
      .A3-Z   Individual.

---

*Tables I-IV for class F, which appear on pages 133-40 of the schedule for Class E-F, have not undergone significant changes and, therefore, are not reproduced here.

Class F

TABLES FOR COUNTRIES, ISLANDS, REGIONS
WITH SINGLE NUMBER OR CUTTER NUMBER

To be used only where indicated in schedules.

VII[4]	VIII[5]	IX	
.A2A-Z	.xA2	.xA2-29	Periodicals. Societies.
.A3A-Z	.xA3-39	.xA3-39	Sources and documents. Collections.
.A5-Z	.xA5-Z	.xA5-Z	General works.
.2	.x2	.x2	Description and travel. Guidebooks. Gazetteers.
.3	.x3	.x3	Antiquities. Indians.
.4	.x4	.x4	Social life and customs. Civilization.
.42	.x42	.x42	Elements in the population.
			History.
.5	.x5	.x5	General works.
.6	.x6	.x6	Biography and memoirs.
			.A1 Collective.
			.A2-Z Individual.
			Political and diplomatic history.
.62	.x62	.x62	General works.
.63	.x63	.x63	Relations with individual countries, A-Z.
			For list of countries, <u>see</u> pp. 605-606.
			By period.
.65	.x65	.x65	Early.
.7	.x7	.x7	Colonial.
.8	.x8	.x8	Independent.
.9	.x9	.x9	Local, A-Z.

---

[4]e.g. Virgin Islands of the U.S.: F2136.A2-2136.9.

[5].x in Table VIII is the decimal part of the class number. The Library of Congress at the present does not have material to class in a decimal number.

Class F

INDIVIDUAL BIOGRAPHY

Use the tables below to subarrange numbers and Cutters for individual
persons under each class number of the F schedule providing for
biography and memoirs, e.g. F1788.22.C3, Castro, Fidel. However,
in cases where individual biography is classed in numbers designating individual periods two Cutters are assigned, one for the name
of the biographee, and one for the author.

X One no.	XI Cutter no.	
.A2	.xA2	Collected works. By date.[6]
.A25	.xA25	Selected works. By date.[6]
.A3-39	.xA3-39	Autobiography, diaries, etc. Alphabeti- cally by title.
.A4	.xA4	Letters (Collections). By imprint date.
.A41-49	.xA41-49	Letters to an individual. Alphabetically by correspondent.
.A5-59	.xA5-59	Speeches (Collective and individual), etc. Alphabetically by title.
.A6-Z	.xA6-Z	Biography and criticism.

---

[6]Class here collected or selected works by the individual on
general historical or political topics pertaining to the period in
which he lived. For his collected or selected works on a special
topic, see the topic.

Class H

TABLES OF GEOGRAPHICAL DIVISIONS   pp. 527-532

I	II	III	IV	V		VI	VII	VIII	IX	X
1	1-2	1-2	1-2	1	America. Western Hemisphere	1				
2	3-4	3-4	3-4	2	North America	2				
3	5-6	5-7	5-8	3-6	United States					
4	7-8	8-10	9-12		Northeastern States. New England					
5	9-10	11-13	13-16		Middle Atlantic States.					
6	11-12	14-16	17-20		Southern States					
7	13-14	17-19	21-24		Central States. Plains States					
8	15-16	21-22	25-28		Great Lakes region					
9	17-18	23-25	29-32		Mississippi Valley					
10	19-20	26-28	33-36		Southwestern States					
11	21-22	29-31	37-40		Northwestern States. Rocky Mountain region					
12	23-24	32-34	41-44		Pacific States					121-130
13	25	35	45		States, A-W					
					Including regions and counties					
14	27	38	49	7-10	Cities, A-Z					
15	29-30	41-43	53-56		Canada	10	11-20	1-10	1-10	151-160
15.25	30.25	43.25	56.25	10.25	Saint Pierre and Miquelon Islands	10.25	20.25	10.25	10.25	160.25
					Greenland, see 99.5 ...					
15.5	30.5	43.5	56.5	10.5	Latin America	11.5	20.5	10.5	10.5	160.5
16	31-32	44-46	57-60	11	Mexico	12	21-30	11-20	11-15	161-170
17	33-34	47	61-64	13	Central America	13	31-35	21-25	16-20	171-175
17.5	35-36	48	65-68	13.5	Belize. British Honduras	13.25	36-40	26-30	20.5	181-185
18	37-38	49-51	69-72	14	Costa Rica	13.5	41-50	31-40	21-25	191-195
19	39	52-54	73-74	15	Guatemala	13.75	51-60	41-50	26-30	201-205
20	40	55-56	75-76	16	Honduras	14	61-70	51-60	31-35	206-210
21	41	57-58	77-78	17	Nicaragua	14.25	71-80	61-70	36-40	216-220
22	42-43	59-60	79	18	Panama	14.5	81-85	71-75	41-45	221-225
22.5	43.5	61	80	18.5	Panama Canal Zone	14.75	86-90	76-80	45.5	226-230
23	44	62-64	81-84	19	Salvador	15	91-100	81-90	46-50	231-235

Class H

TABLES OF GEOGRAPHICAL DIVISIONS

	I	II	III	IV	V	VI	VII	VIII	IX	X
Latin America – Continued										
West Indies. Caribbean area	24	45-46	65-67	85-88	20	16	101-105	91-95	51	241-245
Bahamas	24.5	47-48	68-70	89-92	20.5	16.2	106-110	96-100	53	246-250
Cuba	25	49-50	71-73	93-96	21	16.3	111-120	101-110	56-60	251-260
Haiti	26	51	74-75	97-98	22	16.4	121-125	111-115	61	261-265
Dominican Republic. Santo Domingo	26.5	52	76	99-100	22.5	16.5	126-130	116-120	64	266-270
Jamaica	27	53-54	77-79	101-104	23	16.6	131-140	121-130	66-70	271-280
Puerto Rico	28	55-56	80-82	105-108	24	16.7	141-150	131-140	71-75	281-285
Virgin Islands of the United States	28.3	56.3	83	109	24.3	16.8	150.3	141	75.3	286-290
British West Indies	28.5	56.5	83.5	110	24.5	16.9	151	142	75.4	291
Leeward Islands	28.7	56.7	83.7	110.7	24.7	17	153	144	75.5	293
Windward Islands	28.9	56.9	83.9	110.9	24.9	17.3	154	145	75.6	294
Trinidad and Tobago	29	57	84	111	25	17.4	155	146	75.7	295
Netherlands Antilles. Dutch West Indies	29.3	57.3	84.3	111.3	25.3	17.5	156	147	75.8	296
French West Indies	29.5	57.5	84.5	111.5	25.5	17.6	157	148	75.85	297
Guadeloupe	29.7	57.7	84.7	111.7	25.7	17.7	158	149	75.9	298
Martinique	29.9	57.9	85	112	25.9	17.9	159	150	75.95	299
South America	30	58	86-88	113-116	26	18-19	161-170	151-160	76-80	301-310
Argentina	31	59-60	89-91	117-120	27-30	20-24	171-180	161-170	81-85	311-320
Bolivia	32	61-62	92-94	121-124	31	25-26	181-190	171-180	86-90	321-330
Brazil	33	63-64	95-97	125-128	32-35	28-32	191-200	181-190	91-95	331-340
Chile	34	65-66	98-100	129-132	36	33-37	201-210	191-200	96-100	341-350
Colombia	35	67-68	101-103	133-136	37	38-39	211-220	201-210	101-105	351-360
Ecuador	36	69-70	104-106	137-140	38	40-41	221-230	211-220	106-110	361-370
Guianas	37	71-72	107-109	141-144	39	42-43	231-240	221-230	111-115	371-380
Guyana. British Guiana	37.3	72.3	109.3	144.3	39.3	43.3	240.3	230.3	115.3	380.3
Surinam. Dutch Guiana	37.5	72.5	109.5	144.5	39.5	43.5	240.5	230.5	115.5	380.5
French Guiana	37.7	72.7	109.7	144.7	39.7	43.7	240.7	230.7	115.7	380.7

Class H

TABLES OF GEOGRAPHICAL DIVISIONS

I	II	III	IV	V		VI	VII	VIII	IX	X
					Latin America					
					South America - Continued					
38	73-74	110-112	145-148	40	Paraguay	44-45	241-250	231-240	116-120	381-390
39	75-76	113-115	149-152	41	Peru	46-47	251-260	241-250	121-125	391-400
40	77-78	116-118	153-156	42	Uruguay	48-49	261-270	251-260	126-130	401-410
41	79-80	119-121	157-160	43	Venezuela	50-51	271-280	261-270	131-135	411-420
42	81-82	122-124	161-164	44		52-53	281-290	271-280	136-140	421-430
42.8	82.5	124.5	164.5	44.5		53.5	289.5	280.5	140.5	430.5
					Europe					
					European Economic Community countries					
43	83-84	125-127	165-168	45	Great Britain	54-58	291-300	281-300[1]	141-150[1]	431-440
44	85-86	128-130	169-172	46	England and Wales	60-61	301-310			441-450
45	87-88	131-132	173-176	47	Scotland	62-63	311-320			451-460
45.5	88.5	132.5	176.5	47.5		63.5	320.5			460.5
46	89-90	133-135	177-180	48	Northern Ireland	64-65	321-330	300.3	150.3	461-470
47	91-92	136-138	181-184	49-52	Ireland. Irish Republic	66-67	331-340	301-320	151-160	471-480
47.3	92.3	138.3	184.3	52.3	Austria			320.3	160.3	480.3
47.5	92.5	138.5	184.5	52.5	Czechoslovakia	69.3	340.3	320.5	160.5	480.5
47.9	92.9	138.9	184.9	52.9	Hungary	69.5	340.5	320.9	160.9	480.9
					Liechtenstein	69.9	340.9			
48	93-94	139-141	185-188	53-56	France	70-74	341-350	321-340	161-170	481-490
48.5	94.5	141.5	188.5	56.5	Monaco	74.5	350.5	340.5	170.5	490.5
49	95-96	142-144	189-192	57-60	Germany	75-79	351-360	341-360	171-180	491-500
					Including West Germany					
49.5	96.5	144.5	192.5	60.5	East Germany	79.5	360.5	360.5	180.5	500.5
51	99-100	148-150	197-200	62-65	Italy	85-89	371-380	371-390	186-195	511-520
51.3	100.3	150.3	200.3	65.3	San Marino	89.3	380.3	390.3	195.3	520.3
51.5	100.5	150.5	200.5	65.4	Malta	89.5	380.5	390.5	195.5	520.5
52	101-102	151-153	201-204	65.5	Benelux countries. Low countries	90-94	381-390	391-400	196-200	521-530
53	103-104	154-156	205-208	66-69	Belgium	95-99	391-400	401-410	201-205	531-540
54	105-106	157-159	209-212	70-73	Netherlands	100-104	401-410	411-420	206-210	541-550
54.5	106.5	159.5	212.5	73.5	Luxemburg	104.5	410.5	420.5	210.5	550.5

[1]Class the constituent countries of Great Britain as particular localities of Great Britain in the Local, A-Z number provided.

Class H

TABLES OF GEOGRAPHICAL DIVISIONS

Division	I	II	III	IV	V	VI	VII	VIII	IX	X
Europe - Continued										
Russia	55	107-108	160-162	213-216	74-77	105-109	411-420	421-430	211-215	551-560
Finland	55.3	108.3	162.3	217	77.3	110	421-425	431-435	215.5	561-565
Poland	55.7	108.7	162.7	218	77.7	111	426-429.5	436-439.5	215.7	566-569.5
Scandinavia	56	109-110	163-165	219-220	78	113-114	430	440	216-220	570
Denmark	57	111-112	166-168	221-224	79	115-119	431-440	441-450	221-225	571-580
Iceland	58	113-114	169-171	225-228	79.5	120-124	441-450	451-460	226-230	581-590
Norway	59	115-116	172-174	229-232	80	125-129	451-460	461-470	231-235	591-600
Sweden	60	117-118	175-177	233-236	81-84	130-134	461-470	471-480	236-240	601-610
Spain	61	119-120	178-180	237-240	85-88	135-139	471-480	481-490	241-245	611-620
Andorra	61.3	120.3	180.3	240.3	88.3	139.3	480.3	490.3	245.3	620.3
Gibraltar	61.5	120.5	180.5	240.5	88.5	139.5	480.5	490.5	245.5	620.5
Portugal	62	121-122	181-183	241-244	89	140-144	481-490	491-500	246-250	621-630
Switzerland	63	123-124	184-186	245-248	90	145-149	491-500	501-510	251-255	631-640
Balkan States	64	125-126	187-189	249-252	91	150-154	501-510	511-520	256-260	641-650
Albania	64.5	126.5	189.5	252.5	91.4	154.4	510.5	520.5	260.5	650.5
Bulgaria	65	127-128	190-191	253-254	91.5	154.5	511-520	521-530	261-265	651-660
Yugoslavia	65.5	128.5	192-193	255-256	91.6	154.6	521-525	531-535	265.5	661-665
Romania	67	131-132	196-198	261-264	91.8	154.8	531-540	541-550	271-275	671-680
Greece	67.5	132.5	198.5	264.5	91.83	154.83	540.5	550.5	275.5	680.5
Asia	68	133	199	265	91.85	154.85	541-545	551-555	276	681
Middle East. Near East	68.2	133.3	200	265.5	91.9	154.9	546	556	276.5	682
Turkey	68.25	133.4	200.5	265.7	91.93	154.93	546.5	556.5	276.7	682.5
Cyprus	68.3	133.5	200.6	266	91.95	154.95	547	557	277	683
Syria	68.35	133.7	200.9	266.5	92	155	548	558	277.5	684
Lebanon	68.4	133.9	201	267	92.15	155.15	549	559	278	685
Israel. Palestine	68.45	134	201.3	267.5	92.2	155.2	550	560	278.5	686
Jordan	68.5	134.3	201.6	268	92.25	155.25	551	561	279	687
Arabian Peninsula. Arabia	68.55	134.5	201.9	268.5	92.3	155.3	552	562	279.5	688
Saudi Arabia	68.6	134.7	202	269	92.35	155.35	553	563	280	689
Yemen (Yemen Arab Republic)	68.65	134.9	202.3	269.5	92.4	155.4	554	564	280.5	690

Class H

TABLES OF GEOGRAPHICAL DIVISIONS

I	II	III	IV	V		VI	VII	VIII	IX	X
					Asia					
					Middle East. Near East					
					Arabian Peninsula.					
					Arabia – Continued					
68.7	135	202.6	270	92.43	Yemen (People's Democratic Republic) Southern Yemen. Aden (Colony and Protectorate)	155.43	554.5	564.5	280.7	691
68.75	135.3	202.9	270.5	92.44	Oman. Muscat and Oman.	155.44	555	565	281	692
68.8	135.5	203	271	92.45	United Arab Emirates. Trucial States	155.45	556	566	281.5	693
68.85	135.7	203.3	271.5	92.5	Qatar	155.5	557	567	282	694
68.9	135.9	203.6	271.6	92.52	Bahrein	155.52	558	568	283	695
68.95	136	203.9	271.7	92.53	Kuwait	155.53	559	569	284	696
69	136.3	204	272	92.55	Iraq	155.55	560	570	285	697
69.2	136.4	204.2	272.2	92.56	Iran	155.7	560.2	570.2	285.2	698
69.3	136.5	204.3	272.3	92.57	South Asia	156	560.3	570.3	285.3	700
69.6	136.6	204.6	272.6	92.6	Afghanistan	156.6	560.6	570.6	285.6	700.6
69.7	136.7	204.7	272.7	92.7	Burma	156.7	560.7	570.7	285.7	700.7
69.8	136.8	204.8	272.8	92.8	Sri Lanka. Ceylon	156.8	560.8	570.8	285.8	700.8
69.9	136.9	204.9	272.9	92.9	Nepal	156.9	560.9	570.9	285.9	700.9
71 139–140		208–210	277–280	97–100	India	160–164	571–580	581–590	291–295	711–720
71.3	140.3	210.3	280.3	100.3	Bhutan	164.3	580.3	590.3	295.3	720.3
71.5	140.5	210.5	280.5	100.5	Pakistan	164.5	580.5	590.5	295.5	720.5
71.6	140.6	210.6	280.6	100.6	Bangladesh	164.55	580.6	590.6	295.6	720.6
72	141–142	211–213	281–284	101	Southeast Asia. Indochina Including French Indochina	164.6	580.8	590.8	295.8	721–730
					Burma, see 69.7					
73.3	144.3	216.3	288.3	102.3	Cambodia	164.63	590.3	600.3	300.3	740.3
73.4	144.4	216.4	288.4	102.4	Laos	164.64	590.4	600.4	300.4	740.4

Class H

TABLES OF GEOGRAPHICAL DIVISIONS

I	II	III	IV	V	Division	VI	VII	VIII	IX	X
					Asia					
					Southeast Asia.					
					Indochina – Continued					
73.5	144.5	216.5	288.5	102.5	Vietnam	164.65	590.5	600.5	300.5	740.5
73.55	144.55	216.55	288.55	102.55	Thailand	164.655	590.55	600.55	300.55	740.55
73.6	144.6	216.6	288.6	102.6	Malaysia. Malaya	164.66	590.6	600.6	300.6	740.6
74	145	217	289	103	Singapore	164.67	590.67	600.67	300.67	741
74.3	146.3	218.3	290	103.3	Brunei	164.68	590.68	600.68	300.68	742
75	147-148	220-222	293-296	104	Indonesia	164.7	591-600	601-610	301-305	751-760
76	149-150	223-225	297-300	105	Philippine Islands	164.8	601-610	611-620	306-310	761-770
76.5	150.5	225.5	300.5	106	East Asia. Far East	164.9	610.5	620.5	310.5	770.5
77	151-152	226-227	301-304	107	Japan	165-166	611-620	621-630	311-315	771-780
77.5	152.5	228	304.5	108	Korea Including South Korea	167	620.5	630.5	315.5	780.5
77.6	152.6	228.6	304.6	108.6	North Korea (Democratic People's Republic)	167.6	620.6	630.6	315.6	780.6
77.8	152.8	229	305	109	Outer Mongolia. Mongolian People's Republic	168	620.8	630.8	315.8	780.8
78	154	230	306	110	China	169	621-630	631-640	316-320	781-790
79	155	231	307	111	Macao	170	631-635	641-645	321-325	791-795
80	156	232	308	112	Taiwan. Formosa	171	636-640	646-650	326-330	796-800
81	157	233	309	113	Hongkong	172	641-645	651-655	331	801-805
81.5	160	239	319	116	Arab countries (Collective)	178	656	666	334	816
81.7	160.5	240	320	116.5	Islamic countries (Collective)	179	658	668	335	818
82	161	241-243	321-324	117	Africa	180-181	661-670	671-680	336-340	821-830
82.2	161.2	244	325	118	North Africa	182	671	681	340.5	831
82.3	161.3	244.3	325.3	118.3	Morocco	182.2	672	682	341	832
82.4	161.4	244.5	325.5	118.5	Algeria	182.3	673	683	341.5	833
82.5	161.5	244.7	325.7	118.7	Tunisia	182.4	674	684	342	834
82.6	161.6	245	326	118.9	Libya	182.5	675	685	342.5	835
82.7	161.7	245.3	326.3	119	Egypt. United Arab Republic	182.6	676	686	343	836
82.8	161.8	245.5	326.5	119.3	Sudan	182.7	677	687	343.5	837

Class H

TABLES OF GEOGRAPHICAL DIVISIONS

I	II	III	IV	V	Geographical Division	VI	VII	VIII	IX	X
					Africa – Continued					
82.9	161.9	245.7	326.7	119.5	Northeast Africa	182.8	678	688	344	838
83	162	246	327	119.7	Ethiopia	182.9	679	689	344.5	839
83.2	162.2	246.3	327.3	119.9	Somalia	183	680	690	345	840
					Including British and Italian Somaliland					
83.3	162.3	246.5	327.5	120	French Territory of the Afars and Issas	183.2	681	691	345.5	841
83.4	162.4	246.7	327.7	120.3	Southeast Africa	183.3	682	692	346	842
83.5	162.5	247	328	120.5	Kenya	183.4	683	693	346.5	843
83.6	162.6	247.3	328.3	120.7	Uganda	183.5	684	694	347	844
83.7	162.7	247.5	328.5	120.9	Rwanda	183.6	685	695	347.5	845
83.8	162.8	247.7	328.7	121	Burundi	183.7	686	696	348	846
83.9	162.9	248	329	121.3	Tanzania. Tanganyika. Zanzibar	183.8	687	697	348.5	847
84	163	248.3	329.3	121.5	Mozambique	183.9	688	698	349	848
84.2	163.2	248.5	329.5	121.7	Madagascar. Malagasy Republic	184	689	699	349.5	849
84.3	163.3	248.7	329.7	121.9	Southern Africa	184.2	690	700	350	850
84.4	163.4	249	330	122	South Africa	184.3	691	701	350.5	851
84.5	163.5	249.3	330.3	122.3	Rhodesia	184.4	692	702	351	852
					Including Southern Rhodesia					
84.6	163.6	249.5	330.5	122.5	Zambia. Northern Rhodesia	184.5	693	703	351.5	853
84.7	163.7	249.7	330.7	122.7	Lesotho. Basutoland	184.6	694	704	352	854
84.8	163.8	250	331	122.9	Swaziland	184.7	695	705	352.5	855
84.9	163.9	250.3	331.3	123	Botswana. Bechuanaland	184.8	696	706	353	856
85	164	250.5	331.5	123.3	Malawi. Nyasaland	184.9	697	707	353.5	857
85.2	164.2	250.7	331.7	123.5	Southwest Africa (Namibia)	185	698	708	354	858

Class H

TABLES OF GEOGRAPHICAL DIVISIONS

Africa – Continued

Geographical Division	I	II	III	IV	V	VI	VII	VIII	IX	X
Central Africa. Equatorial Africa	85.3	164.3	251	332	123.7	185.2	699	709	354.5	859
Angola	85.4	164.4	251.3	332.3	123.9	185.3	700	710	355	860
Zaire. Congo (Democratic Republic)	85.5	164.5	251.5	332.5	124	185.4	701	711	355.5	861
Equatorial Guinea	85.6	164.6	251.7	332.7	124.3	185.5	702	712	356	862
São Tomé e Príncipe	85.7	164.7	252	333	124.5	185.6	703	713	356.5	863
French Equatorial Africa French Congo	85.8	164.8	252.3	333.3	124.7	185.7	704	714	357	864
Gabon	85.9	164.9	252.5	333.5	124.9	185.8	705	715	357.5	865
Congo (Brazzaville). Middle Congo	86	165	252.7	333.7	125	185.9	706	716	358	866
Central African Republic. Ubangi-Shari	86.2	165.2	253	334	125.3	186	707	717	358.5	867
Chad	86.3	165.3	253.3	334.3	125.5	186.2	708	718	359	868
Cameroon	86.4	165.4	253.5	334.5	125.7	186.3	709	719	359.5	869
West Africa. West Coast	86.5	165.5	253.7	334.7	125.9	186.4	710	720	360	870
French-speaking West Africa	86.6	165.6	254	335	126	186.5	711	721	360.5	871
Benin. Dahomey	86.7	165.7	254.3	335.3	126.3	186.6	712	722	361	872
Togo	86.8	165.8	254.5	335.5	126.5	186.7	713	723	361.5	873
Niger	86.9	165.9	254.7	335.7	126.7	186.8	714	724	362	874
Ivory Coast	87	166	255	336	126.9	186.9	715	725	362.5	875
Guinea	87.2	166.2	255.3	336.3	127	187	716	726	363	876
Mali	87.3	166.3	255.5	336.5	127.3	187.2	717	727	363.5	877
Upper Volta	87.4	166.4	255.7	336.7	127.5	187.3	718	728	364	878
Senegal	87.5	166.5	256	337	127.7	187.4	719	729	364.5	879
Mauritania	87.6	166.6	256.3	337.3	127.9	187.5	720	730	365	880
Nigeria	87.7	166.7	256.5	337.5	128	187.6	721	731	365.5	881
Ghana	87.8	166.8	256.7	337.7	128.3	187.7	722	732	366	882
Sierra Leone	87.9	166.9	257	338	128.5	187.8	723	733	366.5	883

Class H

TABLES OF GEOGRAPHICAL DIVISIONS

I	II	III	IV	V		VI	VII	VIII	IX	X
					Africa					
					West Africa					
					West Coast – Continued					
88	167	257.3	338.3	128.7	Gambia	187.9	724	734	367	884
88.2	167.2	257.5	338.5	128.8	Liberia	188	725	735	367.5	885
88.3	167.3	257.7	338.7	129	Guinea-Bissau. Portuguese Guinea	188.2	726	736	368	886
88.4	167.4	258	339	129.3	Spanish Sahara	188.3	727	737	368.5	887
					Atlantic Ocean Islands					
					Iceland, see 58 ...					
88.5	167.5	258.3	339.3	129.5	Azores	188.35	728	738	369	888
88.53	168	258.5	340	129.53	Bermuda	188.4	728.3	738.3	369.3	888.3
88.55	168.5	258.7	340.5	129.55	Madeira Islands	188.5	728.5	738.5	369.4	888.5
88.6	169	259	341	129.6	Canary Islands	188.6	728.7	738.7	369.5	888.7
88.63	169.5	259.3	341.5	129.63	Cape Verde Islands	188.7	728.9	738.9	369.6	888.9
88.65	170	259.5	342	129.65	St. Helena	188.8	729	739	369.7	889
88.7	170.5	259.7	342.5	129.7	Tristan da Cunha	188.9	729.3	739.3	369.8	889.3
88.73	171	260	343	129.73	Falkland Islands	189	729.5	739.5	369.9	889.5
					Indian Ocean Islands					
88.75	171.5	260.3	343.5	129.75	Maldive Islands	189.2	729.7	739.7	370	889.7
88.8	172	260.5	344	129.8	Seychelles	189.3	729.9	739.9	370.3	889.9
88.83	172.5	260.7	344.5	129.83	Comoro Islands	189.4	730	740	370.4	890
88.85	173	261	345	129.85	Mauritius	189.5	730.3	740.3	370.5	890.3
88.9	173.5	261.3	345.5	129.9	Réunion	189.6	730.5	740.5	370.6	890.5
88.93	174	261.5	346	129.93	Kerguelen Islands	189.7	730.7	740.7	370.7	890.7
89	175-176	262-264	349-352	130	Australia	190-194	731-740	741-750	371-375	891-900
97.5	192.5	288.5	384.5	130.4	New Zealand	194.6	820.5	830.5	415.5	980.5
97.55	192.55	288.55	384.55	130.43	Pacific Ocean Islands	194.7	820.7	830.7	415.6	980.7
97.6	192.6	288.6	384.6	130.45	Trust Territory of the Pacific	195	821	831	415.7	981
					Including Mariana, Caroline and Marshall Islands					

Class H

TABLES OF GEOGRAPHICAL DIVISIONS

I	II	III	IV		V	VI	VII	VIII	IX	X
				Pacific Ocean						
				Islands – Continued						
				Hawaii, see 13 ...						
97.7	192.7	288.7	384.7	Guam	130.47	195.5	821.5	831.5	416	982
97.8	192.8	288.8	384.8	Papua New Guinea	130.5	196	822	832	416.5	983
98	193	289	385	Solomon Islands	130.53	196.5	823	833	416.7	984
98.3	193.3	289.3	385.3	New Caledonia	130.55	197	824	834	417	985
98.4	193.4	289.4	385.4	New Hebrides	130.57	197.5	825	835	417.5	986
98.5	193.5	289.5	385.5	Fiji Islands	130.6	198	826	836	417.7	987
98.6	193.6	289.6	385.6	Tonga	130.63	198.5	827	837	418	987.5
				Samoan Islands						
98.7	193.7	289.7	385.7	American Samoa	130.65	199	828	838	418.5	988
98.8	193.8	289.8	385.8	Western Samoa	130.67	199.5	829	839	418.7	989
99	195	292-293	389-390	Arctic regions	130.69	200	830	840	420	991-995
99.5	196	294	391	Greenland	130.7	200.5	830.5	842.5	420.5	995.5
100	197	295	393	Antarctic regions	130.9	200.7	830.7	842.7	420.7	996

Class K

SUBCLASS KF

FORM DIVISIONS

I 20 nos.	II 10 nos.	III 5 nos.	IV 5 nos.	V 2 nos.	VI* 1 no.	
1	1	1	1.A1A–Z	1.A1A–Z	.A1A–Z	Bibliography.
.5	.5		.A2A–Z			Surveys of legal research.
2	2	.A3A–Z	.A3A–Z	.A15A–Z	.A15A–Z	Periodicals.
						Class here periodicals consisting primarily of informative material (newsletters, bulletins, etc.) relating to a particular subject.
						For periodicals consisting predominantly of legal articles, regardless of subject matter and jurisdiction, see K1–30.
.5	.1		.A32	.A152	.A152	Yearbooks. Statistics.
						See note below KF178.
3	.3		.A35A–Z	.A16A–Z	.A16A–Z	Society publications.
4	.5		.A4	.A17	.A17	Congresses and conferences. By date.
						Meetings intended to result in concerted action, e.g., recommendations for law revision, new legislation, government action, etc.
						For papers and discussions devoted to the exploration of a subject, including "conferences," "institutes," "workshops," etc., see Symposia, p. 274.
(5)	(3)		(.A5)	(.A2)	(.A2)	Congressional hearings and reports, see KF25 ff.
						For hearings and reports of state legislatures, see KFC10+, KFN5O10+, KFA–KFM, KFZ11+.

*Modifications for state law, see Table IX(A), p. 365.

SUBCLASS KF
FORM DIVISIONS

I 20 nos.	II 10 nos.	III 5 nos.	IV 5 nos.	V 2 nos.	VI* 1 no.	
						Other legislative documents.
5.2	3.2		1.A52	1.A25 By date	.A25 By date	Bills. By date. Including legislative proposals from the Executive Branch.
.4	.4		.A54			Presidential messages. By date.
.5	.5		.A55A-Z			Other (staff reports, research reports, memoranda, individual testimony, etc.)
.8	.8		.A58			Compilations of legislative histories (documents) other than those relating to a particular act. By date of publication.
		1.4.A-Z .5				Statutes. Regulations. Rules of practice.
						Federal legislation. Statutes. Serials.
						Monographs. By date of publication.
						Collections. Compilations. Serials.
						Monographs. By date of publication.
.99.A-Z 6 .5-599	.99.A-Z 4 .5-579		.9.A-Z 2 .1-129	.A29A-Z .A3 .A31-328	.A29A-Z .A3 .A31-328	Particular acts. Arranged chronologically, by means of successive decimal and Cutter numbers, according to date of original enactment or revision of law. Under each:
.A15	.A15		.A15	A15	A15	Legislative history.
.A16A-Z	.A16A-Z		.A16A-Z	A16-169	A16-169	Compilations of documents. By date of publication
						Treatises. Monographs.
						Unannotated texts. Including official editions, with or without annotations.
.A19A-Z .A2	.A19A-Z .A2		.A19A-Z .A2	A19-199 A2	A19-199 A2	Serials. Monographs. By date of publication.

*Modifications for state law, see Table IX(A), p. 365.

Class K

SUBCLASS KF
FORM DIVISIONS

	I 20 nos.	II 10 nos.	III 5 nos.	IV 5 nos.	V 2 nos.	VI* 1 no.
Statutes. Regulations. Rules of practice. Federal legislation. Statutes. Particular acts. Under each--Continued.	6.5-599.A5-Z	4.5-599.A5-Z		2.1-129.A5-Z	1.A31-328A5-Z	.A31-328A5-Z
Annotated editions. Commentaries.	.99.A-Z	.599.A-Z		.19.A-Z	.A329A-Z	.A329A-Z
By author of commentary or annotations.	7	.6		.2	.A33	.A33
Regulations. Rules of practice. Collections. Compilations. Serials. Monographs. By date of publication.	.5-529	.7-719		.25-269	.A35-369	.A35-369
Particular regulations or rules of practice (or groups of regulations or rules adopted as a whole). Arranged chronologically by means of successive Cutter numbers, according to date of adoption or revision of regulations or rules. For rules of practice before a separately classed agency, <u>see</u> the issuing agency. Under each: Unannotated texts. Including official editions, with or without annotations.	.A19A-Z	.A19A-Z		.A19A-Z	A19-199	A19-199
Serials	.A2	.A2		.A2	A2	A2
Monographs. By date of publication. Annotated editions. Commentaries. By author of commentary or annotations.	.A5-Z	.A5-Z		.A5-Z	A5-Z	A5-Z

*Modifications for state law, see Table IX(A), p. 365.

Class K

SUBCLASS KF

FORM DIVISIONS

Description	I 20 nos.	II 10 nos.	III 5 nos.	IV 5 nos.	V 2 nos.	VI* 1 no.
Statutes. Regulations. Rules of practice.						
Federal legislation.	8					
Digests of statutes and regulations.	.3	4.73				.A3692-3694
Citators for statutes and regulations.		.75				
Citators for both cases and legislation are classed with citators for court decisions or decisions of regulatory agencies.						
Indexes to federal statutes and regulations.	.5	.77				
Serials.						.A3697A-Z
Monographs. By date.	.7.A-Z	.78.A-Z		2.29.A-Z		.A3698
Collections of summaries of federal legislation.					1.A37-379	.A37-379
Comparative and uniform state and local legislation. Interstate compacts.						
Collections. Selections.						
Serials.	9.A15A-Z	.8.A15A-Z	2.A15A-Z	.5.A15A-Z	.A39A-Z	.A39A-Z
Monographs. By date of publication.	.A2	.A2	.A2	.A2	.A4	.A4
Particular uniform state laws.	.5-529	.82-829	.2-239	.6-629	.A42-439	.A42-439
Arranged chronologically, by means of successive Cutter numbers, according to date of original adoption or revision of law.						
Enactments by individual states, see .A3-349 in Table IX(A), p. 277, and .A3-39 in Table IX(B), p. 277.						
Under each:						
Drafts. By date.	.A15	.A15	.A15	.A15	A15	A15
Proposed amendments. By date.	.A16	.A16	.A16	.A16	A16	A16
Unannotated texts.						
Including official editions, with or without annotations.						
Serials.	.A19A-Z	.A19A-Z	.A19A-Z	.A19A-Z	A19-199	A19-199
Monographs. By date of publication.	.A2	.A2	.A2	.A2	A2	A2
Annotated editions. Commentaries.	.A5-Z	.A5-Z	.A5-Z	.A5-Z	A5-Z	A5-Z
By author of commentary or annotations.						
History and criticism.	.6.A-Z	.85.A-Z	.25.A-Z	.65.A-Z	.A45A-Z	.A45A-Z

*Modifications for state law, see Table IX(A), p. 365.

Class K

SUBCLASS KF
FORM DIVISIONS

I (20 nos.)	II (10 nos.)	III (5 nos.)	IV (5 nos.)	V (2 nos.)	VI* (1 no.)	
						Court decisions
						Reports.
10.A2A-Z	5.A2A-Z		3.A2A-Z	1.A5-519	.A5-519	Serials.
.A5-Z	.A5-Z		.A5-Z	.A52A-Z	.A52A-Z	Monographic collections.
						Each divided by date of publication.
.3	.3	2.4	.1	.A53A-Z	.A53A-Z	Digests of reports (Case finders).
.5	.5		.15	.A535A-Z	.A535A-Z	Citators.
						Including citators for both cases
						and statutes.
.7	.7		.2	.A54A-Z	.A54A-Z	Indexes.
(.8)	(.8)	(.5)	(.25)	(.A545)	(.A545)	Individual cases. By date.
						Decisions of regulatory agencies. Rulings.
						Reports.
12.A2A-Z	6.A2A-Z		3.A2A-Z	.A6-619	.A55-559	Serials.
.A5-Z	.A5-Z		.A5-Z	.A62A-Z	.A56A-Z	Monographic collections.
						Each divided by date of publication.
.3	.2		.32	.A65A-Z	.A57A-Z	Digests of reports (Case finders).
.5	.25		.34	.A67A-Z	.A575A-Z	Citators.
.7	.28		.35	.A69A-Z	.A58A-Z	Indexes.
14.A-Z	3.A-Z	.8.A-Z	.36.A-Z	.A75A-Z	.A59A-Z	Collections of summaries of cases ("Digests" of cases decided by courts or regulatory agencies). By editor or title.
.5	.4	3	.4	.A8A-Z	.A6A-Z	Encyclopedias.
15	.5	.1	.5	2.A3A-Z	.A65A-Z	Looseleaf services.
16	7	.5	.6	.A35A-Z	.A68A-Z	Form books.
17	.5		4	.A4A-Z	.A7A-Z	Dictionaries.
18	8	4				Casebooks. Readings.

*Modifications for state law, see Table IX(A), p. 365.

Class K

SUBCLASS KF
FORM DIVISIONS

Description	I 20 nos.	II 10 nos.	III 5 nos.	IV 5 nos.	V 2 nos.	VI 1 no.
General works.	19.A1A-Z	9.A1A-Z	5.A1A-Z	5.A1A-Z	2.A45A-Z	.A73A-Z
Collections. Monographic series.	.A2A-Z	.A2A-Z	.A2A-Z	.A2A-Z	.A5A-Z	.A75A-Z
Collected papers and essays. Symposia. Cf. note under Congresses and conferences.						
Official reports and monograph.	.A3-49	.A3-49	.A3-49	.A3-49	.A6-69	.A8-89
Treatises. Monographs.	.A7-Z	.A7-Z	.A7-Z8	.A7-Z8	.A7-Z8	.A9-Z8
Compends. Outlines. Minor works.	.3					
Examination aids.	.5					
Popular works.	.6					
Works for particular classes of users, A-Z. See listing under KF390.	.8	10	.Z9A-Z	.Z9A-Z	.Z9A-Z	.Z9A-Z
Foreign language treatises. By language, A-Z. Translations of works originally published in English are classed with the original.	.9					
Works on comparative and uniform state and local law. Prefer numbers under "General works," supra, in classes for comparative state law, e.g.: KF5390, State civil service; KF6720-6767, State and local, and State finance.	20	.Z95A-Z	.Z95A-Z	.Z95A-Z	.Z95A-Z	.Z95A-Z
Works on the law of individual states. By state, A-Z.*	(.299)	(.299)	(.299)	(.299)	(.299)	(.299)

*Optional arrangement for law libraries using this classification.

Class K

SUBCLASS KF

TABLE VII.   TOPICS REPRESENTED BY CUTTER NUMBERS[*]

Book numbers for works arranged by author are constructed by means of
  successive Cutter numbers.

.A12-129	Bibliography.
.A13-139	Periodicals.
	Class here periodicals consisting primarily of infor- mative material (newsletters, bulletins, etc.) relating to a particular subject. For periodicals consisting predominantly of legal articles, regardless of subject matter and jurisdiction, see K1-30.
.A16-169	Society publications.
(.A2)	Congressional hearings and reports, see KF25 ff.
	For hearings and reports of state legislatures, see KFC10+, KFN5010+, KFA-KFW, KFZ11+.
	Legislative documents other than Congressional hearings and reports.
.A24-249	Serials.
.A25	Monographs. By date of publication.
	Statutes. Regulations.
.A29-299	Serials.
.A3	Monographs. By date of publication.
.A4	Comparative state legislation. By date of publication.
	Decisions. Administrative rulings.
.A49-499	Serials.
.A5	Monographs. By date of publication.
.A8-89	Official reports and monographs.
.A9-Z	Treatises. Monographs. Casebooks.
	Including collected essays, symposia, etc.
.Z95-959	Works on comparative state law.
	Prefer .A9-Z under topics in classes for comparative state law, e.g., KF6720-6767, State and local, and State finance.

TABLE VIII.   FORM DIVISIONS UNDER SINGLE-NUMBER CAPTIONS
FOR GENERAL WORKS

.A1A-Z	Serial publications. Collections.
.A2A-Z	Collected papers and essays. Symposia, etc.
.A3-6	Official reports and monographs.
.A65A-Z	Form books.
.A7A-Z	Casebooks. Readings.
.A75-Z8	Treatises. Monographs.
.Z9A-Z	Compends. Examination aids. Minor and popular works.

---

[*]Modifications for state law see Table, IX(B).

Class K

SUBCLASS KF

TABLE IX. MODIFIED FORM DIVISIONS FOR STATE LAW

(A) Topics Represented by Whole or Decimal Numbers (Table VI)

(.A2)	Legislative hearings and reports, <u>see</u> KFC10+, KFN5010+, KFA–KFW, KFZ11+.
	Other legislative documents.
.A24–249	Serials.
.A25	Monographs. By date of publication.
	Statutes. Regulations. Rules of practice.
	State legislation.
	Statutes.
	Collections. Compilations.
.A29A–Z	Serials.
.A3	Monographs. By date of publication.
.A33–349	Particular acts.

Arranged chronologically, by means of successive
Cutter numbers, according to date of original
enactment or revision of law.
Under each:

.A15	Legislative history (Compilations of documents). By date of publication.
	Unannotated texts.
	Including official editions, with or without annotations.
.A19–199	Serials.
.A2	Monographs. By date of publication.
.A3–Z	Annotated editions. Commentaries. By author of commentary or annotations.

Regulations. Rules of practice.
Collections. Compilations.

.A39A–Z	Serials.
.A4	Monographs. By date of publication.
.A43–449	Particular regulations or rules of practice (or groups of regulations or rules adopted as a whole)

Arranged and divided like .A33–349.
For rules of practice before a separately classed
agency, <u>see</u> the issuing agency.

.A45–459	Digests of statutes and regulations.
	Indexes to statutes and regulations.
.A455–459	Serials.
.A46	Monographs. By date of publication.
.A47–479	Collections of summaries of state legislation.
.A49	Comparative local legislation (Collections, extracts, summaries). By date of publication.

Class K

SUBCLASS KF

TABLE IX.   MODIFIED FORM DIVISIONS FOR STATE LAW

(B)   Topics Represented by Cutter Numbers (Table VII)

(.A2)	Legislative hearings and reports, <u>see</u> KFC10+, KFN5010+, KFA-KFW, KFZ11+.
	Other legislative documents.
.A24-249	Serials.
.A25	Monographs. By date of publication.
	Statutes. Regulations. Rules of practice.
	Collections. Compilations.
.A29-299	Serials.
.A3	Monographs. By date of publication.
	Particular acts and/or regulations.
	Unannotated texts.
.A31-319	Serials.
.A32	Monographs. By date of publication.
.A33-39	Annotated editions. Commentaries. By author of commentary or annotations.
.A396	Indexes to statutes and regulations. By date of publication.
.A397-3979	Collections of summaries of state legislation.

Class L

TABLES OF SUBDIVISIONS

INSTITUTIONS IN AMERICA

(LD-LE)

Use Tables II - V as indicated in the schedules; use Table I for
all other institutions, substituting for .x1 or .x2 of Table I
the initial and first digit(s) of the Cutter assigned to them
in the schedule, and adding a second Cutter for author. For the
first Cutter, expand .x1 and .x2 decimally to provide for additional topics, as shown by the following random examples: for
the Cutter range .G17-26: .G17, .G19, .G197, etc. and .G2, .G24,
.G244, etc.; for the range .G47-56: .G47, .G49, .G497, etc. and
.G5, .G54, .G544, etc. For additional examples, <u>see</u> p. 175.

I	II	III	IV	
x17	0	0	0	Charter (and founding).
x173	.3	.3	.3	Heraldry. Seal.
x175	.5	.5	.5	College statutes, by-laws, etc.
				Administration.
x177	.7	.7	.7	General works. Official reports.
x18	1	1	1	Board of regents, trustees, etc.
x19	2	2	2	President (or head of the institution)
	.5	.5	.5	Treasurer.
	.7	.7	.7	Registrar.
x192	.9	.9	.9	Other administrative reports.
				Special.
x193	3	3	3	Finance
x194	3.5	3.5	3.5	Endowment.
x195	4	4	4	Appropriations and grants.
				By date.
x197	5	5	5	Bequests, donations, etc.
x198	5.5	6	6	Scholarships.
x199	5.8	6.5	6.5	Policy and organization.
x1995	5.9	6.7	6.7	Personnel management.
x1996	5.95	6.75	6.75	Salaries, pensions, etc.

Class L

```
            TABLES OF SUBDIVISIONS
            INSTITUTIONS IN AMERICA
I       II      III     IV
```

I	II	III	IV	
				Catalogs, registers, bulletins, etc.
x2	6	7	7	Annual, semiannual, quarterly.
				Triennial, quinquennial, see Biography.
x2a	7	8	9	Announcements, circulars, etc.
x2b	8	9	10	Directories.
x2d	9	10	11	Requirements for admission.
x2e	10	11	12	Entrance examinations, and accredited schools.
x2g	11	12	13	Curriculum.
x2ga	11.2	12.5	14	Syllabi (Collected).
x2gb	11.25	12.7	14.5	Honors courses.
x2h	11.3	13	15	Graduate work and courses.
x2j	11.7	14	17	Degrees and honors.
x2k	11.8	14.5	17.5	Miscellaneous publications.
				Biography.
x21	12	15	18	Collective.
	12.1	15.1	19	Presidents.
	12.2	15.2	20	Faculty or faculties.
				Alumni.
x21a	12.3	15.3	21	Directories.
x21b	.4	.4	22	General histories.
x21c	.43	.43		Obituary record.
x21d	.45	.45		General special.
x21f	.49	.49	23	General catalogs. Triennial, etc.
x21g	.5	.5	.5	Other catalogs.
.21k	.6	.6	24	By classes.
				Individual.
x213	12.65	15.8	24.5	Founders, benefactors, etc., A-Z.*
x217	12.7	16	25	Presidents, chronogically, by date of inauguration.
x218	12.8	17	26	Other faculty members, A-Z.
x219	12.9	17.5	27	Reminiscences.
				History and description.
				History (including early descriptions).
x22	13	18	28	General.
				By period.
		.3	29	Early.
		.8	30	Recent.
				Description.
x23	14	19	31	General (including guidebooks).
		.2	.2	Y.M.C.A. handbooks.
x233	14.5	19.7	33	Views.
x234	14.6	19.8	34	Dormitories, residence halls, etc.
				Cf. NA 6600-6605, Architecture.
				Laboratories, see Q, T, etc.
				Libraries, see Z.
				Museums, see AM, or special subject.
x238	15	20	35	Individual buildings and places, A-Z.

---

*If founder is first president, prefer the latter classification.

Class L

TABLES OF SUBDIVISIONS
INSTITUTIONS IN AMERICA

I	II	III	IV	
				Student life and customs.
x24	16	21	36	General works.
				Special.
x241	16.2	21.4	36.5	Student societies and clubs.
				Fraternities, see LJ.
				Class days or events.
x242	16.4		(37)	Freshman.
x243	.5		(38)	Sophomore.
x244	.6		(39)	Junior.
x245	.7	22	(40)	Senior.
				Basketball, see GV885.43.
				Football, see GV958
				Religion, see BR561.
				Commencement.
x246	17	23	41	General works.
x247	.2	24	42	Addresses. Orations. Sermons.
				By date.
x248	.5	25	45	Presidential inaugurations.
				By date.
x249	.7	26	46	Other special days and events.
				By date.
				Undergraduate publications.
				Periodicals, see LH.
x25	18	27	47	Annuals.
	.3		.3	Handbooks.
	.5		.5	Calendars.
			.7	Almanacs.
				Alumni activities.
				Alumni magazines, see LH.
x257	18.7	28	48	Graduate class publications (and exercises).
x26	19	29	49	Alumni associations and graduate clubs.
				.A1-4 Resident.
				.A5-Z Nonresident, by name of place.
x265	19.5	29.5	49.5	Special colleges, campuses, etc., A-Z.

Class L

TABLE V

(Institutions to which <u>one number</u>
or <u>Cutter number</u> is assigned)

.A1-7   Official publications.
 .A1-4   Serial.
 .A5-7   Nonserial.
.A8-Z   Other works by author.
             Including student yearbooks, etc.

Class L

TABLES OF SUBDIVISIONS

INSTITUTIONS IN GREAT BRITAIN
(LF1-1257)

I	II	
0	0	Charter and statutes.
.5	.5	Heraldry. Seal.
1	1	Official reports.
2		Finance.
.5		Special funds, etc., A-Z.
3		Policy.
4	2	Catalogs. Yearbooks.
5		Announcements.
6		Entrance requirements and examinations.
7	3	Curriculum. Degrees. Examinations (in course).
	4	Biography.
8	.A2-3	Collective.
		.A2 General catalogues.
9	.A4-Z	Individual.
10		Reminiscences. (5 in Table II)
	5	History.
11		General.
12		Early.
13		Recent.
	6	Description.
15		Guide books.
16		Other works.
17	7	Student life.
.5	.5	Rectorial addresses, etc. (Collected).
18	8	Special days and events. By date.
		e.g. 1884 October 28.
19	9	Other.
.5	.5	Special colleges or branches, A-Z.

For institutions to which <u>one number</u> or <u>Cutter number</u> is assigned
in the schedule, use .A1-7, Official publications; .A8-Z, Other works,
by author. Cutter numbers for institutions in classes arranged by place
should be assigned for the place and the school, e.g. LF795.N45A-Z, New-
castle-upon-Tyne. Royal Grammar School; LF795.N47A-Z, Newcastle-upon-
Tyne. St. Cuthbert's Grammar School.

Class L

TABLES OF SUBDIVISIONS

INSTITUTIONS IN CONTINENTAL EUROPE, ASIA, AFRICA,
OCEANIA

(LF1311-5477, LG)

TABLE I

1.A3	Charters. Constitutions, etc.[1]
.A5	Heraldry. Seal.
.A7	Regulations. Statutes.
.A9	Administration (General works). Official publications.
.B1	Governing board. Reports.
.B3	President. Rector.
.B5	Treasurer.
.B6-9	Other.
.C5	Catalogs. Registers. Yearbooks ("Chronik")
.C7	Announcements ("Verzeichnis der Vorlesungen")
.C9	Directories ("Personalbestand")
	Finance.
	Cf. .B5, Treasurer.
.F3	General.
	Special.
.F5	Appropriations.
.F6	Endowments.
.F7	Bequests, etc.
.F8	Fellowships, scholarships, etc.
.F9	Prizes.
2	Organization. Policy.
	General works.
.A3A-Z	Early through 1800.
.A5A-Z	1801-
.A6-Z	Special topics, A-Z.
	.C8 Curriculum.
	.D4 Degrees.
	.E6 Entrance requirements.
	.E9 Examinations.
	.F3 Faculty.

---

[1]For 1.A3 through .F9 assign second Cutter for author.

Class L

```
                    TABLES OF SUBDIVISIONS
INSTITUTIONS IN CONTINENTAL EUROPE, ASIA, AFRICA, OCEANIA
2.5                 Miscellaneous publications.
                    History.
3.A1-29               Collections. Documents. Sources.
 .A3-Z                General works.
(3.5)                 Anniversaries, jubilees, commemorations
                        of the founding, see subdivision 19.5.
4                     General special. Descriptive.
                          e.g. Architectural histories.
                      Medieval.
5                       General.
6                       Special.
                      16th-18th centuries.
7.A3A-Z                 Early works.
                        Modern.
 .A4-Z                    General.
8                         General special. Policy.
9                         Reminiscences.
                      19th century.
10.A-Z3                 General.
 .Z4A-Z                 Special. Policy.
11                      Reminiscences.
12                    20th century.
                    Biography.
14                  General catalogs. Registers of alumni. Faculty.
                        Official.
 .A1A-Z                   Serials. By title.
 .A2A-Z                   Monographs. By title.
 .A3-Z                  Other.
15                  Other collections.
16                  Individual, A-Z.
17                  Guide books.
18                  Other descriptive works.
19                  Student life.
                      General in LA.
19.5                Special days and events. Anniversaries, jubilees,
                      commemorations, etc.
20                  Other.
 .5                 Special colleges or branches, A-Z.
```

Class L

TABLES OF SUBDIVISIONS
INSTITUTIONS IN CONTINENTAL EUROPE, ASIA, AFRICA, OCEANIA

Use (a) for LF1311+ and (b) for LG where Table
II is indicated.

(a)	(b)	
1	0	Charter and statutes.
.5	.5	Heraldry. Seal.
2	1	Administration (General works). Official reports. Organization and policy.
3	2	Catalogs. Yearbooks. Announcements.
.6	.6	Entrance requirements and examinations.
4	3	Curriculum.
.8	.8	Miscellaneous publications.
5	4	Biography.
		Collective.
	.A2A-Z	General catalogs. Registers of alumni. Faculty.
	.A3A-Z	Other.
	.A4-Z	Individual.
6	5	History.
(6.5)	(5.5)	Anniversaries, jubilees, commemorations of the founding, see subdivision 9 or 8.
7	6	Description.
8	7	Student life.
9	8	Special days and events.
10	9	Other.
.5	.5	Special colleges or branches, A-Z.

For institutions to which one number or Cutter number is assigned
in the schedule, use .A1-7, Official publications; .A8-Z, Other works,
by author. Cutter numbers for institutions in classes arranged by place
should be assigned for the place and school, e.g. LG169.L67A-Z, Lucknow,
India. Isabella Thoburn College; LG169.L7A-Z, Lucknow, India. Reid Christian College.

Class N

Tables I to III-A

I (100)		II (200)	III (300)	III-A (300)
01	America	01	01	01
.5	Latin America	02	02	02
02	North America	03	03	03
03	United States	05	05	05
.5	Colonial period; 18th (and early 19th) century	06	06	06
.7	19th century	07	07	07
04	20th century	08	08	08
05	New England	10	10	10
.5	Middle Atlantic States	.5	.5	.5
06	South	11	11	11
07	Central	14	18	18
08	West	17	23	23
.5	Northwestern States	18	24	24
.6	Southwestern States	.6	.6	.6
09	Pacific States	19	25	25
10	States, A-W[1]	25	35	35
11	Cities, A-Z	27	38	38
12	Special artists, A-Z[2]	28	39	39
	Ethnic groups			
.2	General works	.2	.2	.2
.3	Special, A-Z	.3	.3	.3

```
        e.g.   .A35 Afro-Americans.
                    Negro
               .A4  American Indians
                    For traditional
                    art and crafts,
                    see E-F
               .L3  Latin Americans
               .M4  Mexican-Americans
               (.N5) Negro, see .A35
               .S6  Spanish-Americans
```

---

[1]Each state may be subarranged: .x, General works; .x2, Local (other than cities), A-Z, e.g. .V8, Virginia (General works); .V82F3, Fairfax County, Virginia.

[2]"Special artists" may be interpreted as special individuals, families, or firms.

(Class N continues through page 397)

Class N

N
                              TABLES OF SUBDIVISIONS

I		II	III	III-A
13	Canada	29	41	41
14	Mexico	31	44	44
15	Central America	33	47	47
16	British Honduras	35	50	50
17	Costa Rica	37	53	53
18	Guatemala	39	56	56
19	Honduras	41	59	59
20	Nicaragua	43	62	62
21	Panama	45	65	65
22	Salvador	46	67	67
23	West Indies	47	68	68
24	Bahamas	49	71	71
25	Cuba	51	74	74
26	Haiti	53	77	77
27	Jamaica	55	80	80
28	Puerto Rico	57	83	83
29	Other, A-Z	58	86	86
30	South America	59	89	89
31	Argentine Republic	61	92	92
32	Bolivia	63	95	95
33	Brazil	65	98	98
34	Chile	67	101	101
35	Colombia	69	104	104
36	Ecuador	71	107	107
37	Guyana (British Guiana)	73	110	110
.2	Surinam (Dutch Guiana)	.2	.2	.2
.4	French Guiana	.4	.4	.4
38	Paraguay	75	113	113
39	Peru	77	116	116
40	Uruguay	79	119	119
41	Venezuela	81	122	122
42	Europe[2]	83	125	125
43	Great Britain. England	85	128	128
44	England - Local, A-Z	87	131	131
45	Scotland[3]	89	134	134
46	Ireland[3]	91	137	137
47	Wales[3]	93	140	140
.6	Special artists, A-Z[1]		142	142
	Austrian, German, and Swiss, see 49.6, 98.6, 148.6, 150.6			
48	Austria	95	143	143
49	France	97	146	147
.6	German, Austrian, and Swiss (Collectively)	98.6	148.6	150.6
	German, Flemish, and Dutch, see 52.6, 104.6, 157.6, 162.6			

---

[1]"Special artists" may be interpreted as special individuals, families, or firms of England, Scotland, Ireland, or Wales

[2]Use only the indicated number. Classify material for areas (e.g. Northern Europe, Eastern Europe, Southern Europe) in this number with no area Cutter subarrangement

[3]Under each:
    .A1A-Z General works
    .A3A-Z Special regions, provinces,
       .   etc. A-Z
    .A5-Z   Special cities, A-Z

Class N

N		TABLES OF SUBDIVISIONS			
I			II	III	III-A
	Europe – Continued				
50	Germany		99	149	151
	Including West Germany				
	For Alsace-Lorraine, <u>see</u>				
	49, 98, 147, 148				
.6	East Germany		100.6	151.6	154.6
51	Greece		101	152	155
52	Italy		103	155	159
.6	Dutch, Flemish, and German				
	(Collectively)		104.6	157.6	162.6
53	Low Countries		105	158	163
54	Holland (Netherlands)		107	161	167
55	Belgium		109	164	171
.6	Luxemburg		110.6	166.4	174.6
56	Russia in Europe. R.S.F.S.R.		111	167	175
	For Caucasian republics,				
	<u>see</u> Russia in Asia				
57	Scandinavia		113	170	179
58	Denmark		115	173	183
59	Iceland		117	176	187
60	Norway		119	179	191
61	Sweden		121	182	195
62	Spain. Spain and Portugal		123	185	199
63	Portugal		125	188	203
	Swiss, Austrian, and German, <u>see</u>				
	49.6, 98.6, 148.6, 150.6				
64	Switzerland		127	191	207
65	Turkey		129	194	211
66	Other Balkan states		131	197	215
67	Bulgaria		133	200	219
(68)	Montenegro, <u>see</u> 71, 141,				
	212, 235 (.Ɣ8)		(135)	(203)	(223)
69	Romania		137	206	227

Class N

TABLES OF SUBDIVISIONS

I		II	III	III-A
	Europe			
	Other Balkan states - Continued			
(70)	Serbia, <u>see</u> 71, 141,			
	212, 235 (.Y8)	(139)	(209)	(231)
71	Other countries, A-Z	141	212	235
	.A4 Albania			
	.C9 Czechoslovak Republic			
	.F5 Finland			
	.H8 Hungary			
	.P6 Poland			
	.Y8 Yugoslavia			
72	Asia. The Orient[1]	143	215	237
73	Southwestern Asia. Near			
	East. Levant. Asia			
	Minor[1]	145	218	238
.6	By region or country, A-Z	146	219	239
	.C9 Cyprus			
	.I7 Iraq			
	.J6 Jordan			
	.K8 Kuwait			
	.L4 Lebanon			
	.O45 Oman			
	.S2 Saudi Arabia			
	.S9 Syria			
	.Y4 Yemen			
.7	Israel. Palestine	146.6	220	240
74	Iran. Persia	147	221	241
75	Central Asia[1]	149	224	244
.6	Afghanistan	.6	.6	.6
	Russia in Asia[2]			
.7	By republic, A-Z	150	225	245
	.A7 Armenia			
	.A9 Azerbaijan			
	.D3 Daghestan			
	.G4 Georgia			
	.K3 Kazakhstan			
	.T3 Tajikistan			
	.T8 Turkmenistan			
	.T85 Tuva			
	.U9 Uzbekistan			

---

[1] Use only the indicated number and only for general works on the area as a whole.

[2] For Russia in Asia as a whole, use the numbers provided for Central Asia; for Siberia use local numbers of the R.S.F.S.R., e.g. 56, etc.

Class N

TABLES OF SUBDIVISIONS

I		II	III	III-A
	Asia. The Orient – Continued			
75.8	Southern Asia[1]	150.6	226	246
76	India	151	227	247
.6	Sri Lanka. Ceylon	152.6	230	250
.7	Pakistan	153	231	251
.8	Other countries, A–Z	.6	.6	.6
77	Southeastern Asia[1]	154	232	252
.6	Burma	.6	.6	.6
78	French Indo-China[1]	155	233	253
.6	By country, A–Z	156	234	254
	.C3 Cambodia (Khmer)			
	.L3 Laos			
	.V5 Vietnam. South Vietnam			
	.V55 Vietnam (Democratic Republic, 1946–)			
.7	Thailand. Siam	156.6	235	255
79	Malaysia. Malaya[2]	157	236	256
80	Indonesia. Dutch East Indies[3]	159	239	259
81	Philippine Islands	161	242	262
82	Eastern Asia[1]	163	245	265
83	China[4]	165	248	268
84	Japan	167	251	271
.6	Korea	168.6	253.6	273.6
.7	Korea (Democratic People's Republic)	.7	.7	.7
86	Other countries, A–Z	172	259	279
87	Africa[1]	173	260	280
.6	North Africa[1]	174	261	281
.65	Algeria	.6	.6	.6
.7	Libya	.65	.65	.65
.75	Morocco	.7	.7	.7
.8	Sudan	.75	.75	.75
.85	Tunisia	.8	.8	.8
88	Egypt	175	263	283
.6	Other North Africa, A–Z	176.6	265.6	285.6
	.I3 Ifni			
	.S6 Spanish Sahara			
.7	Ethiopia	.7	.7	.7
.75	Sub-Saharan Africa[1]	.75	.75	.75

---

[1] Use only the indicated number and only for general works on the area as a whole.

[2] Sabah, Singapore and Sarawak and Malaya are treated as locals of Malaysia here.

[3] Java, Sumatra, Kalimantan and West Irian are treated as locals of Indonesia here.

[4] Formosa (Taiwan) is treated as a local of China in this table.

Class N

TABLES OF SUBDIVISIONS

I		II	III	III-A
	Africa - Continued			
88.8	Eastern Africa[1]	176.8	266	286
.9	By country, A-Z	.9	.6	.6
	.B8 Burundi			
	.C6 Comoro Islands			
	.F7 French Somaliland			
	.K4 Kenya			
	.M3 Madagascar			
	.M6 Mozambique			
	.R8 Rwanda			
	.S6 Somali Republic			
	.T3 Tanzania			
	.Z3 Zanzibar			
89	Western Africa[1]	177	267	287
.3	French-speaking West Africa[1]	.3	.3	.3
.6	By country, A-Z	.6	.6	.6
	.A5 Angola			
	.C3 Cameroon			
	.C4 Central African Republic			
	.C5 Chad			
	.C6 Congo (Democratic Republic). Belgian Congo. Zaire.			
	.C7 Congo (Brazzaville)			
	.D3 Dahomey			
	.G25 Gabon			
	.G3 Gambia			
	.G5 Ghana			
	.G8 Guinea			
	.I8 Ivory Coast			
	.L5 Liberia			
	.M3 Mali			
	.M4 Mauritania			
	.N4 Niger			
	.N5 Nigeria			
	.P6 Portuguese Guinea			
	.R5 Rio Muni			
	.S4 Senegal			
	.S5 Sierra Leone			
	.S6 Southwest Africa			
	.T6 Togo			
	.U6 Upper Volta			

---

[1] Use only the indicated number and only for general works on the area as a whole.

Class N

TABLES OF SUBDIVISIONS

I		II	III	III-A
	Africa – Continued			
89.7	Southern Africa[1]	178	268	288
.8	By country, A–Z	.6	.6	.6
	.B6 Botswana			
	.L4 Lesotho			
	.M3 Malawi			
	.R5 Rhodesia, Southern			
	.S6 Republic of South Africa			
	.S8 Swaziland			
	.Z3 Zambia			
90	Australia	179	269	289
93	New Zealand	181	272	292
95	Pacific islands	183	275	293
96	Special, A–Z	184	276	294
	Hawaiian Islands, see 10, etc.			

---

[1] Use only the indicated number and only for general works on the area as a whole.

Class N

TABLES OF SUBDIVISIONS

Table IV

01	America
	American Indians, <u>see</u> E-F
02	Latin America
03	North America
	United States
05	General works
07	Colonial period; 18th (and early 19th) century
10	19th century
12	20th century
15	New England
17	Middle Atlantic states
20	South
22	Central
25	West
26	Northwestern states
27	Southwestern states
28	Pacific states
30	States, A-W[1]
35	Cities, A-Z
36	Collective biography
37	Special artists, A-Z
.5	Ethnic groups (Collectively)
38	Special races and ethnic groups, A-Z
	Afro-Americans, <u>see</u> .N5
	.A4 American Indians
	For traditional art and crafts, <u>see</u> E-F
	Blacks, <u>see</u> .N5
	.L3 Latin Americans
	.M4 Mexican-Americans
	.N5 Negroes. Afro-Americans. Blacks
	.S6 Spanish-Americans

---

[1]Each state may be subarranged: .x, General works; .x2, Local (other than cities), A-Z, e.g. .V8, Virginia (General works); V82F3, Fairfax County, Virginia.

Class N

TABLES OF SUBDIVISIONS – TABLE IV

	America – Continued
	Canada
40	General works
43	Before 1800 (New France)
44	19th century
45	20th century
46	Special divisions, A-Z
47	Special cities, A-Z
48	Collective biography
49	Special artists, A-Z
	Latin America, <u>see</u> 02
50-59	Mexico
	Divided like 40-49
60	Central America
	British Honduras
70	General works
71	Local, A-Z
72	Special artists, A-Z
73-75	Costa Rica[1]
76-78	Guatemala.[1]
79-81	Honduras (Republic).[1]
82-84	Nicaragua.[1]
85-87	Panama.[1]
88-90	Salvador.[1]
91	West Indies
100-102	Bahamas.[1]
103-105	Cuba.[1]
106-108	Haiti.[1]
109-111	Jamaica.[1]
112-114	Puerto Rico.[1]
115	Other, A-Z
120	South America
130-139	Argentine Republic.[2]
140-149	Bolivia.[2]
150-159	Brazil.[2]
160-169	Chile.[2]
170-179	Colombia.[2]

---

[1] Divided like 70-72.

[2] Divided like 40-49.

Class N

TABLES OF SUBDIVISIONS - TABLE IV

South America - Continued

180–189	Ecuador.[2]
190	Guiana
195	Guyana (British Guiana)
196	Surinam (Dutch Guiana)
197	French Guiana
198	Special cities, towns, etc. A–Z
199	Special artists, A–Z
200–209	Paraguay.[2]
210–219	Peru.[2]
220–229	Uruguay.[2]
230–239	Venezuela.[2]
	Europe
250	General works
251	Folios
	Used only for NA951
(252)	Ancient, see Ancient art in general period divisions, N5315–5899, etc.

Class N

TABLES OF SUBDIVISIONS - TABLE IV

	Europe - Continued
253	Medieval
	Used only for NA5453; in other cases <u>see</u> the general period divisions
254	Modern
255	Renaissance
	Used only for NA5455; in other cases <u>see</u> the general period divisions
256	17th-18th centuries
257	19th century
258	20th century
	Special countries
	Great Britain. England
261	General works
262	Ancient
263	Medieval. Gothic
	In NA includes general architectural antiquities
264	Modern
265	14th-16th centuries
	Renaissance, Tudor, Elizabethan periods
266	17th-18th centuries
	Georgian period
267	19th century
	Regency, Victorian, Edwardian periods
268	20th century
	England - Local
269	English counties, A-Z
	For list of English counties, <u>see</u> separate table
270	London
271	Other English cities, A-Z
	Scotland
272	General works
273	Ancient
274	Medieval
	In NA includes general architectural antiquities
275	Modern
276	14th-16th centuries
277	17th-18th centuries
278	19th century
279	20th century
280	Special counties, A-Z
281	Special cities, A-Z
	Ireland
282	General works
283	Ancient

Class N

TABLES OF SUBDIVISIONS - TABLE IV

		Europe
		Special countries
		Great Britain. England
		Ireland - Continued
284		Medieval
		In NA includes general architectural antiquities
285		Modern
286		14th-16th centuries
287		17th-18th centuries
288		19th century
289		20th century
290		Special counties, A-Z
291		Special cities, A-Z
		Wales
292		General works
		Modern
	.7	20th century
293		Special counties, A-Z
294		Special cities, A-Z
295		Other local, A-Z
		e.g. .W6 Isle of Wight
296		Collective biography. British artists
297		Special artists, A-Z
		Austrian, German, and Swiss, see
		359
		Austria
		Including the former Austro-Hungarian empire
301		General works
302		Ancient
303		Medieval. Gothic. Romanesque
304		Modern
305		14th-16th centuries. Renaissance
306		17th-18th centuries
307		19th century
308		20th century
309		Special divisions of Austria, A-Z
310		Special cities of Austria, A-Z
311		Collective biography
	.5	Special artists, A-Z
	.6	Special works, by name (artists unknown)
		Hungary
312		General works
314		Ancient
315		Medieval. Gothic. Romanesque
316		Modern
317		14th-16th centuries
318		17th-18th centuries
319		19th century
320		20th century

Class N

TABLES OF SUBDIVISIONS - TABLE IV

	Europe
	Special countries
	Hungary - Continued
321	Special divisions, A-Z
.5	Special cities of Hungary, A-Z
322	Collective biography
.5	Special artists, A-Z
.6	Special works, by name (artists unknown)
	Czechoslovak Republic
323	General works
325	Ancient
326	Medieval. Gothic. Romanesque
327	Modern
328	14th-16th centuries
329	17th-18th centuries
330	19th century
331	20th century
332	Special divisions, A-Z
333	Special cities of the Czechoslovak Republic, A-Z
334	Collective biography
.5	Special artists, A-Z
	Special cities of Austria-Hungary
(335)	Vienna
(336)	Others, A-Z
(337)	Collective Austro-Hungarian biography
(338)	Special artists of Austria-Hungary, A-Z
	France
341	General works
342	Ancient
343	Medieval. Gothic. Romanesque
344	Modern
345	14th-16th centuries
346	17th-18th centuries
347	19th century
348	20th century
349	Special divisions, A-Z
	e.g. .A4 Alsace-Lorraine
350	Paris
351	Other special cities, A-Z
352	Collective biography
353	Special artists, A-Z
359	German, Austrian, and Swiss (Collectively)
	German, Flemish, and Dutch, see 425
361-368	Germany
	Including West Germany
	Divided like 341-348
	Special divisions
	Including divisions of Germany considered as a whole, divisions of Germany before 1949, and divisions of West Germany, 1949-
369	A - Als

Class N

TABLES OF SUBDIVISIONS - TABLE IV

	Europe
	Special countries
	Germany
	Special divisions - Continued
(370)	Alsace-Lorraine, <u>see</u> 349.A4
371	Als - Bad
372	Baden
.5	Baltic Sea region
373	Bavaria
374	Bav - Hes
375	Hesse
376	Hes - Pr
377	Prussia
378	Pr - Rh
379	Rhine provinces
380	Rh - Sax
381	Saxony
382	Sax - Wu
383	Wurttemberg
384	Wu - Z
(.5)	Democratic Republic, 1949- , <u>see</u> 389
385	Berlin
386	Other cities, A-Z
387	Collective biography
388	Special artists, A-Z
.3	Special works, By name (artists unknown)
	East Germany
389	General works
.2	Local, A-Z
	Berlin, <u>see</u> 385
.4	Collective biography
.5	Special artists, A-Z
391-403	Greece
	Divided like 341-353 (except 400, Athens)
411-423	Italy
	Divided like 341-353 (except 420, Rome)
425	Dutch, Flemish, and German (Collectively)
431-438	Low Countries
	Divided like 341-348
441-453	Holland (Netherlands)
	Divided like 341-353 (except 450, Amster-
	dam)
461-473	Belgium.
	Divided like 341-353 (except 469.F5,
	Flanders; 469.W3, Wallonia; 470,
	Brussels)
474-474.3	Luxemburg
	Divided like 812-812.3
	Slavic art
476	General works
481-488	Russia. R.S.F.S.R.
	Divided like 341-348
	Special divisions of European Russia
	Poland. Polish art, <u>see</u> 755.P6
(491)	General works
	Finland. Finnish art, <u>see</u> 755.F5
(493)	General works

Class N

TABLES OF SUBDIVISIONS - TABLE IV

	Europe
	Special countries
	Russia
	Special divisions of European Russia - Continued
495	Others, A-Z
	Caucasus, see 792.4
	Special cities
496	Leningrad
497	Others, A-Z
498	Collective biography
499	Special artists, A-Z
501-508	Scandinavia
	Divided like 341-348
509	Collective biography
511-523	Denmark
	Divided like 341-353 (except 520, Copenhagen)
541-553	Iceland
	Divided like 341-353 (except 550, Reykjavík)
561-573	Norway
	Divided like 341-353 (except 570, Oslo)
581-593	Sweden
	Divided like 341-353 (except 590, Stockholm)
601-613	Spain and Portugal. Spain
	Divided like 341-353 (except 610, Madrid)
	Moorish art, architecture, decorative arts, see N6270-6271; NA385-387; NK725, 1275
621-633	Portugal
	Divided like 341-353 (except 630, Lisbon)
	Swiss, German, and Austrian, see 359
641-653	Switzerland
	Divided like 341-353 (except 650, Bern)
661-673	Turkey
	Divided like 341-353 (except 670, Istanbul)
675	Other Balkan states
681-693	Bulgaria
	Divided like 341-353 (except 690, Sofia)
(701-713)	Montenegro, see 749, 751
	Divided like 341-353 (710 omitted)
721-733	Romania
	Divided like 341-353 (except 730, Bucharest)
741-753	Yugoslavia
	Divided like 341-353 (except 750, Belgrad)

Class N

TABLES OF SUBDIVISIONS - TABLE IV

	Europe
	Special countries - Continued
755	Other regions or countries, A-Z
	Under each country (using three successive Cutter numbers):
	(1) General works
	(2) Local, A-Z
	(3) Special artists, A-Z
	.A4 Albania
	.F5 Finland
	.P6 Poland
	Asia. The Orient
760	General works
762	Collections. Catalogs. Exhibitions
765	Southwestern. Asia Minor. Near East. Levant
767	Iraq. Mesopotamia
768	Local, A-Z
769	Special artists, A-Z
770	Saudi Arabia. Arabian Peninsula
771	Local, A-Z
772	Special artists, A-Z
774	Armenia
	For historical region only. For Armenian Republic, see 792.6
(775)	Local, see 798
(776)	Special artists, see 799
776.6	Lebanon
.7	Local, A-Z
.8	Special artists, A-Z
777	Israel. Palestine
778	Local, A-Z
.5	Collective biography
779	Special artists, A-Z
.6	Jordan
.7	Local, A-Z
.8	Special artists, A-Z
	Iran. Persia
780	General works
783	Before 1800
784	19th century
785	20th century
786	Special divisions, A-Z
787	Special cities, A-Z
788	Collective biography
789	Special artists, A-Z
.6	Syria
.7	Local, A-Z
.8	Special artists, A-Z

Class N

TABLES OF SUBDIVISIONS - TABLE IV

	Asia. The Orient
	Southwestern. Asia Minor. Near East. Levant — Continued
790	Other divisions, A-Z
	Divided like 755
	e.g. .C9-93 Cyprus
791	Central Asia
	Afghanistan
792	General
.2	Local, A-Z
.3	Special artists, A-Z
	Russia in Asia
	For Russia in Asia as a whole, see Central Asia
.4	Caucasus
.6	Armenia
.7	Azerbaijan
.8	Daghestan
.9	Georgia
793	Kazakhstan
794	Kirghizistan
795	Tajikistan
796	Turkmenistan
797	Uzbekistan
798	Special cities, A-Z
799	Special artists, A-Z
	Southern Asia
800	General
	India. Indic art
801	General works
802	Before 1800
803	19th century
804	20th century
807	Special regions, A-Z
808	Special cities, A-Z
809	Collective biography
810	Special artists, A-Z
.3	Special works, by name (artists unknown)
	Sri Lanka. Ceylon
.6	General
.62	Local, A-Z
.63	Special artists, A-Z
.7-73	Pakistan
	Divided like 810.6-63
.8	Other regions or countries, A-Z
	Divided like 755
	e.g. .N4-43 Nepal
811	Southeastern Asia
	Burma
812	General

Class N

TABLES OF SUBDIVISIONS - TABLE IV

```
                   Asia. The Orient
                     Southeastern Asia
                       Burma - Continued
812.2                    Local, A-Z
   .3                    Special artists, A-Z
813                    French Indo-China
814-814.3                Vietnam. South Vietnam
                           Divided like 812-812.3
814.6-63                 Vietnam (Democratic Republic, 1946-
                           Divided like 810.6-63
815-815.3                Cambodia. Khmer art
                           Divided like 812-812.3
816-816.3                Laos
                           Divided like 812-812.3
                       Thailand. Siam
821                      General
822                      Local, A-Z
823                      Special artists, A-Z
825                    Malaysia
   .6                    Local, A-Z
   .7                    Collective biography
826                    Indonesia. Dutch East Indies
   .6                    Local, A-Z
                           Including Bali, Java, Kalimantan, and Sumatra
   .8                    Special artists, A-Z
827                    Philippine Islands
828                      Local, A-Z
829                      Special artists, A-Z
830                    Other divisions, A-Z
                           Each subarranged by table under 755
832                      Special artists, A-Z
                     Eastern. China, Japan, etc.
836                      Collections. Catalogs. Exhibitions (not A-Z)
837                      General works
                         China
840                        General works
842                        Collections. Catalogs. Exhibitions (not A-Z)
                             Prefer classification by period
                           Before 1800
843                          General works
   .2                          Pre-T'ang
   .22                           Early through Chou dynasty (To 221 B.C.)
   .23                           Ch'in - Han dynasties (221 B.C.-220 A.D.)
   .24                           Three kingdoms, six dynasties - Sui
                                   dynasty (220-618)
   .3                          T'ang - Five dynasties (618-960)
   .4                          Sung - Yüan dynasties (960-1368)
   .5                          Ming - Ch'ing dynasties (1368-1912)
844                          19th century
```

Class N

TABLES OF SUBDIVISIONS - TABLE IV

```
                  Asia. The Orient
                    Eastern. China, Japan, etc.
                      China - Continued
845                     20th century
846                     Special divisions, A-Z
                            e.g.  .M2 Manchuria
                                  .T5 Tibet
847                     Special cities, A-Z
848                     Collective biography
849                     Special artists, A-Z
    .6                  Special works, by name (artists unknown)
                      Formosa
    .8                  General works
    .82                 Local, A-Z
    .825                Collective biography
    .83                 Special artists, A-Z
                      Japan
                        Formosa, see 849.8+
850                     General works
852                     Collections. Catalogs. Exhibitions (not A-Z)
                          Prefer classification by period
                        Early to 1868
853                       General works
    .2                    Early through Tempyo period (To 794 A.D.)
    .3                    Fujiwara (Heian) period (794-1184)
    .4                    Kamakura - Momoyama periods (1185-1600)
                          Tokugawa (Edo) period (1600-1868)
    .5                      General works
854                       19th century
    .5                      Meiji period (1868-1912)
855                       20th century
    .3                      Taishō period (1912-1926)
856                     Special divisions, A-Z
857                     Special cities, A-Z
858                     Collective biography
859                     Special artists, A-Z
    .6                  Special works, by name (artists unknown)
                      Korea. South Korea
860                     General works
862                     Collections. Catalogs. Exhibitions (not A-Z)
                        Before 1900
863                       General works
    .2                    Earliest to 935
                              Silla Kingdom, etc.
    .3                    Koryo (Koryu) period, 935-1392
                          I (Yi) dynasty, 1392-1910
    .4                      General works
864                         19th century
865                     20th century
866                     Special divisions, A-Z
```

Class N

TABLES OF SUBDIVISIONS - TABLE IV

	Asia. The Orient
	Eastern. China, Japan, etc.
	Korea. South Korea - Continued
867	Special cities, A-Z
868	Collective biography
869	Special artists, A-Z
.6	Special works, by name (artists unknown)
870-870.3	North Korea
	Divided like 812-812.3
	Northern
	Russia in Central Asia, see 793-799
	Siberia, see 495
	Africa
880	General
.5	Collections. Catalogs. Exhibitions.
	By author or title
881	Egypt
882	Coptic art
883	Cairo
884	Other local, A-Z
885	Special artists, A-Z
886-886.3	Ethiopia
	Divided like 812-812.3
887	North Africa
	Algeria
888	General works
.2	Local, A-Z
.3	Special artists, A-Z
889-889.3	Libya
	Divided like 888-888.3
890-890.3	Morocco
	Divided like 888-888.3
891-891.3	Tunisia
	Divided like 888-888.3
891.6	Other, A-Z
	Each country subarranged by table under 755
.65	Sub-Saharan Africa. Central Africa[1]
.7	Southern Africa
892	Republic of South Africa
894	Special divisions, A-Z
895	Special cities, A-Z
896	Special artists, A-Z
.6	Other countries, A-Z
	Each country subarranged by table under 755, e.g. .B6-63, Botswana
	.B6 Botswana
	.L4 Lesotho
	.M3 Malawi
	.R5 Rhodesia, Southern
	.S8 Swaziland
	.Z3 Zambia

---
[1]Use only the indicated number.

Class N

TABLES OF SUBDIVISIONS - TABLE IV

```
                Africa - Continued
897               Eastern Africa
    .6              By country, A-Z
                        Each country subarranged by table under
                            755, e.g. .B8-83, Burundi
                        .B8   Burundi
                        .C6   Comoro Islands
                        .F7   French Somaliland
                        .K4   Kenya
                        .M3   Madagascar
                        .M6   Mozambique
                        .R8   Rwanda
                        .S6   Somali Republic
                        .S73  Sudan
                        .T3   Tanzania
                        .Z3   Zanzibar
898             Western Africa
899               By country, A-Z
                        Each country subarranged by table under
                            755, e.g. .A5-53, Angola
                        .A5   Angola
                        .C3   Cameroon
                        .C4   Central African Republic
                        .C5   Chad
                        .C6   Congo (Democratic Republic)
                                Belgian Congo. Zaire
                        .C7   Congo (Brazzaville)
                        .D3   Dahomey
                        .G25  Gabon
                        .G3   Gambia
                        .G5   Ghana
                        .G8   Guinea
                        .I8   Ivory Coast
                        .L4   Liberia
                        .M3   Mali
                        .M4   Mauritania
                        .N4   Niger
                        .N5   Nigeria
                        .P6   Portuguese Guinea
                        .R5   Rio Muni
                        .S4   Senegal
                        .S5   Sierra Leone
                        .S6   Southwest Africa
                        .T6   Togo
                        .U6   Upper Volta
```

Class N

TABLES OF SUBDIVISIONS - TABLE IV

	Australia
900	General
901	Native art
902	Special divisions, A-Z
	e.g. .T2 Tasmania
903	Special cities, A-Z
904	Collective biography
905	Special artists, A-Z
	New Zealand
906	General
907	Local, A-Z
.5	Collective biography
908	Special artists, A-Z
	Pacific islands
	Hawaiian Islands, <u>see</u> 30-35
910	General
911	Special, A-Z
912	Special cities, A-Z
913	Special artists, A-Z

Class N

TABLES OF SUBDIVISIONS

CUTTERS FOR INDIVIDUAL ARTISTS

Use the tables below to subarrange works by and about
individual artists throughout the schedule. Use Table
V for classes reading "Special artists, A-Z" with first
Cutter designating the artist, e.g. ND623.L5, Leonardo
da Vinci. Use Table VI for classes in which a three
Cutter span is assigned for geographical areas, the third
Cutter representing special artists, e.g. ND955.P63A233-
239 (Poland - Aberdam, Alfred- Biography and criticism)

Table V   First Cutter for artist

.xA2	Autobiography. By date
.xA3	Letters. By date
.xA35	Speeches, essays, etc. of the artist. By date
.xA4	Reproductions (Collections). By date Including exhibition catalogs
.xA6-79	Individual works of art. Alphabetically by title of work of art and date
.xA8-Z	Biography and criticism

Table VI   Second Cutter for artist

x	Autobiography, letters, speeches, essays, etc. By date
x2	Reproductions. By date Including collections, individual works of art exhibition catalogs
x3-39	Biography and criticism. Alphabetically by author

Class N

TABLES OF SUBDIVISIONS
TABLE VII
LIST OF ENGLISH COUNTIES

.B4	Bedfordshire	.M6	Middlesex
.B5	Berkshire		
.B9	Buckinghamshire	.N5	Norfolk
		.N6	Northamptonshire
.C2	Cambridgeshire	.N7	Northumberland
.C5	Cheshire	.N8	Nottinghamshire
.C7	Cornwall		
.C9	Cumberland	.O9	Oxfordshire
.D4	Derbyshire	.R9	Rutlandshire
.D5	Devonshire		
.D7	Dorsetshire	.S3	Shropshire
.D9	Durham	.S5	Somerset
		.S6	Staffordshire
.E8	Essex	.S7	Suffolk
		.S8	Surrey
.G5	Gloucestershire	.S9	Sussex
.H2	Hampshire	.W3	Warwickshire
.H5	Herefordshire	.W5	Westmorland
.H6	Hertfordshire	.W7	Wiltshire
.H9	Huntingdonshire	.W9	Worcestershire
.K3	Kent	.Y5	Yorkshire
.L2	Lancashire		
.L5	Leicestershire		
.L7	Lincolnshire		